Thomas D. Ingram

England and Rome

A History of the Relations Between the Papacy and the English State and Church

from the Norman Conquest to the Revolution of 1688

Thomas D. Ingram

England and Rome
A History of the Relations Between the Papacy and the English State and Church from the Norman Conquest to the Revolution of 1688

ISBN/EAN: 9783337162771

Printed in Europe, USA, Canada, Australia, Japan

Cover: Foto ©Lupo / pixelio.de

More available books at **www.hansebooks.com**

ENGLAND AND ROME:

A HISTORY OF THE RELATIONS

BETWEEN

THE PAPACY

AND

THE ENGLISH STATE AND CHURCH

FROM THE

NORMAN CONQUEST TO THE REVOLUTION OF 1688.

BY

T. DUNBAR INGRAM, LL.D.

OF LINCOLN'S INN, BARRISTER-AT-LAW

LONDON
LONGMANS, GREEN, AND CO.
AND NEW YORK, 13, EAST 16th STREET
1892

PREFACE

THE three most ancient and most venerable Establishments in Europe are, the Papacy, the English Church, and the English Monarchy. Of all the Western nations, England has been the most uniform and homogeneous in her growth, and amongst her people a sense of unity, under a central government which represented the national consciousness, was developed far earlier than in the other communities. That feeling hardly existed in France before the English were driven out of the country. In Germany it was impeded and delayed by her fatal connexion with Italy. Spain was consolidated by her long wars with the Saracenic infidels which ended in comparatively modern times. Italy is the newest birth into the family of nations. With respect to the English Church, though the conversion of the Anglo-Saxons dates from the coming of Augustine in 596, yet, if we add to the thirteen centuries of its existence, the period during which the elder branch

—the early British or Welsh Church—flourished, its origin is almost coeval with the foundation of a Christian bishopric at Rome.[1] But it is not only the antiquity of the English Church that commands our attention and respect. Before the smaller States on the Continent had been incorporated into extensive kingdoms, and before their Churches had ceased to be local bodies deriving their importance from their dependence on Rome, the English Church was a great national institution, with a name of its own to distinguish it from the Roman,[2] completely organised, having its recognised representative assemblies, possessing the right of canonically legislating for itself, managing its own affairs, and exercising a powerful influence in the formation or reform of our constitution.[3] It is the object of the following pages to give an account of the Relations which prevailed between the Papacy on the one hand, and the English State and Church on the other, from the Norman Conquest to the Revolution of 1688.

[1] Stillingfleet, *Origines Britannicæ*. Collier follows this author almost word for word.

[2] In our records, statutes, and rolls of Parliament, it is always spoken of as "the Church of England" or "holy Church of England" in opposition to the term "Roman Church."

[3] "The Charter of Runnymede was drawn under Langton's eye; Grosseteste was the friend and adviser of the constitutional opposition. Berksted, the episcopal member of the electoral triumvirate, was the pupil of S. Richard of Chichester; S. Edmund of Canterbury was the adviser who compelled the first banishment of the aliens; S. Thomas of Cantilupe, the last canonized Englishman, was the chancellor of the baronial regency."—Bishop Stubbs, *Const. History*, 2, 299.

It is time that the expression "Tudor Supremacy" should be banished from our histories; for it implies that the ecclesiastical—not spiritual—headship of the English Church was first claimed by that family, and that it did not exist before the reign of Henry VIII. No suggestion could be more unfounded. There is no fact in our history more certain than that, from the earliest period of our monarchy, our Kings exercised a large supremacy over the external regimen and adjuncts of the Church, differing in no respects from that which Henry enjoyed. In the Anglo-Saxon times, the sovereigns both claimed and exercised all the rights which are included in the term of the canonists "external jurisdiction," that is, to execute the ordinances of the Church, to enforce the performance of their duties by the bishops and clergy, to defend the ecclesiastical system from all harm from within and without, and to preserve the purity of the faith. Edgar, the Pacific, declared that he held the sword of Constantine, and that he was, within his dominions, the Lord's husbandman, the pastor of pastors, and the representative of Christ upon earth. In the presence of Archbishop Dunstan, he told his clergy that it was his duty as King " to examine into the morals of both seculars and regulars, whether they lived chastely and conducted themselves with propriety towards the laity, whether they were careful in the administration of their office and assiduous in the instruction of the people;

and to see, that they were moderate in their food, regular in their habits, and equitable in deciding the causes which came before them."[1] Before the Conquest, English sovereigns considered it to be a part of their kingly office to keep their bishops and clergy up to their duties, to remove and punish abuses of whatever kind which had crept into the Church, to appoint bishops and regular prelates without any external interference, to call national councils in which the affairs of the Church were regulated, to preside over them in person, and to confirm by their authority the decrees passed in these assemblies.

The Norman Kings jealously maintained their ecclesiastical supremacy, and guarded their Church from all external intervention. No bishop or abbot was allowed to go to Rome without the King's license. No Papal bull, constitution, or letter could be received into the kingdom unless it were first inspected and approved by the sovereign. A Papal legate or nuncio could not set his foot in England without the royal permission. In 1115 Pope Paschal II. complained, that no communication between England and Rome was allowed by the King and the English bishops, and that all the concerns

[1] " De quorum omnium [ecclesiarum ministri, greges monachorum, chori virginum] moribus ad nos spectat examen, si vixerint continenter, si honeste se habeant ad eos qui foris sunt, si divinis officiis solliciti, si ad docendum populum assidui, si victu sobrii, si habitu moderati, si in judiciis sint discreti. Pace vestra loquor, reverendi patres, si ista solerti scrutinio curâssetis, non tam horrenda et abominanda ad aures nostras de clericis pervenissent."—Spelman, *Concilia*, 1, 477.

of the national Church were settled in the country without his knowledge and without consulting the Papal See. Until the reign of John—with the exception of the anarchy of the times of Stephen—the English Church was exclusively managed at home; but the alliance of the former sovereign with the Papacy seriously affected the royal supremacy and the independence of the Church. During the latter portion of John's reign and the whole of that of his successor, the English Church was delivered over as a prey into the hands of strangers, whose mismanagement laid the foundation of that universal distrust and indignation which brought about the anti-Papal legislation of Edward III. and Richard II.

The accession of Edward I. put an end to the alliance between the Papacy and the Crown of England. In the reign of this King commenced the long struggle between the English State and the Popes, which lasted upwards of a hundred years, and ended in the enactment of the statutes of *Provisors* and *Præmunire.* These Acts re-established the old order of things, restored to the sovereign his ecclesiastical supremacy, and secured to domestic hands the patronage and administration of the Church. After their enactment, no Papal bull, letter, process, or instrument whatever, could be received by any English subject without the King's permission. No one, either lay or cleric, could apply to the Papal Court for any document, or accept from the Pope the smallest office in the Church of the kingdom, without the same permission. If any one did so, he incurred outlawry and forfeiture of all his goods, and it depended wholly on the discretion of the King whether or not these penalties should be exacted. Though the Pope continued to go through the lucrative form of *providing* by his bulls fit persons for English prelacies, as he did even in Cranmer's case, yet his appointments were absolutely worthless until confirmed by the letters-patent of the King. Each prelate, to whom such bulls were sent, was obliged by an immemorial custom to renounce everything in them prejudicial to the royal prerogative or the English laws; and further, after the passing of the Acts of *Præmunire*, it was necessary for him to sue out the King's pardon for having asked, or received, or acted upon such instruments. In 1426, thirty-four years after the enactment of the last of the *Præmunire* statutes, Martin V. declared that the Church of England was governed, not by the Pope but by the King, and that all communication between England and the Papal See was forbidden by the laws of the country.

Henry VIII. was well aware of the nature of the supremacy which had been handed down to him, and was resolved to maintain it. In 1521, Leo X. bestowed on him the title of "Defender of the Faith" for his book against Luther. Notwithstanding his devotion to the Papal See up to this date,[1] Henry would not allow any application to be made to the Roman Court, or any Papal bull or other instrument to be received, published, or executed in England without his previous license granted on the petition of the applicant. The permissions granted in this reign " to accept, read, publish, or execute bulls," or to apply for such instruments, are exceedingly formal, and invariably commence by reciting the clause of the last *Præmunire* Act, which referred to such documents :[2]— " Though it was enacted in the sixteenth year of Richard II. that those, who procured, or caused to be procured, in the Roman Court, any processes, sentences of excommunication, bulls, instruments, or any other thing touching our Crown, or realm, and those who brought them into the kingdom, should be put out of our protection, their lands and goods forfeited and themselves attached, yet We, moved by certain considerations, do, by these presents, give and grant our license, &c."

In 1514, Wolsey was created a cardinal, and in 1518, he obtained from the Pope, with the consent of the King, a commission as legate *a latere*, but without the usual powers granted to such legates. Wolsey was a candidate for the Papal throne, and

[1] When Henry wrote against Luther, and showed his book to Sir Thomas More, the latter advised him not to advance the Pope's authority too much, lest he should diminish his own.

[2] De licentia ad bullas impetrandas et deferendas, 1512.—Rymer, xiii. 340. Pro Priore de Novo Burgo de bullis impetrandis, 1513.— *Ib.* 383. De licentia impetrandi bullas, 1514.—*Ib.* 469.

was not, therefore, likely to diminish the pretensions of the Roman See, or the number of instruments issued by it. Under colour of his commission, he took into his hands the management of the English Church, and acted directly contrary to the statutes of *Provisors* and *Præmunire*, which had been passed to secure for ever the independence of that Church, and its freedom from foreign interference. In his violation of those statutes, Wolsey was abetted by a great number of the clergy. The offences of that body, and their claim to a complete immunity from the criminal law of the country, determined the King to exact an acknowledgment of his headship over them, considered not as spiritual pastors but as citizens. Henry also confirmed and restored to their former vigour the old laws which had been made, before the Reformation was even thought of, to limit the exercise of Papal power. But he did not touch, or wish to touch, the spiritual supremacy of the Popes. What Archbishop Bramhall states is most true, "that Henry VIII. did cast no branch of Papal power out of England but that which was diametrically repugnant to the ancient laws of the land."[1] The spiritual supremacy of the Popes in England was put an end to, not by the King but by Paul III. By his bull, excommunicating Henry and his adherents, interdicting the kingdom, and delivering over its inhabitants as slaves to those who should capture them, Paul destroyed his spiritual

---

[1] *Works*, 2, 449.

authority, lost the affections of the English people, and drove them and their Church out of Catholic unity.

Under Mary, the kingdom was reconciled to the Roman See. The effects of this transaction have been greatly exaggerated. Though the Queen repealed the anti-Papal Acts of her father, which had been passed after the twentieth year of his reign, 1528, yet farther back she did not go. The supremacy of the sovereign and the independence of the English Church were left in the same situation in which they had been before that date. Mary exercised her ecclesiastical supremacy just as her predecessors had done. She made use of the statutes of *Provisors* and *Præmunire* against the Pope himself; compelled her archbishops and bishops to renounce everything in their Papal bulls prejudicial to her prerogative and the laws of the realm; would not allow a legate who had been appointed against her consent to exercise his office; ordered a bearer of Papal letters to be arrested; and issued proclamations about religion, as her father had done.

With the reign of Elizabeth began, on the part of the Popes, a series of aggressions against England, which is without a parallel in history, and which entailed the most disastrous consequences on the Roman Catholics of the kingdom. For upwards of thirty years, the Roman Pontiffs directed all the moral and material resources at their command to the destruction of England, and her conquest by the King of Spain. During all these long years, they never rested for a moment from their hostile attempts. Laying aside all pretence of acting as spiritual teachers, they took into their hands the temporal sword. They invaded English territories with their own troops; encouraged rebellions; instigated conspiracies; fomented civil wars; taught that religion was to be restored by blood and violence; preached crusades against England; organised confederations of the Catholic Powers against her; and despatched missionaries to teach a new faith, which was not the Catholic faith, but a corrupt compound of religion and treason. The four Popes, Pius V., Gregory XIII., Sixtus V., and Clement VIII., destroyed their Church in England; made the country Protestant; shut it out from the Roman Catholic revival which took place in the rest of Europe; and brought down upon their own adherents the afflictions under which they laboured so long.

The thirty years' war waged against England by the Popes and the Spanish Kings, came to an end with the accession of James I. to the English crown. This cessation was not the result of any change in the Papal policy, but of the exhaustion of Spain, and the new strength which England had acquired by her union with Scotland. After the discovery of the Gunpowder plot, James made an attempt to establish a means of distinguishing between the loyal Roman Catholics and the Papistic faction, the members of which entertained the belief that all modes of restoring their religion—however immoral—were justifiable. With this view he drew up an oath of allegiance which referred only to the civil obedience due by subjects to their sovereign. The attempt was defeated by the Popes, who forbade the English Roman Catholics to take the oath, on the ground that it contained many things contrary to faith and salvation. This statement was a mere pretence; their real reasons being (1) that the oath denied the power claimed by the Popes of deposing princes, and (2) the fixed resolution of the Pontiffs, as avowed by themselves, never to allow Roman Catholics to testify their allegiance to a heretical or Protestant sovereign. The effect of the Papal denunciations of the oath was, to prevent a reconciliation between the English Roman Catholics and the government under which they lived, and to necessitate a continuation of the penal enactments.

This obstructive policy of the Popes was persisted in during the reigns of Charles I., Charles II., and after the abdication of James II., throughout the subsequent reigns until the 18th year of George III. We have no reason to believe that this policy would have been departed from by the Papal Court, had not the English Roman Catholics themselves at last cast off the political ascendency of Rome, and its dictation as to their civil duties. In 1778 they presented a petition to the King in which they acknowledged his title to the crown, and assured him of their affection to his government, and their "unalterable attachment to the cause and welfare of this our common country." The First Relief Act in 1780 was the consequence of this petition. The Act contained an oath disclaiming unreservedly the deposing and absolving powers, and also an anti-social doctrine which had long been attributed to Roman Catholics, viz. that no faith was to be kept with heretics. The oath was taken universally by them, and the way was thus cleared for further relief. The apprehensions which had been caused by the long-continued aggressions of the Popes, by the crimes of the Papistic party, and by the errors of the general body of the Roman Catholics in refusing a profession of their allegiance, in holding themselves apart, as a separate body, from their fellow-citizens, and in declining to recognise the Government established by the Revolution of 1688, began to disappear. The impressions of two centuries, however, fade but slowly from the mind of a people, and fifty years had to elapse before the belief, that the Roman Catholic religion was inconsistent with the safety of the State, was entirely removed.[1]

[1] "If, during the present reign [1792], the fatal impression [that the Catholic religion is inconsistent with the government of this country] is in great measure effaced, it is because the Catholics, in both islands, have dared to profess their allegiance, and solemnly abjure the deposing and absolving powers, without even consulting Rome, or regarding its

We, at the present day, are able to discriminate between the words "spiritual" and "ecclesiastical." But in the times of Henry VIII. and Elizabeth, the notions of all men were indistinct on the subject. The claims of the Papacy were so vast and so undefined that it is not to be wondered at if princes, in repudiating those claims, made use of words capable of too great an extension. Yet it is undoubted that all the moderate men in England, during the reign of Henry, attributed to the expression "spiritual or ecclesiastical" the meaning which we give to the single word "ecclesiastical." Fisher himself, who has always been considered as an advocate of the Papal authority, advised his brother bishops to swear obedience to the King " in causes ecclesiastical and spiritual"—advice which most certainly he would not have given if he had believed that the formula included spiritual concerns strictly so-called. Queen Mary restored bishops to what she called "their spiritual and temporal rights." Though the expression " spiritual or ecclesiastical " occurs in Elizabeth's oath of supremacy, yet the Queen published a contemporaneous explanation of it, in which she renounced all spiritual authority, and declared that she only claimed jurisdiction over the persons of all subjects born within her

former vain pretensions and unchristian condemnation. The spirit of 1778 snapped the chains of Papal tyranny. When their social and political principles are concerned, English Catholics will never again be ill-advised enough to resort to any foreign country for directions."— Sir John Throckmorton, *Second Letter to the Catholic Clergy of England*, 72.

dominions, thus merely rejecting the pretension of the clergy to be judged by the Pope alone. We must not forget that princes were willing to limit their ecclesiastical supremacy to the external concerns of their Churches, and that they made infinitely fewer mistakes in confounding the temporal and spiritual provinces than the Popes, who recognised no distinction between things secular and sacred. It was clearly the duty of the Roman Pontiffs to define the nature of the authority which they challenged within the dominions of independent sovereigns, and of the obedience which they required from their subjects. They were themselves temporal princes as well as supreme pastors, and therefore their claims might be misunderstood. It was necessary for the security of governments, and for the peace of their people, that the authority to which such foreign princes declared themselves entitled in the kingdom of another, should be accurately defined, and limited strictly to their spiritual domain. This was not done. On the contrary, the Popes claimed a paramount temporal jurisdiction and suzerainty in England, overriding the laws of the country, and incompatible with its existence as an independent kingdom. In opposing and breaking down the whole mass of the Roman pretensions, political and ecclesiastical, and in confirming the old laws of the land, Henry VIII. and Elizabeth made use of general expressions, which those princes believed could not be applied to things of divine institution, and which were wilfully misinterpreted by Papal advocates, who concealed the fact that Henry limited his claims to a supremacy over the clergy, regarded not as spiritual teachers but as citizens, and that Elizabeth, by her explanation of her oath, followed the same course.

The edition of Rymer made use of in the following pages is the second, 1727-1735, unless where another is mentioned.

CONTENTS

CHAPTER I

THE SAXON AND ANGLO-NORMAN PERIODS UNTIL THE ACCESSION OF EDWARD I . . . PAGES 1–78

CHAPTER II

FROM THE REIGN OF EDWARD I TO THE END OF THE REIGN OF HENRY VII . . . 79–129

CHAPTER III

THE REIGN OF HENRY VIII 131–198

CHAPTER IV

FROM THE ACCESSION OF EDWARD VI TO THE END OF THE REIGN OF ELIZABETH . . . 199–325

CHAPTER V

THE REIGN OF JAMES I 327–375

CHAPTER VI

FROM THE ACCESSION OF CHARLES I TO THE REVOLUTION OF 1688 377–430

CHAPTER I

THE SAXON AND ANGLO-NORMAN PERIODS
UNTIL THE ACCESSION OF EDWARD I

SECTION I

THE words "spiritual" and "ecclesiastical" have been often confounded in our books and in our statutes. Thus we read of spiritual persons, spiritual lords, spiritual courts, and spiritual subjects, when the meaning intended to be conveyed is what we understand by the term "ecclesiastical." In one Act of Parliament, and as late as the time of Queen Mary, we even find the expression "spiritual and ecclesiastical possessions and hereditaments."[1] In almost every case, if not in all, where the word "spiritual" occurs in our legislation, what we more properly call ecclesiastical is meant.

It becomes necessary to distinguish carefully between these words when we apply them to jurisdiction or supremacy. A possible case will show us the difference between them, and explain what a purely spiritual jurisdiction or supremacy is. Let us suppose the existence of a religious body dwelling in a pagan state, and owning obedience to the Roman Pontiff. This body would be governed—not as to civil rights, as these would be exclusively regulated by the law of the country, but as to religious matters—by the Pope, and the authority exercised by him would be purely spiritual. The objects of that authority would be the matters which belong to the soul, such as faith, morals, sacraments, and the like. The only means of enforcing his commands at

[1] 1 & 2 Philip and Mary, c. 8.

the disposal of the Pontiff would be those which appeal to the conscience, viz. monitions, censures, suspensions, and in the last resort excommunication from the flock. No physical or external compulsion would be in his power. For as the law of the country would not recognize the body as a separate community, no temporal means of enforcing his injunctions would be at his disposal. The members of the body who disobeyed his orders would incur no civil inconvenience, as the Pontiff's commands would be ineffectual to deprive them of the smallest legal right. The last punishment in his power, namely, excommunication, would carry with it no temporal or civil loss, for the persons excommunicated would remain with their *status* unchanged, and in the enjoyment of all rights and benefits formerly possessed by them. Such a jurisdiction or supremacy as this would be a spiritual authority in the true sense of the term, acting only on the conscience of the person affected, and unsupported by any external or legal compulsion. This example points out to us the three characteristics of a spiritual supremacy, viz. that its operations are limited to the domain of faith and morals, that it possesses no means of external or temporal coercion, and that the obedience which is yielded to it is voluntary.

For some centuries the ministers of the early Christian Church possessed no means of enforcing their teaching but those which have been mentioned, that is, monition, censure, and exclusion from their society. The Church was composed of members who of their own free will bound themselves to it, and voluntarily submitted to its instruction and correction. Their subsequent separation from it, or their renunciation of it, brought no loss to them either in their lives, their liberty, or their estates. As they were free to join, so were they free to depart, and their withdrawal was not attended with the slightest inconvenience so far as their civil rights were concerned. The sanctions of the early Church were not carnal and temporal, but spiritual. Its arms were prayers, tears, supplications, and excommunications. Its appeals were directed, not to the expectation of worldly advantage, or the apprehension of temporal suffering on the part of its adherents, but to their fear of the unseen, their love for Him who had redeemed them, and their hopes of an everlasting life.

But in process of time, as the nations of the world were converted to Christianity, a close alliance was contracted between the temporal and spiritual authorities. The temporal power incorporated with itself the religious community—which up to that time had been governed within itself and by itself—and lent it a coercive legal power which it did not before possess. Sovereigns and States attached civil sanctions to spiritual judgments, and added external accessories to the essential jurisdiction of the Church. What had formerly been addressed to the conscience was now enforced by the strong arm of the temporal power. An addition was made to the Church from the outside by the State, and there grew up a system of ecclesiastical rights, privileges, and functions, which may be described as its civil establishment. Hence arose those ecclesiastical courts which, by the concessions of Kings and States, exercised a coercive power, and awarded suspensions and excommunications which differed from the early suspensions and excommunications inasmuch as they were followed by the loss of civil rights, and were no longer purely spiritual. The mere fact that a decision of these courts was attended by a legal or civil sanction, proves that the tribunal which gave it was a mixed one, partly spiritual and partly temporal, for the true spiritual jurisdiction of the Church is never followed by an external sanction. An enumeration of the causes which in England came before these courts will show us that a large class of them was purely temporal. These causes were: Blasphemy, Apostasy, Heresy, Schism,

Ordering, Admissions, Institution of Clerks, Celebration of divine service, Matrimony, Divorce, Bastardy, Mortuary claims, Tithes, Oblations, Dilapidations, Repairs of churches, Wills, Administrations, Simony, Incest, Fornication, Adultery, Pensions, Procurations, and Commutation of penance. Even as to those causes which were really spiritual in their nature, the sanction was invariably temporal,—that is, as it was compulsory, it was necessarily derived from the civil establishment of the Church, and from the commission entrusted by the State to the Church to enforce its discipline by the coercion of civil punishment. This compulsory power which was exercised by these ecclesiastical courts was a gift or concession from the State, and might be recalled without touching the spiritual authority of the Church. The portion of authority which the State had given might by the State be revoked. Hence it follows that the Headship or Supremacy of the civil establishment, which was thus conferred on the Church, remained with the State, and the Bishops who presided in the ecclesiastical courts, so far as they exercised a worldly delegated authority, and awarded temporal punishments, were the King's judges; whereas in purely spiritual matters, that is, in teaching, preaching, binding and loosing *in foro conscientiæ*, administering the sacraments, confirming, conferring orders, and chastising by censures only, all Christians have ever agreed that the Church was supreme.

It is of the utmost importance, if we would understand the relations of the English State and Church to the See of Rome, to keep the distinction between the words, spiritual and ecclesiastical, ever before us. Partial writers have taken advantage of the confusion of them to ascribe to our Kings a claim which since the Norman Conquest they have never made—namely, to interfere with things of divine institution —and to affirm that the English Church has allowed a spiritual supremacy to the secular sovereign. It has also led some of our most respectable authorities far astray. Thus, Lord Coke repeats with approval the opinion of an earlier time, that "Kings being anointed with the sacred oil are capable of spiritual jurisdiction." Hume attributes to the English people and parliament, in the reign of Edward III., an inclination to a reformation because they were dissatisfied with the ecclesiastical exactions of the Pope.[1] Froude thinks that the unwillingness of the bishops to pay *annates* in the reign of Henry VIII.—a purely secular matter—shows that they "contemplated a conclusive revolt from Rome." An acquaintance with the distinction between an ecclesiastical and a spiritual supremacy would have saved these authors from mistakes like this. "Spiritual" is limited to the province of faith and morals, and is independent of, and unacquainted with, the exercise of coercion. When applied to jurisdiction or supremacy it means that essential authority of the Church which manifests itself only in the interior court by teaching, monitions, censures, and excommunication, and which is immaterial and unattended by any temporal inconvenience or punishment. "Ecclesiastical" refers to the civil establishment of the Church, to its external vesture, and to the accidental non-essential accessories which it has received from time to time, either by the concessions from sovereigns and states, or by usage and custom insensibly introduced and allowed by these to continue.

[1] "At another time they petition the King to employ no churchman in any office of State; and they even speak in plain terms of expelling by force the Papal authority, and thereby providing a remedy against oppressions which they neither could nor would any longer endure. Men who talked in this strain were not far from the Reformation."

SECTION II

AT the time of the Norman Conquest, and for about two hundred years after it, the Papacy was at the height of its power and pre-eminence; a power and pre-eminence which it had well deserved for its great services in spreading the Gospel, in civilizing the peoples of the Western World, and in assimilating them by breaking down the barriers of national peculiarities. About the commencement of this period, the conversion of Europe had been completed by the propagation of Christianity among the northern nations, the communities round the Gulf of Finland only excepted; and in the south-east Hungary had renounced her idolatry.[1] Paganism had been overthrown, the great revolts from the faith had been put down, and the Papacy had emerged from the contests in the full splendour of its dignity. It was now preparing itself to organize the nations for a joint enterprise to recover the Holy Land, and to erect a perpetual bulwark against the creed of Islam, which had once threatened and was still dangerous to Christendom. While this central authority was consolidating itself and extending its influence in every quarter, political states, with the single exception of England, were crumbling into pieces. The unity embodied in the Carolingian Empire had disappeared. Italy was a

---

[1] Russia is not mentioned here, as she received her Christianity from Constantinople.

congeries of small independent principalities. France was in the same condition. Spain was a mere geographical expression, and as each province succeeded in throwing off the Saracenic yoke a petty and distinct kingdom was formed. In Germany the clergy had obtained great political power with princely rank and jurisdiction. They and the other princes of the Empire were already in the possession of the substantial attributes of sovereignty, and by their claims to complete independence were disintegrating the great Teutonic Union. The Papacy, on the other hand, presented to the eyes of men the view of a firmly compacted power ruling over a body obedient to one head, united for a common purpose, and bound by an internal principle of cohesion. It is hard for us to realize the universal and all-pervading influence which during this period it exercised over the minds of men. Here and there doubt or questionings still lingered, and in sequestered localities murmurings might be heard, but the vast majority in Western Europe yielded a hearty assent to the teaching and to the unity of the Papal authority. The signs of decadence which set in from the middle of the thirteenth century had not as yet made their appearance, and men were satisfied to rest under the faith and morals which emanated from Rome.

What was the position which the English State and Church occupied in relation to the Pope and the Roman Court in the Saxon times, and for nearly two centuries after the Norman conquest?

From its adoption of Christianity the English people had evinced a veneration and devotion to Rome and the Holy See which were shown by no other nation.[1] The Pope was revered as a father, and Rome was regarded as a holy city.

---

[1] "Not only did the doctrine take root in Germanic Britain, but with it a veneration for Rome and the Holy See such as no other country had ever evinced."—Ranke, *Popes of Rome*.

Many of the early English princes retired from the world and assumed the cowl. There was a constant correspondence and communication between the Mother Church and her daughter.[1] Pilgrimages to the threshold of the Apostles were frequent, and the orders and remonstrances of the Pope were always respected, and generally obeyed. His spiritual supremacy was acknowledged, and deference was shown to every Papal suggestion, though occasionally, even in spiritual matters, as in the case of image worship, the teaching of the Roman See was questioned, and at first rejected. The relation of the English Church to the Pope before the Conquest was that of a child to a parent, but it was that of an emancipated child, nor was its attitude to him that of an unintelligent subservience. No jurisdiction on the part of Rome was admitted by the national church save a purely spiritual jurisdiction, and the Papal orders respecting its management were occasionally neglected or passed over in silence. Thus, the constitution of Gregory the Great and of Honorius, which erected York into a province with twelve suffragans, and made it independent of the southern metropolitan, was disregarded. Bishops were nominated and deposed; bishoprics were founded, divided, removed, or given *in commendam*; monks were displaced for prebendaries, and prebendaries for monks; and abbeys were dissolved or restored, without reference to an external authority. There were no appeals to Rome, and everything regarding the discipline and government of the Church was settled at home. The case of Archbishop Stigand affords us a remarkable illustration of the self-government of the English Church. This prelate exercised his jurisdiction as metropolitan without any application to

---

[1] These words refer not to the early British but to the Anglo-Saxon Church.

Rome for his pall.¹ Though he was suspended by Pope Alexander, the English Church paid no attention to the suspension, and did not disown Stigand, for this archbishop received his profession of canonical obedience from Wulstan, on the appointment of the latter to the see of Worcester. The third charter of the Confessor to the Abbey of Westminster is subscribed by twelve bishops and several abbots; yet Stigand signs it next to the Queen and before the Archbishop of York, who had lately received his pall from Nicholas II. No Papal legates, exercising a power of jurisdiction or appointment, were received into the kingdom. There is but one instance of a legate presiding in an English council or synod before the Conquest, viz. the Council of Calcuith, in 787. But if we read the letter sent to the Pope,² in which the joint legates give an account of their mission, we shall see that they were mere occasional envoys or friendly emissaries, directed from one Church to another, for the purpose of monition or advice. They did not convene the council, but the King; nor do they speak of themselves as legates.³ One of them even chose for his helper in the mission an abbot, not sent by the Pope, but by Charlemagne⁴—a fact which shows conclusively that they were not legates in the sense afterwards given to that title. There can be little doubt that these two legates were in the same position in which Germanus, Bishop of Auxerre, and Lupus, Bishop of Troyes, were, when they were called in by a British synod to help it in its dispute with the Pelagians;

---

[1] Stigand was the first secular appointed to Canterbury after Laurentius in 604. He was accordingly hated by the monks. He had received his pall from an intruder on the Papacy calling himself Benedict X.

[2] Spelman's *Concilia*, i. 292.

[3] Quia ut scitis, a tempore sancti Augustini pontificis, sacerdos Romanus nullus illuc missus est, nisi nos.—*Ib.*

[4] Ego autem, assumpto mecum adjutore, quem filius vester excellentissimus Rex Carolus . . . nobiscum misit.—*Ib.*

or in that of John the Abbot, who attended the Council of Hatfield in 680, at the request of Pope Agatho, to give him an account of the faith held by the English Church. It is impossible to read the Anglo-Saxon ecclesiastical laws, and the accounts of the early synods or councils in England without coming to the conclusion that the Church before the Conquest was in the same position towards the Papacy which it occupied when, in the twelfth century, Pope Paschal II. wrote the letters to which a reference will shortly be made, and that its management was purely domestic.

Though in no country the devotion to the Roman See was greater than in England, yet the Church of the kingdom was, before the Conquest, and continued, with the exception of one interval, up to the time of Henry VIII., a thoroughly national and self-governing institution, under the protection of the temporal power, which exercised a large supremacy over its discipline and patronage. The Saxon Kings assumed without question, and as a matter of course, an authority in the Church which differed in no respect from the later Tudor supremacy, so called as if it were peculiar to that family. They carried out a right to correct, to reform, and to legislate in ecclesiastical affairs. They acted as if the general care of the Church, as well as that of the State, was committed to them, and as if it was their business to mark out to the ecclesiastical authorities their several paths and to keep them up to their duties. These sovereigns asserted over the Church in their dominions the same rights which Constantine, who convoked general councils, presided in them, prescribed the subjects of debate, and confirmed their decrees, had exercised in the Empire. This is shown by the celebrated address of Edgar the Pacific to the English clergy.[1] Edward the Confessor, a

---

[1] Ailredus Rievallensis.—Twysden, *Scriptores*, x. p. 360.

canonized saint, claimed as King to be the Vicar of God appointed for the purpose of ruling and defending the Church.[1] No subsequent English sovereign has ever made so large a claim.

As illustrating the large share which the State, up to the Conquest, took in the management of the Church, it should be remembered that there were no separate ecclesiastical courts before that era, and that all Church matters came for decision before a tribunal composed of clerics and laymen. Ecclesiastical and temporal causes were heard, and ecclesiastical and temporal decrees were made in the same assemblies, local and national. The charter of William I., by which the separation of ecclesiastical and civil causes was effected, implies that even those matters which were purely spiritual were adjudicated on by Courts in which laymen sat.[2]

No change as to the supremacy of the sovereign was made after the Conquest, except that the State projected itself, as it were, more and more into the ecclesiastical department, and the rules which defended the national Church from external interference were made stricter. No bishop or abbot was allowed to go to Rome without the King's permission. No Papal constitution or bull could be received into the kingdom unless it were first inspected and allowed by the sovereign.[3] A general council of the bishops could not be called except with his consent, and when such an assembly met, it could not ordain or forbid anything

---

[1] Rex autem, qui vicarius Summi Regis est, ad hoc constitutus est, ut regnum et populum Domini, et super omnia, sanctam ecclesiam regat et defendat ab injuriosis, maleficos autem destruat et evellat . . . Illos vocari decet reges qui vigilanter defendunt et regunt ecclesiam Dei et populum ejus. Leges Edwardi.—Thorpe, *Ancient Laws and Institutes of England*, 193.

[2] Nec causam quæ ad regimen animarum pertinet, ad judicium secularium hominum adducant.

[3] Eadmer, *Hist. Nov.* 10, Rolls series.

that was not agreeable to his will, or had not been previously ordained by him.¹ No excommunication could be pronounced against the servants of the sovereign without his license, inasmuch as such sentences were followed by the loss of civil rights, and it was the duty of the King to protect his ministers against temporal punishments deemed by him to be unjust. The King's supremacy over all persons, and in all matters ecclesiastical and civil, was maintained by the assertion and exercise of the royal prohibition.² The baronies of churchmen were assimilated to those of lay nobles, and were made subject to the public burdens. It was the prerogative of the King to determine in a time of schism which of the claimants was the rightful Pope, and in the exercise of this prerogative the King was ever supported by the English bishops and prelates.³ A closer examination of the laws and customs of England will show us the freedom of the national Church from external interference, and also how largely the State shared in its management and superintendence during the most splendid period of the Papacy. Two things, however, must be kept in mind, namely, first, that for some time in the reign of John, and for the whole of the reign of Henry III., the English Church was delivered up as a spoil to foreign ecclesiastics. From this period, therefore, no precedent is worth quoting. Secondly, that owing to the permission of some of our Kings, who desired the support of

---

¹ *Ib.* 10.

² Episcopos, abbates, et alios principes per totam terram instituit, de quibus indignum judicaretur si per omnia suis legibus, postposita omni alia consideratione, non obedirent, et si ullus eorum pro quavis terreni honoris potentia caput contra eum levare auderet, scientibus cunctis unde, qui, ad quid assumpti fuerint. Cuncta ergo divina simul et humana ejus nutum expectabant.—*Ib.* 9. See also Coke, *Reports*, Part 5, 11.

³ Archbishop Lanfranc in a remarkable letter to an adherent of the antipope Guibert implies the King's right to decide between the competitors to the Papacy [Collier, i. 252]. In the dispute between William II. and Anselm on this point, all the bishops took part with the King,

the Popes for their doubtful titles, or to our civil wars, these laws and customs were occasionally neglected.

I. No Papal legate *a latere* was allowed to enter England except by permission of the King, and after having given security, or taken an oath, not to attempt anything against his will.

There are two senses in which the word legate may be used. It may mean merely a friendly messenger sent by one Church to another for the purpose of informing itself of the spiritual condition of that other, or of strengthening its faith; or it may mean a deputy despatched by the Pope and claiming a visitatorial power of interfering in the management of the Church to which he is sent. Of legates, in the former sense, three instances have been already mentioned— that of the two bishops sent by the Gallic Church to assist a British synod in its dispute with the Pelagians; that of the joint legates of the Pope in 787; and that of John, sent to the Council of Hatfield by Pope Agatho, to give him an account of the faith held by the local Church. It was to legates sent direct from Rome, and claiming a visitatorial power of interference with the management of the national Church that the English sovereigns and clergy objected.[1]

On two occasions in the reign of the Conqueror Roman legates presided in an English ecclesiastical council, but we are informed by our chroniclers that this was done at the

and would not recognise Urban II. until he was acknowledged by the King. In 1378 the King and Parliament by the 2 Ric. II. c. 7, decided legislatively that Urban VI. was the true Pope, and attached the penalty of imprisonment and forfeiture of goods to the recognition of the other claimant Clement, who was supported by France, Spain, Scotland, and Sicily. In 1409 Henry IV. issued a proclamation declaring that Alexander V. was the true Pope, and stigmatising Benedict XIII. and Gregory XII. as heretics and schismatics. All the sheriffs in England were ordered to publish the King's decision.—Rymer, viii. 604.

[1] Sed nec Legati sedis apostolicæ manus suas excutiunt ab omni munere; qui interdum in provinciis ita debacchantur ac si ad ecclesiam

request of the King by whose order the councils had been convened. The first occasion was at the council or synod of Winchester in 1070, when Stigand was deposed.[1] The second was in the same year when, by command of the King, the same legate held a synod at Windsor.[2]

In 1101 Guido, Archbishop of Vienne, afterwards Pope Calixtus II., came into England as legate with a commission from the Holy See. Eadmer tells us that the whole kingdom was amazed at this proceeding, that the archbishop was not recognized by any one as legate, and that he had to depart as he came without having acted in his office.[3]

In 1116 Anselm, a nephew of the late archbishop, came to Normandy to the King, Henry I., who was then in that province, with letters from the Pope, appointing him legate for England. On this being notified by the King to the English nobility, bishops and abbots, a council was called in London, the Queen presiding, to deliberate on the matter. It was resolved unanimously that the Archbishop of Canterbury should proceed to the King, and, having pointed out to

flagellandam egressus sit Satan a facie Domini. Concutiunt angulos, domos, ut prosternant filios et filias ejus qui languores et dolores animarum curavit in cruce. Commovent et conturbant terram ut videantur habere quod sanari oporteat [Johan. Saris. *Fasciculus Rerum Expetend. et Faciend.* 2. 892]. Cardinalibus vestris clausæ sunt ecclesiæ et non patent civitates, quia non videmus eos prædicatores sed prædatores, non pacis corroboratores sed pecuniæ raptores, non orbis reparatores sed auri insatiabiles corrasores [Answer of the Emperor Barbarossa to the complaint of Adrian IV. that the churches and cities of the Empire were shut against his legates.]—*Ib.* 237.

[1] Veniente Angliam Ermenfredo Sedunense episcopo legato Alexandri papæ. Qui ad voluntatem regis coacto concilio Stigandum deposuit. Will. Malmes., *Gesta Pont.* 37, Rolls Series. Jubente et præsente rege Willelmo, domino Alexandro consentiente.—Roger de Hov. 1, 122, R.S.

[2] Cujus [regis] jussu mox in crastino prædictus Sedunensis episcopus Armenfredus synodum tenuit.—Rog. de Hov. 1, 123.

[3] Quod per Angliam auditum in admirationem omnibus venit, inau-

him the ancient customs and liberties of the kingdom, should then go on to Rome, if the King approved, for the purpose of "quashing these novelties."[1] As for Anselm, the King, "unwilling that the ancient customs of England should be infringed," would not allow him to pass into England in his legatine character, and this legate also was obliged to return without having performed any duty of his office.[2]

After the defeat and capture of the antipope in 1121, Calixtus sent legates into all parts of Europe. Amongst these he sent Peter, a noble Roman, into France, with a commission as legate over all Britain. On his arrival in Normandy the legate waited there for the permission of the King to enter England. The King sent a bishop and another ecclesiastic to conduct him to his presence, and commanded them so to order the journey through England, that the legate should not enter any monastery or other religious establishment under pretence of entertainment, or receive supplies from any except the King's immediate servants.[3] When the legate reached the court, and proposed to exercise his legatine authority, the King told him that it could not be done without the consent of the bishops, abbots, nobility, and the parliament of the whole kingdom, and that as for

ditum scilicet in Brittania cuncti scientes, quemlibet hominum super se vices apostolicas gerere, nisi solum archiepiscopum Cantuariæ. Quapropter sicut venit ita reversus est, a nemine pro legato susceptus, nec in aliquo legati officio functus.—Eadmer, *Hist. Nov.* 126.

[1] Placuit omnibus archiepiscopum Cantuariensem quem res maxime respiciebat regem adire, et exposita ei antiqua regni consuetudine simul ac libertate, si consuleret, Romam iret et hæc nova annihilaret.—*Ib.* 239.

[2] Sed rex Henricus antiquis Angliæ consuetudinibus præjudicium inferri non sustinens, illum ab ingressu Angliæ detinebat.—*Ib.*

[3] Quibus etiam ipse rex . . . injunxit, quatinus iter ejus [legati] ita disponerent, ut post ingressum Angliæ nec ecclesias nec monasteria quælibet ad se tendens hospitandi gratia ingrederetur, nec aliunde quam de suis victus necessaria ei ministrarentur.—*Ib.* 295.

himself he was resolved not to give up as long as he lived any of the privileges of his kingdom, one of the greatest of which was that England should be free from the authority of a legate.¹

Two years previously to the arrival of Peter as legate, the King and the Pope had met at Gisors. It was there agreed between them that no Papal legate should exercise his office in England unless the King should desire it upon some extraordinary emergency which could not be decided by the Archbishop of Canterbury and the other English prelates.²

The result of these three attempts to send legates into England is given by William of Malmesbury. "In the beginning of the reign of King Henry, Guido, Archbishop of Vienne, and afterwards Pope, had come to England with the intention of acting as legate, then Anselm, and not long after a certain Peter. All returned without effecting anything, though not without handsome presents. The frequent legations of Romans, who were endeavouring to undermine Ralph,³ were defeated by the cautious conduct of Henry. For the King did not wish to act against the ancient customs, and to receive into England anyone as legate except the Archbishop of Canterbury."⁴ Pope Paschal II. also, in a letter to the King in 1115, among many other things complained that no legates or Papal nuncios were admitted into

---

¹ Super hæc sibi patrias consuetudines ab apostolica sede concessas nequaquam se æquanimiter amissurum fore testabatur, in quibus hæc et de maximis una erat, quæ regnum Angliæ liberum ab omni legati ditione constituerat, donec ipse vitæ præsenti superesset.—*Ib.*

² Si non ipse, aliqua præcipua querela exigente et quæ ab archiepiscopo Cantuariorum cæterisque episcopis regni terminari non posset, hoc fieri postularet a papa.—*Ib.* 258.

³ Ralph of Escures, Archbishop of Canterbury, 1114-1122.

⁴ Nam et in principio regni Henrici venerat Angliam ad exercendam legationem Guido Viennensis archiepiscopus, qui postea fuit apostolicus; tunc Anselmus; nec multo post quidam Petrus. Omnesque reversi nullo effectu rei, grandi præda sui . . . Crebra ergo ad Angliam commea-

the kingdom without the permission of the sovereign. "We are astonished and grieved," wrote that Pope to the King, "that so little regard is paid to St. Peter in your dominions. For neither nuncios nor letters of the Apostolic See can make their way into your kingdom or receive any countenance there without the consent of your Majesty."[1]

In 1124 John de Crema was sent as legate by Honorius II. After having been stopped in Normandy for some time, he was at length permitted by the King to enter England. During his stay he presided at a council of the English clergy held at Westminster. What the public feeling was on this occasion we learn from a monk who was almost a contemporary. "At this time there came into England a certain legate named John, who was pompously received by the archbishops and the bishops of the realm. Having travelled through the kingdom this legate held a council at Westminster, and put the whole nation into no small state of indignation.[2] For there you might have seen a sight hitherto unknown in England, a clerk who had attained no higher grade than that of a priest seated aloft on a throne and presiding over the whole assembly; over archbishops, bishops, abbots, and the whole nobility of the kingdom, while they occupying a lower position composed their faces like men dependent on his nod. Upon Easter

bat legatio Romanorum insidiantium imbecillitati Radulphi, sed effugabantur omnes cautela Henrici. Nolebat enim ille in Angliam præter consuetudinem antiquam recipere legatum nisi Cantuariensem archiepiscopum.—*Gesta Pont.* 128.

[1] Miramur vehementius et gravamur quod in regno potestateque tua Beatus Petrus . . . honorem suum justitiamque perdiderit. Sedis enim apostolicæ nuncii vel literæ præter jussum regiæ majestatis nullam in potestate tua susceptionem aut aditum promerentur.—Eadmer, *Hist. Nov.* 228.

[2] Post modicum idem legatus peragrata Anglia celebravit concilium apud Westmonasterium, et totam Angliam in non modicam commovit indignationem.—Gerv. of Canterbury, 2, 381, R.S.

Day, on his first arrival in the country, he had celebrated the office of that festival in the mother Church instead of the archbishop, seated on high and using the insignia of an archbishop, though he was no bishop but simply a cardinal priest. This occurrence deeply wounded and scandalized the minds of many, and clearly showed not only the novelty of the thing, but also how much the liberty of the ancient realm of England was now violated. For it was notorious to the whole English nation and their neighbours that from Augustine to the present archbishop,[1] all the successors of Augustine were called and regarded as primates and patriarchs, and were never subject to the jurisdiction of any Roman legate."[2] It may also be mentioned that though the legate presided in this assembly, he was too wise a man to call it either in his own name or in that of the Pope. The summons to it ran in the names of the archbishops. The form sent to the Bishop of Landaff is still preserved, and contains a remarkable expression. It gives notice to that prelate that the legate by "the ordering and allowance" of the archbishop intended to hold a synod at London, and requires the bishop to appear at the time specified.[3]

In 1176 Cardinal Vivian was despatched by the Pope as legate to exercise his office in Scotland, Ireland, and Norway. He landed in England, intending to proceed to Scotland.

[1] William of Corbeuil, 1123-1136.

[2] Toti enim regno Anglorum et circumjacentibus regionibus cunctis notissimum est, eatenus a primo Cantuariensi metropolitano sanctissimo, videlicet Augustino, usque ad istum Willelmum, omnes ipsius Augustini successores, monachos, primates et patriarchas nominatos et habitos, nec ullius unquam Romani legati ditioni addictos.—*Ib.* 382.

[3] Willelmus Cantuariensis Archiepiscopus Urbano Landavensi episcopo salutem. Literis istis tibi notum facere volumus quod Johannes, Ecclesiæ Romanæ presbyter cardinalis atque legatus, ordinatione nostraque conniventia consilium celebrare disposuit Lundoniæ in nativitate Beatæ semper Virginis Mariæ. Propterea præcipimus, &c.—1 Collier, *App.* 715.

The King, Henry II., immediately sent the bishops of Winchester and Ely to the legate, to demand by whose authority he had dared to enter the kingdom without his permission. The Cardinal was greatly alarmed, and, to satisfy the King, made oath that he would attempt nothing against the King's will. He was then allowed to pursue his journey to the northern kingdom.[1]

In 1189 Cardinal John of Anagni, who had been sent by the Pope as legate to put an end to the disputes between the Archbishop of Canterbury and the monks of Christ Church, landed at Dover. He was forbidden to proceed any further without the King's (Richard I.) permission. After a settlement of the Canterbury disputes had been arrived at by the English prelates in the presence of the King, it was discussed whether the legate should be driven from the country or courteously received. It was finally determined that he should be solemnly received, but that immediately after his reception he should be conducted to the sea-coast there to embark.[2]

Even in the degenerate days of Henry III. it was not forgotten that by the law of England and the ancient customs of the realm no legate could enter the kingdom without the permission of the sovereign. "Inasmuch as," says Robert Grossetete, Bishop of Lincoln, "a legate cannot be sent into England unless asked for by the King, the Pope

[1] Qui [Vivianus] cum in Angliam veniret, dominus rex Angliæ misit ad eum Ricardum Wintoniensem et Gaufridum Eliensem episcopos, et interrogavit eum cujus auctoritate ausus erat intrare regnum suum sine licentia illius. His igitur interrogationibus prædictus cardinalis plurimum territus, de satisfactione juravit regi, quod ipse nihil ageret in legatione sua contra voluntatem illius, et sic data est ei licentia transeundi usque in Scotiam.—Rog. de Hov. 2, 99.

[2] Sed citissime remitteretur ad mare transfretaturus.—Gerv. of Canterbury, 1, 481. See *post* p. 40, where the ignominious treatment of this legate and his exclusion from all share in the settlement of the disputes between the archbishop and the monks are fully given.

sends false and disguised legates, who, though not clad in scarlet garments, are yet armed with great powers."[1]

We may continue the examination of this point beyond the period of which we are now speaking.

No rule of law or custom of the kingdom was ever observed more strictly or more continuously than this, which prevented a Papal legate from setting his foot in England until he had obtained the license of the king. In the reign of Henry V., Chichely, Archbishop of Canterbury, would not accept the office of legate before obtaining the King's permission.[2] In his letter to the same King this prelate warns him against receiving a Papal legate *a latere*, and tells him that it appeared from the inspection of ancient laws and records that no legates had ever been admitted into England before they had been brought under articles and limited in the exercise of their office.[3] In the following reign, in 1428, Henry Beaufort, Bishop of Winchester, was appointed legate by the Pope. Thereupon, Humphrey, Duke of Gloucester, as "Protector of the realm and of the English Church," together with the Council of the kingdom, publicly protested, on behalf of the infant King and all his subjects against this appointment. They declared that they would not recognise or receive him as legate, " in derogation

---

[1] Et quia non debet mitti in Angliam legatus, nisi a rege postulatus. mittit Papa legatos sophisticos et transformatos, sed non rubeis vestibus redimitos, magnis armatos potestatibus.—Matt. Par., *Chron. Mag.* 5, 406, R.S.

[2] Tierney's Dodd, *Church Hist.* 1, 162.

[3] "Be inspection of lawes and chronicles was there never no legat *a latere* sent into no lond, and specially in to your rengme of Yngland withoute grete and notable cause. And thei whan thei came, after thei had done ther legacie abiden but litul wyle, not over a yer, and summe a quarter or 2 monethes as the nedes requeryd. And yet over that he was tretyd with or he cam into the lond when he schold have exercise of his power and how myche schold bee put in execution."—Twysden, *Vindication*, 57 : Collier, 1, 655.

of the laws, rights, customs, liberties, and privileges of the kingdom," or in any way consent to the exercise of the legatine authority. After protesting against his appearance in England as legate,[1] they go on to draw the right distinction between a legate and a mere envoy from their spiritual father. For they say that if the bishop has anything to propose, not as legate, but as one of the cardinals sent by the Pope for the exaltation of the Catholic faith or the suppression of heresy, he might freely expound it before the King and the council.[2] In the reign of Edward IV. a legate came to Calais intending to come on to England. The King and his council would not suffer him to land in the country until he had taken an oath not to attempt anything against the King or his crown. The same was done to another legate later in the same reign.[3] In the reign of Henry VIII., Wolsey, before he accepted the office of legate *a latere*, was careful to apply to the King for his permission to do so. The 28th article of his parliamentary accusation states, "Where the said lord cardinal did first sue unto your Grace to have your assent to be legate *a latere*, he promised and solemnly protested before your Majesty, and before the lords both spiritual and temporal, that he would nothing do or attempt by virtue of his legacy, that should be contrary to your gracious prerogative or regality, or to the damage or prejudice of the jurisdiction of any ordinary, and that by his legacy no man should be hurt or offended, and upon that condition and no other he was admitted by your

---

[1] Quod nullus apostolicæ sedis legatus venire debeat in regnum suum Angliæ aut alia suas terras et dominia nisi ad regis Angliæ, pro tempore existentis, vocationem, petitionem, requisitionem.—*Fasciculus Rerum Expetend. et Fugiend.* 2, 618.

[2] Quin si dictus Reverendissimus Pater . . . non ut legatus sed tanquam unus de Cardinalibus a sanctissimo domino nostro papa transmissus . . . quicquam habeat dicendum . . . illud . . . dicere . . . libere possit; et præsertim ea quæ ad exaltationem fidei catholicæ, et hæreticorum perfidiam deprimendam vergere queant, &c.—*Ib.*

[3] Coke's *Reports*, part 5, 27.

Grace to be legate within this your realm."[1] Finally, when Father Peto was appointed legate for England in place of Cardinal Pole, Queen Mary availed herself of the old-established custom, and would not allow him to be received in that character. She caused all the seaports to be watched, ordered all letters, briefs, and bulls from the Pope to be intercepted and brought to her, and declared that she would bring Peto and all who owned his authority under the penalties of a *Præmunire*.[2] Mary acted as if a Papal legate was so trammelled by the English law, as indeed he was, that he could not take a step without her permission. For, in 1554, she issued her letters patent allowing Pole to execute his legatine commission.[3] But this general license was not sufficient, for the following year she again issued her letters patent authorizing Pole to summon a convocation, and permitting the clergy to attend it without danger to themselves.[4]

II. Except in testamentary and matrimonial matters no Appeals to Rome were permitted, but all questions concerning the management of the Church were settled in England, unless the king allowed the matter to be referred to the Papal Court.

The word appeal, like the term legate, has a double import. It may mean either an application to an eminent person, such as the Pope, to use his moral influence without jurisdiction on behalf of the applicant, or to give his approval to a line of action; or it may mean a recourse to the adjudication of a Papal Court. It is in the latter sense that the word is here used.

The only precedent for an appeal to Rome from England,

[1] Lord Herbert's *History under Henry VIII*.

[2] Burnet, *Hist. of the Reformation*, 2, 567, Oxford, 1865; Lingard's *History of England*, v. 517, ed. 1849.

[3] Wilkins, *Concilia*, 4, 109.

[4] Strype, *Eccles. Mem.* part 3, 1, 248, 446; Wilkins, *Conc.* 4, 130.

for a thousand years after Christ, is that of Wilfrid of York, about the year 670. But on examination we find that this was no appeal in the sense afterwards given to that word, for the adverse parties were not summoned to Rome. Whether this was an appeal or not, the success of it was so small that no attempt was made to refer an ecclesiastical cause to Rome for upwards of four hundred years. The facts of Wilfrid's case are as follows:—

Theodore, Archbishop of Canterbury, and the English Church,[1] thinking that the diocese of York was too large for the administration of a single prelate—for Wilfrid was not only bishop of York but also abbot of Hexham, Ripon, and Holy Island—resolved to establish new bishoprics within his see. This was done,[2] and Wilfrid was indignant. In the first instance he applied to Egfrid, King of Northumbria, for the restitution of his former extensive jurisdiction. On the King's refusing to reinstate him, Wilfrid declared that he would appeal to Rome; a threat which only moved the laughter of the Court,[3] as an appeal to the Papal Court was a thing unheard of in England. Wilfrid proceeded to Rome, and upon his representation it was there decreed that he should be restored to his see and that the intruders should be removed. Wilfrid returned to Northumbria with the

[1] It was under Theodore that the Anglican Church first became a united body. The unity of the Church preceded, and, what was an inestimable service to the country, stimulated the political unity of the kingdom. During the time of the Heptarchy Englishmen might be the subjects of different Kings, but in relation to the Church they felt that they were fellow-countrymen. A provincial feeling must have been almost impossible among a clergy who were eligible to fill the highest ecclesiastical offices throughout England though born in a different principality from that in which they were promoted.

[2] Three new bishoprics, Lindisfarne, Hexham, and Ripon, were created in Wilfrid's diocese.—Malmesbury, *Gesta Pont.* 220.

[3] Subsannatoribus qui propter regem astarent in risum crepantibus.—*Ib.*

Roman determination and showed it to the King, who thereupon summoned a council to examine it. The bishops refused to acquiesce in the Roman decree, and Wilfrid was thrown into prison.[1]

After an imprisonment of a year Wilfrid was released. He then proceeded to other parts of England, where this eminent prelate distinguished himself by founding religious houses and also by his missionary labours among the South Saxons, who were still heathens. After a period of eight years spent in exile[2] Wilfrid became reconciled to Theodore, who gave him letters to Alfred, the successor of Egfrid, entreating him to recall Wilfrid and to suffer him to live in his dominions. Accordingly Alfred recalled Wilfrid, giving him the abbey of Hexham and the monastery of Ripon, and also permitted him to return to the see of York as limited by the institution of Theodore. But Wilfrid sighed after his old extensive jurisdiction, for on his restoration to York he endeavoured to avail himself of the Roman decree. The King and the bishops charged him with disobedience to the arrangement of Theodore. After four years of contest Wilfrid was expelled from his diocese and again proceeded to Rome. This time he was followed by messengers from Archbishop Berthwald, the successor of Theodore, who stated to the Pope that Wilfrid had committed a "capital offence" in refusing to be bound by the decree of an English synod.[3] The Council at Rome was so puzzled what to do—it being evident that the English Church would not admit Wilfrid on

---

[1] Ille [rex] cum ea [the Roman decree] episcopis contubernalibus suæ factionis legi fecisset, tantum a reverentia Romanæ sedis abfuit, ut spoliatum suis omnibus ... beatum pontificem ... in ergastulum trudendum committeret.—*Ib.* 230.

[2] Ric. Haggalstandensis, 294; Twysden, *Scriptores*, x.

[3] Esse crimen et capitale, quod in concilio in Britannia congregato decretis Berhtwaldi archiepiscopi se non obediturum Wilfridus contumaciter dixisset.—Malmes., *Gesta Pont.* 237.

any terms but her own—that seventy meetings were held on the subject in four months.¹ At last it was resolved that the Pope, John VI., should write advising Berthwald to convene a synod where all parties, both Wilfrid and the new bishops, might be heard.

Wilfrid coming home with Papal legates sent them on to Alfred. But the King, while asserting that he had every respect for these legates as being men of grave life and venerable aspect, refused to assent to their proposal. He declared that it was contrary to reason to hold communication, on account of any Papal letters, with a man who had already been condemned by two English Councils.²

Shortly after King Alfred died. In the reign of his son, Osfrid, a child, Berthwald convened a council at Nidd for the purpose of settling Wilfrid's case. At this Council Berthwald read out the letter of Pope John VI., giving the bishops, under a threat of excommunication, their choice, either to replace Wilfrid in the ancient jurisdiction of his diocese, or to make a journey to Rome and have the case tried in a more numerous assembly. To this proposal the bishops replied that they could see no reason for reversing the decision arrived at by Theodore with the consent of King Egfrid, and afterwards confirmed by a synod at which Archbishop Berthwald, King Alfred, and most of the English prelates were present.³ At last, at the instance of Elfleda, a sister of the late King and Abbess of Streneshalh, a middle course was adopted, though the bishops opposed it,⁴

---

¹ Factum est ut iiii°ʳ mensibus lxx¹ᵃ conciliabula coacta vel propter hoc solum vel propter hoc precipuum.—*Ib.* 238.

² Se quidem legatorum personis, quod essent et vita graves et aspectu honorabiles, honorem ut parentibus deferre; ceterum assensum legationi omnino abnuere, quod esset contra rationem homini jam bis a toto Anglorum concilio dampnato, propter quælibet apostolica scripta, communicare.—*Ib.* 239.

³ Collier, 1, 119.

⁴ Episcopis suo more obnitentibus.—Malmes., *Gesta Pont.* 242.

and a compromise was effected. John of Beverley, one of the intruded bishops, Bosa, the other, having died, was promoted to the see of York, and Wilfrid obtained Hexham and the monastery of Ripon, both of which he had himself founded.[1]

It is impossible to read Wilfrid's case without seeing the sturdy determination of the English bishops to manage the internal affairs of their own Church free from any foreign interference. They yielded so far to the intercession of their spiritual father as to give back to Wilfrid the two religious houses which he had himself founded, but they declined to restore him to his former diocese. Two things are very remarkable in this matter; the length of time it occupied, and the characters of the famous Church personages that were engaged in it. Wilfrid stated in one of the English councils that its members had openly opposed the authority of Rome for twenty-two years. Among those who resisted Wilfrid's claims and sided with the national Church were Theodore, Cuthbert, Berthwald, John of Beverley, Bosa, and the Abbess Hilda, all of whom the veneration of posterity enrolled in the calendar of English saints.[2]

Appeals to Rome were unknown in the reign of William I. and in that of William Rufus. But in the time of the latter King an attempt was made by Anselm, an Italian, not to appeal, but to refer matters within the cognizance of the English Church to Rome for the purpose of obtaining the support and authority of the Holy See. The attempt was defeated by the King and the prelates who acted in strict

[1] Ego tantum monasteria duo in ea provincia posita, Ripis et Hagustaldeie quæ fundavi non amittam.—Letter of Wilfrid to the Pope, *Ib.* 237.

[2] Ut palam sit quanta miseria involvat mortales, quod illi viri quos sanctissimos celebrat antiquitas, Theodorus, Berthwaldus, Johannes, Bosa, necnon et Hilda abbatissa, digladiabili odio impetierint Wilfredum Deo . . . acceptissimum.—*Ib.* 240.

concurrence with him. There was no Pope recognized by the English Church from the death of Gregory VII., in 1085, until the year 1095, there being during that period two rivals, each claiming to be the spiritual head of Christendom.[1] Before the recognition of either in England as Pope, Anselm asked leave to go to Rome to receive the pall from Urban II., whom he had acknowledged while Abbot of Bec in Normandy. The King told him that it was neither his father's custom[2] nor his own to allow any of his subjects to recognize a Pope without his leave, and that if any one presumed to invade this prerogative he should look upon it as an attempt against his crown. Anselm proposed that the question should be examined by all the prelates and nobility of the realm. A council was convened at Rockingham. The bishops and peers advised Anselm to yield to the King and to renounce his intention of going to Rome and recognizing Urban. "The whole kingdom," they said, "is complaining that you are endeavouring to rob the crown of its principal jewel. Cast away your obedience and subservience to Urban"—they would not acknowledge Urban as Pope until he had been recognized according to the customs of the kingdom—"and, as becomes an Archbishop of Canterbury, act as a freeman, submit your will to that of the King, and obey his commands."[3] Anselm declined to follow their advice, whereupon the bishops renounced their canonical obedience to him as

[1] Quæ res [the rivalry of the Popes] . . . per plures annos ecclesiam Angliæ in tantum occupavit, ut ex quo venerandæ memoriæ Gregorius, qui antea vocabatur Hildebrandus, defunctus fuit, nulli loco papæ usque ad hoc tempus [1095] subdi vel obedire voluerit.—Eadmer, *Hist. Nov.* 52.

[2] Non ergo pati volebat [William I.] quemquam in omni dominatione sua constitutum Romanæ urbis pontificem pro apostolico nisi se jubente recipere.—*Ib.* 10. Consuetudo regni mei est a patre meo instituta, ut nullus præter licentiam regis appelletur papa.—Malmes., *Gesta Pont.* 87.

[3] Sed recogita, rogamus te, et Urbani illius . . . obedientiam abjice,

archbishop, and refused all friendship with him.¹ Anselm
then asked for an adjournment, which was granted by the
King, though he was advised by the council to pass judgment
at once upon the archbishop for his contumacy. Shortly
after the council the King sent two of his chaplains to Rome
to inquire into the claims of the rival Popes and to discover
which of the two had been canonically elected. These
agents, when they had found that the right lay with Urban,
recognized him as Pope on behalf of the King. After this
dispute was thus settled, Anselm, being desirous to take the
opinion of the Pope on the state of the country and of
religion in England, and to receive Papal authority in
dealing with these subjects,² sent some of his friends to
inform the King that he felt obliged to proceed to Rome.
He was told that the King declined to give him leave. In
August of the same year he renewed his request, and again
in the October following. On this last occasion Anselm
threatened to leave the kingdom in spite of the King. Before
executing this project he took the advice of some bishops,
whom he selected as he thought that they being ecclesiastics
would favour his design.³ The bishops declined to give him
any assistance. "Your flights are too high for us; if you

subjectionis jugum excute, et liber, ut archiepiscopum Cantuariensem
decet, in cunctis actibus tuis voluntatem domini regis et jussionem
expecta.—*Ib.* 59.

¹ *Ib.* 63. In his exsequendis omnes episcopi Angliæ primati suo
suffragium negarunt, partes agentes mercenarii et libertatis profugi.
Et quasi parum id esset, omnem ei obedientiam et subjectionem abnega-
verunt.—Will. of Malmes., *Gesta Pont.* 87.

² Videns [Anselmus] ecclesias et monasteria solito intus et extra
suis rebus spoliari, omnem in eis religionem exterminari, quosque
sæcularium, tam majores quam minores, corruptæ vitæ semitas tenere,
multa mala ubique fieri . . . Visum itaque sibi, auctoritatem et sententiam apostolicæ sedis super his oportere requiri.—Eadmer, 79.

³ Occurrit animo episcopos æquius esse debere in suo, quod erat Dei,
quam in consilio regis terreni.—*Ib.* 82.

will descend to our level we will consult for your interests as we should for our own, but in nothing will we depart from the allegiance which we owe to the King." At Anselm's request they went to the King, and returned attended by some of the barons with William's ultimatum: "Since it is unheard of in the kingdom, and altogether contrary to its customs that any of the nobility, and especially you, should proceed to Rome without the royal consent, I offer you one of two alternatives. Either swear never to refer to the Papal Court for any cause whatsoever, or leave the kingdom at once."[1] Anselm chose to depart, and remained in exile until he was recalled by William's successor. It is noteworthy that both the people and the prelates sided with the King in this dispute. On his arrival at Rome Anselm told the Pope: "All, both the flock and the bishops who had professed their obedience to me, endeavoured together to induce me to renounce my obedience to the Blessed Peter, lest I should violate the allegiance I owed to an earthly monarch."[2] Anselm was splendidly received at Rome, but the Pope could not or would not effect anything in his favour. William of Malmesbury attributes this to the bribes of the English King. "It was shameful," says the monk, "that in the breast of so great a man—I mean Urban—there was no place for a love of fame or respect for God, and that money should pervert justice. When Anselm saw that he

[1] Inauditum quippe in regno suo est, et usibus ejus omnino contrarium, quemlibet de suis principibus, et præcipue te, quid tale præsumere. . . . aut jurejurando promittas quod numquam amplius sedem Sancti Petri vel ejus vicarium pro quavis quæ tibi queat ingeri causa appelles, aut sub omni celeritate de terra sua recedas.—*Ib.* 84.

[2] Ipsi quos oves, et episcopi quos adjutores habere debebam, et qui mihi obedientiam professi erant, omnes in commune ad hoc me ducere conabantur, quatinus sub obtentu justitiæ contra justitiam facerem, id est obedientiæ Beati Petri abrenunciarem, ne fidem quam debebam regi terreno violarem.—*Ib.* 104.

had nothing to expect from so venal a man he resolved to leave Rome for Lyons."[1]

There were no appeals to Rome in the reign of Henry I. We have this on an authority which cannot be questioned, viz. that of Pope Paschal II. In a letter to Henry that Pope complains that no Papal nuncios or letters were received into England without the King's permission, and that there was no application, no appeal, or recourse for justice, made from his kingdom to the Papal Court.[2] In another letter the same Pope accuses the King and the English bishops of preventing all appeals to him in spite of the decrees of holy councils declaring that all persons aggrieved should have the privilege of appealing to the Roman See.[3] Our early ecclesiastical historians expressly affirm that until the confused times of Stephen appeals to Rome were unknown in England, and that they were first introduced by Henry of Winchester, brother of the King, who was appointed legate in 1139. Gervase of Canterbury informs us that the members of the General Council of London, in 1151, were indignant at the number of appeals, which, up to that time, were unknown in England.[4] The contemporary, Henry of

[1] Indignum factum, ut pectori tanti viri, Urbani dico, vilesceret famæ cura, Dei respectus cederet, et pecunia justitiam præverteret. Visum est ergo Anselmo circa tam venalem hominem expectationem non perdere, sed Lugdunum remeare.—*Gesta Pont.* 102.

[2] Sedis enim apostolicæ nuncii vel literæ præter jussum regiæ majestatis nullam in potestate tua susceptionem aut aditum promerentur. Nullus inde clamor, nullum inde judicium, ad sedem apostolicam destinatur.—Letter of Paschal to the King, Eadmer, 228.

[3] Vos oppressis apostolicæ sedis appellationem subtrahitis, cum sanctorum patrum conciliis decretisque sancitum sit ab omnibus oppressis ad Romanam ecclesiam appellandum.—Letter of Paschal to the King and Bishops of England, *Ib.* 232.

[4] Totum autem concilium novis et inusitatis infrenduit appellationibus. Inusitatæ enim in Anglia appellationes erant usque quo Henricus Wintoniensis episcopus extitit legatus.—Gerv. of Cant. 1, 147.

Huntingdon, declares that till the date of this Council appeals to Rome were not in use, and that they were "cruelly intruded" on the nation by the same bishop.[1]

When the civil war was ended and peace restored under Henry II., the old order of things was re-established, and appeals to Rome were held to be illegal. We have a remarkable instance of this in an ecclesiastical cause which was tried in 1157, and in which Becket, as Chancellor, was one of the judges. The parties were Hilary, Bishop of Chichester, and the Abbot of Battel Abbey. Hilary made a claim over the abbot which the latter denied. To support his case Hilary had applied to Rome, and had obtained a bull from the Pope in his own favour. On the production of this bull by Hilary, Becket drew the attention of the King to the fact that the bishop had appealed to Rome, and declared that it was in contempt of the royal authority. The King's anger was inflamed, and Hilary saved himself by boldly swearing that it was the abbot who had obtained the bull, while Theobald, Archbishop of Canterbury, crossed himself at the audacious perjury. The matter ended by Hilary withdrawing his claim, as he said, of his own free will, and induced thereto by considerations of justice.[2]

In 1164 it was enacted that appeals in ecclesiastical causes should proceed regularly from the archdeacon to the bishop, and from the bishop to the archbishop; if the archbishop failed to do justice, the final resort should be to the

---

[1] In Anglia namque appellationes in usu non erant, donec eas Henricus Wintoniensis episcopus, dum legatus esset, malo suo crudeliter intrusit.—Hen. Hunt. 282, R.S. It is evident that the chronicler was speaking of appeals to Rome, for he goes on to say that in this Council three such appeals were entered against the Bishop himself. Hence the expression "malo suo."

[2] *Chronicle of Battel Abbey.* A summary of the trial is given by Mrs. Green in her *Henry II.*

King.[1] To this enactment, one of the Constitutions of Clarendon, and there recited to be according to the ancient customs and liberties of the kingdom, the archbishops, bishops, abbots, priors, and clergy of England, including Becket himself, swore, and promised "in the words of truth" that it should be observed for ever.[2] Here we have a solemn recognition and declaration assented to by all classes in the realm that it was the ancient custom, and one of the liberties of England, that all appeals in ecclesiastical matters should be decided before a domestic tribunal, and that none should be allowed to proceed farther without the permission of the King. It is true that Becket afterwards withdrew his assent to some[3] of these constitutions; but of what importance is this? How can the action of one man weaken the testimony of a whole nation?

At the same time and place and under similar solemnities it was also enacted that no archbishop, bishop, or dignified ecclesiastic should leave the kingdom without the King's license, and that before they went abroad the King might demand security from them for their conduct while absent. It would be difficult to devise more effectual provisions than

---

[1] Et si archiepiscopus defecerit in justitia exhibenda, ad dominum regem perveniendum est postremo, ut præcepto ipsius in curia archiepiscopi controversia terminetur, ita quod non debet ulterius procedere absque assensu domini regis.—Bishop Stubbs, *Select Charters*, 139.

[2] Hanc recognitionem sive recordationem de consuetudinibus et libertatibus, Archiepiscopi, Episcopi, Abbates, Priores, Clerus, cum Comitibus et Baronibus et Proceribus cunctis, juraverunt et firmiter in verbo veritatis promiserunt, &c.—Spelman's *Codex;* Wilkins' *Leges Ang. Sax.* 322. Et easdem consuetudines recognitas per archiepiscopos et episcopos et comites et barones et per nobiliores et antiquiores regni, Thomas Cantuariensis archiepiscopus &c. concesserunt, et in verbo veritatis viva voce firmiter promiserunt tenendas et observandas domino regi et hæredibus suis, bona fide et absque malo ingenio.—Stubbs, *Select Charters*, 137.

[3] Ten only of the Constitutions of Clarendon were condemned by Alexander III. Six were allowed as tolerable.

these enactments against appeals to a foreign tribunal. If we remember that no Papal legate could enter the kingdom without the royal license; that no bull or rescript of the Pope could be received in England before it was shown to the King, and approved by him; and that the sovereign was entitled to call back to the country those subjects who were in Rome, and to forbid them to remain longer than he desired,[1] we shall begin to understand how the English Church was at this time hedged in from external interference, and how large and wide the protection and authority of the State over it were.

Though Henry II., on his reconciliation with the Pope in 1172, after the murder of Becket, promised that he would not for the future offer any opposition to appeals to Rome, yet he attached to the promise a condition which showed the concession was a favour proceeding from himself, and which in reality nullified the agreement, viz. that if he had any reason to suspect the intention of the person proposing to go to Rome, he might take security from him for his conduct.[2] To render the condition efficient, two writs were framed, either on this occasion or after the enactment of the Constitutions of Clarendon, one to the sheriff of the county, requiring him to take security from any person proposing to depart the realm not to proceed without the special license of the King;

[1] See a proclamation of Edward III.—" Quod omnes Angli, tam Romæ quam alio loco ultra mare existentes, repedare festinarent quantocius sub pœna forisfacturæ corporis et omnium bonorum " [Hen. de Knighton, 260; Twysden, *Scriptores*, x.] In 1301 Richard II. ordered all the sheriffs in England and the Irish justiciary to make proclamation that all his subjects then at the Papal Court should return on pain of forfeiture of life, limb, and all their property, before a certain date, and that no one of whatever rank should bring into the country any bulls, Papal letters, or other instruments contrary to the laws and customs of the realm.—Rymer, vii. 698.

[2] Sic tamen ut, si ei suspecti fuerint aliqui, securitatem faciant quod malum suum vel regni non quærerent.—Gerv. of Canterbury, 1, 238.

the other to the party himself, enjoining him not to go, also without the special leave of the King.[1]

That, by this agreement with the Pope,[2] Henry did not intend to renounce his jurisdiction over appeals is shown by his subsequent conduct in the Hackington case, which occurred in the pontificate of Baldwin, who was Archbishop of Canterbury from 1185 to 1190. In 1186 Baldwin proposed to build a rival church of secular canons at Hackington, about half-a-mile from Canterbury, and to endow it with certain advowsons to which the monks of Christ Church laid claim. The monks were alarmed, and appealed to Rome. The Archbishop, despising the appeal, suspended the prior, and confined the monks to their convent. The Pope, Urban III., by his bull directed to the archbishop, ordered him to declare the sentence of suspension invalid within ten days after notice of the bull, and to undo everything he had done since the appeal. In case of disobedience he appointed a commission consisting of the abbots of Battel, of Feversham, and of St. Augustine's, to relax the suspension, and to serve a mandate on the archbishop to appear at Rome on a given

---

[1] The writ to the Sheriff ran, "Quia datum est nobis intelligi quod A. B. clericus versus partes exteras . . . transire proponit, nos tibi præcipimus ut . . . in brevi de securitate pacis . . . quod ipse versus aliquas partes exteras sine licentia nostra speciali se non divertet . . . compellas ?" That to the individual himself ran, " Quia datum est nobis intelligi quod tu versus partes exteras absque licentia nostra clandestine divertere . . . intendis, in nostri contemptum et præjudicium ac contra proclamationem et inhibitionem nostras sæpius inde factas, nos tibi districte sub periculo quod incumbit prohibemus, ne versus dictas partes exteras absque licentia nostra speciali aliqualiter te divertas."—Gibson's *Codex*, 1, 88 ; see also Rymer, vii. 592, ix. 77.

[2] In this agreement Henry conveyed to the Pope a remarkable threat. He promised not to disown the Pope and his successors as long as he himself was treated by them as a Catholic King. "Juravit etiam quod ab Alexandro summo pontifice et ab catholicis ejus successoribus non recederet, quam diu ipsum sicut regem Catholicum habuerint."—Gerv. of Canterbury, 1, 238.

day. Baldwin was contumacious, and continued the building of his new church. The Pope wrote to him again, ordering him to replace the monks in their rights, and to stay his buildings. At the same time he commanded his commissioners to enforce his mandate. The answer of the archbishop to the order to stop his building was that he commenced to build in stone what had hitherto been compacted in wood. When the Papal commissioners, whom the Pope had chided for their remissness, attempted to execute their commission, they were met by a prohibition from Ranulf de Glanville, the justiciary of England:—" I command you, on behalf of our lord the King, by the allegiance you owe him and the oath you have sworn to him, that you in no way proceed in a suit between the monks of Canterbury and the archbishop of that see, until you shall have conferred with me thereupon, and that you, all delay and excuses being laid aside, appear before me in London on Saturday next after the feast of St. Margaret the Virgin, there to make answer in the premises."[1] Another prohibition was directed to the sub-prior and the convent:—" I command you, on behalf of our lord the King, that you in no way make use of any mandates you may have obtained against the Archbishop of Canterbury, until you shall have conferred with me; and that you, the sub-prior and the council of your convent, without delay or excuse, attend in London on the festival of St. James, there to hear and do what shall be commanded you on behalf of the King; and that you have there with you all mandates which you have obtained against the archbishop."[2] Accordingly, two monks attended the justiciary on behalf of the convent, the sub-prior being ill. To these the justiciary repeated his prohibition:—" Our lord the King has heard that you have received certain mandates from Rome against him and his kingdom, by which you propose to diminish the rights of the

[1] *Ib.* 376.   [2] *Ib.*

realm and to alter his prerogative. Therefore the King commands you, and I on his behalf enjoin you, not to make use of the mandates until you have spoken with him. Further, I order you to send to the King within fifteen days messengers from your community, with copies of your privileges, in order that they may be approved by him, or totally rejected."[1] The three abbots were also prohibited from executing on any occasion the Papal mandates,[2] and thus all proceedings on their part were put an end to. This was the state of affairs at Urban's death. Clement III., on his accession, wrote to Baldwin,[3] expressing his astonishment at his treatment of Urban's mandates, and repeating the command that all things done since the appeal should be undone. The archbishop took no notice of the letter. Clement then issued an order to the prior of Feversham and another ecclesiastic to excommunicate all who had been guilty of violence to the monks. The order was obeyed, but the sentence of excommunication was disregarded by the secular clergy of Canterbury, who, in the name of the King and of the archbishop, exhorted their parishioners in their sermons not to avoid the society of those who were excommunicated by the Pope, and publicly declared that the Pope's sentence had no force in the diocese of the archbishop.[4] Those who refused to hold communication with the excommunicated were imprisoned by order of the King. Clement again

---

[1] Unde præcipio ut infra xv dies ad dominum regem cum vestris privilegiis monachos mittatis, ut ejus arbitrio vel approbentur vel penitus projiciantur.—*Ib.* 377.

[2] Abbatibus quoque tribus minaciter ex imperio regis inhibitum est ne occasione aliqua domini papæ exequerentur mandatum.—*Ib.*

[3] Between Urban III. and Clement, Gregory VIII. occupied the Papal throne for a short time. Gregory confirmed the letters issued by Urban during the last three months of his reign, but excepted from the confirmation those relating to Canterbury.—*Ib.* 302.

[4] Presbiteri etiam Cantuariæ a prophanis canonicis instructi, paro-

wrote to Baldwin, repeating his commands, but without effect. In the next year he renewed his orders to the archbishop. About the same time certain of the monks were sent to the King to implore his assistance. As their convent had lately refused to transfer the cause from the Papal court they obtained an unfavourable reception. On their saying to the King that their community regarded him as their lord, Henry replied, " I have been, am, and will be your lord; away with ye, ye traitors, I will consult with my faithful counsellors."[1] These were the last words of Henry on the matter, as he died a short time after this. Finally, the disputes between the archbishop and the monks were settled before Richard I. and an assembly of English bishops and abbots, on the terms that the monks, being satisfied about the suspension of the prior and the demolition of the new church, should submit wholly to the archbishop. The Papal legate, John of Anagni, who had been sent from Rome to compose these differences, was detained at Dover until after the settlement, by order of the Queen, Richard having gone to Edmundsbury.[2] After the compromise had been effected by the King and the prelates, it was debated whether the legate should be received or driven from the country. Some of the bishops proposed that he should be honourably received, but that he should not be allowed to remain in the kingdom. Others were of opinion that he should be at once dismissed the realm. Ultimately, it was agreed that he should be

---

chianis suis prædicantes prohibebant ex parte regis et archiepiscopi, ne quemquam ex his quos auctoritate apostolica excommunicatos audierant, aliquatenus vitarent, dicentes in diocesi archiepiscopi apostolicam non tenere sententiam.—*Ib.* 425.

[1] Dominus eorum fui, sum, et ero, mali proditores. Sed abite velocius, cum meis enim loquar fidelibus.—*Ib.* 449.

[2] Applicuit interea apud Dovoriam Johannes Anagninus, apostolicæ sedis legatus, sed continuo ex mandato reginæ ne procederet prohibitus est.—*Ib.* 474.

solemnly received, and that immediately after his reception he should be sent to the coast, there to embark.[1] His reception took place at Canterbury, but during his stay there no one was allowed to visit him without the permission of the archbishop.[2] He managed, however, to hold a private conversation[3] with the monks, and told them that he could not help them, "for," said he, "since my arrival in this country I have been so carefully guarded, that I have not been able to speak freely to you or any one, hardly even to leave my chamber for the most necessary purposes.[4] The monks asked him what they were to do as to those who had been excommunicated by the Pope, with whom they were obliged to communicate. The legate told them to do the best they could : "If I take any action I shall incur danger myself, and you will be treated with greater severity. I leave you now, for I am obliged to follow the King to the sea-coast, to-morrow or next day, without any consideration being shown to me."[5] This Hackington case is a good illustration of the manner in which the concerns of the national Church were managed by the King and his prelates a hundred and

[1] Hoc igitur prædicto modo miseræ Cantuariensis ecclesiæ expleto negotio, de vocando vel repellendo legato in præsentia regis et episcoporum sermo consertus est, qui hucusque ad vocem fœminæ apud Dovoriam tremulus subsistebat. Asserebant igitur quidam ex episcopis eum honorifice esse vocandum, sed ne procederet retinendum. Dicebant alii eum ab Anglia citius repellendum. Tandem ex consilio eorum qui regis et archiepiscopi per omnia favebant voluntati, decretum est, ut solemniter cum insigniis susciperetur, sed citissime remitteretur ad mare transfretaturus.—*Ib.* 481.

[2] Ministris archiepiscopalibus undique septus, ne præter eorum licentiam cuiquam ad eum pateret ingressus.—*Ib.* 482.

[3] Conventui tamen seorsum quasi furtim vocato dicebat.—*Ib.*

[4] Nam postquam venimus in hanc terram, ita custoditi sumus quod nec vobis nec alteri libere loqui valemus, sed nec nostram egredi cameram ut ea quæ natura requirit libere possimus expedire.—*Ib.*

[5] Nunc autem vado et crastino vel perendie regem ad mare festinantem inhonorus sequi compellor.—*Ib.* 483.

twenty years after the Norman Conquest. The Papal legate was not allowed to move a finger in the matter, though he had been specially deputed by the Pope to settle it. The whole story throws light upon the complaint of Paschal II., made seventy years before, viz. that all matters relating to the English Church were settled at home without so much as consulting the Papal See.[1]

In the latter end of John's reign and during the unhappy administration of Henry III., appeals to Rome became numerous, though it was never forgotten by the nation that they were illegal. In 1223 when Henry III. was still under the influence of Hubert de Burgh, and before he had delivered himself up as a bondsman to the Pope, he prohibited a reference to Rome. One Nicholas de la Feld sought to recover some lands from the Abbot of St. Thomas's Abbey in Dublin, in the King's Bench, Ireland. The abbot contested his claim on the ground of his illegitimacy. The question of illegitimacy was referred to the ecclesiastical court. The Archbishop of Dublin, then justiciary for Ireland, entered upon the examination of this question, and a third party intervening in the suit, referred the whole case to the Papal Court at Rome. A royal letter was thereupon sent to the archbishop, expressing the King's indignation at the archbishop's conduct, and declaring that he had erred in transferring to "a foreign dignitary" a matter which ought to have been determined before a domestic tribunal. Further, the King commanded the archbishop to give sentence on the question of illegitimacy, notwithstanding the reference to Rome, and to remit his decision to the justices of the King's Bench.[2] In the list of the grievances suffered by the English people at the

---

[1] See *post* p. 60.

[2] Sweetman's *Calendar of Documents relating to Ireland*, 1, 175; Stokes, *Ireland and the Ang. Nor. Church*, 268.

hands of the Pope, and presented on their behalf at the Council of Lyons in 1246, one of the complaints was, that the English were drawn out of their country in appeals and by the Papal authority "contrary to the customs of the kingdom and against its written laws."[1] In the same year the suffragan bishops of Canterbury in their letter to the Pope declared that the summoning of English subjects before a foreign tribunal was contrary to the privileges of the kingdom.[2] As soon as Edward I. came to the throne appeals to Rome were forbidden. Early in his reign he informed the Pope that it was a privilege of the realm that no Englishman should be summoned out of the kingdom by Papal letters; that this had been done of late, and that he had been often and earnestly implored by his subjects to provide a remedy for the evil.[3] He also committed to prison one John of Ibstocke for having a suit at Rome for the rectory of New Church.[4] In 1290 William of Nottingham, an ecclesiastic, petitioned the King in parliament that he might be allowed to prosecute his appeal to Rome, which was refused as being against the King's rights.[5] In the same year Nicholas IV. wrote to Edward complaining that appeals to Rome were prevented, and that ecclesiastics were not allowed to be summoned out of the kingdom by Papal authority. "We have learned," says the Pope, "that it is a frequent occurrence in your kingdom that when Papal letters referring to matters purely ecclesiastical are sent thither, they are not allowed to be presented to your judges,

---

[1] Quod Anglici extra regnum in causis auctoritate apostolica trahuntur, contra regni consuetudines, contra jura scripta, eo quod inter inimicos conveniri non debent.—Matt. Paris, *Chron. Maj.* 4, 528.

[2] *Ib.* 530.   [3] Rymer, ii. 130.   [4] *King James's Works*, 300.

[5] Wills de Notyngham, clericus, . . . petit quod causam suam ecclesiasticam possit prosequi in curia Romana, non-obstante prohibitione de privilegio R. Rex non concessit, quod privilegium suum infringatur.—*Rotuli Parl.* 1, 50.

and that if they are presented a royal writ, to use the English expression, is at once issued, prohibiting any use being made of them under threats and even execution of those threats if the mandate be disobeyed. For those who make use of the Papal letters are arrested even though they be ecclesiastics. For small offences persons of this kind are seized, and, without any consideration for their dignity or rank, are thrown into prison at your will or that of your ministers. No ecclesiastic is allowed to be summoned out of your kingdom by Papal authority, and your courts, scorning the sacred canons, interfere in causes which are undoubtedly clerical, though that should not be done by lay judges." [1]

Edward II. issued letters for the apprehension of the Abbot of Waldon for citing the Abbot of St. Alban's and others to appear in the Court of Rome.[2] In the same reign letters of caption were directed against a prebendary of Banbury for drawing another out of the kingdom by a plea at Rome.[3] Edward on more than one occasion told the Pope that the citation of his subjects out of the realm was to the disherison of his crown and against the royal dignity, and that if he himself were to pass over such a thing, the magnates

---

[1] Intelleximus ... quod frequenter, cum in regno prædicto super negotiis ad ecclesiasticum forum spectantibus literas contingit apostolicas emanare, ... illas judicibus impune præsentare non licet; et si forsitan præsententur, currit statim breve regium—ut patriæ verbis utamur—et usum illarum, sub poenæ comminatione, immo et executione si fiat contrarium, interdicit. Sæpe namque capiuntur illis utentes, etiam si ecclesiasticæ sint personæ. Pro levibus insuper offensis personas hujus modi, absque dignitatis statusque delectu, pro regali et regalium ministrorum libito, regius carcer includit, nec personæ ecclesiasticæ permittuntur extra regnum ipsum auctoritate apostolica evocari; regiaque curia se de nonnullis causis ad ecclesiasticum forum indubitanter pertinentibus, quarum cognitio non cadit in laicum, spretis sacris canonibus intromittit.—Raynaldus, *Annales Eccles.* vol. 14, sub ann. 1290. The title of the section is—"In causarum controversiis provocantes ad sedem apostolicam vexari."

[2] *King James's Works*, 300.   [3] *Ib.*

and noblemen of the kingdom would not allow it.¹ There were many cases in this reign in which the King forbade citations to Rome being obeyed or appeals instituted in the Papal Court.² We also have a long letter from Clement V. to the Bishop of Worcester. In this the Pope complains that the ministers and officers of the King would not allow citations to the Roman Court to be published or served, and, if they were served, would not permit those summoned to obey them or to leave the kingdom.³ In 1325 by his writ, directed to all the bishops of England and thirty-one abbots and priors, the King commanded them not to execute any Papal letters prejudicial to himself, his people, or his crown without consulting him.⁴ Edward III. maintained his rights as strictly as his predecessor.⁵ So carefully was the law, which prevented Papal communications being brought to or published in England, carried out, that the Papal collector himself was obliged to make oath that he would not execute, or permit another to execute, letters or mandates of the Pope to the prejudice of the royal authority, and that he would show all such documents to the King's council before

---

[1] Rymer, iii. 38, 185.

[2] Pro Ricardo de Cornubia contra citationes papales.—*Ib.* iii. 277.

Pro eodem Ricardo, de illis arestandis qui citationes faciunt.—*Ib.*
Ad Papam contra citationes personales.—*Ib.* 216.
De arestando impugnatores jurium coronæ regis.—*Ib.* 466.
De jure regni.—*Ib.* 500.
Contra usurpationes papales.—*Ib.* 784.
Ne quis trahatur in placitum extra regnum.—*Ib.* 795.
De juribus regiis conservandis.—*Ib.* 886, 916.

[3] *Ib.* iii. 187.

[4] Vobis mandamus ... firmiter injungentes quod, si aliquæ literæ papales seu aliæ quæcunque in quibus aliqua nobis, seu juri coronæ nostræ, aut populo nostro præjudicialia sint contenta, vobis delatæ sint seu ex nunc deferri contigerit exequendæ, eas nobis inconsultis executioni nullatenus demandetis.—*Ib.* iv. 184.

[5] *Ib.* 388, 749.

publishing them or delivering them to any person.[1] But the statutes of *Provisors* and *Præmunire* operated powerfully in checking appeals or even the most ordinary applications to Rome. After the passing of these enactments it was illegal for any Englishman, whether a layman or an ecclesiastic, to sue for, bring into the country, accept, publish, or execute, any bull, Papal letter, mandate, or rescript whatsoever, without the previous license of the King. No one could apply to the Papal Court for any document, not even when it became necessary to obtain fresh copies of those which had become rotten from time or neglect, without the royal permission granted on petition of the applicant.[2] In every reign— those only of Edward V. and Richard III. excepted—from Richard II. to the early part of that of Henry VIII., we find petitions to the King for leave to sue at Rome, to make use of Papal bulls, letters, and processes, to proceed in appeals, to remain at the Papal Court for the purpose of prosecuting causes, &c., and also for pardons for applying for, or receiving, or acting on, or bringing into the country, or publishing there, bulls, Papal letters, Papal appointments, or Papal

---

[1] Nullam executionem literarum vel mandatorum Domini Papæ per me vel alium faciam nec fieri permittam, quæ poterit esse præjudicialis regiæ majestati dicti domini nostri regis, aut regaliæ, legibus vel juribus suis, vel eidem regno. Nullas literas papales nec alias recipiam, nisi eas citius quo potero deliberavero concilio dicti domini nostri regis antequam publicentur seu deliberentur alicui personæ viventi.—Rymer, vii. 603. The early form in Norman French to the same effect is given in vol. vi. 709.

[2] See the permission given to the Master and Brethren of the Monastery of Burton in 1439:—Quæ quidem Bullæ Papales, per negligentiam et malam gubernationem custodum earundem, putrifactæ, vastatæ, et destructæ existunt. . . . Nos præmissa considerantes, de gratia nostra speciali, et de avisamento et assensu concilii nostri concessimus præfato Galfrido et confratribus suis . . . licentiam nostram regiam quod ipsi a prædicta sede bullas papales perquirere possint . . . quodque ipsi dictas bullas sic perquirendas acceptare et eas in executionem ponere . . . aliquo statuto vel ordinatione in contrarium factis non obstantibus. —*Ib.* x. 739.

processes.¹ The only exception to this rule of exclusion was the jurisdiction of the ecclesiastical courts in testamentary and matrimonial business. In these matters appeals to Rome were allowed until 1532, when they also were abolished. Testamentary causes were then trifling, as no devise of lands was allowed until the reign of Henry VIII., and the chattel wealth of individuals was small. It is clear that if lands had been alienable by will, the English people would not have permitted the title to them to be decided in a foreign court.² Even the parliament of Mary that passed the Act for the reconciliation of the kingdom to Rome declared "that the title of all lands, possessions, and hereditaments in this your [the Queen's] realm is grounded on the laws, statutes, and customs of the same . . . and in your courts only to be impleaded, ordered, tried, and judged, and none otherwise."³ Appeals in matrimonial suits were permitted, partly on the ground of the sacramental character attributed to the contract of marriage, and partly because they referred to strictly private and personal concerns.

We are not to be astonished if in spite of the most jealous precautions some appeals to Rome—other than in testamentary and matrimonial matters—occurred up to the

¹ For the reign of Richard II. see Rymer, vii. 644, 689, 698, 701, 702; viii. 33. For that of Henry IV. viii, 107, 155, 244, 291, 426, 654, 756. For that of Henry V. ix, 77, 190. For that of Henry VI. x. 739; xi. 14, 19, 48, 54, 212, 226, 256, 259, 468. For that of Edward IV. xi. 638. For that of Henry VII. xii. 648; xiii. 243. For that of Henry VIII. xiii. 340, 383, 469. The last quoted in the times of Henry VIII. is in the 8th of his reign, when he was still devoted to the Pope. Later on there is a pardon to Cranmer for the acceptance and publication of Papal bulls on his appointment to Canterbury. This was in 1533, xiv. 458.

² Edward II. would not allow, as being prejudicial to his crown and dignity, the transference of the personal or real property of the Templars to the Knights of St. John, though a Papal bull had so directed.—Rymer, iii. 337.

³ 1 & 2 P. & M. c. 8, 5, 34.

time when they were finally abolished. Many circumstances favoured their occasional allowance. Several of our Kings were on the best terms with the Pope, and did either tacitly permit appeals or did expressly consent to them. Others had but doubtful titles to the crown and desired the support of the Church. Hence they were unwilling to quarrel with its head until the abuse of appeals compelled them to interfere. At other times their attention was called away by our civil wars or by foreign contests, as in the case of Edward III. and Henry V. It is manifest that under such circumstances examples of appeals taking place are but of little weight to establish a right. One instance of opposition, when a stand is made and the right denied, is worth a hundred precedents which arose from the neglect, the permission, the connivance, or the devotion, of some of our Kings.

III. Until the alliance of King John with the Papacy, the English Church was, and had been from time immemorial, a thoroughly independent and self-managed institution. After the death of Henry III. who continued the alliance, a contest arose between England and the Papacy which ended in the enactment of the statutes of *Provisors* and *Præmunire*, by which all foreign interference with the Church was forbidden, except by leave of the King, and the ancient supremacy of our sovereigns over its external adjuncts was, once for all, re-established.

Before the Conquest perfect concord prevailed between the Church and the State. Ecclesiastical and temporal causes were heard, and ecclesiastical and temporal decrees were made in the same assemblies, local and national.[1] "Wise were also in former days," say the laws of King Ethelred, "those secular witan who first added secular laws

---

[1] Freeman, *Norm. Conq.* 4, 392.

to the just divine laws for bishops and consecrated bodies."[1] "Thrice a year," a law of Canute enacts, "let there be a burh-gemot, and twice a shire-gemot under penalty of the wite as is right unless there be need oftener. And let there be present the bishop of the shire and the ealdorman, and there let both expound as well the law of God as the secular law."[2] From the time of Augustine to the Norman Conquest it was the custom for English Kings with their prelates and temporal nobility to make ecclesiastical laws and to regulate the discipline of the Church within their dominions. The enactments of these mixed assemblies, in which the King usually presided, and which were always called by his authority, extended to many things which were spiritual in their nature. For example it was enacted that children should be baptized within thirty days from their birth;[3] that priests who had neglected to fetch chrism at the due time, or who had improperly denied baptism, should be punished;[4] that all persons should receive the communion at least three times in each year;[5] that all persons should learn the Lord's Prayer and the Creed, and that no person who was not acquainted with them should receive another to baptism or confirmation;[6] that marriages within certain degrees and with certain persons should not be contracted;[7] that widows should not remarry within twelve months of the death of the husband.[8] These assemblies also denounced the punishment of him who marketed or worked, or compelled

---

[1] Thorpe, *Ancient Laws and Institutes of England*, 143. Freeman regards this as a solemn condemnation by the national gemot of the practice of separating ecclesiastical and temporal legislation.—*N. C.* 1, 405, 4, 392.

[2] Thorpe, 165.

[3] *Ib.* 45. The penalty on the priest who neglected this duty was very heavy: thirty shillings if the child lived; if it died without baptism, forfeiture of all his property.

[4] *Ib.* 72. [5] *Ib.* 159. [6] *Ib.* 160, 397. [7] *Ib.* 135, 156. [8] *Ib.* 131, 178.

his servant to work, on Sundays or festival days; and of him who broke a fast day;[1] appointed times to be observed as festivals, and directed how they should be observed;[2] made rules for the payment of tithes and their allocation, and for the rendering of alms and the dues of the Church;[3] exhorted the subject to go frequently to confession and ordained how confessions were to be made;[4] enjoined and rewarded chastity in priests;[5] declared in what cases excommunications should be issued;[6] divided old and created new dioceses, as mentioned before in Wilfrid's case; gave bishoprics *in commendam*;[7] and appointed the saying of masses and other services for the King and his people in churches and monasteries.[8] In addition to these assemblies which legislated both on secular and religious matters, there were others during this period which were called for purely ecclesiastical affairs. Over these the King presided or they were called by his authority, and were also attended by the lay nobility.

The system of regulating the national Church in a mixed assembly of clerics and laymen continued for some of the reigns after the Conquest.[9] This appears from the summoning of many such assemblies, and also from the words of the Charter of William I. which separated the ecclesiastical from the civil courts. "Know ye that I have determined that the episcopal laws which have been in force until my time in the kingdom of England, being not well constituted or according to the precepts of the holy canons, should be

---

[1] Thorpe, 74, 173.   [2] *Ib.* 131, 136.   [3] *Ib.* 111, 146.
[4] *Ib.* 132, 402.   [5] *Ib.* 134.   [6] *Ib.* 16, 27, 149, 407.
[7] Diceto, 456. Twysden's *Scriptores*, x.
[8] Thorpe, 144.

[9] "For some of the first reigns after the Conquest, as well as before, State Councils and Synods were so much alike, that some of those which I have called State Councils and Parliaments and given already an account of as such, may as well be reputed ecclesiastical conventions or synods."—Hody, *Convocations*, pt. 3, 1.

amended in the council of the realm, and with the advice of my archbishops, bishops, abbots, and all the nobility of my kingdom."¹ William, influenced by his personal regard to Lanfranc, allowed him to hold councils or synods which were composed of ecclesiastics exclusively.² This was the first appearance of such assemblies in England.³ But though William permitted these councils to be called, he maintained strictly his prerogative of annulling or confirming their decrees. Eadmer tells us that he would not allow the archbishop in a general council of the bishops " to enact or prohibit anything that was not agreeable to his will, or had not previously been ordained by himself."⁴ The same policy was followed by his Norman successors. William Rufus would not allow a synod to be called during his reign. In that of Henry I. the ecclesiastical councils were either called by the King himself,⁵ or by his authority,⁶ or

---

¹ Thorpe, 213.

² Porro Willelmus rex in omnibus ei [Lanfranco] assurgebat aggaudebatque et ei et aliis quos in bono fervere audisset, permisitque ei concilia congregare.—Will. of Malmes., *Gesta Pont.* 66.

³ For the truth of this observation, examine the enumeration and description of the Anglo-Saxon Councils and Synods given by Hody in his history of Convocations. Freeman says:—" The series of ecclesiastical councils held by him [Lanfranc] get more and more distinguished from those common assemblies of the whole realm, which men of old had looked on as failing in their duty if they did not take order in all causes and over all persons, ecclesiastical and civil, within the English realm."—*Norman Conquest*, 4, 360.

⁴ Primatem quoque regni sui, archiepiscopum dico Cantuariensem seu Dorobernensem, si coacto generali episcoporum concilio præsideret, non sinebat quicquam statuere aut prohibere, nisi quæ suæ voluntati accommoda et a se primo essent ordinata.—Eadmer, *Hist. Nov.* 10. Concilia non sinebat [Willelmus] cogi nec quicquam ibidem statui nisi de voluntate sua omnia procederent.—Gerv. of Canterbury, 2, 63.

⁵ As the Council of London, 1108, was, which made provisions respecting the marriage of those in orders.—Eadmer, 193.

⁶ " Rege annuente," says Anselm, in the acts of the Council of 1102, which he himself drew up.—*Ib.* 193.

their decrees were confirmed by him.[1] But the tendencies of the time were in favour of a distinction between secular and ecclesiastical councils. In 1127 we have the first instance of an ecclesiastical council being held at the same time, but in a different place from the council of the State.[2] In the reign of Henry III. the word "parliament" was first applied to State councils, and "convocation" to synods. In the reign of Edward I. the distinction between the secular parliament and the clerical assembly was fully established. It is from this reign that convocations, used in a specific and not a general sense, and as we now understand the word, date. The origin of convocation and the manner in which it grew and overshadowed all other ecclesiastical conventions in England are curious and interesting.

It has been shown that William I. from his personal regard to Lanfranc permitted the archbishop to call purely ecclesiastical councils. These conventions were known by the name of Provincial assemblies, and at first consisted of bishops only, though in process of time others of the clergy were added for counsel or advice. William Rufus would not allow such assemblies to be called during his reign, but in that of Henry I. they were again summoned by the archbishop for the time being. The King, however, reserved and exercised the right of allowing and confirming their decrees. Provincial assemblies were exclusively ecclesiastical conventions summoned by the archbishop for ecclesiastical purposes only, and in them canons and constitutions were made for the faith and discipline of the Church, and

[1] Sciatis quod auctoritate regia et potestate concedo et confirmo statuta concilii a Willelmo Cantuariensi archiepiscopo et sancto Romanae ecclesiae legato apud Westmonasterium celebrati, et interdicta interdico. Carta Confirmationis Henrici I.—Rymer, i. 8, ed. 1816.

[2] Super his igitur Rex angiaratus concilium tenuit ad Rogationes apud Londiniam; et Willelmus archiepiscopus similiter in eadem villa apud Westminster.—Hen. of Hunt. 247.

remedies were provided for any disorders which had crept into it. They were summoned only occasionally and at irregular intervals, just as it seemed good to the archbishop, and, as long as they were confined to the affairs of the Church, they were not interfered with by the King. They seem soon to have gone out of use, for John de Athon, or Acton, who died in 1350, says that provincial assemblies had been discontinued for a hundred years before his time.[1] At these meetings subsidies and benevolences were granted by the clergy to the King above and beyond what was voted in parliament by the bishops and prelates. But as the clergy increased in number and wealth it was thought reasonable that they should contribute a larger and more regular share to the revenue of the State, and that for this purpose they should be convened as the necessities of the kingdom required. With this view Edward I. made an attempt to incorporate the whole body of the clergy with the parliament by the well-known *Præmunientes* clause. The clergy were reluctant to attend parliament, and preferred to continue to vote their supplies at their own meetings. Our Kings were content to indulge them in this, as all they wanted was to carry their point of obtaining grants. Accordingly they began to request the archbishops, at first without issuing a specific writ for that purpose, but afterwards commanded them by writ, to convene the clergy of their province in convocation for the purpose of voting supplies, and to these meetings the King sent his commissioners to exhort them to a ready and liberal supply. Convocation, we thus see, was a convention of the clergy summoned under the authority of the royal writ, and called entirely for a civil purpose, whereas Provincial assemblies were convened by the authority of the archbishop for the spiritual needs and affairs of the Church.

[1] Archbishop Wake, *State of the Church*, 91. Atterbury, *Convocation*, 7.

But in a very short time the convocations took the place of the provincial assemblies even as to spiritual concerns. Frequent meetings were burdensome to the clergy, and, when they met under the King's writ, it was convenient that they should before separating consider other matters. They took advantage of their grants of aids and taxes, just as the parliament did, to state their grievances to the King and to petition for redress. They laid hold of the opportunity of giving their money to obtain an enlargement of their privileges, and drew ecclesiastical affairs in which the polity and government of the Church were concerned under the cognizance of the convocations. After they had passed their votes of supply and drawn up their statements and petitions, they entered upon the consideration of spiritual matters. This they did under the authority of conciliary letters of the archbishop or by his mere consent, so that they were at the same meeting a convocation called by the King's writ for a purely civil purpose, and a provincial assembly deciding on Church affairs under the authority of the archbishop. Very soon after the establishment of these civil convocations, provincial assemblies as such were but seldom called, and both temporal and spiritual matters were treated in the former. Archbishop Wake informs us that provincial assemblies had been but rarely convened for a hundred years before the submission of the clergy in 1533.[1] Heylyn and Fuller were so struck with the disuse of provincial assemblies that they wrongfully attributed it to the effect of the statutes of *Præmunire*. The fact was that convocation had swallowed up provincial assemblies. Two circumstances, over and above the dislike of the clergy to be called from their homes to frequent meetings, contributed to this. Though convocation was provincially summoned and met in different provinces, yet, being convened about the same time and by

[1] *State of the Church*, 81.

the same authority, it came to be regarded as a national assembly of the whole clergy of England in two conventions.[1] As convocation was called to grant supplies to the King, it consisted of a much larger number than had been called to provincial assemblies, as the whole body of the clergy was represented in it.[2] It would seem as if the very name of provincial assemblies had been forgotten in the time of Henry VIII. For the clergy in their submission speak as if convocation were the only place in which they could make " canons, constitutions, ordinance provincial or other or by whatsoever name they shall be called," and promise that they will make no new canons " in their convocations in time coming" without the assent of the King. If provincial assemblies had not fallen into complete desuetude and oblivion, it is inconceivable that neither the King, who desired to deprive the clergy of *all* power of making canons or constitutions without his consent, or the clergy themselves, should have made no mention of such assemblies in the Act of Submission. From the first and during its whole existence, the convocation of each province has been convened by the King's writ, nor could it be summoned by any other authority,[3] and if its decrees were to the prejudice of the sovereign, his crown, or dignity, the clergy were required to revoke them.[4] In 1279, before provincial assemblies had

---

[1] *State of the Church*, 25.

[2] The earliest writ we have in the 9th of Edward II. runs:— "Requirimus et rogamus quatenus omnes prælatos, tam religiosos quam alios, ceterosque de clero provinciæ vestræ. . . . Convocari faciatis."

[3] "Where the king's humble and obedient subjects, the clergy of this realm of England, have not only knowledged according to the truth, that the convocations of the same clergy is, always hath been, and ought to be assembled only by the King's writ, but, &c. &c."—Preamble to the Submission of the Clergy, 25 Hen. VIII. c. 19.

[4] "If in anything they [the clergy] had exceeded their proper bounds and determined in such cases as did not belong to them to the prejudice

become merged in convocation, Archbishop Peckham called such an assembly at Reading in which certain constitutions infringing on the rights of the Crown were made. Edward I. brought the archbishop before parliament, and compelled him to make a solemn and public renunciation of his constitutions.[1]

Of legatine councils, that is, councils presided over by a Papal legate, and in which the two archbishops and the whole clergy of both provinces appeared, but little need be said. Such councils could be assembled only by the King's permission, as a Papal legate could not set his foot in the kingdom without the royal consent. In addition to this safeguard the clergy, after the enactment of the last statute of *Præmunire*, could not attend a legatine council without the license of the Crown. This is shown by the action of Queen Mary in 1555. In this year the Queen issued her letters patent allowing Cardinal Pole, as legate, to summon a council, and permitting the clergy to attend it. In earlier times, when a legatine council did meet, the King sent his commissioners to it, and by them forbade the legate to attempt the enactment of anything prejudicial to his royal crown or dignity.[2]

Of the independence and self-government of the English Church, and of its free action uninfluenced by external pressure, we have many examples both before and after the

---

of the King, his crown, or dignity, in that case their constitutions were not only accounted void of all force by the laity, but they were sometimes required themselves to repeal them."—Wake, *State of the Church*, 19.

[1] The recantation of Peckham is in Prynne, *Records*, 3, 235.

[2] Concilio jam incœpto, missi sunt ex parte domini regis Comes Lincolniensis Johannes et Johannes filius Galfridi et Willelmus de Ræle canonicus Sancti Pauli, ut dicto legato ex parte regis et regni inhiberent, ne ibi contra regiam coronam et dignitatem aliquid statuere attemptaret.—Matt. Par., *Chron. Maj.* 3, 417, sub ann. 1237.

Conquest. The case of Wilfrid has been already mentioned, in which an English council charged him with contumacy for preferring the judgment of a foreign see to that of a synod of his own country. At the subsequent council of Nidd, when the letters of the Pope in favour of Wilfrid were produced and read, and obedience was enjoined under the penalty of excommunication, the council took no notice of the menace, and pronounced the decrees of the former council to be unalterable. Archbishop Stigand, though he lay under the censures of Rome, was always recognised as Metropolitan by the English Church, until he was removed, at William's request, for political reasons. In 1070 Agelric, Bishop of Selsey, was deposed in the Synod of Winchester. The Pope ordered him to be restored and his case to be reviewed. No attention was paid to the Papal order, and Agelric continued deprived.[1] Archbishop Anselm proposed to introduce into England the Vatican decree that no ecclesiastic should receive investiture from the King's hands, or do him homage, and that no one should presume to consecrate any one who violated this decree.[2] The whole kingdom, the nobility, the bishops, and others of an inferior rank declared that they would rather drive Anselm from the country, and separate from the Roman Church than accept such a decree.[3] And when Anselm did actually refuse to do homage to Henry,

---

[1] Collier, 1, 243.

[2] Postquam revocatus ad episcopatum redii in Angliam, ostendi decreta apostolica quæ in Romano concilio præsens audivi; ne scilicet aliquis de manu regis aut alicujus laici ecclesiarum investituras acciperet, ut pro hoc ejus homo fieret, nec aliquis hæc transgredientem consecrare præsumeret.—Letter of Anselm to Paschal II., quoted by Twysden, *Vindication*, 16.

[3] Quod audientes rex et principes ejus, ipsi etiam episcopi et alii minoris ordinis, tam graviter acceperunt ut assererent se nullo modo huic rei assensum præbituros, et me de regno potius quam hoc servarent expulsuros et a Romana Ecclesia se discessuros.—*Ib.*

and to consecrate those to whom the King had given investiture of their sees, the bishops united with the secular nobility in advising that no obedience should be shown to the Roman Pontiff.[1]

The English prelates, who lived upon the spot, and were acquainted with the nature of the errors complained of, relaxed the rigour of Papal canons as they considered equitable. Thus they dispensed with the vows of those nuns who had taken the veil to preserve their chastity at the time of the Conquest.[2] In 1076, at the Council of Winchester, the decree of a council of Rome was modified. The Roman council had absolutely disqualified all married clergymen, Gregory VII. having declared that no saving grace could be bestowed by the ministration of married priests. The English bishops declined to carry out this decree, and permitted married priests who lived in castles or in country villages to exercise their functions.[3] In 1108 Henry I., wishing to secure the celibacy of the clergy, summoned an assembly of his nobles, and of the archbishops and bishops of England. There the King and his prelates, " with the assent of all his barons," settled the question of the marriage of those in orders.[4] The prelates and dignified

[1] Episcopis regnique proceribus ut sub alio rege solebant verba hinc inde ferentibus et in singulis regiæ voluntati parere certantibus, immo, ne Romani pontificis obœdientiæ subderetur summopere insistentibus.— Eadmer, 131.

[2] *Ib.* 124.

[3] Collier, 1, 249. At this time the larger and better portion of the English clergy were the sons of priests. We learn this from a letter of Pope Paschal to Anselm in 1107. " De presbyterorum filiis quid in Romana ecclesia constitutum sit fraternitatem tuam nescire non credimus. Cæterum quia in Anglorum regno tanta hujusmodi plenitudo est, ut major pene et melior clericorum pars in hac specie censeatur, nos dispensationem hanc sollicitudini tuæ committimus."—*Ib.* 185.

[4] Anselmus ... et Thomas electus ... Eboracensis ... et omnes alii Angliæ episcopi statuerunt in præsentia ejusdem gloriosi regis

clergy of England ever continued to do homage to their sovereign, though by so doing they incurred the danger of excommunication. When, upon their appointment, they applied to the King for the restoration of their temporalities, they renounced everything in the Papal bulls prejudicial to the prerogative of the Crown or to the laws of the land. These renunciations are to be found in every reign, from the first year of Edward II. "Forasmuch as," says Henry VII., on the occasion of his granting the bishopric of Bath and Wells to Cardinal Adrian, in 1504, "all and singular the archbishops and bishops of this our kingdom—whose nominations and promotions to the highest dignities appertain unto us—are bound by a certain peculiar prerogative, and by the laws and customs of the land hitherto undisturbed and inviolably observed, immediately and without delay upon their promotion not only to renounce publicly and expressly all clauses and words in the Papal bulls, which are or may be prejudicial to us, our heirs, our crown, our kingdom, or to the laws and customs of the realm, and to place themselves wholly at our pardon and grace in this respect, but also to take their corporal oath of homage and fidelity."[1] After this recital the King proceeds to appoint

Henrici, assensu omnium baronum suorum, ut presbyteri, diaconi, subdiaconi, caste viverent, et feminas in domibus suis non haberent.—Eadmer, 193.

[1] Cum omnes et singuli archiepiscopi et episcopi hujus nostri incliti regni, quorum omnium nominationes et promotiones ad ipsas supremas dignitates Nobis attinent, ex regali et peculiari quadam prærogativa jureque municipali ac inveterata consuetudine, hactenus in hoc regno nostro inconcusse et inviolabiliter observata, teneantur et astringantur statim et indilate post impetratas bullas apostolicas super eorumdem promotione, ad ipsam nostram nominationem ... non solum palam publice et expresse totaliter cedere et in manus nostras renunciare omnibus et quibuscumque verbis, clausulis et sententiis in ipsis bullis apostolicis contentis et descriptis quæ sunt vel quovismodo in futurum esse poterunt præjudicialia sive dampnosa nobis, hæredibus ... coronæ aut regno nostro juribusve consuetudinibus aut prærogativis ejusdem

three commissioners to take the renunciation and oath of the cardinal, who was then abroad.¹

The independence shown by the English bishops when acting in a body was, on several occasions, equalled by that of individuals of their order. Dunstan, Archbishop of Canterbury, refused to absolve a nobleman whom he had excommunicated, though ordered by the Pope to do so.² Lanfranc was commanded by the same authority, under the penalty of suspension from all the functions of his office, to proceed to Rome. Though he survived this order eight years, he neither went to Rome, nor, so far as it appears, sent an excuse for his disobedience.³ On another occasion Lanfranc, discovering that Baldwin, Abbot of St. Edmund's, had obtained a bull of exemption from Pope Alexander II., took the bull from the abbot and could not be induced to return it until about the end of his life.⁴ In 1150 Walter, Prior of Christ Church, Canterbury, and his convent, appealed to Rome—this was in the disturbed times of Stephen—in a dispute which he and his monks had with Theobald the archbishop. Theobald, "despising the appellant and him to whom the appeal was made," deposed Walter, and imprisoned him in the abbey of Gloucester as long as the archbishop lived.⁵ In 1186 Archbishop Baldwin disregarded the

regni nostri, et quoad hoc totaliter seipsos submittere et ponere in nostra bona venia et gratia, sed etiam juramentum fidelitatis et homagii, ad sancta Dei evangelia per eosdem respective corporaliter tacta, Nobis facere et præstare.—Rymer, xiii. 108.

¹ The form both of the renunciation and of the oath is set out in full in Rymer, and also by Burnet. The oath is well worth reading and considering.

² Collier, 1, 197.

³ *Ib.* 1, 263.

⁴ Quod factum Lanfrancus archiepiscopus moleste accipiens ipsum privilegium abbati abstulit, nec illud ei nisi circa finem vitæ suæ multorum precibus motus reddere voluit.—Eadmer, 133.

⁵ Sed archiepiscopus, suo excandescens impetu, adeo contempsit appellantem et eum ad quem appellatum est, ut conventum canibus

successive bulls of Urban III. and Clement III., respecting his disputes with the monks of Christ Church, and directed his secular clergy to teach in their sermons that Papal excommunications were of no effect in the diocese of Canterbury.[1] A few years later, when these disputes were settled by King Richard and his prelates, the authority of Rome, in the person of its legate, who had been deputed to arrange the quarrel, was carefully excluded. In 1195 Hubert, Archbishop of Canterbury, deposed Robert, Abbot of Thornly, and imprisoned him for a year and a-half in irons, notwithstanding his appeal to Rome.[2] In 1253, Boniface, Archbishop of Canterbury, received a Papal bull forbidding him to disturb the convent of St. Augustine by visiting, suspending, or excommunicating the conventual brethren. The archbishop glanced over the bull, and ordered it to be thrown into the fire.[3]

But the clearest and best evidence of the domestic and exclusive management of the English Church in the twelfth century is to be found in two letters of Pope Paschal II. These letters show beyond all doubt that, at the time when the Papal power was at its zenith, our national Church was a thoroughly self-governing body, possessed of its own system of ecclesiastical law and administration, and also that the Pope's power of visitatorial interference had no existence. The first letter is addressed to the King, and complains, as we have seen before, that no Papal nuncios or bulls were admitted into England without the permission of the sove-

---

compararet, et equos prioris violenter raperet, januas curiæ monachorum clauderet, et armatos custodes apponeret, divinum in ecclesia servitium per manum clerici interdiceret, monachos duos appellationem prosequentes interciperet, captos incarceraret, scripta et privilegia et expensas eisdem auferret.—Gerv. of Canterbury, 1, 145, 146.

[1] See *ante*, pp. 36–39.
[2] Roger de Hov. 3, 299.
[3] Quas literas vix perlectas jussit ignibus præsentari.—Matt. Par., *Chron. Maj.* 5, 415.

reign, and that there were no appeals or applications to the jurisdiction of the Roman See. The second letter is directed to the King and bishops, for the Pope was well aware how close the connexion between the State and the Church was in England. In this, Paschal says, "How the Church of Christ was founded at first it is not at present necessary to examine. But the maintenance and preservation of that Church ought to be referred to our consideration and action. St. Paul commands us to lay hands suddenly on no man, nor to be partakers of other men's sins, which precept of the apostle is thus explained by St. Leo: What is the meaning of sudden laying on of hands? It means, says that doctor of the Church, the giving of the sacerdotal character to those who are not of age for the honour, or who have not passed a proper examination, or who possess no merit or any experience to qualify them. How, then, can we impart the confirmation of the sacerdotal office to English bishops, when we have no knowledge either of their lives or learning? Our Saviour, when he gave over the charge of the Church to the apostle St. Peter, said to him, feed my sheep, feed my lambs. Now, by the sheep are meant the governors of the Church who, by the grace of God, are enabled to beget a spiritual issue. But how can we feed either the lambs or the sheep when we neither are acquainted with them or see them? when we have never heard of them nor they of us? From the apostles St. Peter and St. Paul the custom has been handed down to us, that the more weighty affairs of the Church should be managed or reviewed by our see. But you, in despite of this long-established custom, settle among yourselves the business relating to bishops, without even consulting us, notwithstanding that Victor, Pope and Martyr, declared that, though provincial bishops might examine an accusation against one of their order, they were not allowed to come to a decision without application to the Bishop of Rome.

Zepherinus, also Pope and Martyr, says the trials of bishops and other affairs of great consequence ought to be decided by the Papal Court. You will not allow the oppressed to make their appeal to the Apostolic See, though it has been decreed by the holy fathers in council that all persons aggrieved should have the privilege of appealing to the Papal Court. You venture, without our knowledge, to celebrate councils and synods, though Athanasius told the Church at Alexandria that in the great council of three hundred and eighteen bishops at Nice it was unanimously decided that no councils ought to be held without the knowledge of the Bishop of Rome. You see, therefore, that you have encroached greatly on the authority of the Papal See, and lessened its dignity. You even presume, without our sanction and knowledge, to make translations of bishops, an unwarrantable liberty, as such affairs ought not to be attempted except by our authority. If, for the future, you are willing to pay a due respect to the apostolic see, we shall treat you as brothers and sons; but if you persist in your obstinacy we shall shake off the dust of our feet against you, and deliver you up to the vengeance of God, as backsliders from the Catholic Church."[1]

We may sum up the contents of these letters in the words of a learned and conscientious Church historian[2]:—"Hence it appears that the English prelates held councils and managed the discipline and government of the Church within themselves. And in case of contest they looked upon a national synod as the last resort of justice. The matter was determined at home; there was no appeal in such cases, nor any recourse to a foreign authority. The suffragans, at their consecration, made only a profession of canonical obedience to their primate, without any reservation of submission to the Pope. Neither does it appear that any sees, excepting

[1] Paschal's letters are in Eadmer, 228, 232. [2] Collier, 1, 306.

those of York and Canterbury, made any acknowledgment to his Holiness. Neither was any English prelate obliged to attendance at Rome, unless the two archbishops, who were to go thither for their pall."[1]

It is certain that the decrees of the Pope or of Papal councils never had any force in England without their acceptance and confirmation in this country. The right of examining all external ecclesiastical legislation was always claimed and exercised by our early sovereigns, and until it was approved here, it was of no effect in the kingdom. Eadmer tells us that in the time of the Conqueror no letters from the Pope were permitted to be received by anyone in England until they had been shown to the King.[2] Later on in the twelfth century Pope Paschal states the same thing, and deplores the fact that no communication between the Roman See and England was allowed by the King and the English bishops. When it was proposed in 1235 to receive the canon for the legitimation of children born before the marriage of their parents, it was rejected. The King and parliament made a legislative interpretation of the canon of the Council of Lyons concerning bigamists.[3] Many decrees of the fourth Lateran Council never had the smallest authority in England. By that council it was amongst other things enacted that the goods of clergymen convicted of heresy should be forfeited to the

---

[1] The first ecclesiastic in England, under the degree of an archbishop, who took an oath to the Pope on his admission to office, was John, Abbot of St. Albans, in 1235, during the affliction of the English Church in the reign of Henry III. This oath, one of the conditions of which was that the taker should visit Rome every three years, was at first only required from archbishops when they received their pall. About 1230 it had been imposed also on bishops and abbots by Gregory IX. The oath taken by the abbot of St. Albans is in Matt. Par., *Chron. Maj.* 3, 318.

[2] Non ergo pati volebat quemquam . . . ejus [apostolici] literas si primitus sibi ostensæ non fuissent ullo pacto suscipere.—*Hist. Nov.* 10.

[3] 4 Edward I. c. 5.

Church; that all officers, secular and ecclesiastical, should swear at their admission to office to purge their districts of heresy; that temporal lords neglecting to perform the same duty should be excommunicated, and that in case of contumacy for a year, the Pope should absolve their subjects from their allegiance; that metropolitans should not fail to hold provincial councils every year; that cathedral and regular churches should not be vacant more than three months, and that then a lapse should take place; that no election should be valid that was made by a secular hand; that no one should have two benefices with cure; that, if a patron killed or maimed a clergyman, he should lose his right of patronage; that ecclesiastical persons should be free from taxes; all these were directly contrary to the laws and customs of England, and being such never obtained among us. Ecclesiastics in this country always paid taxes and joined in subsidies. In 1296 Boniface VIII. by his bull, "Clericis laicos," absolutely forbade under the penalty of excommunication the payment by the clergy of any tax whatever on the revenues of their churches.[1] The clergy at a meeting in Canterbury in the following year, pretending obedience to this bull, refused to make a grant to the King. Edward I., anticipating the general punishment of that body in the reign of Henry VIII. for their violation of the statutes of *Provisors* and *Præmunire*, outlawed their whole community, and confiscated the estates of the See of Canterbury.

IV. Previous to the betrayal of the Church by King John, English bishops, abbots, and priors, were nominated, translated, and deposed at home, without any interference on the part of the Papal Court.

Before the Norman Conquest the Anglo-Saxon Kings

---

[1] The bull is given in the Chronicle of William Rishanger, 462, Rolls Series.

appointed bishops and prelates as a matter of course and by their sole authority.¹ Ethelred gave Lichfield to Wilfrid.² Alfred made Asser Bishop of Sherborne, and Deneulphus Bishop of Winchester.³ Edward the Confessor made Robert first Bishop of London, and afterwards Archbishop of Canterbury. Edward also gave the bishopric of London to Robert's successor.⁴ Herman was appointed bishop of Sherborne by the same king.⁵ The legend of Wulstan, Bishop of Worcester, shows us the belief of our earliest ecclesiastical historians that the Anglo-Saxon Kings appointed their bishops by the delivery of the ring and pastoral staff. This prelate was charged by Lanfranc at the Synod of Westminster in 1076 with want of learning, and he was ordered to give up the ensigns of his authority. To this order Wulstan replied, " I know my own insufficiency, and in deference to the sentence of this holy synod I will give up my pastoral staff, not to you, however, but to him who gave it to me." With these words he rose, and, approaching the monument in which the remains of the Confessor reposed, he struck his crozier into the marble.⁶

The Norman Kings from the first claimed and exercised the right of appointing archbishops and bishops after taking

---

¹ "In the earlier ages of Anglo-Saxon history, it has been remarked by a learned antiquarian, that if the people were occasionally allowed to concur in the choice of their chief pastor, the instances of such elections are far less numerous than those which might be adduced to show that the nomination was vested in the sovereign. This power indicated in the earliest age of Saxon Christianity was fully established after the Danish invasion. When Edward the Confessor . . . notified the promotion of a prelate, it was by the promulgation of a charter which stated that he had given and granted the bishopric and all that thereto belonged without any reference to an election."—Hook, *Archbishops of Canterbury*, 1, 480.

² Will. of Malmes., *Gesta Pont.* 235.
³ *Ib.* 162.   ⁴ *Ib.* 145.   ⁵ *Ib.* 183.
⁶ Matt. Par., *Chron. Mag.* 2, 42.

counsel with the prelates and nobles of the kingdom. Thus the Conqueror appointed Lanfranc to the archbishopric of Canterbury by the bestowal of the ring and pastoral staff. Anselm was appointed in the same way by William Rufus. This mode of appointment prevailed during the reigns of William I. and William II., and also, with the exception of a short interval, during the reign of Henry I.[1] During these reigns, with the exception just mentioned, all the bishops and abbots of England, save the Bishop of Rochester, who held his barony of the Archbishop of Canterbury, and was selected by him,[2] were appointed in the same way. Eadmer tells us: "The very cause of the difference between the King [William Rufus] and Anselm seemed a new thing to this our age, and unheard of by the English from the time that the Normans began to reign, that I say not sooner. For from the time that William conquered the land, no bishop or abbot was made before Anselm, who did not first do homage to the King, and from his hand by the gift of the pastoral staff receive the investiture to his bishopric or abbacy, except two bishops of Rochester."[3] Our early ecclesiastical historians are full of instances of appointments to archbishoprics and bishoprics by the sole authority of these Kings. John de Bromton mentions three in one page, those of Canterbury, York, and Winchester.[4] The "Flores Historiarum" affords evidence to the same effect,[5] and Matthew Paris records no fewer than eleven such appointments in the reign of Henry I.

[1] Tunc rex [Henricus] ... exultans et hilaris per dationem virgæ pastoralis illico duos de clericis suis duobus episcopatibus investivit.—Eadmer, 141.

[2] A charter of John's recognising this right in the Archbishops of Canterbury is in Spelman's *Codex*.

[3] Eadmer, 2.

[4] Bromton, 968; Twysden, *Scriptores*, x.

[5] Rex quoque Henricus dedit Symoni clerico reginæ Wygorniensem,

Until the reign of John the Popes never pretended any right or laid any claim to the patronage of the English Church, nor had they any part to act in the appointment of English bishops either in collating, or consenting, or instituting, or inducting, or ordaining.[1] Of all which we have the best evidence, namely, that of Pope Paschal II. in his letters to the King and bishops quoted before. In these the Pope declares that he knew nothing of the English bishops, nor they of him, and that he had never so much as even heard of them; that all matters relating to the Church were settled in England without consulting him, and that bishops were translated without any reference to his authority.

In the reign of Henry I. à dispute arose between the King and Anselm respecting the investiture of prelates. An attempt or first step was made towards the disposal of English bishoprics by the Popes, which was frustrated by the firmness of the King. Anselm, acting under the late decree of the Vatican Council of 1099, which forbade ecclesiastics to do homage or receive investiture from lay persons, refused to consecrate bishops who had been invested by the King and who had done homage to him. We have seen the ill-success which attended Anselm's endeavours to carry out this decree, and that the English bishops and nobility threatened to separate from the Roman Church rather than receive it. The King, however, who had been greatly indebted to Anselm for his support against his brother Robert, was willing to yield something to the archbishop. Accordingly the dispute respecting investitures

---

Johanni archidiacono Cantuarensi Rofensem, Sefrido abbati Glostoniensi Cicestriæ præsulatum.—*Flores Historiarum*, 2, 51, R. S.

[1] In the last years of Stephen's reign Hugh Pusar, Elect of Durham, went to Rome for his consecration, not being able to obtain it from Henry, Archbishop of York, " Romam igitur electus una cum elegentium præcipuis aliquot profectus est, consecrationem ibi quam domi non poterat impetraturus."—Godwin, *De Præsulibus Angliæ*, 735.

was settled by a compromise at the Council of London in 1107, the King relinquishing the investiture by the ring and pastoral staff, but insisting on the homage, to which Anselm assented. Some of the bishops urged the King to stand firm on his ancient rights and to continue the old form of grant.[1] The King soon after, hearing that investiture by the ring and staff was practised by other sovereigns, resumed the old form, and on the death of Anselm conferred the archbishopric of Canterbury on Ralph, Bishop of London, by the gift of the ring and crozier.[2]

The custom that the King should confer archbishoprics, bishoprics, and abbacies by the gift of the ring and crozier appears to have gone out of use in the troubled times of Stephen. From this reign we find bishops elected by their chapters, and abbots by their monks, the royal assent being necessary for the meeting of the electors, and after the election for the purpose of confirming their choice. By the Constitutions of Clarendon in 1164 it was enacted that, when an archbishopric, bishopric, abbacy, or priory became vacant, the King should call together the principal dignitaries of the vacant church, and the election should be made in the royal chapel with the assent of the King and with the advice of such distinguished persons [3] as he might convoke. The manner in which the ceremony took place was, a deputation from the chapter or convent of the vacant church was summoned to court, and there the choice was made under the

---

[1] Quibusdam [episcoporum] ad hoc nitentibus, ut rex eas [investituras] faceret more patris et fratris sui, non juxta præceptum et obedientiam apostolici.—Rog. de Hoveden, 1, 164.

[2] Anno domini MCXIII. Rex Henricus dedit archiepiscopatum Cantuariensem Radulfo Londoniensi episcopo et illum per anulum et pastoralem baculum investivit.—Matt. Paris, *Chron. Mag.* 2, 140. Rex Henricus dedit archiepiscopatum Cantuariæ Radulpho et illum per anulum et baculum investivit.—*Flores Hist.* 2, 43.

[3] Et consilio personarum regni quas ad hoc faciendum vocaverit.

direction of the King. After the assent of the King was given, the elect paid his homage and did fealty to him as to his liege lord.¹ It is evident that this system threw the real nomination and selection of the successor into the King's hands. In this way all the bishops, including Becket himself, were appointed during the reign of Henry II. It is also to be remarked that when, after the murder of Becket, Henry was reconciled to the Pope at Avranches in 1172, no objection was made by the legates of the Pontiff to this mode of election, nor did they suggest any innovation or change in it.²

The first commencement of the quarrel between John and the Papacy arose from an election to the archbishopric of Canterbury. At the request of the King the Bishop of Norwich was elected by the monks of Christ Church. At a previous secret meeting the convent had chosen their subprior Reginald as archbishop.³ Both the elected appealed to Rome. Innocent III. pronounced the elections void and commanded the proctors of the convent who appeared before him to elect in his presence Stephen Langton. The proctors remonstrated with Innocent and told him that they could not proceed to an election without the consent of the King and of their community. At length they yielded, though unwillingly, and gave their assent to the election of Langton.⁴

¹ See Bishop Stubbs' preface to Roger de Hoveden, xix., and the twelfth chapter of the Constitutions of Clarendon.

² The conditions on which Henry made his peace are given by Gervase of Canterbury, 1, 238.

³ The monks of Christ Church had, up to a recent period, exercised the right of electing the primate of all England. On occasion of the three last vacancies the suffragan bishops of the province had claimed a consultative vote in the election. It was to defeat this claim that the monks elected their sub-prior.

⁴ Monachi vero ad hæc [Papæ verba] respondentes asserebant sibi non licere, præter consensum regium et sui conventus, canonicam electionem iu persona qualibet consentire vel sine illis electionem celebrare. . . . .

John at once objected to these proceedings and wrote a strong letter to the Pope.[1] He told Innocent that he had acted improperly in having chosen one who was unknown to him, and who had long lived in close association with his avowed enemies; that, contrary to the liberties of England, his consent had not been asked; that he would stand up for the rights of his crown even unto the death; that the Pope had forgotten how important his support was to his See; that the Papal Court had received richer returns and advantages from England than from all other kingdoms on this side the Alps; and that, as there was in England and the rest of his dominions an abundance of learned and sufficient prelates, he should in future be contented with their services, and not beg for justice or judgment from foreigners.[2] John refused to admit Langton, and for six years held out against interdict, excommunication, and attempted deposition. The long duration of John's opposition to the Pope, his march towards Scotland, his successes in Wales, and his departure for Ireland during this interval, all assure us that the King was supported by English opinion and that he felt himself secure. The country was by no means during this period the scene of pious horror that some writers have described. All things proceeded pretty much as usual, and the people conducted themselves with their

Monachi quoque excommunicationis sententiam incurrere metuentes, licet inviti et cum murmuratione, assensum tamen præbuerunt.—Matt. Par., *Chron. Mag.* 2, 515.

[1] *Ib.* 517.

[2] Compare with these words of John the lofty language of the Act of Henry VIII. in restraint of Appeals. "The English Church . . . . always hath been reputed and also found of that sort, that both for knowledge, integrity, and sufficiency of number, it hath been always thought, and is also at this hour, sufficient and meet of itself, without the intermeddling of any exterior person or persons, to declare and determine all such doubts, and to administer all such offices and duties as to their rooms spiritual doth appertain."

usual loyalty. Notwithstanding his excommunication John observed his wonted religious observances, and distributed his accustomed charities and doles to convents in distress and to the poor; nor is there any mention of these gifts from an unholy hand being refused.[1] He certainly met with but little opposition from the bishops and clergy. He held a convention of all the prelates of England, says the chronicler, in 1210, to which abbots, priors, abbesses, Templars, Hospitallers, &c., repaired.[2] The Cistercian Monks throughout the country continued to celebrate divine service notwithstanding the interdict.[3] Elections to bishoprics and the consecration of the elect took place as usual.[4] Five of that order left the country, but when three of these five by command of the Pope ordered those bishops who remained at home and the other prelates of the kingdom to publish the excommunication against the King, the order was not attended to.[5] The hostility of the Papacy had in no way weakened John's prestige or diminished his resources, for he collected on Barham Downs the noblest army which had been seen in England since the Norman invasion. His fleet, too, was far more powerful than that of France, from

[1] See an interesting note of Lingard in the appendix of his second volume.

[2] Deinde Londonias cum festinatione properans, fecit omnes Angliæ prælatos in sua præsentia convenire. Venerunt autem ad hanc generalem vocationem abbates, priores, abbatissæ, Templarii, Hospitalarii, custodes villarum ordinis Cluniacensis, et aliarum regionum transmarinarum cujuscunque dignitatis et ordinis.—Matt. Par., *Chron. Mag.* 2, 530.

[3] *Ib.* 524.

[4] Hugh to Lincoln, Walter to Lichfield, Henry to Exeter.—*Ib.* 526, 531. Godwin, in his *De Præsulibus Angliæ*, page 504, mentions a fourth, Nicholas de Aquila, who was consecrated in 1209. It is manifest that if the interdict had been observed, no bishop could have been elected or consecrated.

[5] Sed cum episcopi jam dicti confratribus suis qui in Anglia remanserant episcopis aliisque ecclesiarum prælatis publicationem sententiæ auctoritate apostolica commisissent, effecti sunt universi metu regis vel

which an attack was feared, and which he destroyed. But unhappily John irritated his own subjects, and his cruelty and vices drove his barons into a conspiracy against him. To save himself from domestic danger John suddenly altered his policy, contracted a shameless alliance with the Papacy, and betrayed the independence of the English Church.

Immediately on the conclusion of this alliance the Pope sent a general bull to his legate in England authorizing him to fill up at his pleasure all the vacant bishoprics and abbacies in the kingdom, and enjoining him to quell such as might be contumacious by the censures of the Church, all right of appeal being taken away.[1] The legate abused his authority. Acting on this bull, he rejected the advice of the prelates of England, and bestowed the highest offices of the Church upon indigent and ignorant persons. When some appealed to Rome, he suspended them from their benefices, not even allowing them a penny of their own money to pay the expenses of the journey.[2] The parochial churches he distributed among his own followers without regard to the rights of patrons. For which, says the old chronicler, he deserved the malediction of many, inasmuch as he changed justice into injury, and judgment into favouritism.[3]

The proceedings of the legate were so outrageous that Stephen Langton—who had by this time obtained possession of his archbishopric—called a meeting of his suffragans at Dunstable to consider the alarming state of the Church. These prelates were indignant at seeing unworthy and illiterate persons intruded "more by force than by canonical

---

favore canes muti non audentes latrare. Unde injunctum sibi officium exequi dissimulantes, in mandatis apostolicis secundum juris ordinem minime processerunt.—Matt. Par., *Chron. May.* 526.

[1] Si qui vero contradictores fuerint vel rebelles, tu eos per censuram ecclesiasticam, appellatione remota, compellas.—*Ib.* 2, 570.

[2] *Ib.* 571. [3] *Ib.*

election" into the bishoprics and abbacies of England.¹ After consideration the archbishop sent two clerics to prohibit the legate from further appointing to the vacancies and to interpose an appeal to Rome. The legate paid no attention to the appeal beyond sending Pandolph to Rome to counteract the efforts of the English prelates. The subsequent proceedings at Rome illustrate the nature of the alliance between John and the Pope. Pandolph vilified the character of Langton and the English bishops, while he declared that he had never before seen so humble and modest a King as John. Simon Langton, a brother of the archbishop, could not obtain a hearing, and the legate was triumphant.

The alliance between the Crown of England and the Papacy continued during the remainder of John's reign and the whole of that of his son, Henry III., a period of more than fifty years. This interval may be described as the captivity of the Anglo-Catholic Church. An attempt was made to govern our national Church from a distant country and by strangers, and the experiment failed lamentably. We have a full account of the afflictions of the English clergy during this disastrous period in the pages of the *Chronicles of St. Alban's*. Appeals to Rome were multiplied, and beggared the bishops, prelates, and inferior orders. Shameless simony and extortions of every kind prevailed in the Church. The rights of patrons, both ecclesiastical and lay, were disregarded. The authority of ordinaries was rendered insignificant by the constant interference of Rome, by exemptions, appeals, suspensions, and *non-obstantes*,² so that

¹ Moleste enim supra modum ferebant quod legatus . . . illis inconsultis . . . in ecclesiis vacantibus prælatos minus sufficientes posuerat, intrusione magis quam electione canonica.—*Ib.* 571.

² Item gravatur [regnum] ex multiplici adventu illius infamis nuntii, *non obstante*, per quem juramenti religio, consuetudines antiquæ, scripturarum vigor, concessionum auctoritas, statuta, jura, et privilegia,

a bishop who attempted the pastoral administration of his diocese was cramped at every step and was in perpetual danger of excommunication. The parochial system was crippled by the innumerable privileges showered on the mendicant orders, by the loss of the lucrative functions of the priesthood, and by the impropriation of benefices to monkish institutions. Inferior Papal agents, who did not dare, owing to the rule of law, to take the name of legate, suspended the prelates of England until they had satisfied their exactions. On one occasion Papal warrants were sent to *three* bishops to provide benefices for three hundred Italians, and till they had done so, these prelates were suspended from the bestowal of livings.[1] The bishops, abbots, dignitaries, and rectors of England were oppressed, and the wealth of the Church extorted by procurations, interdicts, excommunications, suspensions, provisions, forced loans, and compulsory pensions. Ignorant and unworthy foreigners who did not speak the English language, and who did not reside in the country, were intruded into benefices without even consulting the diocesans. Bishops were created without the consent of the King or State. Nay, anyone who obtained that favour from the Pope was allowed to hold a bishopric and enjoy its emoluments, though not a bishop, but only a perpetual elect.[2] In a letter of remonstrance addressed to the Pope in 1245 by "the community of England," it was stated that the Italians carried from the

debilitantur et evanescunt.—Complaint of the English people to the Pope at the Council of Lyons, 1246, *Ib.* 4, 528.

[1] Misit dominus Papa sacra præcepta sua domino Cantuariensi archiepiscopo Ædmundo, et Lincolniensi et Sariberiensi episcopis, ut trecentis Romanis in primis beneficiis vacantibus providerent, scientes se suspensos a beneficiorum collatione, donec tot competenter provideretur.—*Ib.* 4, 31.

[2] Cæterum quod videre non consuevi, concedit Papa ob favorem sæcularem, ut aliquis episcopatum obtineat, nec tamen episcopus existat, sed electus sempiternus.—Words of Bishop Grossetete, *Ib.* 5, 406. Aymer

kingdom annually more than 60,000 marks, a sum greater than the revenue of the country. In the words of a monk devoted to the Papacy: " England became a spoil and a desolation to strangers, like a vineyard without a wall, common to every wayfarer and to be rooted out by wild boars; illiterate persons of the lowest class, armed with the bulls of the Roman Church and bursting with threats, daily presumed, despite of the sacred privileges we enjoy from our holy ancestors, to plunder the revenues left by pious men for the maintenance of religion, for the support of the poor, and for hospitality to pilgrims, and by thundering forth sentences of excommunication obtained at once what they demanded. Woe to England which, once the chief of provinces, the mistress of nations, the mirror of the Church and the pattern of religion, is now become tributary; ignoble persons have trampled her under foot, and she has fallen a prey to degenerate men."[1] Edmund, Archbishop of Canterbury, who was afterwards canonized, in despair went into voluntary exile rather than look upon the oppression of the Church, and there he was wont to exclaim: " It were better to die than witness the sufferings of one's people and of the saints upon earth."[2]

A single instance will bring home to us, more clearly than pages of narration, the state to which the English Church was reduced, and the manner in which her rights were violated without a hope of remedy either from the Pope or from his ally the King.[3] One day, in 1256, three strangers from Rome entered the Cathedral of York while its officials were

---

de Valence was bishop elect of Winchester, and long enjoyed its revenues, though not consecrated.

[1] *Ib.* 3, 389, 390; 4, 10.

[2] O quam melius esset mori quam videre mala gentis suæ et sanctorum super terram.—*Ib.* 4, 72.

[3] Quibus talia persuadentibus ait [rex] "nec volo nec audeo domino

engaged at dinner. They inquired from a person who happened to be praying there which was the Dean's stall. On receiving a reply two of them conducted the third to the stall, and said to him: "Brother, by the Pope's authority we install you." Thereupon the intruder took possession. When the outrage was reported to the Archbishop, Sewal, and the canons, they were indignant that such a noble prebend and office should be taken possession of by an unknown and despicable person.[1] Sewal at once appealed to the Pope, but the only answer he got was a sentence of suspension.[2] The intruder was neither punished nor removed, for he was supported by Papal favour and protection. At last, after much controversy, he consented to receive an annual pension of a hundred marks—a very large sum in those days[3]—until he was better provided for. As for the good archbishop, the Pope laid a heavy hand upon him, and ordered him to be ignominiously excommunicated throughout England with tapers lighted and bells ringing in order to weaken his determination to support the rights of his Church. Sewal was oppressed, we are told, because he would not bestow the revenues of his cathedral upon unknown and unworthy persons from beyond the Alps, nor would he bend to the will of the Pope, or abandon the rules of justice. On which account, adds the chronicler, the more he was cursed

Papæ in aliquibus contradicere." Et facta est in populis desperatio nimis deploranda.—*Ib.* 4, 10.

[1] Absurdum namque et omni rationi dissonum, immo detestabile, eis merito videbatur, tam nobilem præbendam, tam arduum officium despicabili et ignoto sic intruso conferri permittere.—*Ib.* 5, 586.

[2] Fraudulenti tamen Romanam curiam de qua venerant adeuntes illum bonum verum et modestum, archiepiscopum videlicet, interdici fecerunt.—*Ib.* 586.

[3] Of the value of this pension we may judge if we remember that the salary of Walter de Merton, Chancellor of England in 1260, was 400 marks.

by the Pope, the more was he blessed by the people, though secretly for fear of the Romans.[1]

The manifold oppressions and exactions of the Papacy during this period were not without their fatal effects on the people.[2] The general indignation vented itself in a widespread conspiracy. Letters from "the whole community of those who would rather die than be put to confusion by the Romans" were sent to the bishops and chapters throughout the kingdom. All persons were forbidden, under threats of having their property burned, to pay to the Italians the revenues of churches or the rent of land held from them. The barns of the Roman clergy were pillaged, and the corn collected for their tithes was sold throughout the country by masked armed men for the good of the district or distributed to the poor. An investigation which was ordered on the remonstrance of the Pope revealed the national character of the outbreak. It was discovered that among the principals and abettors of these acts of violence there were bishops, deans, and archdeacons, besides many knights and laymen. Some of the sheriffs and their officers were implicated and imprisoned, or fled to avoid punishment.[3]

But the effects of the mismanagement of the Church were not limited to an explosion of popular excitement. A deep impression was made on the minds of the people and the foundations of doubt were laid. It was in the nature of

---

[1] Matt. Par., *Chron. Mag.* 5, 658.

[2] The letter of the nobles, clergy, and people of England to the Pope in 1246 contains a remarkable expression. They declare that unless the King and kingdom be quickly freed from the grievances mentioned in their complaint "we must make a wall of defence for the house of the Lord and the liberty of the kingdom, which we have hitherto forborne to do out of our respect for the Apostolic See." Nisi de gravaminibus domino regi et regno illatis rex et regnum citius liberenter, oportebit nos ponere murum pro domo Domini et libertate regni. Quod quidem ob apostolicæ sedis reverentiam hucusque facere distulimus.—*Ib.* 4, 534.

[3] *Ib.* 3, 208-18.

things that dissatisfaction with the discipline and external economy of the Church should precede questionings as to its teaching.[1] But the interval between discontent with an institution, and doubt of the principles on which it rests, is short indeed. To use the words of the monkish chronicler: "The devotion of the English clergy and people to their mother, the Church of Rome, and to their father and pastor, the Pope, was fast expiring, and the small fire of the true faith was almost reduced to ashes hardly able to emit a single spark.[2] This feeling however, which was largely due to despair, lasted only till the State, under the first Edward and his successors, again assumed its ancient supremacy over the temporal adjuncts of the national Church, rescued that Church from the domination of foreign ecclesiastics, restored to it order and decency, and thereby increasing its moral and spiritual influence, revived the devotional sentiment which is engrained in an earnest and enthusiastic people such as the English are.

[1] Et quod gravissimum est, diatim inter ecclesiam et populum odium venenosum suscipit incrementum.—*Ib.* 5, 357.

[2] *Ib.* 5, 535.

CHAPTER II

FROM THE REIGN OF EDWARD I TO THE END OF THE REIGN OF HENRY VII

SECTION I

THERE never was a more gradual or more natural progress than that of the Papacy to the eminent position and authority which it so long enjoyed. Much stress has been laid on the False Decretals, and some writers have ascribed this progress to their publication; but it may be asserted with certainty that if these fabrications had never appeared, the result would have been the same. The immediate and universal acceptance of these Decretals was a sign and accompaniment of the growth of the Papal influence, not the cause of it. Doubtless they rendered more determinate and supplied the legal titles for the steps of the Papal advance, but beyond this they effected but little. It is difficult to see how falsifications, not written exclusively in the interests of the Papacy,[1] were followed by such important consequences as have been attributed to them, if there had not been other and far deeper causes at work. It was not by skilfully devised claims and lofty assumptions, but by real deserts, that the early Popes took captive the affection and veneration of Europe, and that a distant bishop imposed a willing and grateful obedience on the Western world. From an early period, and long before the appearance of the False Decretals, all things portended and led up to the rise of a theocracy situated at Rome, and lodged in the hands of a single person.

[1] They were designed to serve the bishops against metropolitans and sovereigns. The bishops everywhere eagerly adopted them.

Confining ourselves to merely human considerations, we can discern many of the causes which contributed to this result. The majestic unity of the Roman Empire had left an impression which was still fresh in the minds of all. So strong was this feeling for the first four centuries after the fall of the Imperial government that separate nationalities were hardly conceivable, and the notion of distinct kingdoms had not as yet overcome the idea of a universal monarchy.[1] The general belief that the Pope was the heir and successor of St. Peter, and that the superintendence of the Church had been bequeathed by its divine Founder to that apostle; the dignity of the imperial city, and the fact that it was the single apostolic Church, and the seat of the only patriarchate in the West; the filiation of the Western Churches to that of Rome, which had planted the majority of them; the eminent position which the Popes enjoyed as the representatives of the Roman republic and the delegates of the Eastern Emperors, and the exercise by them of political power long before the donation of Pepin;[2] the necessity of a spiritual centre to maintain unity of doctrine; the separation of the clergy into a distinct class dispersed throughout all lands requiring their having a common head; the acquisition of an independent temporal sovereignty; the confusion and anarchy consequent on the fall, first of the Roman Empire and afterwards of the Carolingian dynasty; and the universal conviction that there was nothing to control the disorders of the times save the influence of religion:—all these causes tended towards the growth of the Papal authority. At the moment when political unity

---

[1] As late as the beginning of the fourteenth century Dante believed that the only cure for the calamities of the time was a universal monarchy.—See his treatise *De Monarchia*.

[2] The part which Pope Leo the Great played in saving Rome from Attila in 452, and again in 455 in mitigating the ferocity of Genseric, illustrates what is stated in the text.

expired, religious unity arose, and when the nations of
Europe banded themselves as one people for a holy war
against the religion of Mahomet, the movement found its
head and centre in Rome.

The theocracy which thus grew up at Rome was gladly
accepted by the Western nations; and as in an early stage of
society no division between religion and law is recognized,
and the priest is the supreme ruler and legislator, the Popes
exercised a general superintendence over European nations.
This state of affairs continued till the feeling arose—a feeling
which is sure to arise sooner or later in all communities—
that there is a real distinction between the temporal and
spiritual power. Of the growth of such a feeling we have
an example even in the Jewish theocracy when the Israelites
rejected their judges and asked for a king. As early as the
eleventh century this sentiment had acquired force, particularly
in England, as we see by the resistance offered by our Norman
Kings to the Papal encroachments. But the Popes shut their
eyes to the growing change of opinion, and made the mistake
of attempting to maintain their theocratic claims long after
their maintenance was possible. In the presence of a rising
sentiment which was to weaken, if not destroy, their influence
in temporal matters, they insisted that all worldly power
depended immediately on them, and aimed at absorbing
everything, sacred or secular, within their jurisdiction. As
the opposing force gathered strength, their claims rose
higher, and they refused to learn the lesson which temporal
sovereigns were pressing on them, viz. that the subjection
due to the spiritual power by secular governments is a moral
and not a material subjection. Instead of taking this lesson
to heart, the Popes deliberately set themselves to depreciate
the kingly office,[1] and asserted a temporal authority which

[1] "Quis nesciat reges et duces ab iis habuisse principium, qui Deum
ignorantes superbia, rapinis, perfidia, homicidiis, postremo universis pene

menaced every monarch in Europe.¹ Corrupted by the possession of an earthly sovereignty, they mixed up spiritual and temporal jurisdiction, so that in many cases it was impossible to say whether they were acting as secular rulers or as pontiffs. They confounded the affairs of their own principality with religious matters, and diverted their aims from the moral government of Europe to mere schemes of temporal aggrandizement. They aspired to make the kingdoms of Europe feudally dependent on the See of Rome.² They claimed the prerogative of trying, condemning, and deposing sovereign princes, and of interfering civilly with the social economy of every nation in the West. The natural consequences of this conduct on the part of the Popes followed. The necessity of separating the spiritual from the temporal power became evident to all. The supreme priest was lost in the secular prince, and the Roman Pontiffs came to be regarded by sovereigns and States rather as political antagonists than as spiritual fathers and guides. The governments of Europe in self-defence were obliged to take precautions as against the common aggressor, and to vindicate their own temporal authority.

France was the first Continental nation which made a decisive stand against the continuance of the exercise by the Popes of a temporal authority, and proclaimed the independence of her monarchs in secular affairs. Louis IX. took the first step in 1268 when he issued the earliest Pragmatic

sceleribus, mundi principe diabolo videlicet agitante, super pares licet homines dominari, cœca cupiditate et intolerabili præsumptione affectaverunt?—Quoted by Bossuet from the *Epistles of Gregory VII.*

¹ Nos imperia, regna, principatus, et quicquid habere mortales possunt, auferre et dare posse.—Words of Gregory VII. Platina in *Vita Gregorii VII.*

² At the commencement of the fourteenth century the Papacy claimed direct feudal sovereignty over eight kingdoms of Europe, viz. Naples and Sicily, Castile, Aragon and Valentia, Portugal, England, Scotland, Poland, Hungary.—Greenwood, *Cathedra Petri*, 6, 318.

Sanction, which laid the foundations of the self-management of the French Church, and of what have since been called the Gallican liberties. This ordinance secured to the prelates and other patrons their rights of patronage, and freedom of election to the several churches. It also forbade any tax or pecuniary exaction being levied by the Popes without the consent of the King and the French clergy.[1] In 1294 Boniface VIII. ascended the Papal throne. In a bull, *Ausculta fili*, directed to the King of France, Philip le Bel, in 1301, this Pontiff declared in general and figurative language that the King was subject to him, as the sovereign Pontiff of the ecclesiastical order. In the same year a shorter bull, *Deum time*, dated the same day as the longer one, was circulated throughout France, and it was alleged by the King and his chancellor that Boniface was its author. In this shorter bull it was asserted curtly and distinctly that the King was subject to the Pope both in temporal and spiritual matters.[2] Though some French historians assert that the latter bull was the production of Boniface, it is impossible to believe that this was the case, and the Pope and the Roman Curia always denied it.[3] But whether the short bull was the popular version of the longer one, or the official abstract of it, or was a mere forgery, the belief that the Pope had made such claims was sufficient to set France on fire. Philip immediately summoned the States General to take into consideration the pretensions of

---

[1] *Traitez des Droits et Libertez de l'Eglise Gallicane*, 1, 46, 1731.

[2] "Deum time et mandata ejus observa. Scire te volumus quod in spiritualibus et temporalibus nobis subes; beneficiorum et præbendarum ad te collatio nulla spectat, et si aliquorum vacantium custodiam habes, fructus eorum successoribus reserves; et si quæ contulisti, collationem hujusmodi irritam decernimus, et quantum de facto processerit, revocamus; aliud autem credentes hæreticos reputamus." This is the whole alleged bull.

[3] Sismondi in his History, and Drumann in his *Geschichte der Bonifacius* have examined this question. They are of opinion that the

the Pope. The nation was unanimous,[1] and declared that the Pope was not possessed of any temporal jurisdiction or authority in France, and that the King was in secular matters subject to God alone. In 1302 Boniface issued his well-known bull, *Unam Sanctam*, in which it was asserted that both the temporal and spiritual sword were at the command of the Church, and that the subjection of every human being to the Roman Pontiff was an article of faith necessary to salvation.[2] In the following year the States General of France denounced Boniface as an usurper of the pontifical throne, and appealed to a general council of the Church against him. The principal effect of these proceedings was to disclose the decline of the papal authority, and to unite the French people as one man in their opposition to the claims of the Pope.

For the times were changed, and a new epoch had arrived; an epoch which refused to the priest the administration of the commonwealth, and demanded the complete transference of the temporal authority to secular sovereigns. It was felt that a Papal universal monarchy, superintending the Kingdoms of Europe, was no longer possible, and that the Popes

---

short bull was not the production of the Pope. Bossuet, in his *Defensio*, speaks guardedly. At first he implies that Boniface issued the bull, then admits that it has been doubted. Non desunt qui dubitent, verane an falsa sit parva ea epistola Bonifacii VIII., quam an. 1301 toto regno divulgatam, eodemque tempore confutatam a tot gravibus viris, regia quoque autoritate combustam vidimus. Verum id nihil nostra interest, dummodo apud nos constet, omnibus curæ fuisse, ne apud Francos doceretur, regem in spiritualibus ac temporalibus papæ subesse.—Pars 1, lib. 3, cc. 23, 24.

[1] "Quod ergo regia potestas alteri quam Deo in temporalibus subjici diceretur, id non modo regi, sed etiam universæ genti adeo intolerabile visum, ut nulla unquam in re fuerit omnium ordinum tanta consensio."—*Defensio* &c. 1, lib. 3, c. 23. Philip obtained upwards of 700 acts of adhesion from the prelates, nobility, religious houses, and towns of France.

[2] Porro subesse Romano pontifici omnem creaturam, declaramus, dicimus, definimus, et pronunciamus omnino esse de necessitate fidei.

should henceforth be limited to the exercise of their spiritual authority. Mankind had begun to recognize that there were two governments in the world, each of them supreme in its own sphere, and independent of one another. Between the era of Gregory VII. and the reign of Philip le Bel a profound revolution in opinion had silently accomplished itself. How great that revolution was, and what a change had come over the general conception respecting the relation of temporal governments to the spiritual power, will clearly appear if we recall and compare two historical scenes. The one is that of Canossa, where an Emperor, the acknowledged supreme temporal ruler in Europe, with naked feet and in a woollen shirt waited for three days in frost and snow on the good pleasure of a Pope.[1] The other is that of Philip le Bel, persecuting and hounding to death an able and imperious Pope, without a voice in Europe being raised to protest against the iniquitous conduct of the French King.[2] How are we to account for such dissimilar events? The fact was that the Papacy had, to a certain extent, lost its hold on public opinion, and Kings and States had awakened to the perception that there were important interests which lay outside the spiritual domain. The time had come when a theocracy no longer satisfied the wants of society, and the inevitable contest which accompanies the separation of the temporal from the spiritual power had commenced. Sovereigns were resolved to take into their own hands the management of their secular concerns without reference to the judgment of any earthly authority. At the commencement of the fourteenth century the idea of separating the two domains had become general, and had ripened

---

[1] Platina, in *Vita Gregorii VII.*

[2] Even our ecclesiastical chroniclers have not a word of pity for Boniface. Walsingham and Rishanger say that his death was the fulfilment of the prophecy of his predecessor, Celestine V., that he would "die like a dog." Ascendisti ut vulpes, regnabis ut leo, morieris ut canis.

into practical working, as was shown by the almost strictly contemporaneous movements in France, England, and Germany. In 1301 France proclaimed that the Pope possessed no temporal jurisdiction in that country. In the same year a letter was sent to the Pope, Boniface VIII., in the name of the English people, declaring that their King was not bound to submit his rights over Scotland, or in other temporal affairs, to the Pope, and that, if the King were willing to do it, his subjects would not permit him even to attempt it.[1] In Germany, at the diet of Frankfort in 1338, it was laid down as a principle of public law that the imperial dignity was dependent on God alone, and that the election of an Emperor did not require the confirmation of the Pope.[2]

The insular position of England and the national character of its inhabitants had, no doubt, their effects in determining the relation of their Church to the Papacy. But there was another circumstance which more than any other contributed to its independence and self-government. At the time when the Popes, beginning with Gregory VII., commenced their attacks on temporal sovereigns, England was the only strong central government in Europe. France, Italy, and Spain, as united kingdoms, had no existence except on maps; and in Germany the great vassals in alliance with the Pope were undermining the imperial authority. In these countries the local Churches—for the term national can hardly be applied to them—could not expect any support from the civil power,

---

[1] Nec etiam permittimus aut aliqualiter permittemus, sicut nec possumus, nec debemus, præmissa tam insolita, indebita, præjudicialia, et alias inaudita, prælibatum Dominum, nostrum Regem, etiamsi vellet, facere seu modo quolibet attemptare.—Walsingham, *Hist. Ang.*, 1, 96; Rymer, ii. 873. The letter was signed by a hundred and four earls and barons, and it declares that they had authority to represent the whole nation.

[2] The statutes of Frankfort were confirmed at the subsequent Diet of Metz, in 1347, and the encroachments of the Papacy on the liberties of the empire were finally repudiated.

nor was there any authority under the protection of which they could resist the claims of the Popes to monopolize the entire administration of ecclesiastical matters. It was wholly different in England. In this kingdom there was a powerful and compact monarchy, able and willing to repel the encroachments of the Papal Court,[1] and by the side of the monarchy there stood a real national Church, completely organized, with a regular hierarchy appointed by the sovereign, having its representatives in the councils or synods of the kingdom, possessing a large influence in ecclesiastical legislation, and owning the supremacy of the King over its civil establishment. In addition, the visitatorial jurisdiction of Papal legates was jealously excluded, and, as we have seen, no Papal bulls or excommunications could be received into the kingdom until they were examined and approved by the sovereign. It would be hardly possible to find an institution so carefully guarded and hedged round with precautions against external interference. We see, in consequence, that the connexion between the English Church and State and the Papacy was never so close—except during one unhappy period—as that of Continental Churches and kingdoms. There was always a marked tendency in the English policy to confine the Roman Pontiffs to their spiritual authority. We have already considered the supremacy of the Saxon Kings over the Church, and their claims to govern and regulate it. William I. maintained his supremacy over the

[1] The curt and decisive answer of William I. to the request of Gregory VII. that he should do homage for his kingdom is highly illustrative. Gregory had asked for a more regular payment of Peter's pence, and that William should profess himself his man:—" Hubertus legatus tuus, Religiose Pater, ad me veniens ex tua parte me admonuit quatinus tibi et successoribus tuis fidelitatem facerem, et de pecunia quam antecessores mei ad Romanam ecclesiam mittere solebant melius cogitarem. Unum admisi, alterum non admisi. Fidelitatem facere nolui nec volo. Quia nec ego promisi, nec antecessores meos antecessoribus tuis id fecisse comperio. Pecunia, tribus ferme annis in Gallia

external regimen of the establishment intact,[1] and understood perfectly the distinction between that supremacy and spiritual authority. On one occasion, the Abbot of St. Evroul fled from his abbey, and afterwards returned with Papal legates to regain it. William declared that he would gladly receive the Pope's legates as messengers from the common father respecting faith and religion, but that he would hang any monk who questioned his authority. William Rufus followed in his father's footsteps. Henry I. told Paschal II. that, if he attempted to lessen "the dignities and customs of the kingdom of England," he would withdraw his obedience to the Roman See.[2] In the reign of the same King all ranks, including the bishops and the inferior orders of the clergy, asserted that if Anselm persevered in his attempts to introduce into England the Vatican decrees respecting investiture and homage, they would drive him from the kingdom and separate from the Roman Church. Such were the sentiments of our sovereigns and people at a period when the authority of the Papacy overshadowed the world. The lapse of time only strengthened the national jealousy of any external interference with our ecclesiastical and political institutions.

In 1216, when Innocent III. excommunicated the barons who opposed King John, the citizens of London would not allow the bishops to publish the sentence in the city. "The

---

me agente, negligenter collecta est. Nunc vero, divina misericordia me in regnum meum reverso, quod collectum est per præfatum legatum mittitur, et quod reliquum est per legatos Lanfranci archiepiscopi fidelis nostri cum opportunum fuerit transmittetur. Orate pro nobis, &c."— Collier, i., App. 713

[1] As Eadmer has it, "cuncta divina simul et humana ejus nutum expectabant."

[2] Notumque habeat Sanctitas Vestra quod me vivente, Deo auxiliante, dignitates et usus regni Angliæ non minuentur. Et si ego, quod absit, in tanta me dejectione ponerem, optimates mei, immo totius Angliæ populus, id nullo modo pateretur. Habita igitur, carissime pater, utiliori deliberatione, ita se erga nos moderetur benignitas vestra,

ordinance of secular matters," they said, " appertaineth not to the Pope."[1] When Boniface III. tendered his mediation between Edward I. and Philip le Bel, it was accepted on the distinct understanding that Boniface should determine, not as Pope, but in his private and individual capacity.[2] In 1301 the whole kingdom disclaimed the Papal jurisdiction in temporal matters. When Edward III. referred his quarrel with the French King to the arbitration of Clement VI. in 1343, he was careful to tell his parliament that the Pope was chosen not as a judge but as a friend and private person.[3] The King also published a proclamation to the same effect. In 1343 the Commons requested the King and nobles to find a remedy for the oppression of the English Church and realm by Papal provisions and reservations, or else to help them to expel the Pope's power from the kingdom.[5] The archbishops, bishops, and prelates of England declared in parliament in 1392 that Papal excommunications, issued against such bishops as executed the judgments of the King's Court, were in open disherison of the Crown, and that they were resolved to stand by the King and support his rights to the utmost of their power. Accordingly, in the same parliament they voted unanimously for an Act, the last statute of *Præmunire*, the effect of which was to exclude all communications of whatever kind with Rome without the previous license of the king. In 1399 the parliament

ne, quod invitus faciam, a vestra me cogatis recedere obedientia.—Rymer, i. 8, Ed. 1816.

[1] Matt. Par., *Chron. Mag.* 2, 645.   [2] Rymer, ii. 819.
[3] Rotuli Parl. 2, 136.

[4] In this proclamation Edward states that he had commissioned certain persons " ad tractandum coram dicto domino summo pontifice, non ut judice sed ut privata persona et tractatore et mediatore communi, non in forma nec figura judicii sed extrajudicialiter et amicabiliter."—Rymer, v. 366.

[5] Cotton's *Abridgment of Records*, by Prynne, 41 ; Hume 2, 226, ed. 1830.

proclaimed that the crown and kingdom of England had been in all past time so free that neither the Pope, nor any other outside the realm, had a right to meddle therein, and made it one of the charges against the King, whom they deposed, that he had asked the Pope to confirm English statutes.[1] In 1428 the Council of the kingdom would not allow the Papal legate [2] to open his mouth save on purely spiritual matters.[3] We need not pursue the subject any further, for in the fifteenth century the civil governments throughout Europe began to possess themselves of a large share of ecclesiastical privileges and to free their Churches from Papal management. The danger of the Pope's interference was daily lessening, henceforth the Papacy was to be on the defensive to preserve what it had already acquired.

Universal history is an important portion of national history, and in considering the latter we must always keep in mind the concurrent events in Europe. During the interval we are now speaking of, that is, from the reign of Edward I. to the end of that of Henry VII.—a period of about two hundred years—three circumstances contributed especially to weaken the Papal authority and to generate a contemptuous distrust of it. These were, the seventy years' residence of the Popes at Avignon and their subservience during these

[1] Rotuli Parl. 3, 419.

[2] Henry of Winchester. He was made a member of the King's Council in 1429, but on the condition that when any matter relating to the Pope or See of Rome was discussed, he should absent himself.—Cotton, *Abridg.*, by Prynne, 529.

[3] That this opinion [that the Church had power only over spiritual things] was deeply rooted in the English laity of the day is clear from what we read in *Hall's Chronicle* about the general fast ordered by Wolsey on the occasion of the sack of Rome by the Constable Bourbon in 1527, that the clergy in general neglected it; while the laity, to show their grudge against the spirituality, not only refused to observe it, but said that the Pope was worthily served for being such a " 'ruffian' as to exceed his powers in meddling with temporal dominion."—Simpson, *Life of Campion*, 57.

years to the French Kings;[1] the forty years' schism, when
the Church had two or even three heads, and it depended on
the accident of a man's birth in a particular country what
claimant he was to recognize as the divinely appointed head
of the Church; and the open adoption of an exclusively
worldly policy by the Popes, in the interests of their
temporal principality. These three circumstances had the
most fatal effects in destroying the moral influence of the
Papacy. If to these we add the venality and corruption of
the Roman Court, which had become a by-word in Europe;
the innumerable exactions and extortions of the Roman See,
which occasioned universal discontent both among the laity
and clergy; and the degradation of the episcopal office by
appeals, dispensations, exemptions, and *non-obstantes*, we
shall cease to wonder that national Churches, such as those of
England and France, aimed at complete self-management
without breaking their spiritual communion with the head of
Catholicism, and that sovereigns claimed to exercise an
independent supremacy over the temporalities of their
establishments. But in making this claim civil governments were willing to limit their supremacy to the temporal
concerns of their Churches. "Leave us free," was their cry
to the spiritual power, "to manage the domain which lies
outside your jurisdiction, and in return we will let you direct
the conscience of mankind." If they failed occasionally and
in some matters overstepped the limits which divide the
temporal from the spiritual province, a large allowance must
be made for them. For unquestionably in this respect they
made infinitely fewer mistakes than the Popes. The Popes
recognized no distinction between secular and spiritual
things, and attempted to draw all matters, sacred and

---

[1] In the reign of Edward III. there was a proverb current in England
which alluded to the partiality of the Popes to the French, and to our
victories, " Ore est le Pape Franceys et Jesus devenu Engleys."

profane, within their jurisdiction. Above all they sinned in their deliberate endeavours to depreciate and weaken the temporal power, and to teach the revolutionary doctrine that the bond between the subject and the sovereign might be loosed, whereas the civil government recognized clearly the importance to themselves of a great religious institution which had so long regulated the opinions upon which their own authority was largely based. They felt that to weaken it was to attack the foundations of the existing social system. If this consideration stood alone, it would account for the slow and tentative process by which the English Kings recovered their ecclesiastical supremacy which had been seriously affected by the encroachments of the Popes during the reigns of John and his son. It took them upwards of a hundred years to restore the relationship which existed between the Church and State before the alliance which John contracted with the Papacy. This restoration was fully accomplished, as we shall see, by the enactment of the statutes of *Provisors* and *Præmunire*, though the Popes were allowed by our Kings occasionally to appoint to bishoprics and abbacies for about sixty years after the passing of the last of these Acts. It must, however, be understood that this allowance was purely of grace and from respect to the spiritual head of the Church; for, after the passing of these statutes, no one could receive a dignity or benefice in the English Church from the hands of the Pope under the penalties of outlawry and forfeiture of all his goods, unless he had obtained the previous permission of the King. If any person acted without due consideration and accepted such an appointment, it was absolutely necessary for him—as he had incurred an outlawry which at any moment might be objected to him—to apply at once to the King for a pardon of his acceptance and for a confirmation of the appointment, the Papal nomination being in itself of no effect.

SECTION II

THE accession of Edward I. put an end to the alliance between the Crown of England and the Papacy, and to the grinding of the English Church between, as Matthew Paris expresses it, the two millstones of the Pope and the King. Under this sovereign began the long contest between the State and the Pope, which ended in the enactment of the statutes of *Provisors* and *Præmunire*, by which the English Church was freed from external control, and the supremacy of our Kings in ecclesiastical affairs was fully re-established. The issues in this conflict were largely political and chiefly referred to two points, the patronage of the Church, and the finality of the judgments of the civil courts in matters relating to the rights of presentation, and to the temporal possessions of the establishment. At a time when the clerical lords formed the majority of our Upper House, and when our public policy was chiefly directed by that Chamber, it was clearly impossible to allow the nomination of bishops and abbots to rest with a foreign authority. To have permitted the judgments of our civil courts to be questioned or impeached before an external tribunal would have been to abdicate our national life and independence. The object of the statutes of *Provisors* was to secure to domestic hands the patronage of the Church, and to prevent the intrusion of hated and unqualified strangers into it. The original aim of the statutes of *Præmunire* was to preserve the integrity of our civil courts, but by the last of them their scope was so far extended as to forbid all communication with Rome except by permission of the King. Though throughout this long struggle there was no question of faith or dogma involved in it, yet the intolerable exactions of the Papacy, its "tithing and tolling" of England, and its perpetual encroachments on the laws and customs of the country, aroused a feeling of universal indignation and profound distrust, which united the bishops, clergy, nobles, and commonalty, in a determination to limit the Pope to his spiritual province, and to subject all correspondence between him and Englishmen respecting the patronage, the possessions, or the administration of the national Church, to the permission and supervision of the secular sovereign.

We have seen how the patronage of the English Church was abused during the long reign of Henry III., and how the Pope filled up the benefices in the kingdom with ignorant and indigent aliens, who were not even acquainted with the language of the people over whom they were placed. The first to resist these abuses were the great English prelates, among whom may be numbered Grossetete of Lincoln, St. Edmund of Canterbury, and Sewal of York, whose hearts were broken—the expression is not too strong—by the Papal oppressions and exactions. About the commencement of the thirteenth century the Popes took another step, and claimed the direct and general nomination to English bishoprics, abbacies, and benefices.[1] This innovation led to abuses similar in their nature to those which arose from the subservience of John and his son to the Popes. The Roman

---

[1] In 1268 Clement IV. announced to the world that the Holy See "was entitled by virtue of the canons, notwithstanding any antecedent right, to present to all Churches, and that even before vacancy."

Pontiffs had favoured the chapters and monasteries in obtaining the privilege of the free elections of bishops and regular prelates, but no sooner had this been effected, than they began to interfere with the system and to claim the right of appointing these prelates. This they effected by what are known in our legislation under the names of provisions and reservations. As these are technical terms an explanation of them may be desirable.

At first the Popes were content to claim the presentation to all vacancies caused by the death of the incumbent while attending the Court of Rome, or in his journey to or return from it, and also to such as arose from his translation to another church. From this they proceeded to reserve to themselves by way of anticipation the nomination to bishoprics and other benefices before they became void, and while the incumbent was still alive,[1] or simply to direct the patrons of livings to appoint individuals recommended in the Papal instrument. The form of a bull of provision generally stated that the Pope, being anxious to *provide* a fit person for the particular church mentioned, had *reserved* the appointment to himself, and that now that the vacancy had occurred, he had applied himself to find a proper successor. The bull went on to say that the fact of reservation was sufficient to annul all attempts by others to fill up the vacancy, and ended by naming the person appointed.

The statements in each bull varied according to the circumstances of the case. Thus Anthony de Beck was appointed Bishop of Norwich in 1337 by the Pope. His

---

[1] The reservation in the bull of provision appointing William Edendon to the Bishopric of Winchester in succession to Adam de Orlton runs thus:—Dudum siquidem bonæ memoriæ Adam episcopo Wintoniensi regimini Wintoniensis ecclesiæ præsidente, Nos, intendentes eidem ecclesiæ cum vacaret, per apostolicæ sedis providentiam, idoneam præesse personam, provisionem ipsius ecclesiæ Wintoniensis dispositioni nostræ duximus specialiter reservandam.—Rymer, v. 484.

bull of provision recites, that on the late vacancy the chapter had elected Thomas de Hemhale; that the Pope on hearing of the vacancy, and being ignorant of the election, had reserved to himself the appointment, at the same time declaring void all attempts to fill the vacancy; that the said Thomas, on this reservation being brought to his notice, had given up his claims to the Pope, who thereupon began to consider diligently respecting the providing a fit person to the church of Norwich; and that after careful inquiry he had directed his eyes to the aforesaid Anthony.[1] We see from this example that provisions and reservations were identical, being merely separate clauses in the same instrument. These were the provisions so often mentioned in the petitions of parliament and in our anti-Papal legislation; the persons who obtained them were called provisors.

The indignation caused by the abuse of these provisions soon spread from the prelates to the inferior clergy and the people. In 1306 a letter[2] was sent from "the clergy and people of England" to the Pope, remonstrating with him on the numerous evils arising from Papal patronage and exactions. In the letter complaint was made, that by the "extravagant multitude"[3] of provisions which issued from the Roman See, ordinaries were deprived of their rights of collation, and the noble and learned men of England were entirely excluded from Church preferment; that the Pope pretended a right to apply the rents and profits of religious houses which had been founded by English noblemen to the maintenance of cardinals and other non-resident aliens; that he claimed to reserve for his own use the first fruits of vacant benefices, a thing never heard of before, and very

---

[1] Rymer, iv. 732.

[2] The letter was one of congratulation to Clement V. on his accession. It is given in Rotuli Parl. 1, 207.

[3] Effrenatam multitudinem provisionum.

prejudicial to the King, nation, and the support of the poor,
&c. They conclude by saying that such things could no
longer be borne, as they tended to the ruin of the Anglican
Church, the disherison of the King, the enormous loss of the
kingdom, the destruction of the faithful and the scandal of
the nation ; and that as they were bound to defend the laws
of England they were resolved no longer to put up with such
"novelties and intolerable oppressions."[1]

In the following year the first of our anti-Papal statutes
was passed in the parliament of Carlisle. The object of it
was to protect English religious houses from the exactions of
their foreign superiors. The heads of several orders, as the
Cistercians, Benedictines, and others, were in the habit of
visiting and drawing contributions from their branches in
England. The Act forbade abbots and other religious
persons in the King's dominions to pay a tax or impost to
their superiors out of the kingdom, and prohibited the
laying of any payments or burthens on houses in England by their foreign heads on pain of forfeiting all their
estates.

Before the parliament separated, a strong remonstrance
was adopted by the lay Lords and Commons and presented to
the King, in which they petitioned for a legislative remedy
against the vast number of provisions and the other exactions
of the Roman See. They declared that the oppressions of the
Pope, which they set out in full detail, led to the weakening
of faith, the destruction of holy Church, the disherison
of the Crown, the subversion of the laws, and the great
damage and impoverishment of the people. They end their
remonstrance with these striking words : " That unless God
arise and scatter His enemies, unless the mischief be put an
end to by the secular prince and his parliament, the

---

[1] Novitates et oppressiones intolerabiles.

exhaustion of the commonwealth and the ruin of the Church were sure to ensue." [1]

The demand for legislation against provisions and the other exactions of the Papacy ceased for a while in consequence of the death of the King in the same year. Edward II. would not allow his rights to present to English benefices to be interfered with by bulls, provisos, citations, or appeals to Rome,[2] and told the Pope that if he were to show himself remiss in defending the rights of his crown, his nobles would not allow them to be lessened.[3] In 1319 he directed his writ to the archbishops, bishops, abbots, and all other ecclesiastical persons, declaring that it was contrary to the customs of England to cite anyone out of the kingdom for things the cognizance of which pertained to himself. Under the vigorous administration of Edward III.[4] the legislative opposition to provisions was resumed.

In 1342 Clement VI. attempted to confer English benefices on some of his cardinals. The King quashed the appointments, and forbade the introduction of Papal provisions into the country under penalty of capital punishment.[5] Notwithstanding this repulse, the Pope again in the same year conferred some benefices by provisions on two of his cardinals, but when the grantees or provisors sent their

---

[1] A nostre Seigneur le Roy prient Contes, Barons, et tote la communaute de la terre aide et remedie des oppressions southescrites que l'apostoille fait faire en ceste roialme, en abbessement de la foi Dieu, et anyntissement de l'estat de seiute eglise en roialme, &c.—Rotuli Parl. 1, 219.

[2] Rymer, iii. 38, 185, 277, 466, 500, 784, 795, 914.

[3] Profecto, etsi nos vellemus tepescere in præmissis, vel ea permittere sub dissimulationis umbra transire, magnates tamen et proceres nostri, qui ad defensionem coronæ Angliæ juramenti vinculo sunt astricti, jus nostrum hujusmodi taliter deperire minime sustinerent.—Ib. 185.

[4] It was in this reign that the tribute to the Pope agreed to be paid by John was finally refused.

[5] Qua de causa Rex Angliæ offensus, provisiones per dominum papam

agents to England to avail themselves of the gifts, the agents were arrested and driven " with contumely " out of the kingdom.[1] In the following year the Commons petitioned the King to write to the Pope against the promotion of aliens by his provisions and reservations.[2] Thereupon the King wrote what Walsingham calls his "famous letter in defence of the liberty of the Anglican Church."[3] In this letter Edward complains that English benefices were bestowed by provisions on ignorant and mercenary foreigners who did not reside and who were not acquainted with the English language; that his native subjects, persons of great learning and probity, were thus discouraged in their studies, as they despaired of obtaining reasonable promotion in the Church; that the mischiefs growing out of the practice had become intolerable; that he had been requested by his subjects in parliament to apply a speedy and effectual remedy to the evils; and that the Pope should remember that it was his duty to feed, not to shear the sheep. Not content with this remonstrance to the Pope, the Baronage and Commons proceeded to legislate on the subject. An ordinance was drawn up with their and the King's assent, by which it was ordered that no one, either alien or denizen, should bring into the realm Papal letters, bulls, processes, reservations, or other instruments; that no one should by virtue of provisions or reservations accept a benefice, or receive, or make execution of such instruments; and further,

---

factas cassavit. Et ne quis deinceps tales provisiones afferret, sub pœna carceris atque capitis interdixit.—Walsingham, 1, 254, R. S.

[1] Per gentes et officiales regios non solum impediti super eis, quin immo captivati, et tandem de regno prædicto expulsi cum ignominia.— Letter of the Pope to the King. *Ib.* 259.

[2] Rotuli Parl. 2, 144.

[3] Illam famosam epistolam pro libertate ecclesiæ Anglicanæ contuenda. The letter is in Walsingham, and a translation in Collier, 1, 546.

that all those who should be found in possession of such documents, or making use of them by citations or processes against patrons of livings, should be arrested.¹ To carry out this ordinance, writs were despatched to all the sheriffs and to the bailiffs of ports ordering them to make diligent inquiry, and to arrest and imprison all who contravened it.² In the next parliament the Commons petitioned that the ordinance should be affirmed in a perpetual statute.³

The Commons returned to this subject in 1346 and 1347. In the former year we have several petitions against the foreigners who had been intruded on the Church. The Commons pray that all alien monks should be expelled the kingdom by Michaelmas, and that their livings should be disposed of to young English scholars; that the abbeys and priories in which such aliens resided should be seised into the hands of the King; that the benefices of other aliens, including those given to cardinals, should be taken possession of, and their profits given to the King; that aliens buying provisions should be banished and be declared out of the law; that the pensions granted by the Pope to certain cardinals out of the provinces of Canterbury and York should be sequestrated, and such as made suit for them should be outlawed; that no Englishman should take a church or benefice in farm from an alien on pain of perpetual imprisonment; that no money should be sent out of England to the Pope or any other alien; that no person should bring into the realm any bull or Papal letters touching the affairs of aliens, and that those so doing should be outlawed.⁴ In 1347 the Commons again petitioned against provisions. After reminding the King of what had formerly been done against these instruments and the evils resulting from them, they prayed the King that punishments

¹ Rotuli Parl. 2, 145.   ² Rymer, v. 371.
³ Rotuli Parl. 2, 153.   ⁴ Rotuli Parl. 2, 162.

might be enacted against provisors, their agents, promoters, and notaries in a statute "perpetually to indure."[1]

In 1350 was passed the first general statute of Provisors.[2] The wording of this Act is remarkable. Borrowing its language from the remonstrance presented in the parliament of Carlisle in 1307, it recites, "That whereas the holy Church of England had been founded in the estate of Prelacy within the realm, by the Kings of England and their earls, barons, and nobles, to inform the people of the law of God, to make hospitalities and alms, and to perform other works of charity; and for this purpose the Kings and their nobles had endowed it with lands, rents, and advowsons of great value, of which the said kings and their nobles, as lords and avowees, had and ought to have the presentments and collations on vacancies, yet the Pope of Rome, accroaching to himself the seigniories of such possessions and benefices, did give and grant them to aliens and cardinals as if he had been patron of them, as he was not by the law of England." After this recital it enacted that if the Pope collated to any archbishopric, bishopric, dignity, or other benefice, in disturbance of free election, and the rights of clerical or lay patrons, the King should present; and that if any person collated by the King or lawful patron should be disturbed or impeached by holders of Papal provisions, such holders should be arrested, and on conviction imprisoned, without bail, until they had paid fines and ransoms to the King, and made satisfaction to the parties aggrieved. Further, they were not to be released until they had made a full renunciation, and found security never to attempt such things in future, or to sue in the Court

[1] *Ib.* 172.
[2] 25 Ed. III., st. 6. In this same year there had previously been passed a short Act providing that every person purchasing provisions in the Court of Rome, of abbeys or priories, should be out of the King's protection, and that a man "might do with them as of enemies of our sovereign lord the King."

of Rome, or elsewhere, in respect of such renunciation or imprisonment. This statute was confirmed by another in 1364, which repeated the prohibitions and penalties against provisors.[1]

From the year 1350 to that in which the final Act against provisors was passed, the Rolls of Parliament teem with petitions against Papal provisions.[2] Notwithstanding these petitions, and the earnest language of the first statute of *Provisors*, it would be a mistake to suppose that the King and English people desired at this time to put a complete stop to the Pope's power of appointing by provisions. What they objected to was the vast number of these bulls by which non-resident and unqualified strangers were intruded on the best benefices of the Church, and the wealth of the kingdom drained to purchase provisions or to remit the revenues of the churches to their foreign occupants. The latter was a serious evil at a time when the commerce of the country was trifling, and the coin exported could be replaced only after a long interval. In 1376, more than twenty-five years after the first statute of *Provisors*, the Commons complained that the sums paid to the Pope for ecclesiastical dignities amounted to five times as much as the annual tax of all profits which accrued to the King from the whole realm, and that the bishops were so indebted to the Court of Rome for the burthens imposed on them that they were obliged to cut down and sell the timber on their estates.[3] They asserted that there was no King in Christendom so rich as to possess the fourth part of the treasure which was exported from England to Rome. They also complained of the simony of

---

[1] 38 Edw. III. st. 2.

[2] Petitions were presented by the Commons against provisions in 1351, 1353, 1364, 1373, 1376, 1377. In the reign of Richard II., in 1377, 1379-80, 1381, 1383, 1386, 1389.

[3] Rotuli Parl. 2, 337.

"the sinful city of Avignon,"[1] and that its "brokers" promoted many "caitiffs, who knew nothing and were worth nothing, to livings of a thousand marks a year, while learned doctors and masters in divinity could hardly obtain one of twenty marks, whereby clerks lost all hope of advancement, youths were not sent to school. and thus the clergy, who were the substance of holy Church and of the holy Faith, were gradually perishing."[2] If the Popes had shown the slightest moderation, or if they had endeavoured to understand the character of the English people, they might have retained much longer than they did a considerable portion of the patronage of the Church. The veneration for the Papacy was great, and it was felt to be reasonable that the spiritual head of the Church should share in the disposal of its dignities and benefices. But the shameless rapacity of the French Popes defeated itself and exhausted the patience of the people. In 1383 it was enacted that no alien should purchase or occupy any benefice or dignity of holy Church in England without the special license of the King.[3] In 1388 an Act forbade any subject, great or small, to pass over the sea without the special leave of the King, for the purpose of purchasing or obtaining by provision a benefice within the realm.[4] Finally, in the following year, the last and trenchant statute of *Provisors* was passed. This Act,[5] after rehearsing and confirming the prior one of Edward III., provided that every one who should in future accept a benefice in England by way of provision, should be banished for ever, and his lands and goods forfeited to the King. No further legislation was required. The interference of the Pope with the patronage of the English Church was excluded for ever. Henceforth

---

[1] La pecherouse cite d'Avenon.—*Ib.*
[2] *Ib.* 338.
[3] 7 Ric. II. c. 12.
[4] 12 Ric. II. c. 15.
[5] 13 Ric. II. st. 2, c. 2.

everything depended on the character and temper of the King.

The statutes of *Præmunire*—so called from the writ by which they were enforced—were contemporaneous with those of *Provisors*, and were at first intended merely to guard against encroachments by the Papal Court on our civil tribunals. The patronage of parish churches, the title to tithes, and generally speaking the rights to the temporal possessions of the Church, were matters which were decided in the civil courts. It was found that suitors who had been unsuccessful at home had recourse to the Court of Rome for the purpose of qualifying, impeaching, or reversing judgments given in such matters. This abuse was speedily taken up by the Commons. In 1344 they stated in a petition to the King that certain persons sued in the Court of Rome to weaken or annul judgments rendered after due process of English law respecting presentations to churches, prebends, and other benefices; and they prayed that persons so suing in the Court of Rome, "in enervation or destruction of judgments given in the King's Court, or of their effect or execution," should be punished with imprisonment for life or be compelled to abjure the kingdom.[1]

In 1347 the Commons again petitioned the King and drew his attention to the fact that notwithstanding the illegality of such proceedings, and the late efforts made to prevent them, certain persons pursued processes in the Court of Rome for the purpose of impugning or annulling judgments delivered in the King's Court, in prejudice and to the disherison of the King and of the whole community, and they requested that an enactment should be made ordaining penalties against all such offenders.[2]

In 1353 the first statute of *Præmunire* was passed.[3] "On the grievous and clamorous complaint of the Lords and

[1] Rotuli Parl. 2, 153. [2] *Ib.* 172. [3] 27 Edw. III. c. 1.

Commons that divers of the people were drawn out of the realm to answer things whereof the cognisance pertained to the King's Court, and also that the judgments of the same courts were impeached in another court to the disherison of the King and his Crown and of all the people of the realm, and to the undoing and destruction of the common law of the said realm," it was enacted that whosoever should draw any out of the realm in pleas the cognisance of which belonged to the King's Court, should, if he did not appear and conform to the sentence of the civil court, forfeit all his lands and goods and be outlawed and imprisoned.

In 1364 the statute[1] which was passed to confirm the act of *Provisors* also contained a clause against all such as should procure citations from the Court of Rome in causes "whose cognisance and final discussing pertained to the King and his royal court." It was ordained that such offenders should be arrested and, if convicted, should suffer the pains and penalties incurred by those who contravened the statute of *Provisors*.

The history of the last statute of *Præmunire*[2] is contained in its preamble. Its introduction was the occasion of an extraordinary outburst of enthusiasm and national feeling. Shortly before the year in which it was passed, 1392, the Pope had ventured to excommunicate some English bishops for executing the judgments of the civil courts in suits connected with the presentation to benefices. He had also translated some prelates to sees against their will and without the King's consent. When the Parliament met, all ranks were unanimous in their resolution to resist these acts of the Pope as encroachments on the Crown of England, which they declared " to have been so free at all times that it hath been in no earthly subjection, but immediately subject to God in all things touching the regality of the same Crown and to none other, and that the same should not be submitted

[1] 38 Edw. III. st. 2.   [2] 16 Ric. II. c. 5.

to the Pope, nor the laws and statutes of the realm be by him defeated or avoided at his will, in perpetual destruction of the sovereignty of the King, his crown, and regality, and of all his realm, which God defend." The three estates made separate declarations. The Commons declared that these attempts of the Pope were clearly against the King's crown and his regality used and approved in the time of all his progenitors, and that they would stand by the King to live and die with him. The temporal peers asserted, " every one by himself," that such proceedings of the Pope were in derogation of the King's crown and of his regality, and that they would support the King "with all their power." The prelates adopted the language of the Commons, and promised the King to stand by him "in lawfully maintaining his crown and in all other cases touching his crown and regality as they were bound by their ligeance." Accordingly it was enacted that all persons who purchased or procured in the Court of Rome any such translations, processes, sentences of excommunication, bulls, instruments, or any other thing, which touched the King, his crown, regality, or realm, and all who brought them into the kingdom, or received them, or made notification or execution of them, should be put out of the King's protection, their lands and goods forfeited, and themselves attached, or that process be made against them by way of *Præmunire*.

The wide sweep of the enacting clause deserves attention, for it subsequently received the largest interpretation. It includes all Papal instruments, or "other things" which touched the King, his crown, or realm, and all those who brought them into the kingdom or published or executed them. All persons dealing in any way with such instruments were to be outlawed, their property confiscated, and their persons imprisoned. In other words, the act was capable of being applied to every document which issued from Rome. It covered all Papal decisions respecting the external economy of the Church and all rescripts or ecclesiastical appeals. We have seen that in the eleventh century our Norman Kings would not allow a Papal bull or letter to enter the kingdom unless it were first shown to and approved by them. In the reign of Edward I. a subject brought into England a bull of excommunication against another subject and published it. It was held to be treason for which the offender deserved to be hanged, but at the entreaty of the Chancellor and Treasurer of the kingdom he was let off on condition of abjuring the realm.[1] In 1376 Edward III. sent his mandate to Simon Sudely, Archbishop of Canterbury, informing him that many bulls, letters, and other writings had lately been imported into the country "from foreign parts," and ordered him to send all such documents as should be brought to him to the royal council to be there examined and considered. The archbishop wrote back to say that he would reverently obey the King's commands.[2] At the end of this century nearly sixty English prelates, representatives both of the secular and regular clergy, voted unanimously for a statute which, if strictly enforced—and its enforcement depended entirely upon the temporal prince—tended to put a stop to every attempt on the part of the Pope to regulate the smallest ecclesiastical matter in the English Church without the King's consent. It may be asked what difference can be descried between the conduct

---

[1] Coke's *Reports*, part 5, 12.

[2] Wilkins' *Concilia*, 3, 107, 108. Half a century later, when Martin V. sent bulls of censure to Chichely, Archbishop of Canterbury, the King commanded the archbishop to keep the bulls "without notification, publication, or execution," and to send them on to the council for examination. The archbishop wrote to the Pope that he had not even opened the bulls, "bullas ... super præmissis transmissas nunquam perlegerim, nec aperire, obstantibus mandatis regiis, ausus eram ... sed in archivis regiis ... remanent custoditæ."—*Ib*, 3, 474.

of these prelates and that of those who in the reign of Henry VIII. voted as unanimously for the royal supremacy, and afterwards, three years later, renounced the ecclesiastical jurisdiction of the Pope.

The operation of the statutes of *Provisors* and *Præmunire* was immediate and effectual. All communication with Rome, except the small stream of testamentary and matrimonial causes, was at once closed unless by permission of the King. From the year 1389 we have a long series of royal licenses allowing applications to be made to the Papal Court, and of pardons for having done so without the King's previous leave. From this year we may say of our sovereigns what Eadmer said of the Conqueror, "that all things ecclesiastical depended on their nod"; or we may adopt the language of Convocation, of the universities, and of all the religious houses in 1534, "that the Pope of Rome was possessed of no greater jurisdiction in England than any other foreign bishop." Whatever influence the Pope henceforward exercised in this country was a purely moral one, due to the respect felt for him as spiritual head of the Church. He might appoint bishops and prelates by provisions, as Martin V. did in the reign of Henry V., and as Clement VII. appointed Cranmer to the Archbishopric of Canterbury;[1] but these appointments were subject to the good pleasure of the King. What could Roman provisions avail against English laws with their dreadful negative of outlawry, banishment, and forfeiture? The English prelates at least were perfectly alive to the nature of Papal appointments, for on their

[1] Cum Dominus Summus Pontifex, nuper vacante ecclesia cathedrali Cantuarensi per mortem bonæ memoriæ Willelmi nuper archiepiscopi ejusdem ecclesiæ, personam dilecti et fidelis conciliarii nostri Thomæ Cranmer dictæ ecclesiæ nuper electi, in ipsius ecclesiæ archiepiscopum præfecerit et pastorem, sicut per literas bullatas ipsius Domini Summi Pontificis nobis inde directas, nobis constat.—Words of the Privy Seal restoring his temporalities to the new archbishop. Rymer, xiv. 456.

promotion they at once renounced everything in their bulls
which was opposed to the laws and customs of their country,
and hastened to sue out the royal pardon for having received
or published them. The best tests of the effects of statutes
are contemporary records and contemporary accounts of
their working. For this purpose a few of our records are
here quoted, and their testimony will be afterwards confirmed
by extracts from Papal letters. It would encumber these
pages too much to give a long enumeration of the letters
patent granted for licenses to apply to the Roman Court, or
for pardons for having done so. Some only will be given to
show the effects of these statutes on laymen, monks, secular
priests, regular prelates, bishops, cardinals, Papal nuncios,
and Papal legates. In 1448 a license was granted to Andrew
Ogard, lay patron of a priory, to apply to the Pope for bulls,
and when the bulls should be given, to receive, read, pronounce, declare, and execute them without danger to himself.[1]
In 1399 certain of the Carmelites in England, who were
chaplains to the Pope, and prided themselves on their office,
had shown disobedience to their superiors. Thereupon the
Pope issued bulls commanding their obedience. To support
the Pope, the King directed his writ to the provincial and all
the priors of the order in the kingdom. "We knowing,"
says the writ, "that you cannot or ought not in any way to
execute the said bulls or anything contained in them within
our kingdom without our license and authority, do of our
special favour grant unto you authority, license, and power
to correct your brethren according to the form, force, and
effect of the Papal bulls."[2] Henry Chichely, afterwards
Archbishop of Canterbury, had accepted Papal appointments
in the diocese and cathedral of Salisbury; Henry IV. granted
him a pardon for his "transgressions and misprisions in so
doing," and confirmed the appointments.[3] The Prior of

[1] Rymer, xi. 212.   [2] *Ib.* viii. 113.   [3] *Ib.* 244.

Letham asked and obtained a bull from the Pope securing him in the priory for life. The prior petitioned the King for pardon. The King granted him a pardon for his contempt, transgressions, and misprisions in asking for or accepting the bull.[1] In 1449 the Bishop of Hereford had obtained bulls from the Pope respecting the resignation of his see and the payment of an annuity by his successor. The bishop petitioned for his pardon. The King pardoned him " all contempts, transgressions, misprisions, provisions, and forfeitures incurred by reason of applying for, accepting, reading, or proclaiming the said bulls," and permitted the bishop to make use of them.[2] The Pope by his bulls appointed Thomas Kemp to the Bishopric of London. The King granted his license to Kemp " to receive, admit, accept, read and pronounce " the bulls, and to make use of them.[3] In 1410 a license was granted to Cardinal Francisco to accept from the Pope nominations to four benefices in England, not beyond a certain value, and to obtain possession of them, "notwithstanding the Act of *Provisors* of the thirteenth of Richard II. or any other Act."[4] In 1390 license was granted to James Dardain, chamberlain to the Pope and nuncio in England, on his petition to the King in parliament, to make use of a Papal bull appointing him to the Archdeaconry of Norwich, " notwithstanding any statutes or ordinances respecting provisors."[5] In 1460 a license was granted to the Papal legate, Francesco, Bishop of Terni, to receive from the Pope an appointment to an English bishopric, certain sees excepted, and to cause the same to be read and published, " notwithstanding any statutes of parliament or restrictions of the King's predecessors."[6]

---

[1] *Ib.* xi. 48.   [2] *Ib.* 256.   [3] *Ib.* 259.
[4] *Ib.* viii. 654. For other cardinals see viii. 291, and xi. 195.
[5] *Ib.* vii. 689.   [6] *Ib.* xi. 468.

In all these and similar cases the licenses and pardons were granted by letters patent or privy seals, and invariably purported to proceed from the special favour of the King and to protect the recipients from the effects of the statutes of *Provisors* and *Præmunire*. If to these we add permissions to bishops to keep their proctors at Rome;[1] proclamations ordering all English ecclesiastics seeking bulls at the Court of Rome to return by an early date under penalty "of life and limb, and all that they possessed," and forbidding anyone of whatever rank to bring into the country bulls, Papal letters, processes, instruments, or other things contrary to its laws and customs;[2] prohibitions to such powerful bodies as the Knights of St. John not to depart the realm without the special leave of the King, or to send any of their brethren to Rome there to institute proceedings against the laws and customs of England or to the disquiet of the subject;[3] general orders to arrest all persons found in possession of appeals, citations, inhibitions, and processes against ecclesiastical appointments by the King;[4] and commissions to examine, either by a jury or in some other way, the contents of a Papal bull, when its arrival became known to the King;[5] the universal and absolute power of our sovereigns in ecclesiastical matters, a hundred years before Henry VIII. was born, will clearly appear.

These statutes, particularly the last of the *Præmunire* acts, made a profound impression on the mind of the English people. The bishops and prelates, ever until the time of Cardinal Wolsey, himself a candidate for the Papal throne, walked in fear of them. For more than a hundred and fifty years the ordinary Englishman believed that a person convicted of a *præmunire* might be slain with impunity. This was in consequence of the words in them respecting outlawry.

[1] *Ib.* vii. 701, 702.   [2] *Ib.* 698.   [3] *Ib.* viii. 155.
[4] *Ib.* ix. 190.   [5] *Ib.* xii. 269.

I

This belief was so general that it became necessary to extirpate it by a legislative declaration. "Forasmuch as it is doubtful," says an enactment of Elizabeth, "whether by the laws of this realm there be any punishment for such as kill or slay any person or persons attainted in or upon a *præmunire;* be it therefore enacted . . . that it shall not be lawful to any person or persons to slay or kill any person or persons in any manner attainted or hereafter to be attainted of, in, or upon any *præmunire* . . . any law, statute, or opinion or exposition of any law or statute to the contrary in any wise notwithstanding."[1]

From the first the Popes perceived the effects which the statutes of *Provisors* and *Præmunire* were likely to have in checking their interference with the patronage and administration of the English Church. In 1391 Boniface IX. sent a special nuncio to England, and offered to satisfy the King and nation if these Acts were repealed.[2] Seven years later the same Pope sent a bishop, Peter de Bosco, to the King, requesting him to allow his subjects to receive provisions from Rome, and to repeal the Act of *Provisors* and "many similar Acts."[3] But the requests of the Popes were made in vain. The policy of these Acts was adopted and strengthened

---

[1] 5 Eliz. c. 1, s. 21.

[2] In this year proclamation was made in London, that all the English clergy then in Rome should return home, the beneficed on pain of losing their livings, the unbeneficed on pain of forfeiture. "Papa vero, tanto sonitu conturbatus, mittit nuncium sub celeritate, quemdam abbatem videlicet, qui causas exploret harum rerum omnium, simul et statuti parliamentalis nuper editi de provisoribus contra consuetudinem ecclesiæ Romanæ . . . per quem exhortatur, rogat, et requirit, quod rex statuta illa tolli et de capitularibus faciat aboleri, maxime statuta 'quare impedit' et 'præmunire facias' et hiis similia. Et Papa offert, quod si statutarii velint conqueri de aliquo, si mittant ad Papam ambassiatores, erit promptus quantum cum Deo poterit, regi et regno complacere."—*Walsingham*, 2, 200.

[3] *Ib.* 228.

by the legislation of Henry IV. and Henry V.[1] Martin V., who after the healing of the schism in the Church was firmly seated on the Papal throne, directed all his efforts to obtain a repeal of the Act of *Provisors*. In 1426 he wrote to Chichely, Archbishop of Canterbury, severely reflecting on his remissness in not having opposed that statute, and urging him under the penalty of excommunication to use all his influence to effect its revocation. The archbishop was also required under the same penalty to enjoin on his clergy the duty of preaching against it.[2] In addition the Pope wrote to the King, the parliament, and the Duke of Bedford, then regent of France, exhorting and admonishing them to repeal the statute. In his letter to the parliament he told its members, that no one could be saved who was in favour of its observation, required them under pain of damnation to recall it, and offered to secure them in future from any abuses which might formerly have crept in with provisions.[3] But these efforts had no effect. The statutes of *Provisors* and *Præmunire* were never repealed, not even in the days of Queen Mary. It is noteworthy that in the Concordat made by Martin V. at the Council of Constance with the English nation there is no mention made of provisions, reservations, or the other encroachments of the Popes, our ancestors wisely preferring the protection of their own laws to Papal promises which might afterwards be eluded.[4]

[1] By the statutes, 1 Hen. IV. c. 3 ; 7 Hen. IV. c. 8 ; 9 Hen. IV. c. 8 ; 3 Hen. V. c. 4.

[2] " Sub simili pœna mandes et præcipias omnibus rectoribus ecclesiarum quam aliis officium prædicationis obtinentibus, sæcularibus et religiosis, ut frequenter in sermonibus suis populos de prædicta materia instruere non omittant."

[3] The letters to the King, the parliament, and the archbishop are to be found in Burnet's *Collection of Records* and in Wilkins' *Concilia :* that to the Duke of Bedford in Fuller, 148.

[4] This Concordat referred to matters comparatively unimportant, such as the appropriation of churches, the consolidation of vicarages,

The statutes of *Provisors* and *Præmunire* restored to the English Church its domestic management, re-established the royal supremacy over it, and excluded Papal interference with its patronage, though for about sixty years subsequently the Popes were permitted by our Kings to exercise an occasional authority. After the passing of these Acts every one who accepted a preferment in England from the Papal See without the consent of the King was liable to banishment and forfeiture of his lands and goods. It lay therefore entirely in the discretion of the temporal sovereign to determine whether any and what share in disposing of ecclesiastical dignities and benefices should be left to the Popes. Of the way in which these statutes were regarded by English prelates and of their drastic effects, an incident in our history and a Papal letter inform us. In 1432, Henry Beaufort, Bishop of Winchester, great uncle to the King, and a cardinal, perhaps the most powerful man in England,[1] applied to parliament and was secured by a legislative enactment against any pains and penalties under these statutes which he might have incurred whilst acting as Papal legate, and also "for any receipt, acceptance, admission, or execution of Papal bulls."[2] In the letter which Pope Martin V. wrote to Archbishop Chichely respecting the Act of *Provisors*, he thus speaks of it: "In the first place," says the Pope, "by means of this execrable statute the King of England disposes of the Church with his provisions and appointments as if he were the Vicar of Christ. He makes laws for the churches,

---

dispensations for non-residence, &c. The Concordat is given in Wilkins' *Concilia*, 3, 391, and the principal heads of it in Collier, Preface to second vol.

[1] "Yet let us watch the haughty cardinal,
His insolence is more intolerable
Than all the princes of the land beside.
If Gloster be displaced, he'll be protector."
       Second Part, *Henry VI*.

[2] Rotuli Parl. 4, 392.

benefices, clerics, and the ecclesiastical order, draws the
cognisance of ecclesiastical causes into his temporal courts,
and in a word arranges about clerks, benefices, and the
concerns of the hierarchy, as if the care of the Church had
been entrusted to him and not to St. Peter. Besides this
hideous law, he has enacted several terrible penalties against
the clergy,[1] the like of which were never directed against
Jews or Saracens. People of every kind may freely resort
to England; it is only those who have accepted benefices from
the supreme Pontiff, the Vicar of Jesus Christ, that are
banished, seized, imprisoned, and stripped of all their fortunes.
The executors of Papal bulls, and proctors and notaries
carrying censures or processes from the Apostolic See, are
exposed to the most severe punishment, and, being thrown
out of the King's protection, are given up as a prey to all.
Can that be called a Catholic country where such profane
laws are enacted and observed? where application to the
Vicar of God is prohibited, and where St. Peter's successor
is not allowed to execute our Saviour's commission? Christ
said to St. Peter and to his successors, feed my sheep,
but this statute will not suffer him to feed them, but
transfers that office to the King and pretends to give him
apostolic authority in several cases. Our Saviour ordained
that whatsoever the supreme Pontiff should bind on earth,
the same should be bound or loosed in heaven; but this
statute overrules the divine precept, for if the Vicar of Christ
deputes any priests to bind and loose contrary to the intend-
ment of the law, this statute not only forbids their entrance
into the kingdom, but exiles them, seizes their effects, and
makes them liable to further penalties, so that any one
carrying an apostolic censure or process into the kingdom is
punished as for a capital offence. You cannot wonder that
the Church complains of your conduct. Proceed therefore to

[1] This portion of the letter refers to the Acts of *Præmunire*.

instruct the laity and to point out to them the truth. Show them what a snare the said statute is. We command you under the penalty of excommunication to approach the King and his councillors, and to exhort them to repeal the said Act in the next parliament, as it is contrary to the precepts of Scripture and of holy councils, and cannot be observed without the loss of eternal salvation. When the next parliament shall be convened, we command you under the same penalty to use your influence with all who shall have a voice in it. In addition we order you, also under the penalty of excommunication, to enjoin on all rectors and preachers, secular and regular, to preach frequently on this matter, that every precaution may be taken to secure the honour of God and the safety of souls."

One very remarkable circumstance connected with the passing of the statutes of *Provisors* and *Præmunire* was the conduct of the English prelates. No body of men is so homogeneous and compact as an ecclesiastical body. Its members have the same interests and are swayed by the same motives, and in consequence their action is almost always united. In the parliament which passed the last statute of *Præmunire* in 1392 there were "almost sixty ecclesiastical barons";[1] that is to say, the large majority of the Upper House, then by far the more powerful of the two legislative chambers, consisted of prelates. No statute could have been passed against the opposition of such a body. A learned author[2] has asserted that the prelates protested against the Act of 1365, and also against the Act which was passed in the parliament of the 13th of Richard II. This statement is not quite correct. What the prelates did on these two occasions was this. In 1365 they said that they would assent to nothing which was likely to turn to the prejudice of their

---

[1] Fuller, *Ch. Hist.* 148.   [2] Bishop Stubbs.

estate and dignity;[1] a very different thing from protesting against an Act. In the parliament of the 13th of Richard II. they made a general declaration that they in no wise meant or would assent to any law, so far as such law operated in restraint of the Pope's authority, or in subversion of ecclesiastical liberty. But there is no mention of any protest against a particular Act. Their hesitation, if they did hesitate, between the King and the Pope, did not last long, for only four years later, when the last Act of *Præmunire* was introduced in 1392, the prelates voted unanimously for it. It is true that in 1427 the two archbishops and five other bishops, a third of their number, and *two* abbots—there were then twenty-six mitred abbots and priors who sat in Parliament—exhorted the Commons to repeal the Act of *Provisors;* but this was done after the archbishop had been reprimanded and suspended from his legatine functions by the Pope, for having allowed the Act to pass without opposition.[2] In 1441 a motion was made in Convocation to petition the King that the last statute of *Præmunire* might be explained in a sense more favourable, not to the Pope but to the clergy. This motion was made in consequence of the pedantry of the lawyers, who strained these Acts to the disadvantage of the ecclesiastical judges. In the statute of *Præmunire* it was enacted that if any person purchased bulls or instruments in the Court of Rome, *or elsewhere*, he should be liable to the penalties mentioned therein. The word "elsewhere" was inserted to meet the case of the Pope residing at other places than Rome, as Avignon, Lyons, or Pisa. The common-law lawyers insisted that the word applied to all Courts of ecclesiastical jurisdiction, whether

---

[1] Les prelats tout dis fesantz lour protestation de rien assenter ne faire q purra estre ou turner en prejudice de lour estat ou dignite.—Rotuli Parl. 2, 285.

[2] Wilkins, *Concilia*, 3, 483.

native or foreign, and not merely to that of Rome. Accordingly a petition was drawn up, praying the King that the statute of *Præmunire* " and the punishments contained in it, should have relation and be extended only to such processes, sentences, excommunications, bulls, instruments, made and prosecuted in the Court of Rome or elsewhere, outside the kingdom, and not to suits, processes, sentences, bulls, or instruments, made or prosecuted in Courts within the realm, inasmuch as there was a remedy already provided against the errors of the latter Courts by writs of prohibition and attachment."[1] In 1447 the prelates returned to this grievance, and again petitioned the King, for the purpose of restraining this "strange and bitter interpretation" of the Act, as they termed it, "to declare, and make to be declared, by authority of this your present Parliament, that the said statute, made at Winchester the 16th year of King Richard aforesaid, and the pains and punishments contained in the same, have relation only to suits, processes, sentences of cursing, bulls, and instruments made or pursued, or to be made or pursued in the Court of Rome, or in any other places without the realm of England."[2] This was all the action ever taken by the English prelates and clergy respecting these statutes. So far were they from objecting to the Act of *Præmunire* that they assert in their last-mentioned petition that it was passed " in favour of the said archbishops and bishops within the land," and again, that it was " made in favour of the said prelates and spiritual judges in the land."[3]

[1] Que le dit estatut du dit roy Richard et les punishementz contenuz en ycell, eient soulement relacion et entendement as sutez, processez, &c., faitz, pursues, ou a fair et pursuer, en le Court de Rome, et aylours hors du royalme d' Engleterre ... et nemy as sutez, &c., en nul courtes spirituelz ne temporelz deinz le royalme d' Engleterre.—*Ib.* 3, 534.

[2] The Clergie's petition concerning the statute of *Præmunire.*—*Ib.* 3, 555.

How are we to account for the absence of active opposition to these laws on the part of the English prelates and clergy? In truth, they deserted the Pope and clung to the King. They were weary of the exactions of the Court of Rome, and preferred that the patronage of the Church should be distributed by the secular Sovereign. Their idea of what the Church of England should be, was the same as that of their successors in the reign of Henry VIII., that is, an independent, self-governed, and self-organized national Church, in communion with that of Rome, recognizing the Pope as the spiritual head and primate of the Catholic unity, but regarding him as subject to the decrees of General Councils. They were sick of the constant pillaging which they had suffered at the hands of the Roman Pontiffs, and desired that their Church should be free from external control in concerns connected with its civil establishment.

And their desire was fulfilled; for such was the condition of the English Church after the enactment of the statutes of *Provisors* and *Præmunire*. Here is the time and place to ask—What ecclesiastical jurisdiction, as distinguished from his purely spiritual authority by monition and advice, did the Pope possess in England at the accession of Henry VII., that is, forty years before the Reformation was dreamt of? The answer to this question is, the Pope was possessed of none. A general statement like this may be contradicted as generally as it is made. It will, therefore, be better to consider the subject in detail:—

1. The Pope could not appoint, translate, suspend, or depose a bishop, or regular prelate, in England.[1]

2. He could not appoint to an English prebend or

---

[1] Statutes of *Provisors* and *Præmunire*. See also 9 Hen. IV. c. 9, forbidding any Papal or Royal interference with the election of archbishops, bishops, abbots, priors, or deans, but reserving to the King his prerogatives therein.

benefice, and every Englishman who accepted a preferment at home from the Pope, without the King's leave, was liable to banishment and forfeiture of all his property.[1]

3. A Papal excommunication, of itself, had not the slightest effect in England.[2] No one could receive, read, or publish, such a document, or any other Papal sentence, or process, without leave of the King.

4. It follows from these three heads that the Pope could neither reward nor punish a single English ecclesiastic.

5. No Englishman, lay or cleric, could make any application or reference respecting the patronage, possessions, or administration of the Church to the Pope, or receive from him any bull, Papal letter, or other instrument, without the license of the King. If he did so, he incurred, *ipso facto*, outlawry and forfeiture of all his goods, and it depended wholly on the King's good pleasure whether or not these penalties should be exacted.

6. No one could proceed to Rome without the special license of the King.

7. No Papal legate could set his foot in the kingdom without the King's consent and under strict conditions. If a native was appointed to that office, he could not accept the commission without the King's license, nor could he execute the smallest item in it without royal letters authorizing him to do so, as is shown by the cases of Henry Beaufort, Archbishop Chichely, Cardinal Wolsey, and Cardinal Pole.

---

[1] " If any do accept of a benefice of Holy Church, contrary to this statute, and that duly proved, and be beyond the sea, he shall abide exiled and banished out of the realm for ever, his lands and tenements, goods and chattels, shall be forfeit to the King. And if he be within the realm, he shall be also exiled and banished, as afore is said, and shall incur the same forfeiture, and take his way so that he be out of the realm within six weeks next after such acceptation ": 13 Ric. II. st. 2. c. 2, the last Act of *Provisors*.

[2] Coke's *Reports*, pt. 5, 23.

8. The Pope could not convene an English synod or convocation, or do any synodical act, without the King's permission.

9. No canons or decrees of the Pope had any force or effect in England until, and so far only as, they were accepted in the kingdom.

10. The Pope could not exempt any ecclesiastic from his obedience, regular or ordinary;[1] or discharge any one from the payment of tithes;[2] or found an ecclesiastical corporation;[3] or grant the right of sanctuary.[4]

11. The Pope could not summon any English ecclesiastic to Rome without the King's license; and the King could at any moment recall home all his subjects attending the Papal Court.

If we compare with this absence of ecclesiastical jurisdiction the plenary and abounding authority of the Kings of England in all that related to the external regimen of the Church and to those things which were not of divine institution, we shall see that they always—one interval excepted—challenged and enjoyed the political headship of the national Church, and no other was after the Conquest ever claimed by them. If there is one thing clearly brought out by an examination of our Church history, it is this, that whatever ecclesiastical jurisdiction was exercised by the Popes in England was exercised by the allowance and permission of our Kings, and by way of favour, and through respect to the Papacy. None knew this better than the Popes themselves. "If the King of England," said Clement VI., "were to ask for an ass to be made bishop, he must not be denied."[5] "It is not the Pope," said Martin V., "but the King of England that governs the Church in his dominions. With his provisions

---

[1] 2 Hen. IV. c. 3.   [2] 2 Hen. IV. c. 4.
[3] Caudrey's Case, Coke's *Reports*, pt. 5.   [4] *Ib.*
[5] Godwin's *Catalogue of the Bishops of England*, 526.

and appointments he regulates it as if he were the Vicar of Christ. He makes laws for the churches, benefices, clerics, the ecclesiastical orders, and the concerns of the hierarchy, as if the care of the Church had been entrusted to him and not to us. When we send our notaries and proctors into England carrying our censures and processes, the bearers are seized, imprisoned, and stripped of their all; nor is any application to the Apostolic See allowed by the English laws to be made." And when the Roman Pontiffs appointed bishops or regular prelates by provisions, each bull of provision was directed to the King, and ended with a request to him to receive and support by his authority the person appointed, for which favour the Pope promised his hearty gratitude. Let us now see what the King's ecclesiastical supremacy meant:—

1. Though the King could not directly appoint to bishoprics and abbacies, his recommendation to the chapters and conventual brethren, and his subsequent approval of the election, were virtually equivalent to an appointment.[1]

2. It lay with him, and with him alone, to convene English convocations. When the canons of these assemblies infringed his prerogative or the customs of the realm, they had to be retracted, as was done in the case of decrees passed in the Synod of Reading in 1279 under Archbishop Peckham.

3. The King determined the extent of the jurisdiction of the ecclesiastical courts, and by his writs of prohibition restrained them to such matters as the English law allowed.

---

[1] "Henry VII. possessed the undisputed right of nominating candidates to the episcopal sees. He was not satisfied with bestowing all clerical promotions, he also appropriated to himself the half of the *annates*."—Ranke, *Popes of Rome*, 1, 27. "Under Henry VII. and Henry VIII. the royal nominees were invariably chosen."—Stubbs, *Const. Hist.* 3, 317.

4. Decided in what cases bishops should appear in his court to give an account why they excommunicated the subject,[1] and ordered them to recall their sentences.[2]

5. Forbade his bishops to seek confirmation at Rome during a schism, and ordered his archbishops to bestow it on those elected by the chapters.[3]

6. The last appeal in ecclesiastical cases lay to the King, unless he allowed the matter to be brought before the Court of Rome.

7. The King might exempt any ecclesiastic or religious body from the jurisdiction of the ordinary; or grant the privilege of sanctuary; or create an ecclesiastical corporation.

8. Commanded his clergy to reside.[4]

9. If a patron did not present in due time, the presentation lapsed to the bishop, and from him, in default of presenting, to the King, with whom it rested, as universal advowee and patron paramount of the English Church.

10. The revenues of archbishoprics, bishoprics, abbacies, and priories, in the vacancy belonged to the King in the same right; to whom also it pertained to fill up all benefices during the vacancies of the respective dignities.

11. Archbishops and bishops on their appointment were obliged to renounce every clause in their bulls prejudicial to the prerogative of the Crown or to the law of the land.[5]

[1] 9 Edw. II. c. 7.
[2] Prynne's *Records*, 3, 244.
[3] Rotuli Parl. 4, 71. Rymer, ix. 337.
[4] Rymer, x. 84.
[5] Even in the reign of Mary this renunciation was required from Cardinal Pole on his appointment to Canterbury. "Nos, pro eo quod idem Electus, omnibus et singulis verbis nobis et coronæ nostræ præjudicialibus in dictis literis bullatis contentis, coram nobis palam et expresse renunciavit, et gratiæ nostræ humiliter se submisit, volentes

After the last Act of *Præmunire* they sued out their pardons for having received such bulls, and for having published or acted upon them.

It was to the King that the whole nation looked for the protection of the Church and the preservation of the Catholic faith. In 1307 the earls, barons, and "the whole community of the realm" petitioned the King to afford them his aid and protection against the oppressions of the Papal See, which, they declared, tended to the abasement of the faith of God, the destruction of holy Church, the disherison of the Crown, and the impoverishment of the people.[1] It was the same with the bishops and clergy. They held it to be a part of the kingly office to provide that no dissensions, scandals, or divisions should arise in the Church and that the Catholic faith should be preserved. In their supplication to Henry IV. in 1400, the prelates and clergy of the whole kingdom implored the King to remember the glorious actions of his illustrious predecessors, and, in order to save the Catholic faith, sustain divine worship, and preserve the existence, laws, and liberties of the Anglican Church, to provide an opportune remedy for the dissensions, scandals, and dangers to religion which had lately arisen.[2]

The condition and circumstances of the English Church at the accession of Henry VII., and up to that of Henry VIII. may be shortly summed up. It was a national Church completely self-organized and managed at home; with a regular hierarchy practically appointed by the King; possessing the right of canonically legislating for itself, recognizing the

cum eo in hac parte agere et gratiose, fidelitatem ipsius Electi cepimus, et temporalia archiepiscopatus illius prout moris est restituimus eidem."— Rymer, xv. 432.

[1] Rotuli Parl. 1, 219.

[2] Supplicatur ex parte vestrorum humilium oratorum, Prelatorum et Cleri regni.—*Ib.* 3, 466.

supremacy of the King over its civil establishment, having its own representative assemblies, and perfectly guarded and hedged-in from external interference with its patronage and temporal possessions. Its bishops held that they derived their spiritual authority, not from the Pope, but from Christ Himself, a doctrine which lies at the very foundation of the idea of a national Church. They believed that a general council was above the Pope, and had authority to depose him.[1] They acknowledged him as their spiritual head and primate, and as the centre and source of Catholic unity, but they rejected his interference with the patronage of their Church, or with its external regimen. Besides this acknowledgment of his spiritual supremacy, certain payments were made to the Pope by the State, and by the clerical order or individuals of it. Ethelwolf's pension, often confounded with Peter's Pence, was a fixed sum amounting to about three hundred marks, and was paid by the kingdom at large. So also was Peter's Pence, which was "a penny for every chimney which smoked in England," and which Fuller estimated at £7,500 a year. Tenths, or the Tithe of Tithes, was an annual tax contributed by the clergy. *Annates* or first fruits was the payment of a year's revenue imposed on archbishoprics and bishoprics. Both tenths and *annates* had been condemned by the Councils of Constance and Basle, but notwithstanding these decrees were still collected. The amount paid as *annates* by each bishop on his election or translation was formerly very large. The Archbishops of Canterbury paid on their entrance to that see

[1] This was also the belief of Sir Thomas More. " For in the next general council it may well happen that this Pope may be deposed and another substituted in his room, with whom the K. H. may be very well content. For albeit that I have for mine own part such opinion of the Pope's primacy as I have showed you, yet never thought I the Pope above the general council."—More's letter to Cromwell; Strype, *Eccl. Mem.* 1, pt. 2, 202.

for *annates* and their pall fifteen thousand florins.[1] Cranmer was the last English prelate, except those who did so in the reign of Queen Mary, who received Papal Bulls on his promotion. In his case they were eleven in number, for which the Archbishop paid a sum of nine hundred ducats. The smallness of this sum may be accounted for by the late Act which provided that five per cent. only on the first year's revenue should be paid as *annates*. Besides these fixed payments the Popes also derived considerable sums from appeals, in those cases in which they were allowed, dispensations, mortuaries on the death of prelates, legatine levies, indulgences, and pardons.

It is to be observed that the relation of the French State and Church to the Papacy was almost identical with that of England and her Church, as may be seen from the laws and rules which prevailed in that country. No Papal legate was admitted into France but at the request of the sovereign, and before he had taken an oath not to execute his office longer than it should please the King. The sovereign had power at all times to assemble national and provincial synods, and therein to treat of all things concerning ecclesiastical order and discipline. Papal bulls, citations, and sentences of excommunication were not to be executed without the King's permission, and, after permission granted, only by the authority of the King and not of the Pope. Papal provisions, reservations, and expectatives were illegal. The Pope could not exempt any Church, monastery, or religious body from the jurisdiction of the ordinary. General Councils were held to be superior to the Pope, and to possess the power of deposing him. Ecclesiastics might be summoned and convicted before secular judges for the first grievous offence, or for a lesser one after a relapse. Neither the kingdom, the King, nor his officers could be interdicted or excommunicated

---

[1] A florin was four shillings and sixpence.

by the Pope. The Papal authority was limited by the Canons of the ancient councils received in France. The prelates were not allowed for any cause whatever to leave the country without the King's license. *Annates* and tenths had been abolished.[1] Elections to dignities were free. Like their English brethren, the bishops held that they derived their authority immediately from Christ and not from the Pope.[2]

[1] *Annates* were restored to the Pope by the Concordat of 1517.

[2] For these positions and many others see *Traitez des Droits et Libertez de l'Eglise Gallicane*, particularly the commentary of Pierre Pithou.

CHAPTER III

THE REIGN OF HENRY VIII

SECTION I

It is impossible to understand the events which occurred in the reign of Henry VIII. without an accurate knowledge of the nature of the supremacy to which the King succeeded, and which had been exercised by his predecessors in ecclesiastical matters from time immemorial. The historians who start with the idea that the royal supremacy was an invention of Henry, and an innovation in our Church, misconceive, and therefore misrepresent, the occurrences of this reign. To them each step is a new institution or a fresh departure, instead of being a confirmation of the state of affairs which prevailed at the King's accession, and which had been handed down to him from the earliest times. When, in addition, these writers decline to recognize the distinction between a spiritual supremacy and an ecclesiastical one, which latter is, in its essence, of a civil nature, their guidance deserves to be set aside. They neglect the real causes of the English Reformation, and are in possession of but one key to explain its events. Everything is referred to the anger of the King against the Pope; all else is ignored. The tendency of contemporaneous thought, and the effects of the new learning; the indignation at the general mismanagement of the Church; the irritation caused by the Papal exactions, and the venality of the Roman Curia, which had passed into a proverb; the growth of doubt respecting the whole system of mediation between God and man as then taught; the recognition of the sovereignty of the individual conscience; the universal resentment at the political ambition of the Popes; the abuses in converting the sentences of the Church into instruments of extortion; the encroachments on Episcopal rights and discipline by appeals, exemptions, and dispensations purchasable at Rome, and the consequent crippling of the pastoral administration of dioceses: all these are forgotten or passed over in silence. Nor is there any mention of two important considerations which specially influenced the English movement, and without which its history can hardly be understood—(1) that the foundations of the English Reformation were laid by Churchmen who were not Reformers in the popular sense; and (2) that there was behind the King a nation, represented in the House of Commons, urging him to proceed much faster than he himself was inclined to go. The student of our Church history, and particularly of that part of it which occupies this reign, must expect but little aid from our lay historians, from Hallam, inclusive, downwards. If he wishes to comprehend the subject thoroughly, and from the beginning, he must betake himself to our statutes, to the rolls of parliament, to contemporaneous authorities, and to our ecclesiastical writers.

When we are told that the English Reformation was the work of Henry, we are listening to the guesses of children. A sovereign surrounded, as the Turkish Sultans once were, with a celibate and homeless host of Janissaries, could not by his authority alone effect a change in the religious belief of a pious and earnest nation, such as the English; much less could a King make the attempt who did not possess a standing army, and who was supported only by a few yeomen of the guard, in a kingdom where every man was armed. If ever there was a European movement, it was the Reformation, of which the English was but a chapter. It

was the swell of the ocean, not a flood in a river. From
every corner of the Western world there came a cry for the
reform of the Church in its head and members, and the cry
found an echo in the palace of the Popes. "We are well
aware," wrote Pope Adrian VI. to his legate, Chieregato,
whom he sent to the Diet at Nuremberg, in 1522,[1] "that for
a long time many abominations have existed in this sacred
seat;[2] abuses of spiritual things, excesses in the exercise of
its authority; everything has been turned to evil. Nor is
it to be marvelled at if the sickness has descended from the
head to the members, from the supreme Pontiffs to the
inferior bishops. We, the prelates of the Church, have all
gone astray, we have turned every one to his own way, there
is none of us that has done good, no, not one. . . .
Wherein, for so much as concerns us, you shall promise that
we will do our utmost endeavour that in the first place this
court, from whence peradventure the evil has proceeded, may
be reformed; that as the corruption flowed from thence to
all inferiors, so likewise the health and reformation of all
may proceed from the same source. To effect which we
consider ourselves the more closely bound, as we perceive
that *the whole world* ardently desires a reformation of this

[1] It was to this legate that the German princes presented their
"Centum gravamina" or hundred-fold complaint. These may be found
in *Fasciculus Rerum Expetend. et Fugiend.* Lord Herbert gives an
abridged translation of them in his history.

[2] Scimus in hac sancta sede aliquot jam annis multa abominanda
fuisse, abusus in spiritualibus, excessus in mandatis, et omnia denique in
perversum mutata. Nec mirum si ægritudo a capite in membra, a summis
pontificibus in alios inferiores prælatos descenderit. Omnes nos, id est
prælati ecclesiastici, declinavimus, unusquisque in vias suas, nec fuit
jam diu qui faceret bonum, non fuit usque ad unum. . . . Qua in re,
quod ad nos attinet, polliceberis nos omnem operam adhibituros, ut
primum curia hæc, unde forte omne hoc malum processit, reformetur, ut
sicut inde corruptio in omnes inferiores emanavit, ita etiam ab eadem
sanitas et reformatio omnium emanet.—*Fasciculus Rerum Expetend. et
Fugiend.* 1, 345.

kind. . . . Let no one be astonished if we do not at once reform all errors and abuses. Inasmuch as the disease is inveterate, not simple but complicated and multiform, we must proceed carefully and step by step."[1]

Fourteen years later Paul III. issued instructions to nine eminent ecclesiastics to inquire into the state of the Church and to draw up a scheme for its reform. The commission consisted of four cardinals, two archbishops, one bishop, an abbot, and a master of the Papal palace. Among the cardinals were John Peter Caraffa, afterwards Pope Paul IV., and Reginald Pole. These nine drew up a scheme of reform and presented it to the Pope signed by them all.[2] In the opening of this remarkable document, after describing the Church as not merely tottering, but actually fallen in ruin,[3] they accused some of the former Popes of having chosen their ministers, not with a view to learn from them what their duty required, but in order to have cunning advocates to prove that it was lawful for Popes to do what they pleased. "Hence, as flattery attends princes as the shadow does the body, doctors began to teach that, as the Popes were the lords of all benefices, they could not be guilty of simony, inasmuch as they rightfully sold what was their own property. From which source, as from the Trojan horse, so many abuses and such grievous diseases have broken into the Church of God that we now see it labouring almost without a hope of salvation, and the name of Christ blasphemed by the

[1] Ad quod procurandum nos tanto arctius obligatos reputamus, quanto universum mundum hujusmodi reformationem avidius desiderare videmus. . . . Quanquam nemo mirari debebit, si non statim omnia errata et abusus omnes per nos emendatos viderit. . . . Inveteratus nimium morbus est, nec simplex, sed varius et multiplex; pedetentim in ejus cura procedendum est.—*Ib.*

[2] Consilium Delectorum Cardinalium, &c., de emendanda ecclesia Romana jussu Pauli III. Papæ conscriptum.—*Fasciculus Expetend. et Fugiend.* 2, 231.

[3] Labantem, imo vero collapsam in præceps ecclesiam Christi.

unbelieving through our fault; we say it again, through our fault."[1]

From this introduction they proceed to enumerate the abuses which prevailed in the Church.

Abuses in dispensing with its laws.

In ordaining ignorant youths of the vilest birth and of the worst morals. "Hence arise innumerable scandals, contempt for the ecclesiastical order, and the veneration for divine service is not only lessened, but now nearly extinct."

In the bestowal of benefices, and above all, of bishoprics, on non-residents.

In the imposition of pensions on benefices in favour of wealthy ecclesiastics, and the consequent withdrawal of what was intended for the support of divine service and of the incumbents.

Exchanges of livings by agreements, "which are all simoniacal, and in which nothing is regarded but money."

The bequest of benefices and bishoprics by dispensations, nullifying the law that children of priests should not inherit the benefices of their fathers.

Abuses in expectations and reservations.

In conferring several incompatible benefices and even bishoprics on the same person.

In granting, not one, but several bishoprics to cardinals. "We think this matter is of the greatest importance to the Church of God; for the offices of cardinals and bishops are inconsistent. A cardinal assists the Pope in governing the whole Church, whereas the duty of a bishop is to feed his sheep, which he cannot do unless he dwells among them."

[1] Ex hoc fonte tanquam ex equo Trojano irrupere in ecclesiam Dei tot abusus et tam gravissimi morbi, quibus nunc conspicimus eam ad desperationem fere salutis laborare, vel manasse earum rerum famam ad infideles usque, qui ob hanc præcipue causam christianam religionem derident, adeo ut per nos, per nos inquimus, nomen Christi blasphemetur inter gentes.

Non-residence of bishops and beneficed clergymen. "For, in the name of God,[1] what sight can be more afflicting to a Christian man than to see the solitude of the churches. Almost all the pastors have deserted their flocks, and the faithful are given over to mere mercenaries."

Neglect of their duties by the cardinals.

Abuses in the impediments thrown in the way of bishops attempting to govern their dioceses and to punish the guilty. "For bad men obtain exemption from the authority of their bishops, or if they cannot obtain an exemption, they immediately betake themselves to the office of the Datary and there secure impunity for money."

In the religious orders. "We are of opinion that all conventual orders should be abolished, but in order to prevent injury to anyone, it will be sufficient to decree that no new members be admitted."

Public sacrilege in many monasteries.

Impious and irreverent treatment of sacred subjects in the public schools, especially in Italy; "nay, in the very churches."

Abuses in the deception of country and simple folk by the innumerable superstitions introduced by the *quæstuarii*[2] of the Holy Ghost, of St. Anthony, and others of this sort. "We think that these *quæstuarii* should be abolished."

Abuses in absolution for simony. "To what a height, in the name of decency,[3] has this pestilent vice come to in the Church of God, so that some are not ashamed to commit simony and then to seek, nay buy, absolution for the offence, while retaining the benefices they purchased."

In bequeathing the goods of the Church as private

---

[1] Per Deum immortalem.

[2] Hawkers of indulgences, known in England as "pardoners."

[3] Proh pudor.

property, in indulgences, and in the transfer of legacies given for pious uses to the surviving relatives for money.

The scandal given to all foreigners by the corrupt manners of the city of Rome, and by the open exhibition of shameless immorality by ecclesiastics in its streets.

The scheme of reform ends with these words: "If we have not done justice to the magnitude of the trust reposed in us, we have at least satisfied our conscience, not without hope that in your reign we shall see the Church of God purged, fair as a dove, at peace with herself, and united into one body. You have taken the name of Paul: we trust you will imitate his charity. As he was chosen to spread the knowledge of the name of Christ among the heathen, we hope that you were elected to restore, in our hearts and in our works, that holy name which is now forgotten by the nations and by us ecclesiastics, to cure our sickness, to collect the flock into one fold, and to save us from the wrath of God and from the punishment which we have deserved and which is now ready to fall upon us."[1]

Such was the condition of the Church throughout Europe as depicted by Popes and cardinals when Henry VIII. came to the throne,—unsoundness in its head and members; the whole world, as Pope Adrian said, longing ardently for its reform. Revolutions which shake the deepest foundations of society, and destroy old forms of belief; reformations, for which a world is anxiously looking, do not take their rise from the will of a single individual. They are the slow growth of time, the outcome and final result of centuries of forgetfulness of duty, and of infinite and wide-spread mismanagement. It is as great a folly to attribute the English Reformation to the will of Henry as to ascribe the gradual

---

[1] This scheme of reform was put on the Index by Pope Paul IV., though he himself had been a member of the commission which drew it up. This is the only instance of a Pope putting himself on the Index.

and necessary progress of the Papacy to the False Decretals, or to assert that the French Revolution sprang from a single cause. At the time of Henry's accession the Reformation was already in existence, silently working and fermenting in the minds of all men, Popes, cardinals, and laymen. Any occasion might give it birth; at any moment, any individual —a monk in Germany or a King in England—might call it forth and clothe it with a shape and a name. Henry's part in the English movement has been greatly overrated. The hatred of ultramontane writers, his conspicuous position, and the long drama of the divorce, have given him an undue position in its history. We shall find on examining his reign that what Fuller and our other ecclesiastical historians assert is strictly true, "that there was nothing done in the Reformation save what was acted by the clergy in their Convocation, or grounded on some act of theirs precedent to it." Henry's principal achievement was, that he carried the country safely, without massacres, and without a general civil war, through the most tremendous crisis that ever existed in England.

SECTION II

WE have seen the nature and extent of the ecclesiastical supremacy to which Henry succeeded. Two incidents in the early part of his reign, while he was yet recognized as a devoted son of the Church, show us that he was well acquainted with this supremacy, and was resolved to maintain it. There still exists a copy of his coronation oath, altered and interlined with his own hand. The old form runs thus: "The King shall swear at his coronation that he shall keep and maintain the rights and liberties of Holy Church, of old time granted by the righteous Christian Kings of England." The oath as altered stands: "The King shall then swear that he shall keep and maintain the *lawful* right and the liberties of old time granted by the righteous Christian Kings of England to the Holy Church of England, *not prejudicial to his jurisdiction and dignity royal*."[1] The second incident took place in the sixth year of his reign. By a statute[2] passed three years before, which was only to endure till the next Parliament, it had been enacted that the benefit of clergy should be taken from those who were in minor orders, who had been guilty of murder or highway robbery.[3] In 1515 the Abbot of Winchcomb

---

[1] Ellis, *Original Letters*, second series, 1, 176.
[2] 4 Henry VIII. c. 2.
[3] There were five minor orders: subdeacons, acolyths, exorcists, readers, ostiaries.—Gibson's *Codex*, 1, 99.

declared in a sermon at Paul's Cross that the Act was against the laws of God and the liberties of Holy Church; that all who were concerned in making it had incurred the censures of the Church; and that, although only the greater orders were excepted in the Act, all clerks, who had received orders of any kind, were exempt from punishment for criminal causes before a temporal judge. On the other hand it was affirmed by Dr. Standish, before a council of divines and temporal lords, summoned by the King to examine an assertion so derogatory to the laws of the land, that the convening of the clergy before a temporal judge in criminal causes was not contrary to the law of God or the liberties of the Church. For which opinion, among others, he was brought before Convocation and articles there exhibited against him. Standish appealed for protection to the King, who summoned a meeting of the Lords, many of the Commons, the Judges, and the Privy Council, to hear the matter debated. A further and full examination of the question took place, and Wolsey entreated the King, in the name of the clergy, to refer the decision of the matter to the Pope and the Conclave. To this the King replied that he thought Dr. Standish, and others of his council, had given a sufficient answer to the clergy. Warham then urged that divers holy fathers of the Church had opposed the convening of ecclesiastics before a temporal judge, and even suffered martyrdom in defence of that opinion. Fineux, the Chief Justice, then asked by what law bishops could judge clerks for felony, it being a thing determinable only in the temporal court. "Either a clerk," he continued, "must be prosecuted in the temporal court, or escape the punishment due to his crime." The prelates making no answer to this dilemma, the King said, "By the providence and permission of God we are King of England, and the Kings of England in times past had never any superior but God only. Therefore, know you well that we will maintain the rights of our Crown and of our temporal jurisdiction as well in this as in all other points, in as ample a manner as any of our progenitors have done before our time. And as for your decrees, we are well assured that you of the spirituality go expressly against the words of divers of them, as hath been shown you by some of our council ; and you interpret your decrees at your pleasure, but we will not agree to them more than our progenitors have done in former times."

No occurrence in this reign has been so much misunderstood as the acknowledgment of the King's supremacy by the Convocation, in 1531. What the King meant when he demanded this acknowledgment, and what the clergy intended by making it, have been equally misrepresented. Though the King expressed himself clearly on the subject, and though bishops preached, and wrote books, "by the advice and consent of Convocation,"[1] in favour of the royal supremacy, we still affect to be in doubt as to the wishes and intentions of the King and of his clergy. Some writers even appear to think that, in requiring to be recognised as head of the English Church, Henry laid claim to a spiritual supremacy. The bishops, five of whom wrote in favour of the King's claim,[2] had no such idea, either at the time they voted unanimously for it, or six years after. In 1537 a treatise, known as the Bishops' Book, or the "Institution of a Christian Man," appeared, in which both the bishops and the King bore a part, the former in compiling it and the latter in publishing it with his authority. It was addressed to the King, as "supreme head in earth, immediately under Christ, of the Church of England," and was signed by all the archbishops and bishops of England, and by twenty-five others, as repre-

---

[1] Strype, *Mem. Eccles.* 1, 263.
[2] Fox of Hereford ; Gardiner of Winchester ; Stokesly of London ; Tunstall of Durham ; Bonner, afterwards of London.

sentatives of both Houses of Convocation. In this treatise the nature of the spiritual commission claimed by the Church, and that of the temporal authority of the State, are accurately distinguished, and the line between them carefully drawn. " We think it convenient that all bishops and preachers shall instruct and teach the people, committed unto their spiritual charge, that the jurisdiction committed unto priests and bishops by the authority of God's law, consisteth in three special points. The first is, to rebuke and reprehend sin, and to excommunicate the manifest and obstinate sinners, that is to say, to separate, exclude, and repel from the communion and perception of the sacraments, and to reject and cast out of the congregation and company of Christ's people, such persons as have manifestly committed mortal sin and do obstinately persevere in the same: and to absolve and receive them again whensoever they shall return unto the Church by condign penance, &c. . . . The second point . . . is to approve and admit such persons as [being nominated, elected, and presented unto them, to exercise the office and room of preaching the Gospel, and of ministering the sacraments, and to have the cure of jurisdiction over these certain people within this parish or within this diocese] shall be thought unto them meet and worthy to exercise the same; and to reject and repel from the said room such as they shall judge to be unmeet therefor. . . . The third point is . . . to make and ordain certain rules or canons concerning holidays, fasting-days, the manner and ceremonies to be used in the ministration of the sacraments, the manner of singing the psalms and spiritual hymns, as St. Paul calleth them, the diversity of degrees among the ministers, and the form and manner of their ornaments, and, finally, concerning such other rites, ceremonies, and observances as do tend and conduce to the preservation of quietness and decent order to be had and used among the people when they shall be assembled together in the temple. And forasmuch also as great trouble, unquietness, and tumult might arise among the multitude so assembled, in case there were no certain rules, ordinances, and ceremonies prescribed unto them, whereby they should be contained in quietness, and not suffered to do every man after his own fashion or appetite; it belongeth unto the jurisdiction of priests and bishops to make certain rules or canons concerning all these things and for the causes aforesaid," &c.

The ecclesiastical supremacy of the sovereign is thus described and qualified:—" God constituted and ordained the authority of Christian kings and princes to be the most high and supreme above all other powers and offices in the regiment and governance of his people; and committed unto them, as unto the chief heads of their commonwealths, the care and oversight of all the people which be within their realms and dominions without any exception. And unto them of right and by God's commandment belongeth, not only to prohibit unlawful violence, and correct offenders by corporal death or other punishment, to conserve moral honesty among their subjects, according to the laws of their realms, to defend justice, and to procure the public weal, and the common peace and tranquillity in outward and earthly things; but specially and principally to defend the faith of Christ and his religion, to conserve and maintain the true doctrine of Christ, and all such as be true preachers and setters forth thereof, and to abolish all abuses, heresies, and idolatries, which be brought in by heretics and evil preachers, and to punish with corporal pains such as of malice be occasioners of the same; and finally to oversee and cause that the said priests and bishops do execute their said power, office, and jurisdiction truly, faithfully, and according in all points as it was given and committed unto them by Christ and his apostles; which notwithstanding, we may not think that it doth appertain unto the office of kings and princes to preach and teach, to administer the sacraments, to absolve, to excommunicate, and such other things belonging to the office and administration of bishops and priests; but we must think and believe that God has constituted and made Christian kings and princes to be as the chief heads and overlookers over the said priests and bishops to cause them to administer their office and power committed unto them purely and sincerely. . . . And God hath also commanded the said priests and bishops to obey, with all humbleness and reverence, all the laws made by the said princes, being not contrary to the laws of God, whatsoever they be; and that not only *propter iram*, but also *propter conscientiam*." This treatise was again published in 1543 and 1545 with some additions, under the title of "The necessary doctrine and erudition for any Christian man." The King prefaced it with a declaration, the last sentence of which is—"So as, endeavouring ourselves to live quietly and charitably together, each one in his vocation, we shall be so replenished with manifold graces and gifts of God, that after this life we shall reign in joy everlasting with the only head of the universal Catholic Church, our Saviour and Redeemer Jesus Christ." Further on we shall see what the King meant by this claim to be the head of the English Church at the time when the matter was still in debate before the Convocation of York.

The immediate causes of the King's demand, that he should be recognized as the head of the Church—or as he himself explained it, the head of the English clergy regarded as citizens and not as spiritual pastors[1]—were the malpractices of Wolsey and of that clergy, and the fact that the ecclesiastical order claimed to be a body exempted from and above the law of the land.

[1] See the well-known letter of the King to the clergy of the Province of York.—*Cabala*, 2, 1.

There never was a man more justly punished than Wolsey. The first question to be determined in considering whether or not he was guilty of the offences laid to his charge is, what authority he was possessed of under his legatine commission? This question has been overlooked by those historians with whom Wolsey's patronage of learning has covered all his faults, and even his insatiable rapacity. Hume has asserted that he was condemned for taking on himself the character of a legate, and Atterbury and others have repeated the groundless statement. Wolsey was punished, not for obtaining a commission as Papal legate, but for having exercised, under colour of that commission, an authority which was directly contrary to the laws of England. At the time when he was appointed legate, the Pope, who commissioned him, had no ecclesiastical jurisdiction in England, nor could he appoint to the meanest office in the English Church. The Pontiff might, and did, down to and including the case of Cranmer, go through the form of drawing up bulls *providing* bishops for English sees, and regulating the concerns of the English Church; but these bulls possessed no force until quickened into life by the assent of the King, and the recipients of them sued out their pardon for having accepted or read them. As has been said, no Englishman, lay or cleric, could send to, or receive from, Rome, any communication without the previous license of the King, except in testamentary and matrimonial appeals. If he did so, he incurred the penalties of outlawry and imprisonment; and if he accepted, without the same license, a dignity or benefice in England from the Pope, he was liable to banishment for ever, and forfeiture of all his property, real and personal. What the Pope had not, he could not convey to a deputy. In the face of English laws every document which emanated from Rome was waste paper, unless the King, of his special favour, and by his letters patent, ratified and confirmed each particular act and instrument. No one knew better than Wolsey that a Papal bull or letter had not of itself the slightest effect in England, and that it was illegal to act upon or even to receive such instruments without the special license of the King. In 1524, six years after he was appointed legate, he obtained a bull from the Pope authorizing him to suppress the monastery of St. Frideswide, and to convert its revenues to the use of his college at Oxford. "We have inspected," says the King in his letters patent issued on this occasion, "the bull granted to Thomas, Archbishop of York, and legate of the Apostolic See, by Clement, seventh of that name, and believing that it was issued for no other purpose than to convert the revenues of the college to a better use, we, of our special favour, approve and ratify the suing out of the said bull, its presentation, exhibition, acceptance, or reception, and its execution; our intention being that none of our justices or ministers should, under colour of our prerogative or the rights of our Crown, presume to question or institute proceedings by reason of any application for it, or the exhibition, acceptance, execution, or use of the same."[1] In addition to the impotency of Wolsey's commission, and of him who granted it, there is another important fact to be taken into consideration. During the whole period of Wolsey's legation, there was another legate in England, namely, Archbishop Warham, who, in virtue of his archbishopric, was clothed with that office, as all his predecessors had been since the time of William de Corbeuil.[2] Warham was "*legatus sedis apostolicæ*" when Wolsey was appointed "*legatus a latere.*" The expression *a latere* or *missus a latere* meant simply any one coming from the immediate presence of a prince with a

---

[1] Rymer, xiv. 15. The bull is set out at length in the Letters Patent.

[2] Archbishop of Canterbury, 1122-1136.

special commission. Thus, when Becket returned to England in 1170, the young King ordered him, by the mouth of two knights, sent *a latere ejus*, to reside at Canterbury.[1] Wolsey never had a special commission from the Pope such as was granted to legates *a latere*, except when, at the end of his career and by the desire of the King, he was appointed conjointly with Campeggio, to hear and determine in England the case of Henry's marriage. We know too that the first Papal commission to Wolsey did not contain any of the faculties conceded to legates *a latere*. The omission was insisted on by the King. In 1518, the year of Wolsey's appointment, and before it was made, the Pope proposed to send into England a legate *a latere* to urge the King to join a confederation against the Turks. Campeggio was selected at Rome for this mission. When Pace showed the King the letters in which Campeggio's mission was announced, the latter at once remarked, "it was not the rule of this realm to admit legates *de latere*; if, however, he had nothing else except to treat against the Turks he would admit him."[2] Accordingly, Wolsey wrote to the Bishop of Worcester, the English ambassador at Rome, that the King would consent to the coming of Campeggio, on the condition that all the faculties which were usually granted to legates *a latere* should be omitted or suspended in this case, and that his own name, Wolsey's, should be included in the commission, "otherwise the King will in no wise allow Campeggio to enter England."[3] It is clear that the King's conditions were accepted, for the Papal commission to Wolsey merely states that the Pope had sent Campeggio to England to further a confederation against the Turks, and that the Pope, in consideration of

---

[1] Per duos milites qui a latere regis missi fuerant.—Gerv. of Canterbury, 1, 223.
[2] *Letters and Papers of the Reign of Henry VIII.* vol. 2, pt. 2, 1247.
[3] *Ib.* 1263.

Wolsey's influence with the King, had created him legate along with Campeggio.[1] So that it appears that Wolsey's commission as legate, to which the King assented, did not affect to grant him any authority to interfere in Church matters at home,[2] and was a mere honorary distinction which conferred no power or even privilege on him except, perhaps, the fanciful one of having two crosses borne before him in the province of another Archbishop.[3]

It is certain that Wolsey, before he accepted the office of legate *a latere*, obtained the King's permission authorizing him to do so,[4] and that in accepting it with the King's license, he committed no offence against the English law. If Wolsey had not attempted under cover of this office to contravene the statutes of the realm, and if he had kept the solemn promise which he made when he first aspired to the office, he might have safely enjoyed it.[5] What he was

---

[1] *Ib.* 1291.

[2] Yet in the first year of his legateship Wolsey ventured to forbid Warham to hold a council of his suffragans for the reformation of matters in the province of Canterbury. In this prohibition Wolsey writes to the archbishop:—"Being legate *a latere*, to me chiefly it appertaineth to see the reformation of the premises, though hitherto nor in time coming I have nor will execute any jurisdiction as legate *a latere* but only as shall stand with the King's pleasure."—Archbishop Wake, *State of the Church*, App. 208.

[3] The carriage of a cross, or *bajulatio crucis* as it was called, before an archbishop, was an old and fruitful cause of quarrels between the two metropolitans of England. Each considered it an insult to his dignity if the other had his cross carried before him out of his own province. In 1279 the Archbishop of York, coming to the King, had his cross borne before him in the province of Canterbury. Thereupon Peckham prohibited, under the penalty of excommunication, any one from furnishing to the archbishop or his attendants, food, drink, or other necessaries.— Prynne, *Records*, 3, 230.

[4] The 28th of the Articles exhibited against Wolsey in parliament. Wolsey in testimony of his confession subscribed all these Articles.— Wake, 472.

[5] "Had Wolsey kept his word and attempted nothing contrary to

accused of was, that he abused his authority and acted directly contrary to the Acts of *Provisors* and *Præmunire;* that by means of Papal bulls he deprived lay and ecclesiastical patrons of their rights of presentation in favour of his own creatures;[1] that by the same means he appointed to benefices by provision; that he drew into his legatine court all matters cognizable in the ecclesiastical courts belonging either to archbishops or bishops; that by means of the same court he assumed a power of intermeddling with wills and testaments, as Archbishop Warham told him, " not so much as claimed by the Pope himself."

An indictment under the last statute of *Præmunire* was brought against Wolsey, to which the cardinal pleaded guilty, and threw himself on the King's mercy. He also executed a deed to the King by which he acknowledged that on the authority of bulls from Rome he had unlawfully vexed " the greater number of the prelates of the realm, and other of the King's subjects, thereby incurring the penalties of *præmunire*, for which he deserved to suffer perpetual imprisonment, and forfeit all his lands and goods." As some atonement for his offence he prayed the King to take all his temporal possessions, pensions, and benefices, of which he offered to make further assurance when it should be required.[2]

---

the King's prerogative or to the laws of the realm in virtue of it, he might as safely have enjoyed that character without any damage to himself or detriment to the clergy as Cardinal Pole afterwards did or might have done. But he abused it grossly in the exercise of it."—*Ib.* 482.

[1] Two cases of this kind were proved against him to support the indictment; that he had bestowed the church of Stoke-Guilford on James Gorton, though its patronage belonged to the Prior of St. Pancras, and that he had given the church of Galby to Dr. Allen, the true patrons of which were the master and fellows of the hospital of St. Lazarus in Burton-Lazar.—Herbert's *Henry VIII.*

[2] *Letters and Papers of the Reign of Henry VIII.* vol. 4, part 3, p. 2678.

We also have a letter from him to the King at this time asking for mercy, in which these words occur:—"The remembrance of my folly, with the sharp sword of your Highness' displeasure hath so penetrated my heart that I cannot but lamentably cry, *sufficit; nunc contine, piissime rex, manum tuam.*"[1]

The general body of the clergy was punished, not for having submitted to the legatine authority of Wolsey, but for having offended against the laws of *Provisors* and *Præmunire.* Wolsey, by granting faculties and instruments by which benefices were given by provisions, and the rights of lay and ecclesiastical patrons were set aside, had violated these statutes, and the clergy, by purchasing and receiving such instruments and accepting benefices under them, had complied with and favoured his illegal and criminal procedure.[2] That this is an accurate account of the matter, and of the position in which they stood, is proved by the language of the clergy on two occasions; by the words of the pardons which were subsequently granted to them; by the facts that they themselves did not restrain their offence to a mere submission to the legate's authority; and that they never denied their guilt or questioned the justice of their punishment. On the 7th of February, 1531, the clergy of the province of Canterbury debated in Convocation as to the nature of the pardon which should be asked from the King. They described it as a general pardon and remission of their transgressions against the penal laws and statutes of the realm, and also against the statutes of *Præmunire.*[3] And in their petition or grant to the King in the

[1] Brewer's *Reign of Henry VIII.* 2, 379.
[2] "But notwithstanding these laws the Pope still proceeded in his own way, and the clergy were always willing to assist him in it. And by these means there were but very few of any note among them who had not upon some account or other incurred the penalty before mentioned."—Archbishop Wake, *State of the Church*, 481.
[3] Wilkins' *Concilia*, 3, 725.

same year they recite as one of their reasons for making the grant, that the King should extend to all prelates, clerks, religious orders, abbesses, prioresses, and also to all judges, advocates, registrars, scribes, proctors, and apparitors, who had exercised ecclesiastical jurisdiction, his general pardon and remission of all their transgressions both against the penal laws and statutes of the realm, and also those against the Acts of *Provisors* and *Præmunire*.[1] The words of the King's pardon run thus:—"The King ... calling to his remembrance that ... the Archbishop of Canterbury and other bishops, suffragans, prelates, and other spiritual persons of the province ... have fallen and incurred into divers dangers of his laws by things done ... contrary to the order of his laws, and specially contrary to the statutes of *Provisors*, *Provisions*, and *Præmunire* ... is fully and resolutely contented and pleased that the said archbishop, &c., shall be by authority of this present parliament acquitted and discharged all and all manner of offences, contempts, and trespasses committed or done against all and singular statute and statutes of *Provisors*, *Provisions*, and *Præmunire*, and of all forfeitures and titles which may grow to the King by reason of the same statutes."[2] The pardon granted to the clergy of the province of York is in the same terms.[3]

The trafficking with bulls from Rome and with provisions appears to have been general, not only among the clergy but even among the laity;[4] for the Commons besought the

[1] Generalem gratiam et pardonationem de omnibus eorum transgressionibus pœnalium legum et statutorum hujus regni, tum cæterorum, tum etiam statutorum de provisoribus et præmunire.—Wilkins' *Concilia*, 3, 743.

[2] 22 Henry VIII. c. 15.—*Statutes of the Realm*, 3, 334.

[3] 23 Henry VIII. c. 19.—*Ib.* 383.

[4] A pardon was also granted to the laity for their offences "contrary to the statutes of *Provisors* and *Præmunire*," by the 22 Hen. VIII. c. 16.

King to comprehend them also in the pardon granted to the clergy.[1] It is hard to see, how in the face of the concurrent testimony of the clergy and laity, the words of the King's pardon, the confessions of Wolsey, and the parliamentary accusation against him signed by no less a man than More, historians have arrived at the conclusion that Wolsey was punished for accepting a legatine commission, and that the clergy were included in it for merely submitting to his execution of the legation.[2]

So that what we find is this, that in spite of the statutes of *Provisors* and *Præmunire*, there was a general dealing with Papal bulls and provisions, and that the legislative Acts which protected the English Church from external control were being undermined both by Wolsey and the body of the clergy. To understand completely the reasons which induced the King's demand to be formally recognized by the clergy as their head, we must remember these facts and also two other circumstances. The first is, there were then two[3] parliaments in England; an Imperial parliament in which

---

[1] "Accordingly Sir Thomas Audley, Speaker of the Commons, with a number of members along with him, waited on His Majesty, and declared to him that his faithful Commons sore lamented and bewailed their chance in having occasion to think or imagine themselves out of his favour because he had granted his most gracious pardon to his spiritual subjects on the *Præmunire* and not to them."—*Parl. Hist.* 1, 514.

[2] On no occasion did the clergy deny their offence as a body, or question the justice of the King. Shortly after the pardon, a meeting of the London clergy was held at St. Paul's to settle the proportions of the fine to be paid by each. The bishop told them that "through frailty and want of wisdom they had misdemeaned themselves to the King, and had fallen in a *præmunire*." The poorer incumbents refused to contribute, on the ground that they had never meddled with the cardinal's faculties. "Since the bishops and abbots only were guilty, and had good preferments, they ought only to be punished."—Burnet's *Reform.* 1, 114.

[3] Or three, if we count the Convocation of York, but York generally followed the lead of Canterbury.

both the clergy and laity were represented, and a clerical parliament entirely confined to ecclesiastics and representing them alone. Of these two, the clerical parliament exercised a far more general legislative power than the Imperial assembly, and one which affected the lives of the citizens more frequently and more intimately. There was not an Englishman whose every act, from his birth to his death, was not regulated by the laws of the clerical parliament, in which no layman sat. The Acts passed in Convocation bound the laity,[1] and were administered by the Ecclesiastical Courts. In these courts every man might, on mere suspicion or from the malice of an informer, be summoned, and an oath offered to him binding him to discover whatever he knew to want amendment *in rebus et personis*. He was liable to be called in question for every trifling sin and for every offence against the moral law. It is almost impossible for us at the present day to realize the manner in which the enactments of this clerical parliament penetrated into the life of the citizen, or the influence it exercised over the arrangements of his home and family. A hasty word, a profane ejaculation, a remark on the character of a neighbour, absence from church, a loan of money at interest, a suspicion of heresy, or the expression of a doubt, were all sufficient to consign the victim to the tender mercies of courts, the costs of which were enormous and which had long ceased to exercise a true spiritual jurisdiction. Besides these causes all questions concerning testaments, administration,

---

[1] "The prelates and spiritual ordinaries . . . and the clergy have in their Convocations heretofore made and also daily do make many and divers fashions of law . . . unto the which laws your said lay subjects have not only heretofore been and daily be constrained to obey in their bodies, goods, and possessions, but have also been compelled to incur daily the censures of the same, and been continually put to importable charges and expences against all equity, right, and good conscience."—*Supplication of the Commons*, 1529.

marriage, divorce, adultery, &c., were regulated by the legislation of this clerical parliament.¹

The second circumstance is, that the clergy then formed an estate apart from the body of the people. They were exempted in general from the jurisdiction of the temporal courts, and were subject only to such punishments as were awarded by the laws of the Church and by their own enacted in Convocation. On a late occasion, when those in minor orders were for the first time made liable to the ordinary criminal law, Wolsey, who as cardinal was the chief of the English clergy, told the King in a public assembly that "in the opinion of the clergy the convening of ecclesiastics before temporal judges was directly contrary to the laws of God, and that he himself and the rest of the prelates were bound by their oath to maintain this exemption."² The clergy were in fact but half the King's subjects, and in possession of a parliament of their own, to the legislation of which they paid far more regard than to that of the Imperial Parliament, which hardly touched them. The Acts of Convocation did not require the assent of the King as was required in the case of the statutes of the realm.³ Heylyn thus describes the powers exercised by this clerical assembly. "Before this time [25th of Henry VIII.] they acted absolutely in their convocations of their own authority, the King's assent neither concurring nor required; and by the

---

¹ In 1532 the body of Richard Tracy, a gentleman of position, was, by order of Convocation, taken up and burned two years after his death, because in his will he had bequeathed his soul to God through the mercies of Christ only, and had left no money for masses.
² Collier, 2, 7.
³ In Blunt's *Reformation of the Church of England*, vol. 1, 236, note, it is stated that the assent of the King was given to the Acts of Convocation in gross, and not separately, as he assented to Acts of Parliament. Archbishop Wake and Heylyn are of opinion that the assent of the King was not required. The Supplication of the Commons in 1529 states positively that "the prelates and spritual ordinaries of

sole authority which they had in themselves, they did not only make canons, declare heresy, convict and censure persons suspected of heresy, in which the subjects of all sorts, whose votes were tacitly included in the suffrages of their pastors and spiritual fathers, were concerned alike."[1]

It was the existence in England of an *imperium in imperio*, of a class which claimed to be above the ordinary law of the land by the ordinance of God, and Henry's knowledge that this class, behind his back and in the face of stringent statutes, had been availing themselves of Papal bulls and faculties to mismanage the English Church, and to restore the old system of external control over it, which those statutes had been intended to abolish for ever, that determined the King to exact from his clergy an acknowledgment of his supremacy. He meant, as he told them, to be King over both ecclesiastics and laymen, and to maintain his temporal jurisdiction over them. Nor did he value their decrees to the contrary or their interpretation of them. It has been suggested that Henry's reason for making this demand was his desire to put pressure on the Pope in the matter of the divorce, but this surmise will not bear examination. The King had resolved to punish the clergy as early as 1529, for in the Act of General Pardon of that year the clergy were specially excepted from it. " Also excepted and forprised out of his pardon all offences and contempts committed and done against the statute or statutes of

this your most excellent realm of England and the clergy of the same, have in their Convocations heretofore made or caused to be made and also do make many and divers fashions of laws, constitutions, and ordinances, without your knowledge or most royal assent, and without the assent and consent of any of your lay subjects." The answer of the bishops to this Supplication puts the matter beyond doubt.—*Answer of the Ordinaries to the Supplication of the worshipful Commons*, Wilkins' *Concilia*, 3, 750; see also *A Declaration of the Clergy*, Ib. 753.

[1] Heylyn's *Tracts*, 4.

Provisors and *Præmunire*, or any of them, and all forfeitures and titles that may grow to the King's Highness by reason of any of the same statutes."[1] The divorce in 1529 was only in the second year of its prosecution, and four years of it had still to run. It would have been madness on the part of the King to have alarmed the Pope at this stage. Henry was on good terms with Clement and his Court in 1529, and for a long time later, for in 1532 he wrote to the conclave for a cardinal's hat for the Bishop of Worcester, and in 1533 he sent to the Pope for the bulls and pall for Cranmer on his promotion. It is a mistake to suppose that there was anything anti-Papal in Henry's requiring from his clergy a recognition of his headship, or that he intended to touch the spiritual supremacy of the Pope. So scrupulous was he about this, that even after he had assumed the title of head of the Church, Cranmer " was obliged at his consecration to take the usual oath of canonical obedience to the See of Rome."[2] Henry himself had no idea, either at this time or afterwards, that he was encroaching on the Pope's spiritual supremacy. For on the 20th of May, 1533, Henry wrote to the Pope assuring him that, after consultation with the French King, he would do all that he could for the preservation of the faith. The letter is addressed to " our most holy and most clement Lord the Pope." It commences: *Beatissime pater, post humilliman commendationem, et devotissima pedum oscula beatorum;* speaks of the Pope's burning zeal in propagating and preserving the Christian faith, and describes him as the best of pastors. The letter is signed by

---

[1] 21 Henry VIII. c. 1 ; *Stat. of the Realm*, 3, 282.

[2] Dodd's *Church Hist.* 1, 173. His editor, Tierney, adds this note:— " Nor was this a singular instance of the same feeling. Lee and Gardiner, when appointed in 1531 to the Sees of York and Winchester, were compelled to address the Pope for institution, and it was not until the Papal bulls had arrived, that Henry invested them with their temporalities."

the King as "your most devoted and most obedient son."¹ Nor was Clement of opinion that the proceeding was directed against himself, for he never remonstrated with Henry for making this demand. He and the Roman Court were well aware, as we have seen from the letter of Pope Martin V., of the nature and extent of the supremacy which the Kings of England exercised over the national Church, and knew that in making this claim Henry did not transcend his temporal rights.

In 1531 the clergy in the Convocation of Canterbury, after long deliberation,² recognized the King as the only and singular protector of the English Church, and as its supreme head so far as the law of Christ allowed.³ The question was put by Archbishop Warham, and was unanimously adopted, and subscribed by Warham himself, and the eight bishops, and sixty-two abbots and priors, who formed the Upper House, and by eighty-four members of the Lower House, forty-eight being proxies.⁴ What meaning did the clergy and the King attach to this new title, for the term was new, though the fact which it represented was as old as the monarchy? It is clear that the former intended only to acknowledge the temporal authority of the King over the

¹ Sanctissimo Clementissimoque Domino nostro Papae. Beatissime pater, post humillimam commendationem, et devotissima pedum oscula beatorum ... non potuimus Sanctitatis Vestrae ... flagrans studium, sollicitamque mentem non summopere laudare, optimique pastoris pectore dignam existimare. ... Ejusdem Vestrae Sanctitatis devotissimus atque obsequentissimus filius.—Pocock, *Records of the Reformation*, 2, 673.

² Tandem post longum tractatum inter nos, et confratres nostros, praelatosque, decanos, archidiaconos et cleri nostrae Cantuariensis provinciae procuratores.

³ Ecclesiae et cleri Anglicani, cujus singularem protectorem unicum et supremum dominum, et quantum per Christi legem licet, etiam supremum caput ipsius majestatem recognoscimus.—Wilkins' *Concilia*, 3, 742.

⁴ Lewis, *Reformation Settlement*, 22.

civil establishment of the Church, and over themselves as citizens, and did not mean to attribute spiritual jurisdiction to him. It is also clear that the King limited the acknowledgment to his jurisdiction over the persons of his clergy in criminal matters. This appears from a letter which he wrote in answer to one from Tunstall, Bishop of Durham, and the Convocation of York in 1531, while the question was still pending before that assembly. "It were" says the King, "*nimis absurdum* for us to be called *caput ecclesiæ representans corpus Christi mysticum, et ecclesiæ quæ sine ruga est et macula quam Christus sibi sponsam elegit, illius partem vel oblatam accipere vel arrogare.* And therefore albeit *ecclesia* is spoken of in these words, touched in the proem, yet there is added *et Cleri Anglicani:* which words conjoined restraineth by way of interpretation the word *ecclesiam*, and is as much as to say as the Church, that is to say, the clergy of England.... After that ye intend to prove, what no man will deny, the ministration of spiritual things to have been by Christ committed to priests to preach and minister the sacraments, them to be as physicians to men's souls; but in these scriptures neither by spiritual things so far extended, as under colour of that vocabule be now-a-days, nor it proveth not that, their office being never so excellent, yet their persons, acts, and deeds, should not be under the power of their prince ... other crimes we leave to be ordered by the clergy, not because we may not intermeddle with them, for there is no doubt but as well might we punish adultery and insolence in priests as Emperors have done, and other princes at this day do, which ye know well enough; so as in all those articles concerning the persons of priests, their laws, their acts, and order of living, forasmuch as they be indeed all temporal and concerning this present life only, in those we be indeed in this realm *caput*, and because there is no man above us here, be indeed *supremum caput*. As to spiritual things ... forasmuch as they be no worldly nor temporal things, they have no worldly nor temporal head but only Christ that did institute them, by whose ordinance they be ministered here by mortal men, elect, chosen, and ordered, as God hath willed for that purpose, who be the clergy; who for the time they do that, and in that respect, *tanquam ministri versantur in his quæ hominum potestati non subjiciuntur, in quibus, si male versantur sine scandalo Deum ultorem habent, si cum scandalo hominum cognitio et vindicta est.*" Here is the pith of the whole matter. As long, says the King, as the clergy minister unfaithfully, yet without committing an open offence against the law, they are answerable to God alone; if they offend the law, the law is there to punish them.[1]

The only objection made at the time to the recognition of the King's supremacy, after its terms had been settled, by any man in England, was an objection to the words in which it was expressed. Tunstall thought that it should have been drawn so as to point wholly to the civil and secular jurisdiction. "With this explanation," he wrote to the King, "the English clergy, and particularly myself, are willing to go the utmost length in the recognition."[2] It was a wise suggestion, but unhappily its acceptance was hardly possible. The word "spiritual" was then generally supposed to include everything ecclesiastical. As the King himself said, "that vocabule had been too far extended." Tunstall had proposed that to the recognition should be added the words *in temporalibus*. Henry objected that these words were unnecessary. "Whereunto," he wrote back, "in us to be called *ecclesiæ Anglicanæ* [caput] ye at the last agree, so that there were added *in temporalibus*; which addition were superfluous, considering that men, being here themselves earthly and temporal, cannot be head

[1] The King's letter is in the *Cabala*, 2, 1.   [2] Collier, 2, 63.

and governor to things eternal, nor yet spiritual, taking that word *spiritual* not as the common speech abuseth it, but as it signifieth indeed." Had Tunstall's suggestion been accepted, it would have helped to remove doubt on the subject, and might have saved the lives of some men of tender conscience, who believed that the recognition included a spiritual supremacy. If we are to judge of the opinions of individuals by their acts and omissions, we must conclude that the acknowledgment of the King's supremacy was approved by two men whose deaths have been always justly deplored. Fisher, Bishop of Rochester, was present at the Convocation which voted it, and himself subscribed its decree. More than two years later he advised his brother bishops to swear obedience to the King " in causes ecclesiastical and spiritual."[1] More was Chancellor of England at the time when it passed, and continued to be so twelve months after the decree was made.

The Act of 1532[2] in restraint, not for the abolition, of *annates* or first fruits, has also been attributed to the anti-Papal feeling of the King. There is not the slightest ground for this opinion. The Act sprang entirely from Convocation, and from the opposition of the English prelates to the payment of this tax to the Pope. *Annates* were " the entire revenue of one year "[3] of their sees, which the archbishops and bishops paid on their promotion. Their payment

[1] "His inquam aliisque multis rationibus inductus ac deceptus, Roffensis [de quo postea sæpissime gravissimeque doluit] necessitati presenti cedendum ratus, persuasit reliquis qui firmiores adhuc erant in clero, nam plerique jam archiepiscopis Cranmero et Leio, huic Eboracensi, illi Cantuarensi, qui ambo Regis negotium promovebant, adhæserant, ut saltem cum exceptione illa prædicta (quantum per Dei verbum liceret) obedientiam Regi in causis ecclesiasticis ac spiritualibus jurarent."—Sander, *De Origine ac Progressu Schismatis Anglicani*, p. 97; Cologne ed. 1610.

[2] 23 Henry VIII. c. 20; *Stat. of the Realm*, 3, 385.

[3] Fuller's *Church Hist.* 196.

had been forbidden by the Councils of Constance and Basle in 1414 and 1431, and this decree was adopted by the French Council of Bourges in 1438. In other countries they were exacted in the case of all benefices, but in England only in that of archbishoprics and bishoprics.[1] In this kingdom, where they had always been paid with reluctance, they were a comparatively new imposition. They have been ascribed to Pope John XXII., 1316-1334, and also to Boniface IX., 1389-1404. But as long ago as 1306 the clergy and people of England remonstrated with the Pope on his claim to first fruits as being one " never heard of before and very prejudicial to the King, nation, and support of the poor." An Act in restraint of *annates* was passed more than a hundred years before the accession of Henry VIII. By the 6th of Henry IV. c. 1, in 1404, reciting that "a horrible and damnable custom had been lately introduced into the Court of Rome, that no ecclesiastic should have provision for an archbishopric or bishopric until he had compounded with that Court to pay great and excessive sums of money for the first fruits," it was enacted that no person in future should pay greater sums than had been customary in old times. In 1528 Henry's ambassadors to the Pope were in friendly treaty with the Pontiff concerning the freeing of the English Church from this exaction. "Another business of the ambassadors now was, to treat with the Pope concerning taking away the burden of first fruits from the clergy of England.[2] The first moving thereof to the Pope happened seasonably upon

---

[1] Hanc autem consuetudinem omnes admisere præter Anglos, qui id de solis episcopatibus concessere ; in cæteris beneficiis non adeo.—Platina, in *Vita Bonifacii IX*.

[2] In the reign of Queen Mary, the Lower House of Convocation presented an address to the Upper, in which it was prayed that the clergy might be delivered from the "importable burden of the first fruits, tenths, and subsidies."—Burnet, *Collection of Records*, 5, 402.

the Pope's communication with them concerning the bishops of England, and the great age of some of them, and particularly Norwich, who was then about eighty years old. Of him they told the Pope, that he had a motion to the King and cardinal for the taking away these first fruits in his diocese. The Pope asked how and after what manner it might be done. They answered, by redemption, and then showed him a device of the King and cardinal which he liked very well, and so did the cardinals then present."[1] Shortly before the passing of the statute, a petition was presented by Convocation to the King praying for "an Act to take away *annates* exacted by the Court of Rome."[2] In this petition the Convocation made use of the very same arguments which were afterwards inserted in the Act itself. They set forth how the Papal Court exacted first fruits before the bishops could obtain their bulls out of the said court; the mischief their payment caused to the nation; the decay of the land, and the great impoverishment of the bishops; that owing to these exactions the bishops were not able to repair their churches, houses, and manors, and that this was the cause of their decay; and that they could not bestow the goods of the Church in hospitality and charity, as they were bound to do by the law, and the intentions of

---

[1] Strype, *Memor. Eccles.* 1, 168.

[2] It has been lately asserted that this petition against *annates* proceeded from parliament and not from Convocation, on the ground that a similar petition has been found in our records entitled "from parliament." But to this it may be answered:—(1) there is no account in any of our histories of such a petition being presented by parliament: (2) there is no mention of a petition from parliament in this reign; mention is made of petitions from one of the Houses, but a petition from parliament, if assented to by the King, would be a legislative act: (3) what settles the matter is, the Commons were at first opposed to the Act [Stubbs' *Lectures*, 280-1]. The mistake has probably arisen from the words recording a petition, which ran thus:—*Quædam petitio exhibita est domino regi in parliamento.*

the donors of their endowments. The Convocation ends their petition with this prayer:—" First to cause the said unjust exactions of *annates* to cease and to be foredone for ever by Act of this his Grace's high court of parliament. And in case the Pope will make any process against this realm for the attaining those *annates*, or else will retain bishop's bulls till the *annates* be paid; forasmuch as the exaction of the said *annates* is against the law of God, and the Pope's own laws forbidding the buying or selling of spiritual gifts and promotions; and forasmuch as all good Christian men be more bound to obey God than any man, and forasmuch as St. Paul willeth us to withdraw ourselves from all such as walk inordinately; it may please the King's most noble grace to ordain in this present parliament, that then the obedience of him and the people be withdrawn from the See of Rome, as in like case the French King withdrew the obedience of him and his subjects from Pope Benedict, the XIIIth of that name, and arrested by authority of his parliament all such *annates*, as it appeareth by good writing ready to be showed."[1]

This petition of Convocation is well worth our attention. It was a revival of the old English policy to limit the Pope to his spiritual authority, and to prevent the impoverishment of the English Church. The assembly which governed that Church called upon the secular prince and his parliament to come to their aid, and in defence of the bishops to ordain that, should the Pope not cease to impoverish them by his exactions, the obedience of the kingdom should be withdrawn from the Pope so far as concerned his aggressions on the temporal possessions of the Church. The members of Convocation were willing to pay, as they express it, the competent charges for the writing and sealing of bulls, and

[1] Strype, *Memor. Eccles.* 1, 222, Appendix, 158; Wilkins' *Concilia*, 3, 760.

to remunerate the labour of the Papal officers, but they required that the amount of their payments should be determined, not by the Roman Curia, but by the laws of their country. If the Pope did not agree to their terms, they were prepared to face the consequences, and content that their bishops should perform the functions of their sacred office without the Pope's confirmation. This was not by any means the first occasion on which the English Church manifested its hostility to Papal pressure. There is a wonderful continuity in our ecclesiastical history. In the reign of Henry I., as we have seen, all ranks, including the greater and lesser clergy, declared that if Anselm persevered in his attempts to introduce the decrees of the Vatican Council respecting the investiture and homage of English bishops, they would drive him from the kingdom and separate from the Roman Church. In 1392 the archbishops and bishops adopted the language of the Commons, and asserted that Papal excommunications, issued against those prelates who carried out the English law respecting presentations to benefices, were in open disherison of the Crown, and subversive of the laws of the realm, and that they, for their part, would stand by the King. In the sixteenth century, four hundred years after the national declaration in the reign of Henry I., the English Convocation, representing all ranks and orders of the Anglo-Catholic Church, both secular and regular, petitioned the King that, in case the Pope should continue to exact the *annates*, and to put pressure for their payment on the bishops by delaying their bulls, he would ordain that the obedience of him and his people should be withdrawn from the Roman See.

We must not, however, push the thing too far, and attribute to the members of this Convocation wishes and intentions which they did not entertain. Such expressions as "separating from the Roman Church," and "withdrawing their obedience from the See of Rome," had a very different meaning in the reign of Henry I., or in that of Henry VIII., from that which would be attached to them if used at the present day. Those who then used such terms had no intention of separating themselves from Catholic unity, or of denying the spiritual supremacy of the Pope. To the members of the Convocation which drew up the petition to take away *annates*, the payment of them was a mere secular matter, wholly unconnected with the spiritual authority of the Pope. And because they looked upon it in this light, they called upon the State to protect them, and to provide for the continuation of the episcopal functions, in case the Pope should withhold his confirmation of those prelates who were appointed by the King. The Convocation of this reign meant only the same thing which the clergy meant in that of Henry I., viz. to refuse obedience to the Pope when he exceeded his true spiritual authority, and attempted to regulate such matters as lay without it.

The Act in restraint of *annates* was eminently fair. It did not abolish them at once, but only if the Pope did not accept the compromise offered in it. "To the intent our said holy father the Pope and the Court of Rome shall not think that the pains and labours . . . about the writing, sealing . . . of any bulls . . . shall be irremunerated or shall not be sufficiently and condignly recompensed, it is enacted . . . that every spiritual person of this realm named and presented to any archbishopric or bishopric . . . shall and may lawfully pay for the writing and obtaining of his bulls . . . five pounds sterling for and after the rate of the clear and whole yearly value of every hundred pounds sterling above all charges of any such archbishopric or bishopric." The final confirmation of the Act was suspended until Easter, 1533, or the next meeting of parliament. If the Pope should in the meantime " amicably, charitably, and reasonably compound, or else by some friendly, loving, and tolerable composition" moderate the *annates*, the agreement respecting them between him and the King was to have the effect of a law "inviolably to be observed." To allow time for the proposed arrangement and to enable the King to carry it out when accepted, a power was given to him to declare by his letters patent, at any time before the expiration of the period limited, how much of the Act should have effect. The Roman Court was " informed and certified "[1] of the contents of the Act and of the proposal in it, " to the intent that by some gentle ways the said exactions might have been redressed and reformed." But the Pope made no proposals. Accordingly, in 1533, a second Act was passed confirming the former, and also containing provisions for the consecration of prelates in England —provisions which had been suggested in the petition of Convocation.

The first Act originated in the Lords, and was thence sent down to the Commons, and being agreed to there, received the royal assent, though it had not its final confirmation till July, 1533. At this time there sat in our Upper House twenty-one archbishops and bishops, and thirty abbots and priors.[2]

The enactments against appeals to Rome—first for their restraint,[3] and afterwards for the abolition of all such appeals[4] —have also been ascribed to the King's wish to put pressure on the Pope. This is a result of the theory which attributes everything to the King and nothing to the nation, though

---

[1] 25 Henry VIII. c. 20, s. 2.

[2] There is a *lacuna* in the Lords' *Journals* between the parliament of 1515, and that of 1533, the one in which the second Act against *annates* passed. On the first day of the latter parliament the names of nineteen archbishops and bishops, and thirty abbots and priors, are given as being present in person or by proxies. The number of lay lords present on the same day is fifty-one.—Lords' *Journal*, 1, 58.

[3] 24 Henry VIII. c. 12. 1533.   [4] 25 Henry VIII. c. 19. 1531.

the French ambassador about this time informed his master that "the whole country was in a blaze against the Pope." A historian[1] even tells us that the Act—he is referring to the first—"had a special as well as a national bearing, and here it is less easy to arrive at a just conclusion. It destroyed the validity of Queen Catherine's appeal; it placed a legal power in the hands of the English judges to proceed to pass sentence upon the divorce; and it is open to the censure which we ever feel entitled to pass upon a measure enacted to meet the particular position of a particular person." All this is a mistake. The Act had not, and could not have, any effect on Catherine's cause, nor did it give power to English judges to pass sentence upon the divorce. The Act referred only to causes which were depending, or thereafter to be commenced, in English Courts. Catherine's cause had never been before such a Court, nor was her application to evoke the cause to Rome, an appeal in the sense intended by the Act, namely, an application to a foreign Court to review, and finally decide, a cause already decided in an English Court. Catherine's motion, so often spoken of as an appeal, was merely an application or petition to the same Court in which the cause had commenced, to hear the cause itself, and not by commissioners or deputies appointed by it. It was an appeal in no sense of that word, either under the Act, or as generally understood when we are speaking of matters of jurisdiction. Even in the section which refers to the special appeal given in causes in which the King was concerned, the words restrain the effect of the Act to causes "now depending or that shall come in contention in any of the foresaid courts," that is, English courts.

Surely, we may leave conjectures aside when the history of the English Church, and the Act itself, supply us with sufficient reasons for these enactments. These provisions

[1] Mr. Froude.

against appeals to Rome were but the confirmation of the ancient law of the land. It was enacted by the Constitutions of Clarendon, which had never been repealed, that appeals in ecclesiastical causes should proceed from the archdeacon to the bishop, and from the latter to the archbishop; if the archbishop failed to do justice, the last resource was to the King. Appeals to Rome were always disliked by the bishops and prelates, and for the reasons given in the Act—the enormous costs, the long delay, and the great difficulty of forwarding the proofs and witnesses to a distant city. In the reign of William Rufus all the English bishops sided with the King against Anselm, who proposed to refer matters relating to the English Church to Rome. Pope Paschal II. tells us, in 1115, that the bishops of England prevented persons from appealing to Rome. At the Council of Lyons, in 1246, the suffragan bishops of Canterbury told the Pope that the summoning of English subjects before a foreign tribunal was contrary to the privileges of the kingdom. Though the law against appeals to Rome was constantly violated in the reign of John and his son, yet that arose from the alliance between the Pope and the King, in whose power it lay at any moment to prevent this. But on the accession of Edward I. they were again regarded as illegal, and as such forbidden. From the time of this monarch, and especially from the passing of the last *Præmunire* Act up to the period we are now considering, appeals to Rome depended entirely upon the temper of our Kings.

We are so accustomed to hear every occurrence of Henry's reign referred to his irritation about the divorce, that we are tempted to ask why it was, that this particular juncture was selected to forbid absolutely appeals to Rome, when up to this period they had been occasionally allowed? It must be remembered that the clergy had been lately punished for their offences against the laws of *Provisors* and *Præmunire*, and for accepting benefices by provisions from Wolsey, who being himself a candidate for the Papal throne, was not likely to weaken the influence of the Papacy, or to restrain the number of instruments issuing from it. We may be certain that with the increase of Papal bulls, faculties, and provisions, during Wolsey's tenure of the legatine office, appeals to Rome were multiplied in proportion. The Act may have been a consequence of the misbehaviour of the clergy, and it may have been necessary to make a legislative declaration against the custom of appealing to Rome. It is remarkable that the final prohibition of appeals is contained in the Act which forbade the Convocation to meet or consult without the express sanction of the King. To us, at this distance of time, there appears to be no connexion between the legislative power of Convocation and appeals to Rome. But the parliament may have taken a different view of the matter. This association of the restraint of the clerical legislation with the custom of appealing to Rome, looks as if the parliament not only remembered the recent transgressions of the clergy, but also considered that appealing to Rome was a part and parcel of the special and exclusive *status* to which the clergy then laid claim. However this may be, it appears that the clergy heartily concurred in the abolition of appeals, for, if the Acts did not meet their approbation, how did it come to pass that, although fifty-one of their prelates sat in Parliament, there is no mention in our histories of any one of them speaking or protesting against them?

The Act[1] abolishing Peter's Pence and payments to Rome for dispensations of "human laws made and used within this realm," is noteworthy for the memorable declaration made by the King and parliament, that they were acting politically, and not meddling with things in their nature spiritual. The

[1] 25 Henry VIII. c. 21. 1534.

Act recited that as the King was the head of the Church of England, and had been recognized as such by the clergy in their synods, it lay within his power, with the assent of the Lords spiritual and temporal and the Commons, to ordain, "upon all such laws as have been made and used in this realm," that no person should in future pay any pensions, censes, portions, Peter's Pence, or any other impositions, to the See of Rome. Lest their proceedings should be misinterpreted, and it should be thought that they intended to touch or weaken the spiritual supremacy of the Pope, they thus explain themselves: "Provided always that this Act, nor any thing or things therein contained, shall be hereafter interpreted or expounded, that your Grace, your nobles, and subjects, intend by the same to decline or vary from the congregation of Christ's church in any things concerning the very articles of the Catholic faith of Christendom, or in any other things declared by Holy Scripture and the Word of God necessary for your and their salvation; but only to make an ordinance by policies necessary and convenient to repress vice, and for good conservation of this realm in peace, unity and tranquillity, from ravin and spoil, insuing much the old ancient customs of this realm in that behalf; not minding to seek for any relief, succours, or remedies for any worldly things and human laws in any cause of necessity, but within this realm at the hands of your Highness, your heirs and successors, Kings of this realm, which have and ought to have an Imperial power and authority in the same, and not obliged in any worldly causes to any other superior."

Though this declaration of the King and parliament is limited in words to the present Act, it can hardly be doubted that it was intended to be an explanation of the policy they were then carrying out. That is, that their ordinances were temporal, and referred only, as they say, to worldly things and human laws, and that they did not mean to assume a spiritual jurisdiction or to claim an interference in matters connected with the faith of Christendom. They professed that they were making no change, but only "insuing" the ancient customs of the realm, to which an abolition or translation of a spiritual power was unknown, in order to guard it from ravin and spoil which are material. They acknowledged that they were bound by the Holy Scriptures, yet they knew that in these the power of the Keys was given, not to sovereign princes or secular assemblies, but to the Apostles and their successors. If we compare this solemn announcement with the previous statement of the King, that he claimed only a supremacy over the persons of ecclesiastics for their crimes, and with the expressions in the "Bishops' Book" published three years after this Act, we are forced to conclude that the King made no claim to a spiritual jurisdiction in the Church, and that the bishops and English Convocation were satisfied that he did not.

Almost contemporaneously with this Act—for there was only a week between the two events—Clement, on the 23rd of March, 1534, gave a definitive sentence in Henry's divorce. By this judgment the marriage with Catherine was pronounced to be valid, and the King was commanded to accept her as his wife. In case of his refusal to obey, excommunication was denounced against him,[1] and the Emperor was made the executor of the sentence.[2]

The Emperor was perfectly willing to undertake the execution of the Papal sentence, if his numerous other engagements and the threatening aspect of affairs in Germany had not prevented him and saved England from

[1] In this bull, as given by Sander, the issue of Henry and Anne were declared bastards, and the King was pronounced to have fallen to his own damnation under the censure of the greater excommunication, but time for repentance was granted until the end of the following September.—Sander, *De Origine Schismatis Anglicani*, p. 101.

[2] Lord Herbert.

the danger of an invasion.[1] Among the kingdoms and nations which owned Charles as lord, were the Netherlands, a country with which Englishmen were familiar, for the trade between England and the Low Countries was very great, and there were fifteen thousand Flemings resident in London. In these provinces Charles had, for twelve or fourteen years, been busy in burning, beheading, hanging, and burying alive, thousands of dissentients from the faith of Rome. The number of these unhappy victims of persecution has been placed as high as a hundred thousand by Grotius, and has seldom been put at a lower mark than fifty thousand.[2] These proceedings must have been perfectly well known in England, and must have taught its inhabitants what the execution by a foreign sovereign of a Papal sentence against their King meant. But Henry and his people were not daunted. The beacons throughout the realm were repaired; the fortresses near the coast were put in order; the artillery and munitions of war were cleaned and made ready; orders were sent to veteran seamen to see the ships thoroughly overhauled, and preparations were made to repel an invasion.[3]

The fear of an excommunication and of its consequences drove the King to take the next step he did. Henry knew what the results of such a sentence were; that the Roman Canonists held that excommunicated Kings ought not to be obeyed, that an interdict on his kingdom would follow, and that his own deposition would be proclaimed. He was therefore desirous of knowing the opinion of the English Church respecting a sentence which, if approved by the clergy, would have plunged the country into the miseries

[1] The Emperor always declared that "he would not fail in what was necessary for the execution of the sentence."—Minutes of a Consultation at Toledo, 12th April, 1534, *Letters and Papers of Henry VIII.*, 7, 195.

[2] Motley, *Rise of the Dutch Republic.*

[3] *Letters, &c., of Henry VIII.*, 7, 177.

of a civil war. Accordingly he consulted the universities, "the greatest and most famous monasteries in the kingdom,"[1] the prelates, and the two Convocations on the question: "Whether the Roman Pontiff had a greater jurisdiction within the Kingdom of England, conferred on him by God in Holy Scripture, than any other foreign bishop."[2] On the 2nd of May, 1534, the University of Cambridge resolved the question in the negative. On the 5th of May the Convocation of York passed a decree to the same effect. On the 7th of June the University of Oxford followed with a similar declaration, and in November following the Convocation of Canterbury adopted the same proposition. The general agreement was remarkable. The answer was unanimous in the case of the University of Oxford and the Convocation of York. The words of the Cambridge declaration are, *illis igitur persuasi, in unam opinionem convenientes . . . decrevimus*. In the Convocation of Canterbury[3] four voices affirmed the question, one doubted, and thirty-four decided in the negative. Wharton tells us that he had in his possession a hundred and seventy-five such instruments transcribed from the records in the Exchequer; that these transcripts contained the subscriptions of all the bishops, chapters, monasteries, colleges, hospitals, &c., of thirteen dioceses, and that to his certain knowledge the original subscriptions of the remaining dioceses were lodged elsewhere. All these instruments answered the

---

[1] Heylyn's *Tracts*, 7.

[2] An Romanus Pontifex habeat aliquam majorem jurisdictionem, collatam sibi a Deo in Sancta Scriptura, quam alius quivis externus episcopus.

[3] The date of the Canterbury declaration is generally given as of March, but from a careful consideration of the report [Wilkins' *Concilia*, 3, 769] I think it took place in November following. November is the date fixed in the Appendix of Lewis's translation of Sander's *De Origine Schismatis Anglicani*.

question in the negative, and also acknowledged the ecclesiastical supremacy of the King. This statement of Wharton has since been more than corroborated, for we find upwards of five hundred of these documents noted in a recent volume of our records.[1]

Notwithstanding the many assertions which have been made on this subject, it is clear that neither the question nor the answers to it referred to the spiritual supremacy of the Pope, but to his claims of temporal power. The answers were a renunciation of his pretensions to interfere with the external regimen of the English Church and with the civil duties of the subject. Henry himself never questioned the Pope's spiritual supremacy, but he denied, as his predecessors had done, that it invested the Pontiff with a right to dispose at his will of the temporal possessions of the Church, or to regulate the allegiance of the people. There can be no doubt that the belief of the individuals and bodies to whom the question was propounded was the same as the King's, viz. that the Pope, as spiritual head and primate of the Catholic Church, was the bond and principle or source of unity, which kept its members within one communion, irrespective of the diversity of nations which composed it. If this be so, the question and answers must refer to something else than the Pope's spiritual supremacy. The word used is "jurisdiction," and the answers limit themselves to this term. "Jurisdiction" is a word of art, and a technical expression, and was well understood to be such by the learned persons and bodies to whom the question was put. Two extracts from the "Bishop's Book," published three years later, will illustrate what is here said:—"Forasmuch as after the mind of certain doctors of the Church, this whole power and authority belonging unto priests and bishops is divided in two parts, whereof the one is called *potestas ordinis* and

[1] *Letters and Papers of Henry VIII.*, vol. 7.

the other is called *potestas jurisdictionis*;[1] and forasmuch also as good consent and agreement hath always been in the Church concerning the said first part, and contrary much controversy for this other part of jurisdiction. . . . Christ did by express words prohibit that none of his apostles, or any of their successors, should, under the pretence of the authority given unto them by Christ, take upon them the authority of the sword, that is to say, the authority of Kings or of any civil power in this world . . . if any bishop, of what estate or dignity soever he be, be he Bishop of Rome or of any other city, province, or diocese, do presume, or take upon him authority or jurisdiction in causes or matters which appertain unto Kings and the civil powers and their courts, and will maintain or think that he may do so by the authority of Christ and His Gospel, although the Kings and princes would not permit and suffer him so to do; no doubt that bishop is not worthy to be called a bishop, but rather a tyrant and an usurper of other men's rights . . . and, therefore, sith Christ did never seek nor exercise any worldly kingdom or dominion in this world, but rather . . . did leave the said worldly governance of kingdoms, realms, and nations to be governed by princes and potentates . . . and commanded also His apostles and disciples to do the *semblable* . . . whatsoever priest or bishop will arrogate or presume

[1] "But I am sure the noble Duke knows enough of our ecclesiastical matters to be apprised of the distinction between 'the power of order' and the 'power of jurisdiction.' The 'power of order' these Roman Catholic prelates [of Ireland] possess. But the 'power of jurisdiction' does not of necessity attach upon the 'power of order.' A man may be a bishop, and yet it follows not of necessity that he is bishop of a diocese. The two powers, that of order and that of jurisdiction, are quite distinct and of distinct origin. The power of order is properly a capacity of exercising the power of jurisdiction conferred by a competent authority. And this power of order is conveyed through the hierarchy itself, and no other authority but that of the hierarchy can give it."— Bishop of St. Asaph, Debate in the Lords on the Catholic Petition, 1805.

upon him any such authority, and will pretend the authority of the Gospel for his defence therein, he doth nothing else but crowneth Christ again with a crown of thorns," &c. It was not the power of order, but that of jurisdiction, which the English Church denied to the Pope. By the word jurisdiction in the question and answers was meant, not the spiritual authority which is exercised over the conscience and manifests itself in the interior court by absolving, censuring, and excommunicating, but the material ecclesiastical power of the external court, which is in truth rather political than spiritual and is followed by civil consequences. The meaning of the answers is this—"Although the Pope is spiritually supreme, yet he has no power of issuing edicts which entail a civil effect or political consequences." We must remember, too, that only a month previously the King and parliament had made a solemn declaration that they did not intend to decline or vary from the congregation of Christ's Church in any things concerning the articles of the Catholic faith of Christendom. The English bishops who answered the question of the King in the negative, and who wrote and preached in favour of his supremacy, were unconscious that they were touching the spiritual supremacy of the Pope, or breaking the bonds of Catholic unity. Some months after this question was propounded, and before the final breach with Rome, Archbishop Lee, one of the antireformers, wrote to Cromwell inclosing his profession to that minister.[1] In his letter, as abstracted, we find the following words:—" Is ready in this and all other things, as his conscience and learning will suffer, to follow the King's pleasure and commandment, so that our Lord be not offended, and the unity of the Faith and the Catholic Church saved; for saving whereof he perceives the King's Christian and

[1] *Letters and Papers, Henry VIII.* vol. 8, 114.

Catholic mind in a statute, 25 Henry VIII. c. 21."[1] Two years later Tunstall wrote to Reginald Pole a letter in which these expressions occur—" Ye presuppose for a ground, the King's grace to be swerved from the unity of Christ's Church, and that in taking upon him the title of supreme head of the Church of England, he intendeth to separate his Church of England from the unity of the whole body of Christendom; taking upon him the office belonging to spiritual men, grounded in the Scripture, of the immediate cure of souls, and attribute to himself that belongeth to priesthood, as to preach and teach the Word of God and to minister the sacraments; and that he doth not know what longeth to a Christian King's office and what unto priesthood: wherein surely both you and all other so thinking of him do err too far.... For his full purpose and intent is, to see the laws of Almighty God purely and sincerely preached and taught, and Christ's faith without blot kept and observed in his realm; and not to separate himself or his realm any wise from the unity of Christ's Catholic Church, but inviolably at all times to keep and observe the same."[2]

To unite the laity and clergy a civil sanction was, at the end of this year 1534, given to the acknowledgment of the King's ecclesiastical supremacy, which had been made by the two Convocations and by the whole kingdom. By a statute, which declares that it was passed "in corroboration and confirmation" of the recognition of the clergy, it was enacted that the King should be accepted and reputed the only supreme head on earth of the English Church.[3] This was the last Act, to which an anti-Papal colour can be given before the breach with Rome. On the 30th August, 1535,

---

[1] This was the statute containing the declaration of not declining or varying from the faith of Christendom.

[2] *Collection of Records*, Burnet, 6, 179.

[3] 26 Henry VIII. c. 1.

Paul III. drew up his bull against Henry and the kingdom at large.[1] By this extraordinary document the Pope deprived Henry of his crown; dissolved all leagues of princes with him; gave away his kingdom to any invader; interdicted his dominions; required all clerical and monastic bodies to retire out of his territories; commanded his nobility to take up arms against him; freed his subjects from all oaths of allegiance; cut off their commerce with foreign states; and declared it lawful for any one to seize them, to make slaves of their persons, and to convert their effects to his own use.

Up to the moment when Paul III., abusing and exceeding the office of a judge in a matrimonial cause, declared what was virtually war against England, and issued his invitation to foreign princes to invade her soil, and to enslave her inhabitants, not a word had been spoken, or a thing done, against the spiritual supremacy of the Pope. Without a crime and without an accusation, the whole kingdom was involved in the offence—if there was an offence—of one; and the English Church, which had never varied a tittle from the Catholic faith, was driven out of the unity of Christendom. Every change which had been hitherto made related to secular matters, or to what lay within the authority of a national Church to alter or regulate. Even the confirmation of bishops at home, the only thing which wears a spiritual aspect, was first suggested by an English Convocation, and was but a return to the state of affairs which prevailed at an earlier period. For in the twelfth century Pope Paschal II. declared that he knew nothing and had never even heard of the English bishops. Nor could the Papal Court complain of the nomination by the King of his bishops. The nomination of bishops by

[1] Though not formally published until 1538, it was known immediately in England.—Dodd's *Church Hist.* 1, 225, note by the Editor.

a sovereign is exactly similar to the institution by secular patrons to parish churches, a matter which has never been questioned in the Latin Church. These incumbents on their institution receive the secret and divine influence, which capacitates them for the performance of their sacred functions, not from the patron, but from the episcopal ordination. It was the same with the bishops appointed by the King. They received their benefices and temporal possessions from the King, but their office from Christ. The King nominated, but bishops ordained them. The custom of royal appointment to bishoprics had existed in England from the Saxon times to the reign of John, and for the forty years before this period had been exercised absolutely without an objection from the Pope. The nomination of bishops by the secular prince was not peculiar to England. A similar right had always been exercised by the Kings of Castile, and afterwards by those of Spain. By the late Concordat with Francis I. the same privilege had been conceded by the Popes themselves to the French Kings. The mere enumeration of the subjects of the English enactments prior to the bull of Paul III. shows us that they were secular, and that there was not one of them which concerned spiritual authority. *Annates*, appeals to Rome, Peter's Pence, plurality of benefices, tenths, dispensations "of the human laws of this realm," licenses, faculties, &c.—they all referred to the external regimen of the Church, and to mere pecuniary payments which had been forbidden by the decrees of General Councils. The Council of Constance declared that it was not lawful for the Bishop of Rome to impose any indictions or exactions upon the Church, or upon ecclesiastical persons in the nature of a tenth, or in any other way. The Council of Basle passed a like decree. England had committed no fault beyond declining to continue the payment of exactions which she believed to be of human institution, and to concede to the

Pope a supreme jurisdiction over the temporal possessions of her Church and the allegiance of her citizens. There was no dispute on any matter of faith, such as in earlier times had been the cause of division. The movement in England was commenced and carried out by men "who were sound, according to Roman doctrines, in all other points."[1] The sole question at this time between the Papacy and the English Church was, whether the innumerable direct and indirect payments to the Pope were of divine right, and therefore could not be subtracted, or whether they were of human ordination, and might be refused. The Roman Court was not ignorant of the consequences that would follow a sentence which, either by express words, or necessary implication, declared the issue of Henry and Anne to be bastards, defeated the national hopes of a tranquil succession, and subjected England to the horrors of a religious war. Wolsey had warned the Pope that he might lose the English realm if he delayed giving a just decision. Henry himself had told Clement that there "never was any prince so handled by a Pope as your Holiness hath entreated us," and that though the Pontiff had sent him a written promise not to revoke the commission, he had yet in violation of his word unjustly revoked it.[2] In 1530 the nobles of England, among whom were the two archbishops, four bishops, and twenty-

---

[1] See note, next page.

[2] Clement's promise to the King ran as follows:—"Promittimus et in verbo Romani pontificis pollicemur, quod ad nullius preces, requisitionem, seu instantiam, merove motu aut aliter, ullas unquam literas, brevia, bullas, aut rescripta ... quæ materiam emissarum antehac in causa prædicta commissionum ... inhibitoria, revocatoria, aut quovismodo prejudicialia quacunque ratione contineant, atque ut dictarum commissionum ... plenam perfectam finalem et effectualem executionem remorentur, impediant, aut in aliquo contrarientur, illave aut eorum aliqua revocent, aut eisdem vel eorum aliquibus in toto vel in aliqua parte eorundem præjudicent, concedemus."—Lord Herbert, *History;* Burnet, *Records,* 6, 26.

two abbots, had remonstrated with the Pope against his delay in granting what was desired by the whole kingdom, and had threatened, if his Holiness should refuse to grant their demand, "to find relief some other way."[1] The members of the Roman conclave knew what the excommunication of a King meant; that it entailed the deposition of the sovereign, and the withdrawal of the allegiance of his subjects. They were aware that entrusting the execution of that excommunication to a foreign prince against whom England had lately declared war,[2] and with whom she was then in a state of armed neutrality, was a declaration of hostilities against the country, and that a high-spirited people would resent the management of their affairs being delivered over to the hands of a stranger. Yet in the face of all these things, and though the Church of England had never departed even by a hair's-breadth from the Catholic truth, and though not one word had been uttered, or a thing effected, against the spiritual supremacy of the Pope, the Pontiff and the Roman Court took a step which necessarily led to the separation of England from the unity of Christendom. If it be schism, as it undoubtedly is, to drive from the universal fold, without a just and necessary cause, a faithful Church which had ever kept the Catholic verity, the Pope in issuing this bull, and the imperial cardinals who urged him to do it, were guilty of this offence.[3]

---

[1] Rymer, xiv. 405.   [2] November, 1527.

[3] Cardinal Manning was once of opinion that the schism did not proceed from the English King and Church, but from Rome, and as logical deductions from historical facts do not vary with a change in religion, his words are here quoted:—" The Crown and Church of England with a steady opposition resisted the entrance and encroachment of the secularized ecclesiastical power of the Pope in England. The last rejection of it was no more than a successful effort after many a failure in struggles of the like kind. And it was an act taken by men who were sound, according to the Roman doctrines, in all other points. . . . There is no one point in which the British Churches can be attainted of

It was not the English King or the English Church, but the Popes themselves, who put an end to their spiritual supremacy. By their interdicts and invitations to foreign sovereigns to invade England and enslave her inhabitants, they practically declared war against the kingdom and lost their dominion over the hearts of its people. The English were unable to distinguish between the Catholic Pontiff and the Italian prince, who, mixing up things divine and secular, endeavoured as far as in him lay to excite a crusade against their country, and to extend to its soil the bloody work which the Emperor was carrying on in the Low Countries. Silent resentment took the place of filial obedience, and the remembrance of the spiritual father faded from the minds of the people. Without a word against the Pope's spiritual supremacy in our statutes, or a reference to it in the decrees of our Convocations, it died away spontaneously and without external impulse.

What was the Church of England, thus driven out of Catholic unity, to do but what she did? It was then the almost universal opinion of churchmen out of Italy, that the Pope was subject to a General Council; that he could not of himself alter the articles of religion; and that he was placed in his seat to govern the Church, and not to introduce new creeds. The essentials of the Christian faith, "once for all delivered unto the saints,"[1] had been cleared from doubt in those General Councils which had been held before the Popes, corrupted by the possession of an earthly principality,

either heresy or schism. She [the Anglican Church] has rejected—what the Eastern Churches rejected before—the arrogant pretence of a universal pontificate rashly alleged to be of divine right, imposed in open breach of apostolical traditions and the canons of many councils. The Churches of the East are not schismatical for their rejection of this usurpation; neither are the Churches of Britain. But *they* are guilty of the schism that obtrude this novelty as the condition of Christian communion."—*Unity of the Church*, 361-3.

[1] Τῇ ἅπαξ παραδοθείσῃ τοῖς ἁγίοις πίστει.

arrogated to themselves a temporal authority and a right to monopolize the management of national Churches. The Church of England naturally recurred to those times when the universal Church was a real spiritual congregation, and to the traditions of an institution which was a true Church of God, undisturbed by dreams of worldly ambition and unentangled in European politics. In the opinion of all men, including Popes and Cardinals, a reformation was necessary, and it was the duty of the Church of England to set about it.[1] Left to her own guidance and deserted by her pastor, she necessarily took into her own hands those matters of discipline which every national Church has a power and a right to reform, such as the marriage of the clergy, communion in one or two kinds, prayers in an unknown tongue, and the regulation of public worship.

It was inevitable that in carrying out this necessary reformation a large share of influence should fall to the lot of the secular prince. The Kings of England had from time immemorial exercised a pre-eminent authority in ecclesiastical matters, and it was to them that the clergy had, for hundreds of years, looked as to their protectors against the oppressions and exactions of the Papacy. The great position of the King in the commonwealth furnished a point of union without which at this juncture the English Church might have dissolved away into separate and hostile bodies of sectaries. Our lay writers have in general asserted that the share which fell to the King was too large, and that he overrode the Church and took into his own hands the exclusive manage-

[1] Cardinal Bellarmine thus speaks of the state of the Church before the Reformation. "Some years before the rise of the Lutheran and Calvinistic heresy, according to the testimony of those who were then living, there was almost an entire abandonment of equity in the ecclesiastical judgments, in morals no discipline, in sacred literature no erudition, in divine things no reverence; religion was almost extinct."— Quoted by Blunt, *Reform. of the Church of England.*

ment of religion. Our ecclesiastical historians have always denied this, and declared that the changes were not forced upon the Church, but that they sprang from the bosom of the Convocation. Thus Fuller states: "Upon serious consideration it will appear that there was nothing done in the reformation of religion save what was acted by the clergy in their Convocations, or grounded on some act of theirs precedent to it, with the advice, counsel, and consent of the bishops and most eminent churchmen; confirmed upon the post-fact, and not otherwise, by the civil sanction according to the usage of the best and happiest times of Christianity."[1] Heylyn tells us: "Nor was there anything done here in that reformation, but either by the clergy in their Convocations, and in their Convocations rightly called and canonically constituted, or with the counsel and advice of the heads thereof in more private conferences, the parliaments of these times contributing very little towards it, but acquiescing in the wisdom of the sovereign prince and in the piety and zeal of the ghostly fathers."[2] Sir Robert Cotton says: "If any shall object that many laws in Henry the Eighth's time had first the ground in parliament, it is manifested by the dates of their acts in Convocation that they all had in that place their first original."[3] And Atterbury complains that Burnet adopted such an order of narration as shut out this truth. "That history," says he, "is by its very method apt to mislead an unwary reader in inquiries of this nature; the way of it being, to set down first the proceedings of parliament in every case, and then those of Convocation; which makes it look oftentimes as if the parliament led the way to the Convocations in their debates, when the contrary to that is most certainly true, and would have appeared so to be, had his Lordship thought fit to follow the pattern set by

---

[1] Fuller, *Church Hist.* 188. [2] *Tracts*, 5.
[3] Quoted in *Rights of an English Convocation*, 179.

Antiquitates Britannicæ, and given the precedence always to the Acts of Convocation, when the business was first agitated there, and afterwards brought into parliament."¹

Did, then, Henry VIII. assume greater powers in managing and directing the Church during his reign than his predecessors, or did he merely follow the steps which the earlier kings of England had marked out for him?² Before considering this question it is necessary to recall to our remembrance how those Kings acted and what powers they exercised over the National Church from the beginning of our history. "First for the King's right to make laws," says Archbishop Bramhall, "not only concerning the outward regiment of the Church, but even concerning the keys of order and jurisdiction, so far as to oblige those who are trusted with that power by the Church to do their duties, it is so evident to everyone who hath but cast his eyes upon our English laws, that to bestow labour on proving it were to bring owls to Athens. Their laws are extant, made in all ages, concerning faith and good manners, heresy, holy orders, the Word, the Sacraments, bishops, priests, monks, the privileges and revenues of Holy Church, marriages, divorces, simony, the Pope, his sentences, his oppressions and usurpations, prohibitions, appeals from ecclesiastical judges, and generally all things which are of ecclesiastical cognizance; and this in those times which are acknowledged by the Romanists themselves to have been Catholic."³

If we examine the subject calmly and impartially, undeterred by Ultramontane clamour or religious rancour, we

---

[1] *Ib.* 181.

[2] Henry VIII. never assumed any authority at all approaching to the power exercised by Charles V. in the Interim or Declaration of Religion of 1543. By this declaration Charles prescribed what was to be believed throughout Germany on all matters of religion until the meeting of a General Council. The Interim comprised twenty-five heads or articles.

[3] Bramhall's *Works*, 2, 430.

shall find that Henry's part in the settlement of doctrine was of the smallest, and that he limited himself to lending his authority, and giving a civil sanction, to the determinations of the spirituality,[1] a part which everyone then believed to belong to the office of a sovereign, and which was required by the Act for the Submission of the Clergy. There were in this reign four attempts made to secure uniformity in belief and also in rites and ceremonies. Three of these were formularies of faith, and the fourth was the well-known Act of the Six Articles. All of these had their first inception and approval in Convocation. The first is, as its title tells us, " Articles about Religion set out by the Convocation, and published by the King's authority." This appeared in 1536. At the commencement of these Articles, we are informed by the King that he, " being credibly advertised of much diversity of opinions in such things as doth concern our religion, caused our bishops, and other the most discreet and best learned of our clergy of this our whole realm, to be assembled in our Convocation for the full debatement and quiet determination of the same : Where, after long and mature deliberation and disputations had of and upon the premises, finally they concluded and agreed upon the said matters, as well those which be commanded of God and are necessary to our salvation, as also the other touching the honest ceremonies and good and politic order. . . . And for because we would the said articles and every of them to be taken and understanden of you after such sort, order, and degree as appertaineth accordingly, we have caused by the like assent and agreement of our said bishops and other learned men the said articles to be divided into two sorts, that is to say, such as are commanded expressly by God, and are necessary to our salvation, and such other as, although

---

[1] " It is also worthy of remark that this settlement of Doctrine was entirely the work of the clergy."—Blunt's *Reformation*, 1, 480.

they be not expressly commanded of God, nor necessary to our salvation, yet being of a long continuance, for a decent order and honest policy prudently instituted, are for that same purpose and end to be observed." These Articles are signed by Cromwell on behalf of the King, by the two archbishops, sixteen bishops, and forty abbots and priors of the Upper House of Convocation, and by fifty-one deans, archdeacons and proctors of the clergy in the Lower House.¹

The second is "The Institution of a Christian Man," published in 1537, and also known as the "Bishops' Book." This treatise is dedicated to the King, as "supreme head in earth, immediately under Christ, of the Church of England," by the two archbishops, and "all other the bishops, prelates, and archdeacons of this your realm." The preface tells us that "your Highness commanded us now of late to assemble ourselves together, and upon the diligent search and perusing of Holy Scripture, to set forth a plain and sincere doctrine concerning the whole sum of all those things which appertain unto the profession of a Christian man, that by the same all errors, doubts, superstitions, and abuses might be suppressed, removed, and utterly taken away, to the honour of Almighty God, and to the perfect establishing of your said subjects in good unity and concord, and perfect quietness both in their souls and bodies.... And, therefore, calling to our remembrance how the whole pith and sum of all those things which be at great length contained in the whole canon of the Bible, and be of necessity required to the attaining of everlasting life, was sufficiently, exactly, and therewith shortly and compendiously, comprehended in the twelve Articles of the common Creed, called the Apostles' Creed, in the seven Sacraments of the Church, in the Ten Commandments, and in the prayer of our Lord called the Paternoster, ... we

¹ *Formularies of Faith in the Reign of Henry VIII.* Oxford, 1825. By Bishop Lloyd.

have, after long and mature consultation had amongst us, compiled a certain treatise, wherein we have employed our whole study, and have therein truly and purely set forth and declared in our mother tongue the very sense and meaning, and the very right use, virtue, and efficiency of all the said four parts." This dedication is signed by all the archbishops and bishops, by eight archdeacons, and seventeen doctors of divinity. It was signed by the bishops, and by the archdeacons and doctors, as Committees of both Houses of Convocation.[1] It was not even read by the King before its publication, for "he sent it back with the order to have it printed, saying that he had not time to read it, but trusted to them for its being according to Scripture."[2]

In 1539 there was an Act of Uniformity passed, the Act known as that of the Six Articles.[3] This also commenced in Convocation, and the doctrines set forth in the statute were considered and determined there before they were submitted to Parliament. The Bill was not brought in until the 7th of June. The articles had been debated and settled on the previous 2nd of the same month.[4] Indeed the Act itself informs us of this. It recites that the King "commanded that the said articles should deliberately and advisedly, by his said archbishops, bishops, and other learned men of his clergy, be debated, argued, and reasoned, and their opinions therein to be understood, declared, and known. . . . Whereupon, after a great and long deliberate and advised disputation and consultation had and made concerning the said articles, as well by the consent of the King's Highness as by the assent of the Lords spiritual and temporal, and other learned men of his clergy, in their Convocation, and by the

[1] Heylyn's *Tracts*, 11 and 549.
[2] Blunt, *Reformation of the Church of England*, 1, 465.
[3] 31 Henry VIII. c. 14, "An Act abolishing Diversity of Opinions."
[4] Wilkins' *Concilia*, 3, 845.

consent of the Commons in this present parliament assembled, it was and is finally resolved, accorded, and agreed in manner and form following."

The fourth was "A necessary Doctrine and Erudition for any Christian Man," first published in 1543. This treatise was "nothing more than the 'Institution' in a varied form, with some additional articles on the subjects of Free Will, Good Works," &c.[1] It was the last attempt in this reign to secure the much-desired uniformity. In 1540 a committee of divines had been appointed to frame a declaration of belief, and an order of the rites and ceremonies to be observed in churches. The committee consisted of the archbishops, sundry bishops of both provinces, and also of a great number of "the best learned, honestest, and most virtuous sort of the doctors of divinity." A short Act was passed in this year declaring that the decrees and determinations set forth by this committee, or else by the whole clergy of England, if approved by the King, should be binding on the people.[2] Great care was taken and much labour expended to make the attempt as perfect as possible. Three years were employed in the new work.[3] Questions respecting different points were circulated, and individuals separately consulted, and the answers were collated and laid before the King. Henry himself had also suggested some corrections in the "Institution," and had sent it so corrected to Cranmer, who laid it before Convocation to be examined and reviewed by that body.[4] The new Formulary was the result of these varied labours. The original treatise, of which it was but an enlarged edition, was the work of Convocation. It is certain, says Atterbury, that all the alterations and additions

---

[1] Bishop Lloyd, in Preface to *Formularies of Faith*.
[2] 32 Henry VIII. c. 26, "Concerning Christ's Religion."
[3] Lingard, 5, 161.
[4] Heylyn's *Tracts*, 549. Atterbury, 188.

which appeared in this edition, were debated and approved in the same body.[1]

Not only were these four attempts at uniformity the work of the Convocation, but many of the King's injunctions and proclamations respecting religious matters proceeded in the first instance from the same source. Thus the order for a new translation of the Bible was the consequence of a petition from Convocation. That from the Upper House is still extant, in which the bishops, abbots, and priors requested the archbishop to press upon the King that he would decree that the Holy Scriptures should be translated into the English tongue.[2] The proclamation for the setting up of large Bibles was the result of this petition. The injunction to bring in erroneous and suspected books, printed beyond or within the seas, was founded on a petition from Convocation to this effect.[3] The proclamation concerning the rites and ceremonies to be observed in churches was the result of the action taken by a committee of bishops and divines who sat to consider this matter by the authority of Convocation.[4] The proclamation respecting the abrogation of a number of holidays was previously settled in the same body.[5] The injunction respecting the service in the English tongue arose from the revision, by a committee of Convocation, of the ancient service books, which revision received the final sanction of the whole body in March, 1544.[6] Two sets of injunctions were published by the King, or Cromwell, as his representative, enforcing on the clergy the "Articles about Religion," which had been set out by Convocation. It will be found that the injunctions and proclamations, which have been considered to be the work of Henry himself, were either based on acts

---

[1] Heylyn's *Tracts*, 549, 569. Wilkins' *Concilia*, 3, 868. Atterbury, 188.
[2] Atterbury, 183.
[3] Wilkins' *Concilia*, 3, 776.
[4] Atterbury, 188, 9.
[5] Strype, *Eccles. Memor.* 1. 494.
[6] Blunt, 1, 494–8.

of the Convocation, or on books set forth by them, such as the "Articles about Religion," "Institution," &c.; and that the King merely lent his name to them to prevent a contravention of the late statute which enacted that no canons, constitutions, or ordinances of Convocation should be binding unless they were assented to by the King, and published by his authority.[1]

Nothing is more remarkable in this reign than the perfect concord which prevailed between the King and his clergy after Rome had cast them off. Some writers, as Sander, who cannot deny the existence of this concord, ascribe it to the cowardice and servility of the prelates and Convocation. General indictments against communities or large bodies are easily made and hardly deserve an answer. We know that the members of Convocation were invincibly constant in their refusal to acknowledge the King as head of the Church, though they were then entangled in the meshes of a *præmunire*, until their scruples had been removed by the acceptance of the qualifying words; that the bishops resolutely declined, whatever might be the consequences, to consent to the King's terms respecting a revision of the old canons;[2] and that there were at this time many in Convocation who have since been regarded by both parties as martyrs, and who afterwards gave up all for their convictions, or sealed with their blood the faith that was in them. The real reason of this accord was, that the King, while guarding his ecclesiastical supremacy, left the settlement of doctrine and the regulation of divine service to the spiritual body in the national Church,

---

[1] "Be it, therefore, enacted that they [the clergy] shall not promulge or execute any such canons, constitutions, or ordinances provincial, by whatever name or names they may be called, in their Convocations ... unless the same clergy may have the King's most royal assent and license to make, promulge, and execute such canons."—25 Henry VIII. c. 19, s. 1, 1533.

[2] Hook, *Archbishops of Canterbury*, 6, 413. Blunt, 1, 227.

the prelates and clergy in their Convocations, who, after the abdication by the Pope of his true supremacy, necessarily took the management of religion into their own hands. But it was not only the clergy who were in accord with the King—the whole country was with him. There is no evidence of coercion on the part of the King, or of reluctance or hesitation on the part of all the learned individuals and bodies in England when, in 1534, the Papal jurisdiction was denied. Gardiner, a witness of no ordinary weight, tells us in 1536—"All who have been born and reared in England, learned and unlearned, men and women, are agreed upon this point, that they have nought to do with Rome. All with one consent embracing the truth, acknowledge, reverence, and venerate the King as supreme head of the Church on earth."[1] In the same year Tunstall wrote to Reginald Pole: "One thing yet resteth that I thought convenient to advertise you of, wherein I do perceive ye be ignorant, which is this. Ye write in one part of your book, that ye think the hearts of the subjects of this realm greatly offended with abolishing of the Bishop of Rome's usurped authority in this realm, as if all the people or most part of them took the matter as ye do. Wherein I do assure you ye be deceived. For the people perceive right well what profit cometh to the realm thereby, and that all such money as before issued that way now is kept within the realm; whereas before, all that went that way, which was no small share but great and excessive, and daily the said issue increased more and more, never returned again hither any part thereof, which was to the great impoverishing of this realm. So that, if at this

---

[1] Omnes plane constantissimo consensu in hoc convenerunt, docti pariter atque indocti, tum viri tum fœminæ, nihil ei cum Roma esse negotii, quem Anglia genuit et educavit; omnes summo consensu veritatem amplexantes atque exosculantes principem, supremum in terris ecclesiæ caput agnoscunt, colunt, et venerantur."—*De Vera Obedientia, Fasciculus Rerum Expetend. et Fugiend.* 2, 817.

day the King's grace would go about to renew in his realm the said abolished authority of the Bishop of Rome, granting him like profits as he had before through this his realm, I think he should find much more difficulty to bring it about in his parliament, and to induce his people to agree thereunto, than anything that ever he proposed in his parliament since his first reign." [1] It is even absurd to speak of the existence of coercion at a time when the King, the two Universities, the two Convocations, all the monasteries, colleges, chapters, hospitals, &c., in the kingdom, and the two Houses of Parliament, were of the same mind. And that, too, when the prelates, owing to the absence of some of the temporal lords in the wars, had almost invariably a majority in the Upper House.

It is not the fact that the bishops of England ever admitted by word or deed that they derived their spiritual authority from the secular sovereign. The Commission which they accepted in this and the following reign has been cited to prove this, but on examination it establishes the direct contrary. In this commission the ecclesiastical power which the bishops derived from the King, as judges or as lords of parliament, is accurately distinguished from the spiritual authority which they obtained by ordination. "Forasmuch as the King," thus it runs, "is the fountain of all authority, both ecclesiastical and secular, and the head and source of all the *magistracies* in the kingdom." The Commission then proceeds to confer certain powers upon the bishop, "over and above those powers which the Holy Scriptures do testify are given to you by God." [2] The Commission does not assume to grant these things, but only the civil powers and privileges

---

[1] Burnet, *Collection of Records*, 6, 181.

[2] "Ac alia quæcunque autoritatem et jurisdictionem episcopalem quovis modo respicientia et concernentia, præter et ultra ea quæ tibi ex sacris literis divinitus commissa esse dinoscuntur."

which were by the laws of the land annexed to the sacred office. As these were the gifts of the State, they might by the State be recalled or modified.[1] The Church of England has always and from the first denied, as all other Christian denominations have done, that the spiritual authority of the Church proceeded from the sovereign. We have in this reign "a declaration made of the functions and divine institution of bishops and priests" signed by Cromwell, then vicegerent of the King in ecclesiastical matters, the two archbishops, eleven bishops and twenty-four divines and canonists, which declares, that the power of the Keys and other Church functions were distinct from the civil power. "Christ and His apostles did institute and ordain in the New Testament, that beside the civil powers and governance of kings and princes, which is called in Scripture *potestas gladii*, the power of the sword, there should also be continually in the Church militant, certain other ministers or officers, which should have special power, authority and commission under Christ to preach and teach the Word of God unto His people, to dispense and administer the sacraments of God unto them; and by the same to confer and give the grace of the Holy Ghost, to consecrate the blessed body of Christ in the sacrament of the Altar, to loose and absoile from sin all persons which be truly penitent and sorry for the same; to bind and excommunicate such as be guilty in manifest crimes and sins and will not amend their defaults, to order and consecrate others in the same room, order, and office whereunto they be called and admitted

[1] "And therefore it was and shall be always lawful unto the said kings and princes and their successors, with the consent of their parliaments, to revoke and call again into their own hands, or otherwise to restrain all the power and jurisdiction which was given and assigned unto priests and bishops by the license, consent, sufferance, and authority of the said kings and princes, and not by the authority of God and His Gospel."—*Institution*, or *Bishops' Book*, 1536.

themselves; and finally to feed Christ's people like good pastors and rectors, as the apostles calleth them, with their wholesome doctrine, and by their continual exhortations and monitions to reduce them from sin and iniquity, so much as in them lieth, and to bring them unto the perfect knowledge, the perfect love and dread of God, and unto the perfect charity of their neighbours. . . . This office, this power and authority was committed and given by Christ and His apostles unto certain persons only, that is to say, unto priests or bishops, whom they did elect, call, and admit thereunto by their prayer and imposition of their hands." There is also the judgment of eight bishops including Cranmer, concerning the King's supremacy, which asserts that the commission which Christ gave His Church had "no respect to a king's or prince's power," and that the Church had it by the Word of God, to which Christian princes acknowledge themselves subject.[1] The 37th of our Articles of religion, drawn up in 1562, is to the same effect. "Where we attribute to the Queen's Majesty the chief government, by which titles we understand the minds of some dangerous folks to be offended; we give not our princes the ministering either of God's Word or of the Sacraments, the which thing the Injunctions also set forth by Elizabeth our Queen do most plainly testify; but that only prerogative which we see to have been given always to all godly princes in Holy Scripture by God Himself, that is, that they should rule all estates and degrees committed to their charge by God, whether they be ecclesiastical or temporal, and restrain with the civil sword the stubborn and evil-doers."

From what has been said in the preceding pages certain conclusions may be drawn. These are:—

1. That the supremacy of our Kings in ecclesiastical

---

[1] Both these documents are in the collection of Records in Pocock's *Burnet*, 4, 335-340.

matters was not an invention of Henry VIII. or an innovation in our Church, but that it existed from time immemorial.

2. That Henry VIII. did not override the English Church, but that he left the settlement of doctrine and the regulation of divine worship to the clergy; he himself doing nothing more than lending his authorization to the publication and promulgation of the canons and decrees of Convocation, as was required by the statute made on the Submission of the Clergy.[1]

3. That inasmuch as the King made no claim to a spiritual headship, the oath of supremacy was a political test, and was understood to be such by the vast majority of English Churchmen, as was shown by the fact that it was taken almost universally in this reign, in that of Edward VI., and in the commencement of the reign of Mary.

[1] 25 Henry VIII. c. 19.

CHAPTER IV

FROM THE ACCESSION OF EDWARD VI TO THE END OF THE REIGN OF ELIZABETH

SECTION I

Two distinct stages in the English Reformation which ought to be kept separate are sometimes confused by our historians. These stages are (1) the revolt of the Anglo-Catholic Church against the ecclesiastical exactions and oppressions of the Popes, and (2) a modification of the doctrines of that Church. The first, though completed in the reign of Henry VIII., had commenced as far back as the time of Edward I., and was in no way connected with faith or dogma. We have traced the long struggle between the Papacy and the English State and Church, which ended in the restoration of their old ecclesiastical supremacy to our Kings by the statutes of *Provisors* and *Præmunire*, and in the freeing of the national Church from external control. Though the Pope's patronage was legally abolished by these statutes, occasional appointments by him were for some time allowed by our Kings, but even these died away with the reign of Edward IV. This first stage was initiated and carried out by men whom at the present day we should call Roman Catholics. Though some writers have branded Henry VIII. and his bishops as schismatics, no one has ventured to say that they were unorthodox.[1] The final

---

[1] "King Henry contended only with the See of Rome about the article of the supremacy, being orthodox in all other points."—Tierney's *Dodd*, 2, 64. Cardinal Allen asserted the same thing.

acknowledgment of the royal supremacy was made by bishops and by a clergy who had no idea that in so doing they were departing from the unity of the Catholic Church. The names of Warham, Lee, Tunstall, Gardiner, and Fisher, are our guarantees for this. Not only did Fisher subscribe the decree of Convocation recognising the royal supremacy, but nearly three years later, as Sander informs us, he advised his brother prelates to take the oath of succession, which, as modified by Henry himself, when required from the clergy, declared that the King was the supreme head of the Church of England, and that the Bishop of Rome had no more jurisdiction within the realm than any other foreign bishop.[1]

With respect to a modification in doctrine, nothing in this direction was effected until after the death of Henry, and long after the final accomplishment of the first stage. The commencement of the English Reformation, properly so called, therefore dates from the accession of Edward VI. Henry left his people united among themselves and satisfied with the alterations which had been made in his reign. It was the duty of the succeeding Government to see that the changes in religion, which it proposed, should be gradual and should carry the people with them. At such a time above all others the strong hand of repression was required, rather than the indiscreet fervour of the enthusiast. The Administration had abundance of warning in the very beginning of Edward's reign. The fanatics outran the discretion of the State, and ventured on reforms without public authority. It was necessary, in the first parliament, to denounce penalties against such as spoke irreverently of the Sacraments, and to issue a proclamation against those who

---

[1] Lingard, 5, 33, edit. 1849. See also the form when required from the clergy in Rymer, xiv. 487-527. The acceptance of Henry's supremacy and the renunciation of the Pope's jurisdiction made by a hundred and seventy heads of religious houses are there given.

altered or omitted of their own will any rite or ceremony of the Church. Gardiner, a real statesman, was of opinion that there was but one way to preserve peace, namely, to follow "such laws and orders in religion" as the late King had left. He advised Somerset to make no changes until Edward had attained his full age. Gardiner's advice was neglected, and the Reformation was hurried forward with a precipitancy which for the time was fatal to it. Yet, in spite of the prevailing spirit of reckless innovation, the alterations made in the first years of the boy-King were moderate, and referred principally to those matters of discipline which lie in the discretion of every national Church, such as the marriage of the clergy, service in the mother-tongue, and Communion in both kinds. In the Injunctions of 1547, and in the Office for the Communion, 1548, prayers for the dead were admitted, auricular confession was left to the choice of the individual, the sign of the cross and the rite of unction were retained, while the question of the corporal presence in the Sacrament was expressed in such general terms that each might believe that they represented his own opinion. The changes made so far were approved by Gardiner. The order for the Communion was published with a royal proclamation on the 8th of March, 1548. On the 29th of the following June, Gardiner preached before the King at Paul's Cross. In his sermon he renewed his adhesion to the abolition of the Pope's supremacy, commended the young King's proceedings, thought that images might have been inoffensively used, yet that their removal was justifiable, was of opinion that the receiving the Sacrament in both kinds by the laity and the taking away a great number of masses were satisfactory, and expressed himself pleased with the new order for the Communion. This new order was inserted in the Liturgy which was drawn up in the following year, and received the sanction of parliament under the name of the Book of Common Prayer, in the first Act of Uniformity, 1549. Immediately after the passing of this Act the reins were drawn tighter, and a hard and fast line was laid down. The hand and counsel of the foreign reformer became more and more visible, and the reasonableness of the native character, at once reforming and conservative, was laid aside. In the Injunctions issued later in the same year, 1549, harmless and non-essential ceremonies, such as kissing the altar, breathing on the bread or chalice, ringing or sacrying bells, &c., were forbidden as " abuses and superstitions." A violent Act was also passed in this year " for the abolishing and putting away of divers books and images." It provided that the old service books should be called in and burnt, and that "all images of stone, timber, alabaster, or earth, graven, carved, or painted, which heretofore have been taken out of any church or chapel, or yet stand in any church or chapel," should be defaced and destroyed. In 1552 the forty-two articles were published. In these, purgatory was declared to be " a fond thing, vainly invented," and transubstantiation was explicitly denied, as " repugnant to the plain words of Scripture." These changes, hasty as they were, inasmuch as they were made within a period of five years, might have been acquiesced in if they had stood alone, and if any attempt had been made to render the transition insensible. Reasonings on abstract theological doctrines have very little immediate effect on the majority of a nation. But unhappily no care was taken to conciliate the affections of the people, and innovations were pressed forward without the slightest regard to the feelings or prejudices of those who were affected by them. Everything was done to outrage the devotional sentiments of a grave and conservative nation. The whole outward aspect of religion was altered, as it were, in a moment, and the ancient practices, however innocent and inoffensive, were banned as superstitious. Customs and ceremonies, consecrated by immemorial antiquity, and endeared by a thousand associations, were scornfully " reformed "—such was the expression. Contemporaneously with the changes in discipline and doctrine, England presented a scene of havoc and desecration never before witnessed in a Christian country.[1] Churches were demolished for their materials, their lead was stripped off for exportation, their bells were taken down and sold. The sacred utensils, ornaments, and plate were purloined by private persons, encouraged by the example of the Government, or were seized by the State. Shrines, altars, and images were ruthlessly destroyed, monumental brasses were torn from tombs, horses were watered in stone or marble coffins from which the bodies had been ejected, altar cloths and copes were displayed in the houses of the gentry as carpets or coverings, chalices were used as carousing cups, and libraries were scattered to the winds. No English Protestant can read the first chapter of our religious reformation, as distinguished from the politico-ecclesiastical movement, without pain and indignation. The civil outlook at this period was equally forlorn. The kingdom was full of misery. The value of money had fallen in consequence of the Spanish importations from the mines of South America, and the currency had been debased by frequent issues of impure coin, so that it was hardly possible to effect the common processes of buying and selling. Great and general distress had arisen from the rise in prices and rents, the inclosure system, the increase of pasturage to the exclusion of tillage, and the new relations between landlord and tenant following on the weakening of the feudal principle. The yeomanry were starving, and the country was held down by foreign mercenaries. The moral deterioration of the kingdom kept pace with its material decline, for the external disorder was but the sign and consequence of the relaxation

[1] The *Bildersturm* of the Netherlands did not take place till 1566.

of belief and the disturbance of customs which had hitherto regulated conduct. Irreligion and open profligacy prevailed, blasphemous ribaldry was common, duty was forgotten, the laws were unexecuted, the courts were venal, the patronage of the Church was scandalously abused, and the clergy were reduced to destitution by the nobility and gentry appropriating the profits of the benefices of which they had in law only the presentation. The upper classes hastened to increase their possessions, while the mass of the people saw all the institutions intended for their benefit disappearing. Grammar schools were closed, alms-houses, founded by the piety of former generations for the relief of the poor, were in decay, and the endowments of hospitals and other charities were fraudulently made away with. England was not merely disorganized, she was rapidly falling to pieces, or as Camden expresses it, she seemed to be " in a downright phrensy, miserably languishing at the very heart by reason of rebellions, tumults, factions, embasing of her money, and all the mischiefs and maladies which are wont to happen under an infant-King." Nothing similar to her condition had been seen since the reign of Henry III. The kingdom had been so mismanaged during the short reign of Edward, by the two adventurers, Somerset and Northumberland, and by the rash policy of the reforming bishops, who wished to break at once and for ever with the past, that at the close of his reign universal discontent prevailed. The eloquence of facts which appeal to the eye is convincing, and the state of the country appeared to be the result of the Reformation. A consideration of the moral and material anarchy, to which England had been reduced during the minority of the King, may explain the apparent levity with which the people agreed to the alterations in religion made in the reign of Mary, and may account for the reaction which then took place.

During the reign of Edward the Popes did not intermeddle with the internal affairs of England. At the accession of the young King, Paul III. urged the Emperor to assert by arms the title of his sister Mary to the crown, on the ground that Edward, having been born when the kingdom lay under an interdict, could not be considered as legitimate. The Papal request was not attended to. The Oath of Supremacy, recognizing the sovereign as the head of the Church, was taken by all without scruple, even by those who afterwards as bishops refused to take that of Elizabeth.[1] It may be remarked here that the terms "Protestant" and "Roman Catholic" have been improperly used to distinguish the parties in England during this reign. There were no Protestants and no Roman Catholics: all were members of the Anglo-Catholic Church. The unity which had been bequeathed by Henry VIII. was still unbroken. In Edward's time a rigid line between those who were afterwards known as Protestants and Roman Catholics was not established. There were differences of opinion, one party meditating a further advance, the other desiring to remain as it was, but two sects did not stand out clear and distinct from each other, and the nation was not divided into two hostile communions. That division was effected in the following reign by the fires in which the martyrs were consumed.

The alterations in religion made by Mary may be classed under two heads,—those concerning the relations of England to the Papacy, and those referring to the administration of religious matters at home. The extent and importance of the former have been greatly exaggerated. Mary repealed all the Acts against the authority of the Papal See made

[1] If we remember how short the reign of Mary was, and the mature age at which men are promoted to bishoprics, it will be evident that the prelates, who refused to take the oath of supremacy in Elizabeth's reign, must have taken the stricter oath of Henry and Edward over and over again.

subsequently to the twentieth year of Henry VIII., but farther back she did not go. We have seen that long before that date the Popes had ceased to exercise any authority save a spiritual one, over the English Church, and that they could not directly or legally appoint to a benefice or dignity in England. The legislation of Mary made no alteration in this respect. Though she renounced the title of head of the Church—but not until her marriage with Philip—she maintained resolutely her ecclesiastical supremacy in spite of her devotion to the Pope as spiritual father of the Church, and her desire to secure his approbation. The statutes of *Provisors* and *Præmunire* were preserved untouched, and in one instance at least she called in their aid against the Pope himself. Paul IV. disliked Cardinal Pole. In 1557 he appointed Peto, the Queen's confessor, a cardinal, and revoking Pole's legatine authority, transferred it to Peto. Mary at once issued orders that every messenger from abroad should be detained and searched. The bearer of the Papal bulls was arrested at Calais, and the bulls themselves were forwarded to the Queen, who quietly laid them past or destroyed them. She also declared that she would prosecute under the statutes of *Præmunire* any who would recognise Peto's authority. Further, the statute by which England was reconciled to the Papacy was by no means the general surrender it is commonly represented to be. Important rights of the nation and of the Crown were declared in it and were secured anew. The 35th section, relating to the assurance of ecclesiastical property to the new possessors, while it recites that the Pope by his dispensation had removed all impeachment arising from the *canon* law, asserts "that the title of all lands, possessions, and hereditaments in this your Majesty's realm and dominions is grounded in the laws, statutes, and customs of the same, and by your high jurisdiction, authority royal, and crown imperial, and in your courts only to be impleaded, ordered, tried, and judged and none otherwise." The admission of Papal bulls, dispensations, and privileges was strictly guarded, "all bulls, dispensations and privileges obtained before the said twentieth year [of Henry VIII.] or at any time since, or which shall hereafter be obtained from the See of Rome, not containing matter contrary or prejudicial to the authority, dignity, or pre-eminence royal and imperial of these realms, or to the laws of this realm now being in force and not in this parliament repealed, may be put in execution."[1] The statute also provided that nothing in it should diminish the liberties, privileges, pre-eminences, authorities, or jurisdictions of the Crown, and carefully restricted the authority and jurisdiction of the Popes to what they had exercised before the twentieth year of Henry, when, as we have seen, the Roman Pontiffs could not have directly appointed a sexton to an English parish church.[2] It would appear that the reconciliation with Rome was limited to a formal and public acknowledgment of the Pope as the spiritual head of the English Church, and the restoration of certain payments formerly made to him as fees on the confirmation of bishops, *annates*, Peter's Pence, &c.[3] Of one thing we may be certain, viz. that Queen Mary exercised to the full the ecclesiastical supremacy which her predecessors had enjoyed. She authorized her bishops to grant licenses to clergymen to preach in

[1] 46th section, 1 & 2 Phil. and Mary.

[2] "The Pope's Holiness and See Apostolick to be restored, and to have and enjoy such authority, pre-eminence, and jurisdiction, as his Holiness used and exercised, or might lawfully have used and exercised by authority of his supremacy, the said twentieth year of the reign of the King your father, within this your realm of England and other your dominions, without diminution or enlargement of the same, and none other."—53rd sec.

[3] It is very doubtful whether Peter's Pence was collected in England during Mary's reign.—Twysden, *Historical Vind.* c. 4, s. 5; Sarpi, *Hist. of Council of Trent*, sub ann. 1555.

any cathedral or parochial church throughout England;[1] restored bishops of her own authority to their "spiritual and temporal rights;"[2] presented more than two hundred and fifty incumbents to rectories and vicarages in the first year of her reign;[3] commanded chapters to elect to bishoprics learned, devout, useful and loyal persons;[4] deprived of her own motion bishops and other ecclesiastics for being married, though the law of the land permitted them to contract matrimony;[5] published her license to elect, and signified her assent to the election of prelates;[6] received an oath of allegiance from her archbishops and bishops, and compelled them to renounce everything in their Papal bulls prejudicial to her prerogative or crown;[7] issued an edict that all foreign heretics should depart the realm within twenty-four days;[8] promulgated proclamations "about religion" and ordered that no one should keep heretical books in his possession; directed her justices of the peace "to have one or more honest men secretly instructed in every parish to give information of the behaviour of its inhabitants;" would not allow a Papal legate sent against her will to be recognized, and set aside the bull appointing him; adopted the Acts of *Provisors* and *Præmunire;* put forth injunctions that none of her subjects should preach or expound scripture, or print

---

[1] Rymer, xv. 337.   [2] *Ib.* 340.

[3] *Ib.* 342–350. In the year 1556 she also presented a hundred and ninety-eight to livings.—*Ib.* 442–448.

[4] "Mandantes quod talem vobis eligatis in episcopum et pastorem qui sacrarum literarum cognitione ad id munus aptus, Deo devotus, nobis et regno nostro utilis et fidelis, ecclesiæque nostræ prædictæ necessarius existat."—*Ib.* 369, 374, 375, 403.

[5] *Ib.* 370.

[6] *Ib.* 375, 376.

[7] *Ib.* 425, 426, 427, 428, 432.

[8] "Dicuntur autem ex hoc decreto abiisse, supra triginta millia hæreticorum, variarum nationum et sectarum."—Sander, *De Schismate Ang.* 291.

any books, without her special license;[1] and directed the bishops how they were to proceed in the pastoral administration of their dioceses.[2] Her conduct in Ireland was similar. In that country she did not abate by one jot the authority in ecclesiastical matters which her father and brother had exercised before her. She created bishops by letters-patent, refused to admit the Papal power of appointing by provision, and granted away the property of the Church as freely as Henry VIII. or Edward VI.[3]

The really important alterations made by Mary, and which affected the life of the people, consisted in the repeal of her brother's religious enactments, the revival of the old Acts against heretics, and the restoration to the bishops and their courts of their former independence of the civil government.

Some canonists, as Bellarmine, contended that the exemption of the clergy from appearing before temporal courts was a rule of the Divine law; others held that the Pope had the power to command it. In England this exemption was always more or less limited, and never extended to treason. Before the time of Henry VIII. we find many instances of ecclesiastics being executed for this offence, and Henry IV. put to death Scrope, Archbishop of York, on the charge of having levied war against him. Henry VIII., in his well-known letter to Tunstall, declared that the State punished in its secular courts some crimes committed by the clergy, while it left others to the ecclesiastical tribunals. "And as for the living of the clergy, some notable offences we reserve to our corrections, some we remit by our sufferance to the judges of the clergy; as murder, felony, and treason, and such like enormities we reserve to our examination, other crimes we

---

[1] Burnet, 2, 395.
[2] Ib.; *Collection of Records*, 5, 381.
[3] Richey, *Hist. of the Irish People*, 425-7, edit. 1887.

leave to be ordered by the clergy." In the sixth year of Henry's reign, the question, whether clerks were exempt from the cognizance of temporal courts in criminal matters, was solemnly debated before the King and Council, all the judges being present. Dr. Standish, counsel for the King, asserted in this assembly that the prosecution of clerks before temporal judges was customary practice, and conformable to the laws of the kingdom. It would, therefore, seem that in some cases there was no clerical exemption. The law at this time appears to have been that ecclesiastics enjoyed no privilege whatever in treason, or in certain grave crimes. In the case of other offences committed by a clerk, the rule was, that the accused should be first arraigned, and might then claim his privilege either by way of plea to the jurisdiction, or after conviction by way of arresting judgment. The accused was then discharged from the sentence of the law in the King's Court, and was delivered over to the bishop to be dealt with according to the canons. The clergy, however, were by no means satisfied with this state of the law, and claimed a total immunity from secular jurisdiction, as a right inherent in their order by divine law.[1] Wolsey told the King himself, on the occasion before alluded to, that "in the opinion of the clergy the convening of clerks before temporal judges was directly contrary to the law of God, and that he himself and the rest of the prelates were bound by their oath to maintain the exemption." It was this claim of the clergy that principally determined Henry to exact from them a recognition of his supremacy in all matters civil and criminal. The result was the recognition in Convocation, and the subsequent sanction given to this recognition by the Legislature. This enactment put an

[1] Bellarmine denied that secular princes were princes in the case of the clergy:—"Principes seculares respectu clericorum non sunt principes."

end to the claims of the clergy to be exempt in all cases from the criminal law administered in the royal courts, while for some offences they were still left, by the consent of the King, to the jurisdiction of the ordinary. The Supremacy Act of Henry was repealed by Mary, together with that for the " Submission of the Clergy," renouncing their power of legislating without the approbation of the Sovereign. The effect of this repeal was to revive all the old pretensions of the clergy to a complete exemption, and to establish a class claiming to live wholly under their own peculiar laws.[1] Elizabeth, like her father, was resolved to maintain her temporal jurisdiction over all her subjects, lay and clerical, and to restore the regal supremacy as settled by the decree of Convocation and the subsequent Act of Parliament. With this object her Supremacy statute and the oath contained in it were framed.

The title of this statute is "An Act to restore to the Crown the ancient jurisdiction over the Estate, ecclesiastical and spiritual, and abolishing all foreign powers repugnant to the same." It differs in some important particulars from the Act of Supremacy in the reign of Henry VIII. By that Act the oath of supremacy might have been offered to any one at the pleasure of the King's Commissioners, and the refusal to take it was treason. By the Act of Elizabeth, the oath could be administered only to ecclesiastics, temporal judges and ministers, those receiving the Queen's fee or wages, persons suing out livery of their lands, and those taking degrees in the universities. The penalty of refusing the oath was deprivation or incapacity merely. In the Acts of Henry and Edward, the sovereign was described as " Supreme head in earth of the Church of England and Ireland." Elizabeth disliked the expression " head of the

[1] Mary ordered her bishops not to make use of the clause, " regia auctoritate fulcitus."

Church," as she believed such a title was to be given to Christ only.[1] Accordingly, instead of these words the following were substituted: "Supreme governor of this realm, as well in all spiritual or ecclesiastical things or causes as temporal." Charles Butler explains the general scope of the Act: "None, however, except persons holding ecclesiastical or civil offices could be required to take the oath; and none but those who voluntarily denied the Queen's supremacy were subjected to other penalties."[2]

The oath at length is: "I do utterly testify and declare in my conscience, that the Queen's Highness is the only supreme governor of this realm and of all other her Highness' dominions and countries as well in all spiritual or ecclesiastical things or causes as temporal; and that no foreign prince, person, prelate, state, or potentate hath or ought to have any jurisdiction, power, superiority, pre-eminence, or authority ecclesiastical or spiritual within this realm; and therefore I do utterly renounce and forsake all foreign jurisdictions, powers, superiorities, and authorities, and do promise that from henceforth I shall bear faith and true allegiance to the Queen's Highness, her heirs and lawful successors, and to my power shall assist and defend all jurisdictions, pre-eminences, privileges, and authorities granted or belonging to the Queen's Highness, her heirs and successors, or united and annexed to the Imperial Crown of this realm." It will be observed that the oath does not call upon the taker to declare that Elizabeth was the head of the Church.

To clear away all doubts as to the nature of the claim she made, and as to the obligation imposed by the oath, the

---

[1] "Regina non vult appellari aut scribi caput ecclesiæ Anglicanæ: graviter enim respondit, illam dignitatem soli attributam esse Christo, nemini autem mortali convenire."—Jewel to Bullinger, 22 May, 1559.

[2] Butler, *Hist. Memoirs of the English Catholics*, 3rd ed. 1, 346.

Queen published, contemporaneously with the statute, an Admonition to her people explaining the sense in which the oath was to be understood. In this she renounced all spiritual authority and declared that she claimed jurisdiction only over the persons of all born within her dominions. "And further, her Majesty forbiddeth all manner her subjects to give ear or credit to such perverse or malicious persons which most sinisterly and maliciously labour to notify to her loving subjects, how by the words of the said oath it may be collected, that the Kings or Queens of this realm, possessors of the crown, may challenge authority and power of ministry of divine offices in the Church, wherein her said subjects be much abused by such evil disposed persons. For certainly Her Majesty neither doth or ever will challenge any other authority than that was challenged and lately used by the said noble Kings of famous memory, King Henry VIII. and Edward VI., which is and was of ancient time due to the imperial crown of this realm; *that is, under God to have the sovereignty and rule over all manner of persons born within these her realms and dominions and countries so as no foreign power shall or ought to have any superiority over them.* And if any person that hath conceived any other sense of the form of the said oath shall accept the said oath with this interpretation, sense, or meaning, Her Majesty is well pleased to accept every such in that behalf as her good and obedient subjects, and shall acquit them of all manner of penalties contained in the said Act against such as shall peremptorily or obstinately refuse to take the same oath."[1]

The greatest care was taken to make this interpretation generally known. The explanation was repeated in the Declaration enjoined to be read in churches before the Thirty-nine Articles were drawn up. The fifth paragraph

[1] Admonition annexed to the Queen's injunctions, 1559, Sparrow's *Collection of Articles, Injunctions, &c.*; Wilkins' *Concilia*, 4, 188.

of this declaration is: "I do acknowledge the Queen's Majesty's prerogative and superiority of government of all states and in all causes, as well ecclesiastical as temporal, within this realm and other her dominions and countries, to be agreeable to God's Word, and of right to appertain to her Highness in such sort as is in the late Act of Parliament, and sithence by her Majesty's injunctions declared and expounded." Two years later, in 1562, the explanation was again repeated by Convocation in the 37th article: "We give not to our princes the ministering either of God's Word or of the Sacraments, the which thing the injunctions lately set forth by Elizabeth our Queen do most plainly testify; but that only prerogative which we see to have been given always to all godly princes in Holy Scripture by God Himself, that is, that they should rule all estates and degrees committed to their charge by God, whether they be ecclesiastical or temporal, and restrain with the civil sword the stubborn and evildoers." Lastly, in the same year the explanation received the sanction of the Legislature, "provided also that the oath, expressed in the said Act made in the said first year, shall be taken and expounded in such form as is set forth in an admonition annexed to the Queen's Majesty's injunctions passed in the first year of Her Majesty's reign ; that is to say, to confess and acknowledge in Her Majesty, her heirs and successors, none other authority than that was challenged and lately used by the noble King Henry VIII., and King Edward VI., as in the said admonition more plainly may appear."[1]

The Puritans were satisfied with the Queen's explanation and took the oath "as only restoring Her Majesty to the ancient and natural rights of sovereign princes over their subjects."[2] So did the vast majority of the clergy, as they had done in the reign of Henry and Edward, less than two

---
[1] 5 Eliz. c. 1. s. 14.   [2] Neal, *Hist. of the Puritans*, 1, 124, ed. 1

hundred out of nine thousand four hundred declining to take the oath of supremacy. After the first refusal of the bishops and a small minority of the clergy to acknowledge the supremacy of Elizabeth, her oath was taken generally by her Roman Catholic subjects during the first twelve years of her reign, as is shown by the silence as to any prosecutions against them on this matter. In truth, they had taken a much stricter oath without a word of complaint throughout the latter years of Henry, the whole reign of Edward, and at the accession of Mary.[1] There was no disposition on their part to refuse the oath until Pius V. issued his bull of excommunication and deposition, a bull, says a Roman Catholic author,[2] "ever to be condemned and ever to be lamented." As this bull cut off from the Church all who recognized Elizabeth as Queen or obeyed her laws, tender consciences began to doubt whether they could acknowledge her as their sovereign. This hesitation was greatly increased by the arrival of the Jesuits and seminary priests, who, educated in foreign schools and deeply imbued with ultramontane doctrines respecting the temporal authority of the Pope, objected to every oath which denied him the possession of the deposing power.

Many eminent Roman Catholics, historians and others, have recognized the truth, namely, that Elizabeth's oath of supremacy had no reference to spirituals, but was merely a political test. Feckenham, the last Abbot of Westminster, was satisfied

---

[1] In her first parliament Mary is described as "supreme head of the Church of England and of Ireland."—See Statute Book.

[2] "Such was this celebrated bull, ever to be condemned and ever to be lamented. It is most clear—that the Pope assumed by it a right, the exercise of which Christ had explicitly disclaimed for himself—that it tended to produce a civil war between the Queen's Protestant and Catholic subjects, with all the horrors of a disputed succession; and that it necessarily involved a multitude of respectable and conscientious individuals in the bitterest and most complicated distress."—Butler, *English Catholics*, 1, 349.

with the Queen's explanation, and declared himself willing to take the oath in the sense of her admonition. "It will, I believe, be readily admitted," says Sir John Throckmorton, "that the words of the oath, interpreted in this manner [by the Queen's admonition], affect not any part of that authority which Christ delivered to his Church, and which the pastors of it exercise independently on any civil power."[1] "By the oath of supremacy," writes Father Walsh, "no other authority or power is attributed to the King save only civil or that of the sword; nor is any spiritual or ecclesiastical power denied therein to the Pope, save only that which the. General Council of Ephesus under Theodosius the younger in the case of the Cyprian bishops; and the next Ecumenical synod of Chalcedon, under the good Emperor Martianus, in the case of Anatolius, Patriarch of Constantinople; and the two hundred and seventeen bishops of Africa, whereof St. Augustine was one, both in their canons and letters too, in the case of Apiarius, all denied unto the Roman bishops of their time."[2] Dr. O'Conor says: "The Act of Supremacy was really nothing more as to its intent than the Act of *Præmunire*. Its object was to restrain the exercise of illegal jurisdiction, and to confine within due limits the arbitrary proceedings of men who, under pretence of religion, claimed a power of exclusively deciding on all matters, whether mixed or unmixed, relating to the Church; men who claimed exemption from the law courts, pretending that they could be judged only by the Pope; who frequently made the very sacraments subservient to their passions, forbidding divine service, and interdicting the benefits of Christianity to all those who refused to comply with their arbitrary injunctions and decrees."[3] The Rev. Joseph Berington, in 1793, ad-

---

[1] Throckmorton, *Letters to the Catholic Clergy of England*, 88.
[2] *Hist. of the Irish Remonstrance*, Introd. 18.
[3] O'Conor's *Historical Address*, 2, 272.

vised the Roman Catholics of England to take the oath of supremacy, and thus qualify themselves for the exercise of their full rights of citizenship.[1] "Why should we," he asks, "importune Government for the further redress of grievances, or complain that we are aggrieved, if the remedy be in our own hands? One bold man, by taking the oath, may dissipate the whole charm of prejudice, and restore us to the most valuable privilege of British citizens."[2]

After the conspiracy of the Poles in 1562, it was enacted that the oath of supremacy should be tendered to classes of persons not included in the original Act, and the penalties for refusing it were rendered more severe, but no change was made in the wording of it. It was this Act[3] which gave a legislative sanction to the interpretation of the oath by Elizabeth.

The next Act is that of Uniformity, a revival of similar laws in the reign of Edward, which during his life were obeyed by all without reluctance.

Though we are unwilling to confess the truth to ourselves, toleration is not the child of reason, but the result of experience or indifference. The principle of toleration was not admitted in the times of which we are speaking. In the language of Scripture, zeal for what our fathers considered the house of God had eaten them up. All men, both reformed and unreformed, believed that uniformity was desirable and attainable. They were for one religion,

[1] *Memoirs of Panzani*, Introd.

[2] " James II., though a Catholic, was head of the Church of England in the same sense as Queen Elizabeth, and exercised all the powers annexed to the Crown by the Act of the first of Elizabeth. These powers then cannot be of a spiritual nature, nor can the acknowledgment of them in the King infringe any article of Catholic belief, unless we suppose that a Catholic sovereign may conscientiously exercise powers which a Catholic subject cannot conscientiously acknowledge."—Sir John Throckmorton, 92.

[3] 5 Eliz. c. 1.

one uniform manner of worship, one mode of Church discipline for the whole nation, with which all must comply. Freedom of conscience, as we understand it, was unintelligible and hateful to all, as it was the universal conviction that it was the duty of the State to enforce what it believed to be the truth.[1] It is important to remember that Elizabeth's Act of Uniformity was not directed against any class in particular, but against all non-conformists, and that it was as rigidly executed against the reformed as against those who adhered to unreformed Catholicism.[2]

The Act of Uniformity enjoined all beneficed clergymen —under penalties ascending from imprisonment for six months, and forfeiture of a year's value of their benefice, to imprisonment for life and deprivation—to use the Book of Common Prayer. Unbeneficed offenders were to be imprisoned for the first offence during twelve months, and for the second during life. Persons speaking in derogation of the established Service were to suffer forfeiture for the first and second offence, and for the third, imprisonment for life.[3] Besides these regulations for ministers of the established religion, it was enacted that any person omitting, without reasonable cause, to attend his parish church on Sundays and holidays, should be subjected to a fine of twelve pence.

The legal enforcement of a uniformity in religion is undoubtedly opposed to our modern ideas. But there can

---

[1] In Germany the "Recess" of Augsburgh proclaimed the principle of "cujus regio ejus religio." This was in 1555.

[2] "The independent spirit of the Puritans . . . both disgusted and alarmed Elizabeth; she perceived that their dislike to any ecclesiastical restraint was accompanied by strong sentiments of political liberty. One object of the statute of Uniformity certainly was to guard the Church and State against these religionists."—Butler, *English Catholics*, 1, 290.

[3] "The operation of this statute was also limited: it affected only the Protestant clergy, and persons in general who should speak against the Common Prayer-book."—*Ib.* 1, 346.

be no greater mistake than to judge the actors in the past by a standard framed on the experience of ages which were to them future. To blame the Act of Uniformity because it is not consonant to our feelings, is to ignore the slow growth of opinion which has made us what we are, and the convictions of the times at which it was passed. To condemn Elizabeth and her government for not adopting a toleration which was then inconceivable, and was regarded by all as a sin against God, is as unreasonable and contrary to the historical spirit, as it would be to blame them for not making use of inventions then unknown. Both were impossible, the one in the moral, the other in the material world. The conduct of the English administration at this juncture should be compared, not with modern practice, but with that of the neighbouring governments of Europe, in every one of which uniformity was enforced by the stake, burying alive, the wheel, the gibbet, or by drowning. Let us for a moment cast our eyes on those nations. In Italy the Inquisition, on the advice of Cardinal Caraffa, afterwards Paul IV., had been lately re-established by Paul III. on the model of that of Spain. Commissioners, of whom Caraffa was one, were at once appointed as general inquisitors in matters of faith with power to imprison the *suspected*, and to punish the guilty with death and confiscation of goods. A reign of terror broke out in every part of Italy. Many fled, while those who could not escape fell victims to the terrific persecution which ensued. In Venice, where the inquisitors were not wholly emancipated from civil control, the unhappy sufferers were drowned. At Rome they were burnt alive in front of the Church of Santa Maria alla Minerva.[1] In Spain, the possession of a forbidden book, or mere suspicion, was sufficient to consign the victim to torture and the stake. Even death did not put an end to the vengeance of the

[1] Ranke's *Popes*, 1, 140-6.

Inquisition. If subsequent evidence was forthcoming, the memory of the dead was declared to be infamous, his house was razed to the ground, his property was confiscated, and his bones were dug up and committed to the flames. In France, similar means of compelling uniformity, the short and ill-kept truces with the Huguenots excepted, were adopted.[1] In 1568 the Inquisition condemned to death as heretics all the inhabitants of the Low Countries, with the exception of a few specified individuals, and ten days later Philip II. confirmed the sentence by a royal proclamation from Madrid.[2] At the moment when the Uniformity Act of Elizabeth was passed, four months had not elapsed since even in England the slightest divergence from the religion of the State was punished by Mary with the stake, and the magistracy of the country was hounded on by her council to search out for heretics, and to employ secret informers to help them in the discovery. In her reign bishops, gentlemen, artisans, servants, women, and boys were burned for opinions in speculative matters, without the least pretext of the violation of any civil duty, while in the reign of her successor all classes of the laity were corrected for non-conformity by a fine of twelve pence. If we remember that Elizabeth made no examination into conscience, but at the most required an outward conformity, and if we compare her conduct with that of contemporaneous sovereigns, we are constrained to acknowledge, that the

[1] "It was believed that the severity exercised during the last few months, in Paris and many other French cities, against persons condemned for their religion, of whom very great numbers were burnt alive, would have so terrified the survivors, &c."—Venetian Ambassador to the Doge, 6 March, 1560. *State Papers, Venetian*, 7, 153.

[2] The sentence of the Inquisition is dated 16th February, 1568. It and its confirmation by Philip are given in *Meteren*, folio 54. On one occasion Philip II. told the Papal Nuncio that "all his subjects must either believe what he believed or be utterly destroyed."—*Cal. of State Papers, Venetian*, 7, 428.

compulsory uniformity of the reformed government of
England was the most wonderful and most sudden advance
in humanity recorded in history. It was the mildest form
of religious coercion which had ever been shown up to that
period since the time when religion first became incorporated
with the State. Surely it is inconsistent, and very like a
concealment of the truth, for Roman Catholic writers to cry
out against the milder form of coercion adopted by the
English government, and at the same time to withhold all
condemnation, or even mention, of the savage persecutions
of the Popes, who ransacked the consciences, and burnt the
bodies of their non-conformists. These writers should reason
concerning religious penalties, enforced in Roman Catholic
countries, as they reason concerning them when imposed by
the government of Elizabeth. If they did so, we should
hear from them nothing but praise of the gentleness of her
administration.[1]

The statutes of Supremacy and Uniformity were the
only ones relating to religion which affected in any way
the Roman Catholics during the first twelve years of
Elizabeth's reign; that is, up to two years subsequent to
1569, the fatal date when the Popes entered upon their

---

[1] Compare the English Act with the remorseless severity of the rules which secured uniformity in the Papal dominions:—

"(1) In affairs of faith there must not be a moment's delay, but on the slightest suspicion proceedings must be taken with the utmost diligence.

"(2) No regard must be paid to any potentate or prelate, whatever be his power or dignity.

"(3) On the contrary, the greatest severity must be shown to those who seek to shelter themselves under the protection of a ruler; only when confession is made, are leniency and fatherly compassion to be shown.

"(4) To heretics, and especially Calvinists, no toleration must be granted."

Rules drawn up by Cardinal Caraffa, afterwards Pope Paul IV., for the Roman Inquisition.—Ranke, *Popes,* 1, 142.

machinations against England and English institutions. During this period, there were no penal laws against any particular class of the Queen's subjects, for the oath of Supremacy, as explained by the Queen's admonition, was considered by all to be a political test, and the Act of Uniformity was as strictly enforced against the reformed as against those who adhered to the unreformed religion. The bloody statutes[1] against heretics which had been revived by Mary, and which might have been strained against Roman Catholics as they had been strained against the Protestants, were repealed by Elizabeth. There was no difference made between any of her subjects, and equal laws were administered to all. Roman Catholics and the rising sect of the Puritans were treated alike. By those among both who were liable to it, the oath of supremacy was willingly taken, and offences against uniformity were impartially punished. It may be asserted with certainty, that if the Popes had not fomented rebellions, abetted treason, invaded English territory, attempted to loosen the social bonds which kept the nation together, and, when these projects failed, organised crusades against England; if an active party among the Roman Catholics at home, which the government was unable to distinguish from the general body, had not lent itself to schemes of invasion, treason, and assassination; above all, if those emissaries of sedition, the Jesuits and seminary priests, had not been despatched to England and Ireland to stir up insurrections, and to teach the doctrine of the deposing power, no penal laws would ever have been enacted against English Roman Catholics.[2] That body

---

[1] 5 Ric. II. st. 2, c. 5. [Sheriffs to apprehend preachers of heresy]. 2 Hen. IV. c. 15. [For the repression of heresy and burning of heretics]. 2 Hen. V. c. 7. [Magistrates to assist ordinaries in extirpating heresies and punishing heretics].

[2] " Had these men [the Roman Catholic clergy who retired to foreign schools] remained at home, patient of present evils and submissive as

would have continued to occupy at least as favourable a position as other dissenters. We may even go farther and say that it would soon have been placed in a much better situation. For Elizabeth and her government recognized its Church as a true Church, whereas the Puritans and other dissidents were looked upon as recusants, who for small and trifling differences had deserted the pale of the reformed establishment, and by their bickerings had brought discredit upon the Reformation itself.

We have seen that the Roman Catholics were, during the first twelve years of Elizabeth's reign, in exactly the same position as other non-conformists. All the evidence which has come down to us, including their own, shows us that their condition during these quiet and peaceful years was not only comfortable but even happy. Though the Marian persecution had for ever divided the people of England into Protestants and Roman Catholics, no thought of retaliation on the latter was ever entertained. Their bishops after their deprivation were treated with leniency and forbearance. A very different fate had overtaken the reformed bishops in the late reign, five of them having been burned in Mary's time. Archbishop Heath lived in his own house at Chobham, where he was often visited by the Queen. Tunstall, of Durham, and Thirlby, of Ely, lived in the palace of Lambeth; and Bourne, of Wells, with his old friend Carew, Dean of Exeter. White, of Winchester, after a short imprisonment—he had threatened to excommunicate the Queen, an offence little short of

far as might be to the laws; had they continued the practice of their religion in retirement and distributed without clamour instruction to those who claimed it, the rigour of the Legislature would soon have relaxed; no jealousy would have been excited, and no penal statutes, we may now pronounce, would have entailed misfortunes upon them and their successors."—Rev. Joseph Berington. "Had these seminaries never existed, we had not heard of the seditious doctrines which I have mentioned, nor should we have been oppressed by the subsequent cruel laws enacted against our religion."—Sir John Throckmorton.

treason—was allowed to live among his friends, as was Turberville, of Exeter. Poole, of Peterborough, also resided with his friends, and died on one of his own farms. Christopherson, of Chichester, experienced a like indulgence. Watson, of Lincoln, who had also threatened to excommunicate the Queen, after a short restraint spent his time with the Bishops of Rochester and Ely, but being accused of practices against the State he was finally committed, after nearly twenty years of liberty, to Wisbeach Castle in 1580. Pates, of Worcester; Goodwell, of St. Asaph's; and Scot, of Chester, left the country. Oglethorpe, of Carlisle; Bayne, of Lichfield; and Morgan, of St. David's, died soon after their deprivation, " but all of them in their beds and in perfect liberty."[1] Bonner alone was imprisoned for life, as many thought, to save him from the indignation of the populace. Of the many hundred priests[2] who during these twelve years ministered to the religious wants of the Roman Catholics, few or none, after the refusal of a small minority to take the oath of supremacy and their consequent deprivation, were disturbed by the Government so long as they were contented to exercise their functions in private. In 1601, towards the end of Elizabeth's reign, there was published a treatise or circular letter in the name of the secular priests of England.[3] In this we find the following statement:—" It cannot be denied but that for the first ten years of Her Majesty's reign the state of Catholics in England was tolerable, and after a sort in some good quietness. Such as for their consciences

[1] Berington, *Panzani*, 12.

[2] Charles Butler states that in a manuscript perused by him the number is given at a thousand.—*Memoirs of the English Catholics*, 1, 308.

[3] Its title is "*Important Considerations which ought to move all true and sound Catholics, who are not wholly Jesuited, to acknowledge, without all equivocation, ambiguities, or shiftings, that the proceedings of her Majesty and the State with them, since the beginning of her Highness' reign, have been both mild and merciful.*"

were imprisoned in the beginning of her coming to the crown, were very kindly and mercifully used, the state of things then considered. Some of them were appointed to remain with such of their friends as they themselves made choice of. Others were placed, some with bishops, some with deans, and had their diet at their tables, with such convenient lodgings and walks for their recreation as did well content them." In 1602 William Watson, a seminary priest, published "Questions Concerning State and Church."[1] He says: "How great quiet the State and Court was in for twelve years! No talk of treasons or conspiracies, no jealousies nor suspicions, no envy nor supplantations, no fear of murderings nor massacrings, no question of conscience or religion. All lived in great content, and right good fellowship was amongst them." In 1593 Robert Parsons issued his *Responsio ad edictum Reginæ Elizabethæ*. In this he addresses the Queen in the following words:—" In the beginning of thy reign thou didst deal more gently with the Catholics. None were then urged by thee or pressed either to join thy religion or to deny the ancient faith. All things indeed did seem to proceed in a far milder course; no great complaints were heard, no unusual dissensions or repugnance was observed."[2] In another of his books, the same author introduces among his characters a lady of the court, and puts these words into her mouth: " I do well remember the first dozen years of Her Highness' reign; how happy, pleasant, and quiet they were, with all manner of comfort and con-

---

[1] *Dechacordon of Ten Quodlibetical Questions concerning State and Church*, p. 266. Watson was executed for his share in a conspiracy against James I.

[2] Dum enim initio regni tui mitius aliquantum cum catholicis ageres, dum nullum adhuc vehementissime urgeres; nullum admodum premeres vel ad sectæ tuæ participationem vel fidei antiquæ abnegationem. Omnia sane tranquilliori longe cursu incedere videbantur, nec audiebantur magnæ querelæ, nec insignis aliqua dissentio aut repugnantia cernebatur.—p. 81, ed. 1593.

solation. There was no mention then of factions in religion, neither was any man much noted or rejected for that cause, so otherwise his conversation were civil and courteous. No suspicion of treason, no talk of bloodshed, no complaint of troubles, miseries, or vexations. All was peace, all was love, all was joy, all was delight."[1] On the accession of James I. a petition was presented to him by the Roman Catholic laity in 1604 for toleration of their religion. In this we find it stated: "And that [the result of mild and tolerant measures] appeareth most evidently by the first twelve years of the late Queen's reign, which, as they were free from blood and persecution, so were they fraught with all kind of worldly prosperity. No prince was for that space better beloved at home or more honoured or respected abroad, no subjects ever lived with greater security or contentment; never was the realm more opulent or abundant, never was both in court and country such a general time of triumph, joy, and exultation."[2] We shall see in the sequel why it was that these happy and prosperous years did not continue, and how it came to pass that the tranquil scene of peace, love, joy, and delight, as described by Parsons, the irreconcilable enemy of Elizabeth and her government, was so soon overclouded.

In 1560, in the commencement of Elizabeth's reign, Pius IV. had sent Vincentio Parpalia, Abbot of St. Saviour, to Flanders as his nuncio, with orders to pass over into England and exhort the Queen to return back into the bosom of the Church. Heylin, Burnet, and Sir Roger Twysden, have asserted that Parpalia was commissioned by

[1] Leicester's *Commonwealth*, p. 162, ed. 1641.
[2] *An Apology or Petition of the lay Catholics*, p. 14. This is commonly known as the *Petition Apologetical*. Charles Butler says, that the same expressions regarding the lenity of Elizabeth at the beginning of her reign, are to be found in another petition of the Catholic clergy presented to James at the same time.—*English Catholics*, 3, 189.

the Pope to offer a confirmation of the English Prayer-book, an allowance of communion in both kinds, and a declaration of the Queen's legitimacy. But this is uncertain. Camden merely says that he did not believe that Parpalia's instructions were put into writing, and declines to guess what they may have been. All that is certain is, that in the Papal letter to the Queen of which Parpalia was the bearer, the Pope entreated her to give the same credit to his agent which she would do to himself, a clause which suggests that the abbot had secret instructions not mentioned in his letter of recommendation. Parpalia was not admitted. In the following year, Pius invited the Queen to send ambassadors or representatives to the Council of Trent, and despatched the abbot Martinengo to Brussels, who from thence requested that he might be allowed to present letters from the Pope and other princes to the Queen. The English Council was summoned, and it was debated whether the nuncio should be admitted. Among the reasons given for not allowing the Papal messenger to enter England was one which was unanswerable; "the Pope hath, even at this instant time, in Ireland a legate, who is publicly joined already with certain traitors and is occupied in stirring a rebellion, having already by open acts deprived the Queen's Majesty of her right and title there as much as in him lieth."[1]

We are now about to enter upon the consideration of a series of aggressions which, for its long continuance, its iniquity, and the evil consequences which flowed from it, is unexampled in history; aggressions, too, not upon a religious sect but upon a whole nation. For upwards of thirty years the Popes of Rome directed all the moral and material resources at their disposal towards the destruction of England and the conquest of the country by

[1] Note of the Consultation held at Greenwich, May 1, 1561, Tierney's *Dodd*, 2, Append. 322.

the King of Spain. There is hardly an offence known to international law, and which one State can commit against another, which was not committed by the Roman Pontiffs during this period against the Sovereign of England and her people. They attempted to exclude Elizabeth from the comity of European nations,[1] invaded her territories, instigated civil wars amongst her subjects, organised combinations of the Catholic powers to attack her, and preached religious crusades against her. The Popes have been for more than a thousand years mixed personages, compounded of a secular prince and of a supreme priest. In whichever character we consider those who sat upon the Papal throne during this reign, their conduct to Elizabeth and the English nation is equally indefensible. If we regard them merely as Italian princes, no excuse can be offered for their behaviour to an independent sovereign, against whom they had not declared war, and who had never intermeddled in their quarrels. If we view them as supreme priests and vicars of the Prince of Peace, their proceedings are even more blameable. What has the preaching of the Gospel to do with the Sword, or the restoration of religion with subornation of treason and rebellion, instigation of civil war, and actual invasions? The four Popes, Pius V., Gregory XIII., Sixtus V., and Clement VIII., deliberately put aside their spiritual duties, and neglecting the divine precepts of which they claimed to be the supreme expounders, took into their hands the weapons of the flesh. By their plots and intrigues against England, by continual attempts against her and her institutions they harassed her people, drove them to madness by perpetual threats of revolution, rendered

---

[1] "The unceasing representations which the nuncio of the Pope is constantly making to his Majesty [of France] and also to the King of Spain to recall the ambassadors who represent them in England." — Venetian Ambassador to his Signiory, *State Papers, Venet.* 7, 467.

their own adherents the objects of the hatred of their fellow-citizens, destroyed their communion in the kingdom, and from a multitude reduced it to a remnant. It was these Popes that brought down upon the English Roman Catholics the afflictions under which they laboured so long, and sacrificed their Church to the maintenance of the dogma of the deposing power. Well might Urban VIII. declare, in 1641, that he bewailed with "tears of blood" the conduct of his predecessors of the sixteenth century towards England and her people.[1]

[1] Cardinal Newman, *Letter to the Duke of Norfolk*, p. 34; Simpson, *Life of Campion*, App. 371.

SECTION II

For the first eleven years of Elizabeth's reign the Popes did not interfere in the internal affairs of England. They did not even make an attempt to create bishops, or to provide any ecclesiastical organization for the English Roman Catholics. This abstention lasted up to 1569, when Pius V.[1] suddenly, and without any immediate cause, became the aggressor. This was the year in which the Northern rebellion broke out under the Earls of Northumberland and Westmoreland. The Pope had drawn up his bull of excommunication against Elizabeth in the February of this year, though it was not promulgated till 1570. In the summer of 1569 he despatched Dr. Morton to the north of England, with the ostensible purpose of imparting spiritual faculties to the Roman Catholic clergy, "to declare by apostolic authority that Elizabeth was a heretic, and therefore had lost all right to the dominion and power which she exercised over Catholics, and might be treated by them as a heathen and publican, and that thenceforth they owed no obedience to her laws or commands."[2] Pius also sent a letter

---

[1] "Pius V. was beatified by Clement X. in 1672, and canonized by Clement XI. in 1712. His festival holds its place in the Roman Calendar on the 5th of May; but, in canonizing a saint, the Church is far from canonizing all his actions."—Butler, *English Catholics*, 1, 350.

[2] Sander, in his *De visibili Monarchia*, states that Morton was sent by the Pope "ut certis illustribus et catholicis viris authoritate apostolica

to the insurgent earls assuring them of his zealous support " in their holy and religious endeavour to free themselves and their country from the shameful slavery of female lewdness." The Earls had evidently informed the Pope of their intended rebellion, for the Papal letter ends with these words, " which, that it may succeed, we will not only assist you in performing those good offices with the Christian princes which you desire, but we will also contribute as large a sum of money as is in our power at present to supply, of which you shall be more clearly and fully informed by our beloved son, Robert Ridolfi."[1] The Pope also wrote to Alva on the 3rd of November, eleven days before the rebellion broke out, exhorting him to invade England and restore the Catholic religion in that country.[2] The rebellion was a complete failure. The Earls sent letters to the Roman Catholics throughout the kingdom, entreating them to join their standard. So far were the persons addressed from associating themselves with the enterprise, that the majority of them sent on the letters to the Queen. Everyone, says Camden, from all parts of the country, strove to be foremost to offer his person and his purse to resist the rebellion—a testimony to the mild government of Elizabeth and its popularity, which ought not to be forgotten.

Sander, the future Papal legate, and instigator of rebellion in Ireland, informed the Pope that the failure of the Northern insurrection was to be attributed to the

denunciaret, Elizabetham, quæ tunc rerum potiebatur, hæreticam esse, ob eamque causam omni dominio et potestate quam in catholicos usurpabat jure ipso excidisse, impuneque ab illis velut ethnicam et publicanam haberi posse, nec eos illius legibus aut mandatis deinceps obedire cogi."
—Quoted by Tierney. Camden, Strype, and Simpson [*Life of Campion*], assert the same thing.

[1] The letter is given by Sir John Throckmorton in his *Letters to the Catholic Clergy*, p. 100; and also by Blackerby in his *History of the Penal Laws*.

[2] Mignet, *Marie Stuart*.

ignorance of the English Roman Catholics that he had excommunicated the Queen, and to their feeling that they were bound by their oath of allegiance until the Pontiff had absolved them from it. To remove all doubt on this head, Pius in February, 1570, launched his bull *Regnans in Excelsis* against Elizabeth. In this bull the Papal claims to supreme temporal jurisdiction were asserted in the strongest language. After declaring that the Pope alone is appointed "prince over all nations and all kingdoms, to destroy, to scatter, to crush, to plant, and to build,"[1] it terms Elizabeth "the pretended Queen of England, and the servant of wickedness." It proceeds:—"We do out of the fulness of our apostolic power declare the aforesaid Elizabeth, as being a heretic and a favourer of heretics, and her adherents, to have incurred the sentence of excommunication, and to be cut off from the unity of the body of Christ. And, moreover, we declare her to be deprived of her pretended title to the kingdom, and of all dominion, dignity, and privilege, whatsoever; and also the nobility, subjects, and peoples of the said kingdom, and all others who have in any way sworn unto her, to be for ever absolved from any such oath, and all manner of duty, allegiance, and obedience. And we do also by authority of these presents absolve them, and deprive the said Elizabeth of her pretended title to the kingdom, and all other things before named. And we command and charge all and every the noblemen, subjects, peoples, and others aforesaid, that they presume not to obey her, or her orders, mandates, and laws, and those that shall do the contrary we include also in this sentence of anathema."[2]

---

[1] These words, usual in Papal depositions, were borrowed from Jeremiah, 1, 10: "See, I have this day set thee over the nations and over the kingdoms, to root out, and to pull down, and to destroy, and to throw down, to build, and to plant."

[2] Anathema is the most dreadful form of excommunication, and

This bull deserves a more careful consideration than it receives in our general histories; for it was the source, and to those who adopted it, the justification, of all the subsequent plots, conspiracies, and invasions, which distracted the remainder of Elizabeth's reign. It entailed the most disastrous effects on the Roman Catholics of England,[1] whom it divided into two parties, the Patriotic and the Papal party, between which the Government, as it could not pry into conscience, was unable to discriminate. The bull of Paul III. against Henry VIII. had fallen harmless principally for two reasons. The first was, that Henry and his subjects were practically agreed on matters of religion, and there was no party in the kingdom that desired to give effect to the bull. The second was, that divergence of opinion had not then become inveterate, and hopes were entertained of a re-union. But all this was changed in the time of Elizabeth. The separation was now complete, and had been greatly embittered by the Marian persecution. The Reformed and the Roman Catholics of England were severed for ever by the fires in which the Protestant martyrs had perished. There was now a large body in the country to which the bull of Pius appealed. Roman Catholic authors are fond of magnifying the number of their communion in the beginning of Elizabeth's reign, and tell us that it amounted to half or even two-thirds of the population. To every one of these the bull was directed, and called upon him, under the awful sanction of an anathema, to offer a perpetual hostility to Elizabeth and her government.

Coming as it did from their head, who claimed as the

separates the offender, "a societate omnium Christianorum et a liminibus sanctæ matris ecclesiæ in cœlo et in terris."

[1] "The claim of the Popes to temporal power by divine right has been one of the most calamitous events in the history of the Church. Its effects since the Reformation on the English, Irish, and Scottish Catholics have been dreadful."—Charles Butler, 1, 347.

Vicar of God, supreme temporal power, and who was then busy in planning invasions to restore religion by violence, the bull of Pius was a command, under the penalty of being cut off from the unity of Christ, to the Roman Catholics of England to prepare for a war of religion, and a contest for the succession to the crown, with their Protestant fellow-subjects. It proclaimed that there was no Queen, no magistrates, no laws, or lawful authority in England. It exalted rebellion into a religious duty, and sedition into a proof of faith, while it declared that thenceforward no Englishman could be a sincere Roman Catholic without being a traitor. It was a solemn pronouncement by the Pontiff himself that the Roman Catholic form of belief was inconsistent with the safety of the country, and the obedience of the subject. Like her father, Elizabeth had no choice but either to abdicate with the hope of receiving back her crown as John did from a Papal legate, or to hold her own in spite of the Popes, and in direct and avowed hostility to them.[1] Till this bull was recalled, or publicly repudiated by the class to which it was addressed, it was not possible to consider Roman Catholics as mere non-conforming subjects. It justified Elizabeth in regarding everyone who did not disown the bull as a soldier of the Pope and of the Spanish King, for it was well known in England that Pius was urging Philip to invade the kingdom. "What King in the world," ask the secular priests, "being in doubt to be invaded by his enemies, and fearing that some of his own subjects were by indirect means drawn rather to adhere unto them than to himself, would not make the best trial of them he could, for his better satisfaction whom he could trust to? In which trial, if he found any that either should make doubtful answers, or peremptorily affirm that they would leave him their prince and take part with them, might he not

[1] Simpson, *Life of Campion*, 63.

justly repute them for traitors, and deal with them accordingly? Sure we are that no King or prince in Christendom would like or tolerate any such subjects within their dominions if possibly they could get rid of them."[1] We may illustrate the position of Elizabeth after the publication of this bull by a reference to modern times. The head of the Muhammedan religion claims to be the vicegerent of the Almighty, and is venerated as such by every Mussulman. If he were to proclaim that the English government in India was against the law of God and ought to be overthrown, those who now take such different views of the conduct of Elizabeth in similar circumstances, would unite in declaring that the preachers of such a gospel should be restrained by the sword.

After Pius had issued his bull the Queen endeavoured by means of powerful intermediaries to obtain its revocation.[2] But the Pope refused to recall it unless Elizabeth would return to the obedience of the Roman See. Finding that her efforts to obtain a revocation of the bull were fruitless, she resolved to put an end to all communications between her subjects and the Papal Court. The publication of the bull in London by Felton, and the fear that the introduction of similar instruments in future might lead to mischief, was the occasion of the Act of 1571. Its title is, "An Act against the bringing in and putting in execution of bulls, writings, or instruments, and other superstitious things from the See of Rome." It provided that it should be treason to

---

[1] *Important Considerations*, 1601.

[2] This is asserted by Sander and Tierney, though denied by Fuller. The question appears to be settled in the affirmative by a letter from the Pope to the Emperor Maximilian, quoted from Theiner by Simpson in the appendix to his *Life of Campion*:—"Why she [Elizabeth] makes such a stir about this sentence," says the Pope, "we cannot quite understand, for if she thinks so much of our sentence and excommunication, why does she not return to the bosom of holy mother Church?"

put in use any bull, &c., the effect of which was "to absolve and reconcile those who will be content to forsake their due obedience to our lady the Queen, and to yield and subject themselves to the feigned, unlawful, and usurped authority of the Bishop of Rome." The introduction of *Agnus Dei*, crosses, and beads from Rome was also forbidden under the lesser penalty of a *præmunire*. Some of our historians have negligently asserted[1] that this Act was directed against conversions to the Church of Rome. This is a mistake. Conversions are not effected by the instantaneous exhibition of declamatory documents but by teaching and holy example. Pius had included in his anathema all who obeyed the laws of Elizabeth, or recognized in any way her government. It was found that some persons procured bulls and other documents absolving them for disobedience to the Pontiff's commands, that is, from the religious penalties imposed by the bull for obedience to the Queen, and the consequent disobedience to the orders of the Pope. It was against such instruments as these that the Act was directed, and not against conversions to the religion of Rome. No one living in those times considered that the statute was enacted against religious conversions. Bacon did not, nor did Walsingham. The secular priests speak of it as having been made only against the importation of bulls, &c. They say: "Her Majesty called a parliament in the thirteenth year of her reign, 1571, wherein a law was made containing many branches against the bringing into this land after that time of any bulls from Rome, any *Agnus Dei*, crosses, or pardons, and against all manner of persons that should procure them

---

[1] As Hallam. Charles Butler, a lawyer of great eminence, and well qualified to interpret an Act of Parliament, is careful to avoid such a misreading. He says:—"In the construction of this Act it appears to have been understood that the absolutions which it mentions did not denote absolutions given in sacramental confession, but those absolutions only which were granted by special faculties."—*English Catholics*, 1, 352.

to be so brought hither, with many other particularities thereunto appertaining."

This Act has been described as the first of the penal laws against Roman Catholics.[1] This description requires to be largely qualified. The statute consists of two parts. The first, that against the introduction of Papal bulls was general, and a declaration only of the old law which had prevailed in England from the Norman conquest,[2] but more particularly from the passing of the *Præmunire* Act of Richard II., enacted more than a hundred and fifty years before Elizabeth's accession. It is undoubted that during this interval it was illegal for any English subject to bring into the kingdom, or accept, or even sue for, a Papal bull, letter, or rescript without the license of the sovereign first asked and obtained. We have in our records, as we have seen, many letters-patent granting permission to persons to sue for or to receive such instruments, and also examples of pardons for having accepted them without a previous license. The only portion of the statute which was new, was that against bringing in tokens and remembrances from Rome. The English Government had endeavoured to obtain a revocation of the bull deposing the sovereign, and had failed to do so in consequence of the obstinacy of the Pope. Its offer of peace had been rejected. The Pontiff by his bull had denied it the name and rights of a lawful government, and was now corrupting the fidelity of its subjects. For these reasons the Administration considered it incumbent to cut off all communication between those subjects and the Papal Court. It feared, as the secular priests say, that the Roman Catholics of England might be " by indirect means

[1] Simpson's *Campion*, App. 370.
[2] Edward I. was with difficulty persuaded to spare the life of one who had brought a Papal bull into the kingdom. Edward III. put to death several persons for this offence. See Walsingham. *Historia Anglicana*, 1, 286. Sub ann. 1358.

drawn to adhere to their enemies," or, as Bacon and Walsingham put it, that by such "love tokens as are well known not to be any essential part of the Romish religion, the affections of the people might be enchanted from their allegiance to their natural sovereign."[1] The Roman Catholics themselves did not consider this Act as one of the penal laws, and dated the first of these laws ten years later, viz. in 1581. In a book[2] which was addressed to Clement VIII. in the name of the English Roman Catholic clergy in 1601, the following paragraph occurs:—"Father Parsons was the principal author, the incentor, and the mover of all our garboils at home and abroad. During the short space of nearly two years that he spent in England [from June, 1580, to the end of 1581] so much did he irritate by his actions the mind of the Queen and her ministers, that on that occasion the *first* severe laws were enacted against the ministers of our religion and those who should harbour them." This Act against the introduction of Papal bulls was allowed to sleep harmlessly on the statute book for six years.

One of the consequences of the bull of Pius was, as has been said, to divide the Roman Catholics of England into two parties; Roman Catholics, properly so called, who, true to the traditions of the old national Church, knew how to reconcile their belief with loyalty to their sovereign, and Papists,[3] who added to their faith two new articles, that the

---

[1] *Observations on a Libel.* Bacon's expressions in this are borrowed by him from a letter written by Walsingham in defence of Elizabeth's administration. Walsingham's letter is given in Collier, 2, 607.

[2] *Declaratio Motuum*, &c., written by John Mush, a seminary priest. Berington's *Memoirs of Panzani*, 28.

[3] "To the appellation of *Papistic Party* some persons may object.... It is not new; it has always been used to distinguish those who by their obsequiousness and too great adherence to the Papal power, have supported and given strength to the exorbitant pretensions of the Court of Rome." Throckmorton, *Letters to the Catholic Clergy of England*, preface.

Pope was invested by divine right with the power of deposing Kings, and that to obey a heretical prince was to betray the cause of religion. This division made its appearance immediately after the publication of the bull of Pius. The English Government was alarmed at the doctrine of the deposing power set forth in that document. Accordingly in 1570 it convened a meeting of the deprived bishops, and of "many abbots and deans" of their persuasion. To this assembly the following questions were submitted :—

"Whether the Queen was divested of the kingdom by the deposing bull of Pius? or by any other sentence passed, or to be passed? or whether her subjects were discharged from their allegiance?"[1] To these questions a unanimous answer was given : "Notwithstanding this bull, or any other declaration or sentence of the Pope, passed or to be passed, we hold Queen Elizabeth to be the lawful Queen of England and Ireland, and that obedience and fealty are due to her as such by all her English and Irish subjects."[2] In process of time the rift between the parties became wider. In 1587, when Cardinal Allen published his disgraceful letter to the officers of Stanley's regiment, praising them for having betrayed Deventer and for having deserted to the Spanish King, the "chiefest" of the English Roman Catholics drew up an answer to it. In this reply they repudiated the opinion expressed by Allen, that the "rendering of such towns of the

[1] "Utrum per bullam illam Pontificis depositoriam, aliamve declarationem vel sententiam latam vel ferendam, sentirent Reginam Elizabetham jure regnorum suorum devestitam esse? aut subditos ab illius obedientia et fidelitate exemptos?"—Caron, *Remonstrantia Hibernorum*, pars. 1, c. 5, s. 4.

[2] The answer was signed by Watson of Lincoln; Feckenham, Abbot of Westminster; Cole, Dean of St. Paul's; Harpsfield, Dean of Canterbury, and N. Harpsfield, Archdeacon of the same. Of this opinion also were Archbishop Heath, Bishops Poole, Tunstall, White, Oglethorpe, Thirlby, Turberville, *plurespue abbates ac decani.—Ib.*

Low Countries as be in any English custody was necessary to be done under pain of mortal sin and damnation," and "declared to the whole world that they utterly defied the seditious doctrine of his resolution."[1] Some years later, in 1601, when the designs of the Jesuits and the seminary priests had become better known, the secular priests asserted that they were ready to receive any person from the Pope on a purely spiritual mission, "but if he [the Pope] come or send hither an army, under pretence to establish the Catholic religion by force and with the sword, we will ever be most ready, as native-born and true subjects to Her Highness, with the hazard of our lives, and with all our might, to withstand and oppose ourselves against him, and to spend the best blood in our bodies in defence of our Queen and our country." Further on they say to their flocks: "We desire you, by the mercies of God, to take heed of novelties and Jesuitism, for it is nothing but treachery, dissimulation, ambition, and a very vizard of most deep hypocrisy. . . . Never give ear to any private whisperers or Jesuitical persuasions that shall tend to allure you from your duties and allegiance unto her Majesty or your native country. All arguments that can be brought to corrupt you in either, assure yourselves are false and unlearned sophistications."[2] Unfortunately for England and the English Roman Catholics the Papists were by far the more active and enterprising party. They were supported by all the influence of the Papal Court, by Philip in Spain, and by his Viceroys in Flanders. Their leaders were William Allen and Robert Parsons, the respective heads of the two missionary bodies, the seminary priests and the Jesuits, who preached and

---

[1] "The Answer of divers Catholic English gentlemen to a certain seditious book, veiled with the name of Dr. Allen."—*Letters and Memorials of Card. Allen*, 299.

[2] *Important Considerations.*

taught that Elizabeth should be deposed and religion restored in England by rebellion or by invasion. To these two, of all men, after the Popes of Rome, the subsequent misfortunes of the English Roman Catholics were principally due.

In 1568 Allen founded at Douay the first foreign seminary for the education of English priests. Dodd and other authors tell us that he did so to preserve the succession of Roman Catholic priests, who otherwise might have died out. It is only too certain that Allen's real intention was, to establish schools from which he might despatch apostles to spread his seditious doctrines. There was not then the slightest necessity for establishing colleges abroad, for in 1568 Roman Catholic schools might have been founded at home. "I cannot admit," says Throckmorton, "that we are under any obligation to these men [Allen and Parsons] for procuring the foundation of foreign seminaries. At the time they did it, the universities were, indeed, shut against the Catholics,[1] as they now [1792] are, but it was not therefore necessary to fly to a strange land for education. No law then existed to debar the Catholics from educating their children in England. Had these seminaries never existed, we had not heard of the seditious doctrines which I have mentioned, nor should we have been oppressed by the subsequent cruel laws enacted against our religion." "Our ancestors were unwise," says the Rev. Joseph Berrington, "in founding foreign houses of education, not only because they took the place of better establishments, which in the course of a few years we might have formed at home, but also because, from their views, some real and some imputed by their enemies, on the ground of their foreign connexions and

---

[1] Sir John Throckmorton means by the Oath of Supremacy. As a matter of fact, this oath was then considered by Roman Catholics as a political test, and was freely taken by them. The stricter Oaths of Henry and Edward did not prevent them flocking to the Universities.

their avowed designs against the religion of the country, they soon excited in the breasts of our governors a suspectful jealousy . . . It will not be denied that . . . our foreign houses soon imbibed an Ultramontane spirit which, as it flattered, and by flattering secured the favour of Rome, so did it offend . . . the government. The doctrine of deposing princes and disposing of their crowns, with other concurrent maxims of a like tendency, were the *pabulum* on which that Ultramontane spirit fed."[1] Not only might English schools and colleges have been established for Roman Catholics, but the succession of their bishops, and therefore of their priests, might have been secured in the regular way. Many of their deprived prelates, after a short imprisonment, or none at all, were practically left at liberty. Archbishop Heath dwelt in his own house, and died there in 1579, twenty years after the accession of Elizabeth. Poole, of Peterborough, was at first merely restricted to within three miles of London,[2] and died on one of his own farms. White of Winchester and Turberville of Exeter lived with their relations, and Bourne of Wales with an old friend. Watson of Lincoln, after a short restraint, was at liberty among his friends for nearly twenty years, and acted as a kind of Pope's legate in England,[3] until he was suspected of political intrigues, and sent to Wisbeach in 1580. There was nothing to prevent these bishops from meeting and consecrating successors as vacancies occurred. No danger was to be apprehended from the Government, at least the Pope and the Roman Catholic clergy believed so. In 1580 the Pope sent Goldwell, formerly of St. Asaph's, to take upon himself the charge of religion in England, though the bishop did not get farther than Rheims. In the same year Parsons himself wrote to

[1] Berington, *Panzani*, Introd. 23.
[2] *Cal. of State Papers, Elizabeth*, Addenda, 1547-65, p. 52.
[3] Berington, *Panzani*, p. 37.

Agazzarius, rector of the English College at Rome, describing the spiritual wants of the Roman Catholics, and expressing a hope that a bishop would speedily be nominated. Goldwell also at this time wrote to the Pope, remonstrating with him for not appointing bishops for England : " I cannot but marvel how it is . . . you make so many difficulties about creating three or four titular bishops to preserve and propagate the Catholic faith."[1] In 1596 the clergy in England resolved to supplicate the Pope to restore their hierarchy and to appoint bishops, " being now sensible when it was too late how culpable had been their remissness in not having induced the old bishops to leave successors behind them."[2] When Blackwell was appointed by the Pope Arch-priest in 1598, with jurisdiction over England and Scotland, he exercised his office without molestation from the Government. In Ireland the succession of both bishops and priests was kept up. What was possible in Ireland was surely not impossible in England. If this had been done, and if the spiritual care of the Roman Catholics of England had been entrusted to clergymen educated at home, instead of being committed to a large extent to seminary priests and Jesuits nourished on the foreign doctrine of the deposing power, the whole history of that communion would have been different.

Charles Butler denies that the English government was opposed to the appointment of bishops by the Pope as vacancies occurred, and points out the advantages that would have resulted from such institution. "After bishops are installed in their Sees, they are only removable for a canonical crime and by a canonical proceeding. Such bishops therefore, might disregard, and even resist with impunity,

[1] Letter quoted from Theiner by Simpson in his *Life of Campion*, 106.
[2] Berington, *Panzani*, 42.

such illaudable bulls as those of Paul the Third, of St. Pius the Fifth, Gregory, and of Sixtus Quintus, which had so greatly injured the Catholic cause, and guard their flocks against them. In fact so generally was it understood that the appointment of bishops would be acceptable to Elizabeth and her ministers, that the Catholic opposers of the measure used this very circumstance as an objection to it, observing that it was impossible to suppose that any plan could be acceptable to their adversaries if they did not foresee that it would essentially prejudice the Catholic religion."[1] Another Roman Catholic author, Charles Plowden, tells us that the Pope refused to appoint bishops for England because the measure was patronised by Elizabeth.[2]

The foundation of the English seminary at Douay[3] was succeeded by that of others at Rome, Valladolid, Seville, Louvain, and St. Omer, under the protection of the Pope and the Spanish King, who contributed largely to their support. All these were established by the labours of Allen and Parsons. From these centres of sedition, books and treatises were poured into England teaching that every Act of Elizabeth since her excommunication was void, and that her subjects were bound to depose her under the pain of damnation. A few extracts from the writings of Allen and Parsons, who were the heads of the two missionary bodies, the seminary priests and the Jesuits, will show us what the teaching in these colleges must have been, and the absolute necessity of preventing the entrance of its apostles into England. During the war in the Low Countries, Sir William Stanley was in command of the town of Deventer, which he betrayed into the hands of the Spaniards, and

---

[1] *Memoirs of the English Catholics*, 2, 252.   [2] *Ib.* 253, note.

[3] The establishment at Douay was removed to Rheims in 1578, where it flourished for fifteen years under the patronage of the Guises, the inveterate enemies of England, and then returned to Douay.

deserted with his regiment to the service of Philip. This act of treachery excited the indignation of all honest men; but Allen hastened to address a letter[1] to the officers of Stanley's regiment in which he justified the betrayal, and exhorted the Roman Catholics in all other regiments to do the same. "To come then to your purpose, though I have already by my letters to Sir William given my own opinion, I will yet, for better clearing the cause, set here down my mind more largely and distinctly. Therefore, first, I say that, the rendering up of such towns and places of the Low Countries as be in any Englishmen's custody, is not only lawful but necessary to be done, under pain of mortal sin and damnation.[2] . . . Yea, I say more to you, gentlemen, seeing your desire to know my meaning fully on this point, that as all acts of justice within the realm done by the Queen's authority ever since she was by public sentence of the Church and See Apostolic declared a heretic and an enemy of God's Church, and for the same by name excommunicated and deposed from all royal dignity; as, I say, ever since the publication thereof all is void by the law of God and man; so likewise no war can be lawfully denounced or waged by her though otherwise in itself it were most just. Because that is the first condition, that it be denounced by one that hath lawful and supreme power to do the same, as no excommunicate person hath, especially if he be withall deposed from his regal dignity by Christ's own Vicar, which

---

[1] "*The copy of a letter written by M. Doctor Allen, concerning the yielding up of the citie of Daventrie unto his Catholic Majesty. Wherein is shown both how lawful, honourable, and necessary that action was and also that all others, especially those of the English nation, that detain any towns or other places in the Low Countries from the King Catholic, are bound upon pain of damnation to do the like.*"—Reprinted by the Chetham Society, 1851.

[2] Sir William Stanley's conduct was also justified by Parsons in his "Manifestation."—Butler's *English Catholics*, 2, 20.

is the supreme power on earth. And all subjects are not only absolved and discharged of their service, oath, homage, and obedience, but specially forbidden to serve or obey any such canonically condemned person."

In 1587 Allen was created a cardinal, and in the same year he drew up an admonition or manifesto,[1] which was dispersed among the Roman Catholics of England before the arrival of the Armada. The tone of this publication is almost inconceivable. If copies did not still exist, it would be incredible that such a document was ever issued by a minister of religion. Here are some paragraphs: "She [Elizabeth] is indeed taken and known for an incestuous bastard, begotten and born in sin of an infamous courtesan, Anne Boleyn, afterwards executed for advoutery, treason, heresy, and incest, amongst others with her own natural brother; which Anne Boleyn, her said supposed father kept by pretended marriage in the life of his lawful wife, as he did before unnaturally know and keep both the said Anne's mother and sister." After describing the Queen as a perjurer, persecutor, a destroyer of the ancient nobility, an oppressor of her subjects "with manifold exactions not only by ordinary means, but also by sundry shameful guiles of lotteries, laws, decrees, and by falls of money and such like deceits," and a "seller of laws, licenses, dispensations, pardons, and permissions to the enriching of herself and servants," it accuses her of the most shameful licentiousness. "With the aforesaid person [Leicester] and divers others, she hath abused her body against God's laws, to the disgrace

[1] "*An Admonition to the nobility and people of England and Ireland concerning the present wars made for the execution of his Holiness's sentence by the high and mighty King Catholic of Spain.*" The substance of this address was also compressed into a smaller compass and printed as a broadside, with the title "*A Declaration of the sentence of deposition of Elizabeth, the usurper and pretended Queen of England.*"

of princely majesty and the whole nation's reproach, by unspeakable and incredible variety of lust, which modesty suffereth it not to be remembered, neither were it to chaste ears to be uttered how shamefully she hath defiled and infamed her person and country, and made her court a trap by this damnable and detestable art to entangle in sin and overthrow the younger sort of the nobility and gentlemen of the land; whereby she is become notorious to the world and in other countries a common fable for her turpitude, which in so high degree, namely, in a woman and a Queen, deserveth not only deposition, but all vengeance both of God and man." " She could never be restrained from this incontinence, though the principal peers of the realm and others of high authority, as deputies from the whole parliament and estates, made humble suit and supplication to her, that for pity and compassion of their desolate case and of the danger that the whole realm and specially the nobility should be in if she deceased without lawful issue . . . . she would therefore marry and procure . . . . lawful heirs of her body . . . . to whom sometimes she merely and mockingly answered that she would die a maiden Queen, but afterwards in contempt and rebuke of all the states of the realm and to the condemnation of chaste and lawful matrimony . . . . whereunto as to a bridle of her licentiousness she is an enemy, she forced the very parliament itself to give consent and to provide by a pretended law . . . . that none should so much as be named for her successor during her life saving the natural, that is to say, bastard born child of her own body." . . . " Now therefore my lords and dear countrymen, if you list, follow this God's ordinance and happy provision that He hath of His great mercy made for your honours, liberty and salvation. If you without delay join yourselves, as God, conscience, and nature bindeth you; if you take part one with another in so goodly and honourable a quarrel, you shall attain your purpose without all bloodshed, where otherwise if you should either sit still or refuse to help, or sever yourselves one from another, or any of you seek to uphold—which God forbid—the usurper or her complices, being thus cursed by the Church and forsaken of God and of all good men, you that do so shall first incur the Angel's curse and malediction upon the inhabitants of the land of Meros,[1] who sat still and would not help God nor venture their lives in His quarrel, and secondly be as deeply excommunicated as she is, and so you shall be guilty of your own ruin and the blood of the people, and yet shall not prevail. You shall fight against God and against His anointed, against your next lawful King, against truth, faith, religion, conscience, and your dear country. You shall bootless defend, yea to your own present destruction and eternal shame, a most unjust usurper and open injurer of all nations, an infamous, depraved, accursed, excommunicate heretic, the very shame of her sex and princely name, the chief spectacle of sin and abomination in this our age, and the only poison, calamity, and destruction of our noble Church and country. Fight not for God's love, fight not in that quarrel in which if you die you are sure to be damned."

The writings of Parsons were equally dangerous and subversive of all secular sovereignty. In one of his works he says: "The whole of divines and canonists do hold that it is certain and *of faith*,[2] that any Christian prince whatsoever, if he shall manifestly deflect from the Catholic religion and

---

[1] "Curse ye Meroz, said the angel of the Lord, curse ye bitterly the inhabitants thereof; because they came not to the help of the Lord, to the help of the Lord against the mighty."—Judges v. 23.

[2] "Et est certum et de fide, quemcunque principem christianum, si a religione catholica manifeste deflexerit, et alios avocare voluerit, excidere statim omni potestate et dignitate, ex ipsa vi juris tum divini tum humani."

endeavour to draw others from the same, does immediately fall from all power and dignity by the very force of human and divine law, and that also before any sentence of the supreme pastor or judge denounced against him, and that his subjects whatsoever are free from all obligation of that oath which they had taken for their allegiance to him as their lawful prince; and that they may, and ought, if they have forces, drive out such a man as an apostate or heretic and a backslider from the Lord and Christ, and an enemy to the commonwealth, from all dominion over Christians, lest he infect others, or by his example or command turn others from the faith, and that this certain, definite, and undoubted opinion of the best learned men is wholly agreeable and consonant to the apostolical doctrine."[1]

Similar tenets were upheld in their books by Stapleton, first professor of divinity at Douay, and afterwards at Louvain; by Bristowe, prefect of studies, and occasionally regent, at Douay; by Sander, and many others. It is certain that these opinions were inculcated in the colleges founded by Allen and Parsons, and presided over by their friends. There is no room for the least doubt. For, as Parsons informs us, they were held by all divines and canonists as of faith, that is, as truths necessary for salvation. Such doctrines were universally maintained by the doctors and canonists of Italy and the Spanish dominions, where these colleges were situated, so that it was impossible that these opinions should not be taught in the seminaries. It is trifling with our intelligence to say that the laws, which prevented the apostles of such doctrines from corrupting the allegiance of the English people, were not necessary, or that Elizabeth was not bound first to warn them not to enter the kingdom, and if they persisted, to draw the sword against them. Such laws were then necessary when every art and

[1] Throckmorton's *Letters to the Catholic Clergy*, 129.

every menace were unremittingly employed to stimulate the English Roman Catholics to abandon their loyalty, and to disturb the government of the land. Similar laws may be necessary again. A modern Roman Catholic government[1] has found it requisite to direct penal enactments against those ministers of religion who abuse their sacred functions for the purpose of spreading political views, and, under the pretence of exercising their office, enjoin opinions hostile to the State.

The celebrated Cardinal D'Ossat,[2] writing in 1601 to the King of France from Rome, where he had resided for more than twenty years, thus describes these seminaries:—"For this purpose [to support the claims of Philip II. and his successors to the English crown] colleges and seminaries have been expressly established for English youths by the Spaniards at Douay and St. Omer. Young gentlemen of good families are received into these institutions in order that they may influence their relations and friends in England. The principal aim of these schools has been to catechise, educate, and rear young English gentlemen in the belief and firm faith that the late King of Spain had, and that his family now has, the true right to the crown of England, and that the furtherance of this claim would be advantageous to the Catholic religion not only in England but throughout Christendom. When these young men have finished their secular studies in the Low Countries, they are removed to Spain, where there are other colleges for them, in order that they may be made thorough Spaniards. There, they are instructed in philosophy and theology, and confirmed in the holy faith that the kingdom of England

---

[1] The Italian Government.

[2] "He [Cardinal D'Ossat] was one of those extraordinary personages who have united every voice in their praise."—Butler, *English Catholics*, 2, 49.

belonged to Philip II. and now belongs to his family.
When the young men have gone through these studies,
those of them who are considered to be the most hispaniolated,
and the firmest believers in the "credo Espagnol," are sent
to England to spread that faith, to gain converts to it, to
act as spies in the country, and to give information to the
Spaniards of the readiest means of subjecting the kingdom
to Spain; and also, if necessary, to undergo martyrdom as
much or more for the said Spanish faith as for the Catholic
religion."[1] In the following year, 1602, Thomas Bluet, a
seminary priest, wrote to the Cardinals Borghese and
Aragon:—" In the Spanish seminaries he [Parsons] forced
English students to subscribe to the Infanta as their lawful
Queen, that on their return they might persuade their
relatives to accept no other. Can it be wondered at that the
Queen should rage against priests so educated? and when
they slay and torment us, they declare that it is not for
religion but for treason. Parsons himself acknowledges
that the Queen is forced to these proceedings."[2]

Undeterred by the failure of the insurrection of 1569,
the Pope immediately recommenced his intrigues against
England, and in 1570 and 1571 endeavoured to stir up
another civil war, and to bring about an invasion by the
Spaniards. Ridolfi, as we have seen from the Papal letter
to the insurgent earls, was the secret agent and correspondent of the Pope in England. He was a banker, and
director of the company of Italian merchants in London.

[1] *Lettres du Cardinal D'Ossat*, 5, 30, ed. 1708.
[2] *Cal. State Papers, Domestic, Elizabeth*, 1601-3, p. 170. The secular priests also assert that Parsons urged the English students in the Spanish seminaries to acknowledge the Infanta as their Queen. "To which purpose he [Parsons] framed and afterwards published a book, wherewith he acquainted the students in those seminaries in Spain, and laboured nothing more than to have their subscriptions to the said Infanta's title, therein promising unto her their present allegiance as unto their lawful sovereign."—*Important Considerations.*

He had been justly suspected of a connexion with the northern rebellion, and had been imprisoned for some months, but his professed occupation enabled him to give explanations which satisfied the English Government. This person was sent with full powers from the Pontiff to Mary Stuart, and was also well furnished with money and credit.[1] He, Norfolk, and the Queen of Scots, arranged among themselves the plan of a rebellion for the purpose of restoring religion and delivering Mary. If this conspiracy had succeeded, Elizabeth would infallibly have been deposed. Ridolfi proposed that Elizabeth's person should be seized by the Roman Catholic lords attending parliament, but Norfolk was of opinion that nothing should be done until answers had been received from abroad from those princes who favoured the enterprise.[2]

Accordingly, Ridolfi was despatched to the Pope and King of Spain, with full instructions from Mary and the Duke of Norfolk. In her instructions, Mary expressed her resolution to have recourse to all Christian princes, and especially to the Pope and King of Spain, for the purpose of restoring the Catholic religion. She mentioned that the nobles of England had determined to take up arms under the leadership of Norfolk to uphold her rights, and to oppose by force the projected marriage between Elizabeth and the Duke

[1] "From his [the Pope's] nuncio there were letters also of the good disposition of the Pope to help the Queen of Scots, and that, any time that she could make a party here in England, he would bestow 100,000 crowns beside any other aid and help he could procure."—*Evidence of Barker*, Murdin, *State Papers*, 126. The secular priests in their *Important Considerations* say:—"Had not the Pope and King of Spain assigned the Duke of Norfolk to be the head of this rebellion? Did not the Pope give orders to Ridolfi to take 150,000 crowns to set forward this attempt?" Catena in his *Life of Pius V.* also states that Ridolfi was sent from the Pope with 150,000 crowns.—See Camden, sub anno 1572.

[2] "Barker did report to me that the duke did no wise like of such

of Anjou ; assured the Pope of the devotion of Norfolk to the Catholic religion : and requested him to use all his influence with the King of Spain, and to urge that monarch to support an enterprise so advantageous to Christendom and to himself personally ; proposed to marry her son to one of the infantas, and to place him in the meantime in the hands of Philip as a guarantee of her good intentions ; and offered, in case an expedition should be sent, the Castle of Dumbarton or Edinburgh, in order to secure the success of the landing.[1]

The instructions of the Duke of Norfolk were fuller and more specific than those of Mary : " So great is the confidence which the Queen of Scots, I, and other nobles of the realm repose in you, that we have resolved to entrust to you a matter of the greatest importance not only to the safety of our persons but to the greater number of the inhabitants of these two kingdoms, and to the whole of Christendom. We authorize you to hasten to Rome to our lord the Pope, and from him to Spain, to explain the calamitous state of this island, and to propose a certain means of freeing its inhabitants from their miseries. You have received instructions from the Queen of Scotland what you should propose on her behalf. I also, in my own name and in that of the majority of the English nobles, a list of whom you take with you,[2] hereby declare our intentions. You will represent to our

Italian devices, and could attempt nothing before he should get answer from these princes beyond the seas that were reputed to be friends."— *Exam. of the Bishop of Ross*, Murdin, 44.

[1] The instructions of Mary and the duke are in Prince Labanoff's *Lettres, Instructions, et Memoirs de Marie Stuart*, extracted from the Vatican archives, and attested by the pontifical prefect of the library. They are undated, but must have been drawn up before the 24th of March, 1571, on which day Ridolfi set out for Brussels on his way to Rome.

[2] This list contained the names of sixty-three English noblemen, forty as favourable to the enterprise, seventeen as neutral, and six only as hostile. No Scotch noblemen were mentioned.

lord the Pope and the Catholic King the miserable condition of this island, and the probability of its becoming worse, unless they intervene to restore the Catholic religion and to support the rights of the Queen of Scotland to the English crown. You will make known to our lord and the Catholic King the good and prompt disposition of the English Catholics—who form the larger and more powerful party in the realm—and the opportunity now offered to restore the whole country to the Catholic faith, and to advance the just title of the Scotch Queen, inasmuch as the Protestants will assist the enterprise, moved thereto by their hatred to her competitors, and the question of the succession to the Crown. And since our lord the Pope and his Catholic Majesty have up to this time entertained doubts of me as professing Protestantism, you will explain to them that I have done so, not from any disaffection to the Holy See, but to be able on a fitting opportunity like the present to do service to the country and the whole of Christendom.[1] You will kiss the feet of our lord in my name and that of all the Catholic noblemen, and assure him that if this enterprise succeed I shall be satisfied to do anything that he, the Catholic King, and the Queen of Scotland, shall order me to do." After further assurances of his devotion to the Spanish King, the duke explained what succours he would require. He asked for six thousand musketeers, four thousand muskets to arm volunteers, two thousand cuirasses, twenty-five pieces of artillery, a supply of ammunition and money, and an experienced commander. He desired, if possible, that the force might be increased to ten thousand men, in order that diversions in Scotland and Ireland might be effected. He promised on his side to furnish twenty thousand infantry

[1] Yet on the scaffold the duke made use of these words:—"God is my judge before whom I stand; I thank God I was never a Papist since I knew what religion meant."—*State Trials*, 1, 1034.

and three thousand cavalry, and suggested Harwich or Portsmouth as convenient places for landing.¹

Furnished with these credentials Ridolfi left London on the 24th of March, 1571. On his way to Rome he had an interview with Alva at Brussels and explained to him the plan, the resources, and the requirements of the conspirators who had despatched him. Alva at once took the measure of Ridolfi, whom he described as a babbler. Regarding the enterprise itself, Alva wrote on the 7th of May a long letter to Philip II., in which he expressed a strong opinion that it ought not to be commenced with the open assistance of that King. The first step in the matter should be taken by the English confederates. If however, he added, the Queen of England should die a natural or any other death, or if her person should be seized, there would be no difficulty in the affair. The proposal of a marriage between her and Anjou would then drop of itself, the French would no longer fear that Philip intended to make himself master of England, and the Germans would not distrust him, as his only object would be to sustain the Queen of Scots against the rival claimants to the crown. Should any one of the three cases happen, that is, the natural death, the assassination, or the capture of Elizabeth, " your Majesty may then promise to assist them with six thousand men from the Netherlands. For myself I look upon this as so convenient, so honourable, and so easy for your Majesty, that, if one of the three cases

¹ Dr. Lingard has attempted to throw doubts on these instructions of Norfolk. It is certain that they were authorized by the duke. (1) Copies of them exist in the Vatican and Simancas archives. (2) Alva, on learning that the conspiracy was discovered, wrote to the Spanish Ambassador in London to keep carefully the instructions of Mary and the duke, which had been deposited with him. (3) Mary, in her correspondence with Alva and Norfolk, often refers to these instructions. (4) The Bishop of Ross affirmed that they were authorized by Norfolk [*Murdin*, 25]. (5) In her instructions, Mary mentions those given by the Duke: " Io

happens, I shall not hesitate to act without fresh instructions, and I shall do so unless you order to the contrary."[1]

From Brussels Ridolfi proceeded to Rome, where he received a warm welcome from the Pope. In the preceding January, Pius had remonstrated with the Spanish ambassador on the neglect of his master to effect anything for the deposition of Elizabeth and the restoration of the Catholic religion in England. On the present occasion the Pope at once adopted the plans of Ridolfi, and placed at his disposal a sum of money to advance them.[2] In addition he gave him a letter to Philip, imploring that King to furnish Ridolfi with the means of carrying them into execution. The letter is as follows:—"Our dear son, Robert Ridolfi, by the help of God, will lay before your Majesty certain things which affect not a little the honour of Almighty God and the advantage of the Christian commonwealth. We require and beseech your Majesty to grant him, on this account and without hesitation, your most entire confidence, and we conjure you especially by your fervent piety towards God to take to heart the matter on which he will treat with your Majesty, and to furnish him with all the means which you may judge most suitable for the execution of his plans. Meanwhile we beseech your Majesty to do this, submitting the affair to the judgment and prudence of your Majesty, and from the bottom of our heart praying our Redeemer in His mercy to

---

mi remetto alla particulare instructione che il Ridolfi portera del duca di Norfolk." Lastly, about the same time Norfolk wrote to Philip that he had determined to put himself at the head of the English and Scotch nobility, in order to restore the Catholic religion in both countries.— Labanoff, 3, 247, 254.

[1] The letter is given in Mignet's *Marie Stuart*. In it Alva mentions the instructions of Mary Stuart and the Duke of Norfolk:—"Despues vino el dicho Ridolfi secreto con cartas de creencias de la dicha Reina y del duque."

[2] Lingard, 6, 260, Ed. 1849.

grant success to that which is projected for His honour and glory."

In June Ridolfi arrived in Madrid, and on the 7th of July he was questioned regarding the enterprise by the Duke of Feria, who had been deputed to examine him. On the same day, the Council of State met and discussed the projects for the assassination or capture of Elizabeth and the invasion of England. All its members agreed as to the necessity of interfering at once in English affairs, but differed as to the manner of so doing and the feasibility of the plans offered for their consideration. The Papal nuncio alone was sanguine as to the success of the enterprise, and mentioned that Cipiano Vitelli,[2] one of Alva's officers, had offered to go in person, with a dozen or fifteen resolute men, and seize the Queen of England at one of her country houses. He was also of opinion that Alva possessed sufficient means for securing the success of an invasion, and advised that he should proceed under the authority of the bull deposing Elizabeth, and act in the Pope's name. But the Duke of Feria opposed this, and maintained that they should found their intervention on the claims of the Scottish Queen. Finally the Council was of the same opinion as Alva, viz. that the English conspirators should first show their strength and do something for themselves.[3] On the 14th of September Philip wrote to Alva: "Perceiving that you are firmly persuaded that it is not advisable to proceed in this matter unless the confederates show themselves in force, and considering the careful attention you have given to the subject, I am led to leave it in your hands, in order that,

[1] *The Pope to the Catholic King*, Rome, 5 May, 1571. The letter, in Latin, is in Mignet, from the Simancas archives.

[2] Marquis of Cetona, Campmaster-General to Alva.

[3] The rough notes of this discussion still survive and are given by Mignet from the Simancas records.

after examining into all points, you may act as you may consider advantageous to the service of God and of ourselves, and I feel assured that you will direct this great enterprise with all the zeal, solicitude, and prudence which it requires." In the meantime the conspiracy had been discovered in England and Norfolk sent to the Tower. In the following January he was put on his trial and convicted of treason, though he was not executed for some months later.

In 1572, the whole reformed world was horrorstruck by the news of the massacre of St. Bartholomew. For upwards of forty years, the Protestants of England had been hearing of the burning, beheading, and burying alive of tens of thousands of dissidents from the Roman faith in the Netherlands by the Spaniards.[1] The memory of their own persecution in the time of Mary was still fresh, and its revival was an ever present terror before their eyes. They were well aware that the Pope and the King of Spain were plotting the invasion of their country, and the destruction of their institutions. They believed that the success of these plans would entail a persecution upon them as severe as those in the Netherlands and in Spain. While they were in this state of mind, the news suddenly arrived that fifty thousand[2] French Protestants had been shot, stabbed, or hacked to pieces at their own firesides by their countrymen, and that the homes of the victims had been polluted by every crime which attends the taking of a city by storm. But this was not all. It was known that the Pope had adopted the massacre; that, on receiving information of it from the Cardinal of Lorrain, he had set apart a day of

---

[1] In 1535 an imperial edict was issued at Brussels condemning all heretics to death—repentant males to be executed by the sword; repentant females to be buried alive; the obstinate of both sexes to be burned alive. The bloody work had commenced as early as 1522.

[2] "The number of the victims was fifty thousand."—Ranke, 1, 404.

public thanksgiving to God the just avenger, and had published a bull of extraordinary indulgence to such as should pray for the heavenly assistance to the King and kingdom of France;[1] and that he and his cardinals had walked in procession from sanctuary to sanctuary to celebrate the great event. One thought flashed through the minds of all Protestants. Was there then a universal plot among the Roman Catholics of Europe for the general murder and extermination of the reformed? Nothing is more wonderful in this remarkable reign than the fact that, threatened, harassed, and tortured with apprehensions of invasion and persecution as the English Protestants were, there was no retaliatory outbreak. The extraordinary woman who was then at the head of our affairs was incapable of panic. She and her minister Burghley calmed the natural fears of her subjects, and took precautions against any act of violence. Not a single Roman Catholic lost his life on this occasion, nor was there any restrictive law passed against that body.

Gregory XIII. had succeeded Pius V. in 1572, for it was this Pope who adopted the French massacre. Gregory, says Ranke, "did not conceal that he wished to bring about a general combination against England. Year after year, his nuncios endeavoured to negotiate this matter with Philip II. and the Guises. It would be an interesting labour to collect and arrange all these negotiations and projects which were often unknown to those whose ruin they were designed to accomplish, and which at length led to the grand enterprise of the Armada." In 1574 this Pope urged Philip to restore Catholicism in England by sending thither an expedition under the command of Don John of Austria. He proposed that Mary Stuart should marry this young prince, to whom, said the Pope, the zealous

[3] Strada, Book 7.

Catholics of England had turned their attention.[1] Gregory asserted that the hero of Lepanto and Tunis "would marvellously serve this enterprise by his valour and by the success which constantly attended his arms." A debate took place in the Spanish council on this double proposal of invasion and marriage, and the project was rejected.

In the following year, 1575, Gregory urged Philip to send Don John into the Netherlands as governor, that he might have an opportunity of invading England with a Spanish army from that country. The Pope despatched Ormanetti, Bishop of Padua, to Philip with this proposal, and again pressed that Mary, Queen of Scots, should be married to Don John, with the kingdom of England for her dowry.[2] Philip promised the nuncio to send his brother into the Netherlands as governor, which was done on the death of Requesens in March, 1576. In 1577 it was arranged between the Pope and Don John, then in the Netherlands, that the latter, after he had pacified that country, should undertake the invasion of England, and place Mary Stuart on the throne. To aid the proposed expedition, Gregory sent his nuncio, Sega, to Don John with 50,000 crowns.[3] A few months later in the same year he sent Sega on to Madrid, expressly with the view of gaining Philip over to this design, and offered on his own part to supply an auxiliary force of 4000 or 5000 men.[4] Owing to the suspicions which Philip

---

[1] Letter of the Pope's nuncio to Philip, 10th January, 1574, quoted by Mignet from the Simancas records.

[2] Strada, Book 8.

[3] "Au commencement de janvier [1578] le nonce Philippe Sega vint en Flandre, muni d'une somme de cinquante mille écus que le pape avait destinée pour les frais de l'expédition progetée contre l'Angleterre. Mais le nonce à son arrivée trouva toute la Frandre en armes, et il fut obligé d' employer l'argent . . . a soutenir don Juan contre ses ennemis." —Labanoff, 5, 16.

[4] *Letters and Memorials of Card. Allen*, Introd. 29.

entertained of the ambitious designs of his brother, or to his fear of awakening the jealousy of his rivals, or more probably to the fact that his hands were then full, this scheme was also rejected by the Spanish King.

On the 6th of November, 1577, Sander, the future Papal legate to Ireland, wrote from Madrid to Allen a letter in which the following occurs: "I beseech you take hold of A [the Pope], for the X [Philip] is as fearful of war as a child of fire, and all his endeavour is to avoid all such occasions. The A will give two thousand [men], when you shall be contented with them. If they do not serve to go to England, at least they will serve to go into Ireland. *The state of Christendom dependeth upon the stout assailing of England.*"[1] A copy of this letter fell into the hands of the English Government and was read at the trial of Campion.[2] At the date when this letter was written, nineteen years of the reign of Elizabeth had elapsed, during which period not a single Roman Catholic, priest or layman, had been put to death for any matter touching religion.[3] Even the 13th of Elizabeth, passed in 1571, against the introduction of Papal bulls into England, had been allowed to sleep for six years. Gregory now entered upon a course of actual war and invasion against England; a policy which had the most fatal effects upon the Roman Catholics of the country, and which necessarily transformed, in the eyes of the English government, every seminary priest into a recruiting officer for the Papal army. Throwing aside the character of a spiritual

[1] *Ib.* 38. The italics are not in the original.

[2] It is described wrongly in the report of Campion's trial as being from Allen to Sander.—*State Trials*, 1, 1058. In the subsequent proceedings on the death of the Earl of Northumberland it is referred to its true author.—*Ib.* 1116.

[3] The first mentioned by Bishop Challoner in his *Catholic Martyrology* is Cuthbert Maine, who was executed on the 29th of November, 1577, for publishing a Roman bull.

father, and neglecting the true arms of the Church, prayers, tears, and persuasion, Gregory, who never abandoned the idea of restoring by force the British Isles to his obedience, stood forth as a secular prince and organized invasions of his own. With this view, he, in the early part of 1578, equipped at his expense an expedition into Ireland, and gave the command of it to Thomas Stukely, an English adventurer, whom he created Marquis of Leinster, Earl of Wexford and Carlow, Viscount Morrogh, and Baron of Ross. The expedition consisted of Italian soldiers, well found and armed, to the number of 800 men, and cost the Pope 40,000 crowns.[1] It set sail from Civita Vecchia, and on its way from the Mediterranean to Ireland put in at Lisbon. Sebastian, the young King of Portugal, was then on the point of leaving for Africa to conduct a war against the sovereign of Morocco. Sebastian induced Stukely to suspend his enterprise against Ireland and to accompany him to Africa, with the promise that on their return from Morocco he would either join him in his invasion of Ireland, or furnish him with large resources.[2] Stukely complied, and added his forces to those of Sebastian, and with him fell at the battle on the plain of Tamita, or, as it is called by some, the Battle of the Three Kings,[3] on the 4th of August, 1578.

In the following year, 1579, Gregory was again busy in organizing another Papal invasion of Ireland. An Irish rebel, James Fitzmaurice, who had been pardoned for a former insurrection, addressed himself to the Pope and offered him the kingdom of Ireland. Fitzmaurice had made the same offer to Henry III. of France and to Philip II.,

---

[1] Ranke, 1, 418.

[2] Rex a Stucklio, ut in Mauritaniam secum transmittat, petit, pollicitus post reditum vel seipsum cum Stucklio in Hiberniam trajecturum, vel certe copias uberiores daturum ad asserendam illam insulam in libertatem.—O'Sullivan, *Hist. Cathol. Hib. Compendium*, 113, ed. 1850.

[3] So called from the death of Sebastian and of the two Moorish rivals.

but had received scanty encouragement from either King.
He betook himself to the Pope, who ardently entered into
the plan of assailing England from the side of Ireland.
Fitzmaurice obtained money from Gregory, and a commission
in the Pope's name to raise troops for the proposed enterprise. Sander was appointed Papal legate to accompany
him, with a consecrated banner, and a bull addressed to the
nobility, clergy, and people of Ireland. The bull granted a
plenary indulgence and remission of all sins, " such as was
given to those warring against the Turks, or for the recovery
of the Holy Land," to those who should aid Fitzmaurice
" with counsel, favour, supplies, arms, or in any other way "
against the English heretics.[1] Fitzmaurice and Sander set
out for Ireland, where they landed in July, 1579,[2] and raised
a fort at Smerwick. After a short time Fitzmaurice was
killed in a quarrel by one of the Burkes. In the meantime
the Pope was getting ready at an immense expenditure an
expedition on a large scale, which was to take with it
money, ammunition, and arms for 5000 men.[3] Corrado, the
Venetian ambassador at Rome, reported to his government
that Gregory had spent 230,000 crowns upon its preparation.[4]
Gregory had learned that James Fitzmaurice was slain; he
therefore renewed his bull, and granted the same indulgence
and remission of sins which he had given to the followers of
Fitzmaurice to all those who should aid his cousins John
and James Geraldine, who had joined Fitzmaurice in his
rebellion.[5] The Papal expedition consisted of " five ships of

[1] A copy of the bull is given in Ellis, *Original Letters*, second series, 3, 93 ; and a translation of it in Phelan's *Remains*, 2, 204.

[2] Camden says they landed about the 1st of July. Froude makes it the 17th.

[3] Cox, 367.

[4] Simpson's *Campion*, 102.

[5] This second bull is in O'Sullivan's *Compendium*, p. 121. It refers to the former bull.

the largest class, full of soldiers and munitions of war," as an Irish agent of the Vatican described it in a letter to the Papal nuncio at Paris.[1] It landed in September, 1580, and its commander San Josepho, who had been appointed by the Pope, took possession of the fort which had been erected at Smerwick by James Fitzmaurice. Sander was in Smerwick when the invaders arrived,[2] and remained with them until news was brought that Lord Grey was advancing to invest the fort. Grey on his arrival summoned the garrison and asked them who they were, and who sent them to erect fortifications in the Queen's dominions. They answered that they were sent, some from the Holy Father, and some from the King of Spain to whom the Pope had given Ireland, as Queen Elizabeth had justly forfeited her title by heresy.[3] The defence was contemptible, and the fort was surrendered at discretion. On being asked to show his commission, its commander confessed he had none. As Grey had but a small force with him, and it would have been dangerous to convey a numerous body of prisoners through the disturbed districts, the strict laws of war were enforced against them. With the exception of their officers, they were put to death as filibusters, that is, as persons who invade a country on their own private account without a commission from a sovereign prince.[4] As for Sander, after wandering about for some months exposed to all the rigours of an Irish winter, he perished according to Camden of starvation, but O'Sullivan says that he died unexpectedly of dysentery.[5]

[1] "Quinque naves grandissimas, armatis militibus et munitionibus bellicis onustas." The agent adds:—"idcirco tremit miserabiliter flagitiorum serva Angla et tota suorum hæreticorum caterva."—Theiner, *Ann.* 3, 217.

[2] *Ib.*

[3] Camden, sub ann. 1580.

[4] Spenser's *View of the State of Ireland* in Thom's *Collection of Tracts and Treatises*, vol. 1, p. 529.

[5] Morbo fluentis ventris occupatus.—O'Sullivan, p. 121.

The Papal invasion of Ireland was but a part of a larger scheme which had been hatched at Rome, and which embraced not only that country but also England and Scotland. Contemporaneously with the despatch of troops into Ireland, two Jesuits, Parsons and Campion, with a number of seminary priests, were sent into England to see how the land lay and to prepare the minds of the Roman Catholics for a triple invasion. Dates are here of importance. The second bull intended to be published in Ireland and which accompanied the expedition under San Josepho, is dated the 18th of May, 1580. On the 18th of the preceding month, April, Parsons and his party left Rome for England.[1] Nine months before their departure, in the early part of July, 1579, Sander had landed at Smerwick with a commission as Papal legate, and had published circular letters, announcing that his coming was to be followed by a Papal army.[2] Parsons and Campion arrived in England separately in June, 1580, Parsons disguised in the uniform of a captain, and Campion passing himself off as a jeweller under the name of Edmunds or Hastings.[3] The English Government was well served by its spies, and was perfectly acquainted with what had taken place between the Pope and these two Jesuits before their departure from Rome. Parsons and Campion had applied to Gregory to modify, in a manner suggested by them, the bull of deposition which had been

---

[1] Simpson's *Campion*, 108.

[2] " What will ye answer to the Pope's lieutenant, when he, bringing us the Pope's and other Catholic princes' aid, as shortly he will, shall charge you with the crime and pain of heretics for maintaining an heretical prætensed Queen against the public sentence of Christ's Vicar." Letter of Sander " *To the right honourable and Catholic lords and worshipful gentlemen of Ireland.*"—Ellis, *Original Letters*, second series, 3, 94.

[3] Mr. Simpson says that Campion's assumed name was Edmunds. At his trial Campion was asked by the Queen's counsel why he had taken the name of Hastings.

issued by Pius V. against Elizabeth. The Pope consented, and these two were commissioned to tell the English Roman Catholics that they might profess themselves loyal subjects until circumstances allowed the original sentence to be executed. The bull of Pius cut off from the unity of Christ's body all the subjects of Elizabeth who observed her laws, recognized her government, or obeyed her commands. Parsons and Campion asked, that the bull might be mitigated so far as not to bind the Roman Catholics, while it remained in full force against Elizabeth and those who adhered to her. In other words, they petitioned the Pope to grant a general absolution from the pains and penalties of the bull to those Roman Catholics who should temporarily obey the laws of their country and observe their allegiance to their sovereign. This was a direct violation of the late Act which forbade the introduction of such absolutions for the performance of civil duties in opposition to the commands of the bull. In addition, it is manifest that, as the mitigation of the bull left untouched the sentence of deposition against Elizabeth contained in it, Parsons and Campion accepted that sentence as being still in force against the Queen and her adherents. Consequently, it was an act of treason on their part to communicate or publish the bull, thus altered in an immaterial point, while the substance of it was left unimpaired, to any English subject. The effect of the bull, as altered by this modification, is well put by the latest biographer of Campion. "The famous mitigation, obtained by Campion and Parsons, did not in the least affect the substance of the bull, whereby the Queen still remained excommunicated and deposed, but merely allowed the English Catholics to exhibit to her a temporary and conditional fealty and obedience, *rebus sic stantibus*, as long as they could not help themselves; but the moment they could, or thought they could, or were told by the Pope that the time was come, then their obedience and fealty were to end; the censures were to resume their full force, and the Queen was to be violently assailed. The mitigation would thus be made to appear like a truce obtained upon false pretences by one belligerent party only, in order to gain time to recruit his forces for a new attack."[1] A reprieve was to be granted to the Queen of England until the instruments of death were got ready, and in the meantime the victim was to remain decorated with the trappings of royalty. It was at least natural that her ministry should not be satisfied with these ominous honours, and should demand an unequivocal recognition of her title.[2]

The petition of Parsons and Campion to the Pope for a modification of the bull of Pius, and the answer to it are as follows:—" Let there be asked of our most holy lord an explanation of the declaratory bull made by Pius V. against Elizabeth and her adherents; which bull the Catholics desire to be understood in this manner, that the bull shall always bind her and the heretics, but the Catholics it shall by no means bind as matters now stand, but only hereafter when the public execution of that bull may be made." "The supreme Pontiff has granted these aforesaid graces to Father Robert Parsons and Edmund Campion, who are now about to set out for England, the 14th day of April, 1580."[3] A consideration of these graces or indulgences will enable us to estimate at their true value the declarations of allegiance to the Queen made by Campion and by the others who

[1] Simpson's *Campion*, 130.   [2] Phelan's *Remains*, 2, 187.
[3] Petatur a summo domino nostro explicatio bullæ declaratoriæ per Pium Quintum contra Elizabetham et ei adhærentes, quam Catholici cupiunt intelligi hoc modo, ut obliget semper illam et hæreticos, Catholicos vero nullo modo obliget rebus sic stantibus, sed tum demum quando publica ejusdem bullæ executio fieri poterit, &c. Has prædictas gratias concessit summus pontifex patri Roberto Parsonio et Edmundo Campiano in Angliam profecturis, die 14 Aprilis, 1580.—Somers' *Tracts*, 1. 197.

suffered with him. Doubtless they considered Elizabeth to be their Queen, as they said, but only provisionally, and until the Pope had otherwise ordered. Even Roman Catholic authors have given up affecting to attach any value to these protestations. "Nothing, certainly," says the Rev. M. A. Tierney, "can be more unsatisfactory than the declarations in question. When Parsons and Campion were about to proceed to England they applied to Pope Gregory XIII. and obtained from him a modification of the bull, to the effect that, although it must still continue to be binding on Elizabeth and her adherents, the Catholics might be relieved from its operation, in other words, might continue to acknowledge her authority, but only until an opportunity should offer of carrying the sentence into full effect. It is clear that, with this dispensation in their possession, no protestation however explicit, either from Campion or his associates, could possibly be received as an indication of their real opinion on the subject of the deposing power claimed by the Pope."[1] With this indulgence or mitigation in their possession, Parsons and Campion set out for England and arrived there, Parsons on the 12th, and Campion on the 25th of June, 1580.

The advent of the Jesuits was far from being desired by the secular priests of England.[2] Some prudent men, also, among the Roman Catholic laity, suspected that their coming was connected with the contemporaneous invasion of Ireland, or with other political combinations then rumoured abroad. It became necessary to conciliate the resident clergy and to

[1] Tierney's *Dodd*, 3, 12.

[2] "These good fathers ... came into England and intruded themselves into our harvest, being the men, in our consciences, we mean both them and others of that society with some of their adherents, who have been the chief instruments of all the mischiefs that have been intended against her Majesty since the beginning of her reign, and of the miseries which we or any other Catholics have upon these occasions sustained."—*Important Considera-*

allay these patriotic suspicions. Parsons and Campion convened a synod or meeting at Southwark, in July, 1580. There the fathers exhibited their instructions, and took a solemn oath before God—(1) that they had never heard of Sander's expedition to Ireland until they were at Rheims, on their way to England, and (2) that their mission was purely spiritual, without political pretence, or knowledge of State matters. The first assertion is simply incredible. Parsons and Campion left Rome on the 18th of April, and occupied nearly six weeks on the journey to Rheims, which they reached on the last day of May.[1] During the whole of this time, Campion was in the company of Parsons, who was perfectly acquainted with the secret designs of the Papacy, and was steeped to the lips in every intrigue against England. Nine months before the pair left Rome, Sander, as has been said, had publicly landed at Smerwick as Papal legate, and Fitzmaurice, the Pope's general, had been killed shortly after. The news of these transactions reached London in July, 1579, and yet Parsons and Campion declared in July, 1580, that they were ignorant of matters which must have been publicly known and discussed at Rome for months before they left that city. Their other assertion is equally incredible; for, in the first place, they brought with them a politico-religious manifesto, granting a Papal indulgence to English Roman Catholics for the fulfilment of their civil duties; and, secondly, Campion, within a few months of his arrival, published a challenge[2] to, amongst others, the lawyers, to a " discourse of religion so far as it toucheth the commonwealth and your

---

tions. "A very grave and ancient priest, named Mr. Wilson, not so much in his own name as of others by whom he was sent, proposed to Parsons, that the fathers should leave England again until a calmer time."—*Letters, &c. of Cardinal Allen*, 303, note.

[1] Simpson's *Campion*, 117.

[2] The challenge was triple—to the Council, to the Doctors and Masters of the Universities, and to the Lawyers.

nobilities," a proceeding entirely inconsistent with his profession of not meddling in matters of State. Further, the latter assertion is also disproved by the subsequent conduct of Parsons, the superior of the mission, who, during the eighteen months that he remained in England, spent his time in spreading his treasonable doctrines under the vizard of religion, and in stirring up rebellion under the seal of the confessional. Of this we have the best evidence. Two years later, in May, 1582, Parsons paid a visit to Tassis, the agent of Philip II., at Paris, and assured him that the English Roman Catholics were prepared to take up arms and to join a Spanish expedition then spoken of. Tassis asked him what authority he had for making this assertion: Parsons replied that "he knew all this from what many of the Catholics had declared when he had treated with them of their consciences."[1] The secular priests, in their circular letter of 1601, thus describe Parsons' conduct during his stay in England: "Upon their arrival, Master Parsons presently fell to his Jesuitical courses, and so belaboured both himself and others in matters of State, how he might set her Majesty's Crown upon another head . . . that the Catholics themselves threatened to deliver him into the hands of the civil magistrate except he desisted from such kind of practices."[2] Camden asserts the same thing: "Parsons tampered so far with the Papists about deposing the Queen, that some of them, I speak upon their own credit, thought to have delivered him into the magistrate's hands."[3]

It is therefore impossible to believe that the mission of Parsons and Campion was intended at Rome to be a spiritual one.[4] A belief to this effect is untenable if we put all the

[1] *Letters, &c., of Card. Allen*, Introd. 39.
[2] *Important Considerations.*
[3] Sub ann. 1580.
[4] "The mission of 1580 into England was ultimately a spiritual failure because it was not purely a spiritual mission. The intention of its chiefs was not single. They doubtless had the intention to save souls;

contemporaneous facts together and reflect on them. Jesuits and seminary priests were sent into England, where there was a powerful party consisting of Protestants and the loyal Roman Catholics, to deceive the Government by smooth and deceptive professions of allegiance, while at the same time Sander and Allen[1] were despatched to Ireland, where dissimulation was only an incumbrance, to stir up, with the stimulant of a plenary indulgence, its excitable people to rebellion and a war of religion. When Parsons and Campion arrived in England in June, 1580, a Papal fleet and army were actually on their way to Ireland, where they landed in the following September. This was by no means all. Two months before Parsons and Campion left Rome, the Pope had entered into a league for the invasion of England, Scotland, and Ireland. It cannot be doubted that, as the Papal invasion of Ireland in 1580 had been heralded by the advent of Sander as Papal legate in 1579, so the Jesuits were sent into England to feel the dispositions of the Roman Catholics, and to prepare them for the reception of the simultaneous invasion of the three kingdoms, which the Pope, the King of Spain, and the Grand Duke of Tuscany were preparing at the very moment when Parsons and Campion left Rome for England. This plan of invasion, which had been agreed to by the Pope and the ambassadors of Philip and of the Grand Duke, included the conquest of Scotland in order that a descent from the north might be made into England; a Spanish fleet was to arrive from the south; the Prince of Parma was to lead an attack from the east; while a diversion was to be effected on the west in

but they took a perspective view of all these souls, and looked on them also as the moving forces of bodies that might be useful soldiers in the coming struggle."—Simpson's *Campion*, 334.

[1] Not the future cardinal. This Allen was a Jesuit, and was killed at the battle of Monaster Neva, near Limerick, where he displayed the Papal standard.—Leland, 2, 274.

Ireland in order to distract the counsels and forces of Elizabeth.[1] Early in 1580 the English Government had obtained information of the league which had been concluded between the aforesaid powers on the 18th of February of that year, that is exactly two months before Parsons and Campion left Rome for England. The treaty consisted of ten articles, of which the following were the principal[2]:—

1. The Pope was to furnish ten thousand infantry and one thousand cavalry; the King of Spain fifteen thousand infantry and fifteen hundred cavalry; the duke eight thousand infantry and one hundred cavalry; to these were to be added the Germans who had gone to Spain, and who were to be paid *pro rata* by the aforesaid princes.

2. The Pope, as sovereign lord of England, was to grant power to the Catholic nobles of the kingdom to elect a Catholic King, who should render obedience and fealty to the Roman See, as the former Kings had done before the time of the last Henry.

3. Elizabeth was to be declared an usurper and incapable of reigning, because she was born of an illegitimate marriage and because she was a heretic.

4. Mary Stuart was to be liberated and restored to her own kingdom.

5. The Pope was to use all his influence with the French King to prevent him or his brother from giving assistance to Elizabeth.[3]

6. The bull of excommunication issued by Pius was to be published in the courts of all Christian princes.

In addition to the forces to be contributed by the Pope,

[1] Simpson's *Campion*, 230.
[2] *Cal. of State Papers, Venetian*, 7, 650.
[3] A marriage between Elizabeth and the Duke of Alençon was then projected.

the King of Spain, and the Duke of Tuscany, the Knights of Malta and their vessels were to be employed in the invasion, to which the Pope had given the name of the " sacred expedition."[1] To afford further encouragement to it, Gregory renewed the bull which Pius had issued against Elizabeth excommunicating and deposing her.[2] The danger to England was great and imminent. Fortunately for her, at this juncture the Cardinal King of Portugal died without direct heirs, leaving a more tempting field for the ambition of the Spanish King. Philip without losing a moment seized the opportunity, and poured the forces which had been intended for England into Portugal. The alarm of the English government had been great, and the relief afforded by the information that Philip had turned aside to Portugal was proportionate to the fears which it had entertained.[3] The Venetian ambassador in Paris, writing to his Signory at this time, says:—"This morning, early, the English ambassador called upon me to learn what news I had concerning the death of the King of Portugal . . . and he said to me with a most cheerful countenance, God be praised that my Queen is now free from a great anxiety. We were advised that the Spanish fleet was to sail for England, and we knew exactly

[1] Labanoff, 7, 152-161.

[2] It has been doubted whether Gregory XIII. ever renewed the bull of Pius. Contemporaneous authorities remove this doubt. " While these practices were in hand in Ireland, Gregory XIII. renewed the said bull of Pius Quintus, and denounceth her Majesty to be excommunicate, with intimation of all other particulars in the former bull mentioned."— *Important Considerations.* Cardinal Allen in his admonition, 1587, says:—" She [Elizabeth] hath been in person justly deposed by the sentences of three sundry Popes, whereunto if we add the two former censures condemning her incestuous nativity and generation, we shall find that she hath been condemned by five declaratory sentences of God's Church."

[3] "And its fears were not chimerical. Statesmen, who knew the circumstances of the case, were nearly unanimous in attributing the salvation of Elizabeth's government to the death of the old King of Portugal."—Simpson's *Campion,* 231.

the course the galleys were to take, and where they were to land forces in England and Ireland. We also knew that the Pope had made fresh denunciations against England, besides those which Pius V. had pronounced, to liberate all our people from their oaths of allegiance. We also knew that certain priests had been sent to England to negotiate secretly, and I have given the Queen information of their proceedings, and by this time I hope that they are in her hands. . . . He added, that his Queen was well aware that the Grand Duke of Tuscany had taken part in the combination formed against her by the Pope and King of Spain, and that although he and his states were situate at a great distance from England, still the Queen would not fail to retaliate."[1]

Campion and thirteen seminary priests were arrested, Campion himself in July, 1581.[2] Up to this date the English government had been singularly lenient, in spite of the bull of Pius and its renewal by Gregory, and though the administration was well aware that it was in constant danger from foreign invasions and domestic treason. Till this month, but three Roman Catholics had been executed for politico-religious reasons,[3] namely, for the introduction of Papal bulls, an offence which Lord Coke declares was punishable capitally even in the days of Edward I.[4] When the English Roman Catholics were told by him whom they regarded as the Vicar of God, that it was a duty to rebel, and a sin to obey their Queen, her Executive had merely replied by introducing an

[1] *State Papers, Venetian*, 7, 630.
[2] Parsons escaped from England.
[3] "The first execution under this Act [13 Elizabeth, c. 2, against the introduction of Papal bulls] was that of Cuthbert Mayne in 1577; the second that of Nelson and Sherwood, who suffered at the beginning of the following year."—Tierney's *Dodd*, 3, 15. Bishop Challoner claims only three martyrs before July, 1581.
[4] Coke's *Reports*, pt. 5, 12.

Act against the importation into the kingdom of Papal bulls. For six years this Act was allowed to remain as a threat rather than as an effective weapon. This was the only penal enactment against Roman Catholics until January, 1581, if indeed a statute which had been necessitated by the mad conduct of Felton, who set up the bull of Pius on the gate of the Bishop of London, can be considered as directed against any particular class. But the Papal invasions of Ireland, and the Confederation of Catholic Powers with Gregory at its head, opened the eyes of the English Government to its danger, and showed that the Pope had entered the lists against it and the kingdom as a secular prince and the leader of armies. All the moral and material resources which he could command, his money, his blessings and cursings, his soldiers, and missionary priests, were directed by him against England. He was labouring, in order to effect what he called the restoration of the faith, to excite a war of religion among Englishmen, to subvert their institutions, to break up their homes, to slay their young men, and to subject their wives and daughters to the outrages of a foreign and fanatical soldiery. A word from the Pope would have induced Elizabeth—who alone among the sovereigns of Europe extended to her non-conforming subjects a toleration up to that time unknown—to establish a *modus vivendi* between herself and the members of a communion which she respected.[1] But he disdained the paths of peace, and the ancient ways of spreading the faith by preaching, prayers, instruction, holy example, and the exercise of the priestly functions. He

---

[1] "The Queen also at my request freed or mitigated the captivity of many other priests ... if I, a mere worm and a captive, have obtained so much of the Queen, what might the Pope, the most Christian King helping him, do towards relieving the afflictions of the Catholics? What have wars, invasions, and books done these 20 years?"— Letter of Thomas Bluet, a seminary priest, to Cardinals Borghese and Aragon, *State Papers, Domestic*, 1601–3, 167.

declared for open war and the weapons of the flesh. His taking the field as a secular prince, and his recourse to physical force, effected a sudden and profound change in the attitude of the English government to its Roman Catholic subjects. Up to the time of Gregory, when the Roman Pontiffs pronounced the deposition of an English King, they left the execution of their sentence to temporal princes, and confined themselves to exhortations. Seated aloft and unstained with the dust of the arena, they pronounced judgment, and called upon the neighbouring sovereigns to obey the voice of the Church and to carry its sentence into effect. But Gregory abdicated the position of a supreme judge for that of a military commander, and in so doing he clothed the English government with new rights against those who favoured his temporal claims, and justified it in treating them as mere secular soldiers. His bulls and admonitions were no longer the voice of the Church, but the orders of a captain in command of an army, and those who obeyed him were rebels against their country. Obedience to his directions was a desertion of the English citizen to the ranks of an enemy who threatened the conquest of his country and challenged its government to a mortal combat with temporal arms. Elizabeth was obliged to take up the challenge, and to enact most rigorous laws against those who identified religion with treason, and preached, at the same time, allegiance to a belligerent Pope and disloyalty to England.

The only question is, were these laws necessary for the safety of the commonwealth? Parsons himself acknowledged that Elizabeth was forced to take the steps she did against the seminary priests. William Watson, one of them, asserted in 1602 that it was a matter of wonder, considering the provocation that had been given to her government, that a single Roman Catholic had been left alive in England.

"The affliction of Catholics in England," says Watson, "hath been in very deed extraordinary . . . so also hath the cause thereof been extraordinary, and so far beyond the accustomed occasions of persecutions given to any prince in Christendom or monarchy that is or ever was in the world, . . . as rather it is to be wondered at, all things duly considered, that any one Catholic is left in life in England, than that our persecution hath been so great ; for name one nation —I know none can—under heaven, where the subjects, especially if they were Catholics, ever sought the death of their sovereign though of a different religion from them, the conquest of their native land, the subversion of the State, the depopulation of the weal public, the alteration and change of all laws, customs, and orders, and, in few, the utter devastation, desolation, and destruction of all the ancient inhabitants of their land in so unnatural, unchristian, uncatholic a manner as the Spanish faction have sought it in our own flesh and blood against this realm."[1] In 1601 the secular priests declared that the burdens under which they laboured were " far less than any prince living in her Majesty's case would have inflicted upon us." " Yea," they continue, " there have been amongst us of our own calling who have likewise said, that they themselves, knowing what they do know, how under pretence of religion the life of her Majesty and the subversion of the kingdom is aimed at, if they had been of her Highness' Council, they would have given their consent for the making of very strait and rigorous laws to the better suppressing and preventing all such Jesuitical and wicked designments." If, then, these laws were necessary, the subsequent afflictions of the English Roman Catholics must be ascribed to the Popes, and the death of every Jesuit and seminary priest, who was executed under them in the reign of Elizabeth, lies at the door of the Roman Pontiffs.

[1] *Dechacordon*, p. 276.

"For," say the secular priests, "if the Popes from time to time had sought her Majesty by kind offices and gentle persuasions, never ceasing the prosecution of those and such like courses of humanity and gentleness; if the Catholics and priests beyond the seas had laboured continually the furtherance of those most priest-like and divine allurements . . . if we at home . . . had possessed our souls in meekness and humility, honoured her Majesty . . . and dealt as true Catholic priests . . . most assuredly the State would have loved us or at least borne with us . . . there had been no speeches amongst us of racks and torments, nor any cause to have used them, for none were ever vexed that way simply for that he was either priest or Catholic, but because they were suspected to have had their hands in some of the said most traitorous designments."[1]

It is important to observe that Campion and the twelve[2] seminary priests, who were convicted with him, were arraigned under the old statute of treasons which had been passed in the reign of Edward III., two hundred years before, when England was still Papal.[3] So anxious was the English government to save these men, and to avoid the obloquy of their execution, that it drew up six questions in their nature wholly civil and entirely unconnected with faith or discipline. Speaking of these questions, a Roman Catholic author said, in 1822: "Among the six questions, there is not one which the Catholics of the present time have not fully and unexceptionably answered in the oaths which they have taken in compliance with the Acts of the 18th, 31st, and 33rd years of his late Majesty's reign."[4] An answer to the effect that

---

[1] *Important Considerations.*

[2] Thirteen were put upon their trial, but John Colleton was acquitted.

[3] It is stated in the *Letters and Memorials of Cardinal Allen*, p. 112, that the Judge who presided at Campion's trial, Sir Christopher Wray, was his uncle.

[4] Charles Butler, *English Catholics*, 1, 429.

Elizabeth was their lawful Queen, and that her subjects were not dispensed from their allegiance by the bull of Pius, would have saved them all, as it did actually save three of them, even after their conviction.[1] Cardinal Allen himself admitted that those who were put to death after their answers to the six queries suffered for maintaining the deposing power.[2]

The questions were:—

1. Whether the bull of Pius Quintus against the Queen's Majesty be a lawful sentence and ought to be obeyed by the subjects of England?

2. Whether the Queen's Majesty be a lawful Queen, and ought to be obeyed by the subjects of England notwithstanding the bull of Pius Quintus, or any bull or sentence that the Pope hath pronounced or may pronounce against her?

3. Whether the Pope have or had power to authorize the Earls of Northumberland and Westmoreland and others her Majesty's subjects to rebel or take arms against her, or to authorize Dr. Sander or others to invade Ireland or any other her dominions and to bear arms against her, and whether they did therein lawfully or no?

4. Whether the Pope have power to discharge any of her Highness' subjects, or the subjects of any Christian prince, from their allegiance or oath of obedience to her Majesty or to their prince for any cause?

5. Whether the said Dr. Sander in his book of the *Visible Monarchy of the Church,* and Dr. Bristowe in his book of *Motives,* writing in allowance, commendation, and

---

[1] John Hart, James Bosgrave, Edward Rishton, the editor of Sander's *De Schismate Anglicano.* Orton, a layman educated at Douay, also saved himself.

[2] Throckmorton, 114. Charles Butler, 1, 428.

confirmation of the said bull of Pius Quintus, have therein taught, testified, or maintained a truth or falsehood?

6. If the Pope do by his bull or sentence pronounce her Majesty to be deprived and no lawful Queen, and her subjects to be discharged of their allegiance and obedience unto her, and after the Pope or any other by his appointment and authority do invade this realm, which part would you take, or which part ought a good subject of England to take?

When Campion was asked whether Elizabeth was a lawful Queen or only a pretended and deprived one, he said that depended upon the bull of Pius, whereof he was not to judge, and refused to answer any further. Of the others, one affirmed that the Queen was his sovereign lady, but could not say she was so lawfully.[1] One refused to answer any questions.[2] Three merely said they believed what the Church taught, and would not answer further.[3] Four were of opinion that the Pope could depose princes and discharge their subjects from their allegiance, and that Papal sentences ought to be obeyed.[4] John Hart saved himself by an ambiguous answer, viz. that the Queen was a lawful sovereign notwithstanding the bull of Pius, but whether she ought to be obeyed and taken for a lawful Queen notwithstanding *any* bull or Papal sentence he could not say. James Bosgrave, a Jesuit, and Edward Rushton acknowledged that the Queen was their lawful sovereign, and that the Pope had no authority to discharge subjects from their allegiance. These two with Orton were afterwards deported. Campion and the rest had all pursued their studies or had been employed as teachers in the Seminary of Douay.

In 1569 Dr. Morton had been despatched by the Pope to

[1] Alexander Briant. [2] Ralph Sherwin.
[3] Thomas Cotton, Laurence Richardson, John Short.
[4] Luke Kirby, Thomas Ford, Robert Johnson, William Feltic.

the north of England to declare by apostolic authority that Elizabeth was a heretic and usurper, who might be treated by her subjects as a heathen and publican. In 1579 Sander was sent into Ireland as Papal legate to teach that Elizabeth was " an enemy to God and man,"[1] and that she ought to be deposed. And now Campion,[2] who had come direct from Rome, declared that the fact of Elizabeth being a lawful Queen, or a pretended and deprived one, depended on the bull of Pius. In addition, out of twelve priests and Jesuits educated or pursuing their theological studies at Douay, ten asserted positively or implied by their silence that the Pope could depose the Queen and discharge her subjects from their oath of allegiance. There was no longer room for doubt as to the sentiments of the Seminarists who were pouring into England. They seemed to consider themselves as the subjects of a foreign master whose sovereignty was paramount, and would give no assurance that they regarded Elizabeth in any other light than as an usurper and a fit object of punishment by the Pope. They maintained the validity of the bull of Pius declaring that Elizabeth was not a lawful Queen. They held that the laws of England constituting her Queen were of no effect unless approved by the Pope, and that her title was to drop whenever he declared that the time was come. Such doctrines were directly opposed to the traditions and teachings of the old unreformed Church of England, and had been expressly

[1] " Quæ, Deo pariter et hominibus infesta, in Anglia et ista Hiberniæ insula superbe et impie dominatur." The words of the bull which Sander took into Ireland.

[2] Campion was by no means the mild and gentle character he is represented to have been by his biographers. He applies to Bishop Jewel such terms as craft, ignorance, roguery, and impudence. Of the Protestant martyrs he thus expresses himself: "for a few apostates and cobblers of theirs burnt, we have bishops, lords, knights, the old nobility," &c. This unchristian language resembles too closely that of Bristowe, who calls the Protestant confessors "stinking martyrs."

repudiated as late as 1570 by the deprived bishops and doctors of that communion. Principles subversive of the rights of an English sovereign and of the English nation could never have originated in a native school. They were the fruits of foreign seminaries planted in the dominions of Philip or in Rome, in which the supreme authority of the Pope in temporal matters was maintained. It is evident that wherever this doctrine was taught, a corresponding hostility to the secular prince who controverted it, and held her own in opposition to the Papal bull enunciating it, *must* have been inculcated, either directly or indirectly, intentionally or unintentionally. The idea, that Elizabeth was an obstruction to the spread of the truth, must have been ever present in the thoughts of those who were educated in these institutions. To the tender mind of the student, or the exaltation of the convert, the mere teaching, that the Queen of England was resisting the efforts of the Vicar of God to exercise a power vested in him by divine appointment, must have engendered feelings of hatred and disaffection.

England, ever slow in self-defence, was at last thoroughly alarmed by a propaganda of treason which walked in darkness. Menaced with crusades, and harassed with the ever-present fear of a persecution which a successful attack would most certainly have entailed, she had borne with the invasions of her territories by Papal forces, and the deposition of her sovereign by Papal bulls. Her strength lay in a people bound together in the ties of a common allegiance. Of help from abroad there was no hope. There was not even a European public opinion to which she could appeal, for the world was against her. As long as she could rely on the united affection of her inhabitants, open force did not daunt her. Of the arrow which flieth by day she was not afraid, but the terror by night appalled her. A gospel of treachery preached within her own borders, and which threatened the dissolution of every social tie, roused her to fury. When more than one half of her people were bidden by " their most holy lord " to disarm her by a pretence of devotion, while they cherished smothered treason in their hearts; and when an army of Jesuits and seminary priests was let loose upon her shores to teach doctrines subversive of all authority and of all political morality, it was time to think of her own preservation. It is not to be wondered at that her government, taking the same views which the Pope and the King of Spain did, regarded every convert as a future soldier against her, and adopted rigorous measures to prevent the introduction of a new faith, which was not the Catholic faith, but an impure compound of religion and treason.

Before the advent of the Jesuits and seminary priests in 1580, intelligence had been received in London of the landing of Sander in Ireland as Papal legate, and of his seeking to enforce a new bull of deposition in that country. After the arrival of the Jesuits and their associates, and before their arrest, further information had come in of the Papal invasion in September, 1580. The English government, rightly connecting the arrival of Campion and the others with the proceedings in Ireland,[1] issued in January, 1581, a proclamation denouncing the principles inculcated in the foreign seminaries, commanding all persons whose children were receiving their education abroad, to recall them within four months, and forbidding anyone to harbour or conceal a Jesuit or seminary priest.[2] When parliament assembled about the same time, a statute[3] was passed enacting that all

[1] " That the Pope intended the great mission of priests into England to subserve the purpose of this invasion [of Ireland] there can be little doubt."—Simpson's *Campion*, 310.

[2] Strype, *Annals*, 3, 57. Sander, *De Schismate Anglicano*, 382.

[3] 23 Eliz. c. 1. *An Act to restrain the Queen's Majesty's subjects in their obedience.*

persons possessing or pretending to possess, or exercising, the power of absolving or withdrawing others from the obedience of the Queen, or withdrawing them *for that intent* from the Established "to the Romish religion," or suffering themselves to be so absolved and withdrawn, should suffer the penalties of treason; that every person saying mass should forfeit two hundred marks and be imprisoned for one year, and everyone hearing mass should pay one hundred marks and be imprisoned for the same time; and that absence from church should be punished by a fine of £20 a-month for all persons above the age of sixteen. In the following year, after the trial of Campion and his associates, another proclamation was issued against Jesuits and seminary priests. In this it was declared that all such persons "coming into these dominions in such secret manner" were and ought to be considered as traitors. Further, it ordered all English subjects then residing in the foreign seminaries to return within three months, or in default to be taken and reputed as traitors.[1]

Respecting the last-mentioned statute it is to be observed that no priest was ever punished for merely converting persons to the Roman Catholic faith, and that none of the old Marian clergy were disturbed under its provisions. The statute was directed not against the Roman Catholic religion, but against the new creed which declared that it was necessary to salvation to believe that the Pope was possessed of supreme temporal power, and which introduced a political immorality leading to numerous plots, and finally to the Gunpowder conspiracy.[2] This is shown by the facts: that it was passed immediately

---

[1] Strype, *Ann.* 3, 120. Sander, 386.

[2] "He [Parsons] might have told how he had planted, at Lapworth Park and other places round Stratford-on-Avon, the seeds of a political Popery that was destined in some twenty-five years to bring forth the Gunpowder Plot."—Simpson's *Campion*, 178.

after the Government had learned that the Pope had sent Jesuits to preach a corrupt doctrine, and to sow, under the cover of that doctrine, the seeds of sedition; that twenty-two years of Elizabeth's reign had elapsed without any special Act against Roman Catholics save that against the importation of Papal bulls; and by the wording of the statute itself. It included only those who withdrew persons from the established religion with the intent " to absolve, persuade, or withdraw any of the Queen's subjects, or any within her Highness' realms and dominions, from their natural obedience to her Majesty." It is obvious that mere conversion would not have sufficed to satisfy this clause, and could not have led to a conviction. In addition to the circumstance that this is the only possible construction of the statute, we have strong evidence that its interpretation was not strained. King James asserted, in 1607, that Queen Elizabeth " had never punished any Papist for religion." The secular priests, twenty years after the passing of this Act, declared that no one had ever been vexed simply for that he was either priest or Catholic, but " because they were suspected to have had their hands in some of the said most traitorous designments." They could not have made this assertion if even one priest had been condemned for merely doing his duty. Secondly, the provision respecting the fine of £20 a-month for non-attendance at Church applied to all dissenters, whether Roman Catholic or Protestant. " Till the statute of 35 of Elizabeth," that is, till 1593, says Charles Butler, " Protestants and Catholics were equally considered as recusants, and equally subject to the penalties of recusancy."[1] Recusancy was the offence of non-attendance at church.

When Philip II. had secured possession of Portugal, the plan of a triple invasion of the British islands was revived by the Pope and the Spanish King, who adopted the Duke of

[1] *Memoirs of English Catholics*, 1, 292.

Guise as a partner in the enterprise. The years 1582, 1583, and a portion of 1584, were spent in the development of this project.

In 1579, Esme Stuart, a Roman Catholic, had arrived in Scotland from France. King James, whose cousin he was, received him with favour, appointed him his chamberlain, and finally created him Earl and Duke of Lennox. Lennox soon acquired supreme influence, and the government of Scotland passed into his hands. This unscrupulous adventurer calmed the apprehensions of the Presbyterian ministers by professing a Protestantism of the most extreme kind, and flattered the young King[1] by ascribing his conversion to the royal arguments. In March, 1582, Lennox sent to Tassis, the Spanish agent in Paris, by the hand of a Jesuit, Creighton, who had been despatched to Lennox by the Pope and Philip, a letter in which he offered his services for the restoration of religion, and the liberation of Mary Stuart.[2] Creighton, having conferred with Mary's ambassador[3] and Dr. Allen in Paris, went to Parsons at Rouen, and then with the latter proceeded to Eu, where he delivered the letter to the Duke of Guise. The Duke of Guise and Creighton returned to Paris, leaving Parsons ill of a fever which detained him for a few days at Rouen. On the 8th of May, the Papal nuncio at Paris wrote to the Pope that Guise had made up his mind to invade England from certain seaports of his, from which it was possible to cross over in six or seven hours. That for this part of the undertaking the Duke required no aid, "having a good understanding with the Catholics of England." That little was required to raise the Catholics of Scotland, but that Lennox thought it

---

[1] James was then thirteen years of age, having been born June 19th, 1566.

[2] *Letters and Memorials of Cardinal Allen*, 35.

[3] The French government recognised Mary's ambassador as the Scotch envoy till her death, notwithstanding her imprisonment.

to be desirable to stir up the Irish against Elizabeth, that she might be obliged to send her ships and troops to that country, and "thus leave the frontier towards France unprovided." That to effect these diversions, the Duke of Guise estimated it would be necessary to have for Scotland and Ireland from six to eight thousand infantry, together with corslets, pikes, and arquebuses, to arm such of the English as would rebel. The letter proceeds:—"This is what the duke desires me to signify to our lord for the moment, as nothing further can be done at present owing to the illness of Father Parsons, who has arrived from England, where he has had this affair in hand for the last two years, and has in his mind all that should be done."[1]

On his recovery, Parsons hastened to Paris, where he and Creighton had an interview with the Spanish agent, who on the 18th of May sent a report of it to Philip. The agent informed his master that Lennox asked for 20,000 men, consisting of Spaniards, Italians, Germans, and Swiss, together with munitions of war, artillery, and money both to raise troops and to fortify a number of strongholds. When Creighton had explained at length the demands of Lennox, Parsons assured Tassis that the Catholics of England were extremely desirous that this scheme should be adopted, and that they were ready to hasten to the camp to be formed in Scotland. Tassis asked him what reason he had for thinking that the English Catholics would join in the enterprise. Parsons answered "that he knew all this from what many of them declared when he had treated with them of their consciences, and that, in regard to this, things had gone so far that there could be no doubt about it, and that most certainly England was very well disposed at the present time for this movement being attempted there." Parsons also informed Tassis that in a few days Guise, the Scotch

[1] *Letters, &c. of Cardinal Allen*, 36.

ambassador, and Allen would meet again and come to a decision about the affair, when Creighton would leave at once for Rome, and he himself for Spain, to give an account of the plan to the Pope and to Philip.[1]

The remainder of the month of May was spent in discussing the design. Finally, at a meeting held at Paris towards the end of the month, at which the Duke of Guise, his confessor, the Scotch ambassador, Allen, and Parsons were present, a draft scheme of invasion was proposed. Creighton was despatched with it to the Pope, and Parsons was deputed to carry it to Philip. Creighton took with him to Rome a letter from Allen to the Pope, informing him that Creighton had just returned from Scotland " with very full mandates and instructions from the chief men of that country for his Holiness and the King of Spain, but as the matters also concerned the welfare of England, Creighton had been ordered to communicate them fully to the Scotch ambassador and to himself."[2]

In the summer of this year, 1582, the progress of the conspiracy was arrested by an occurrence which took place in Scotland, and which had an important bearing on the projected enterprise. The person of the King was seized by the Earl of Gowrie and the confederate lords, and a few months later, Lennox was compelled to leave the kingdom and return to France, where he died in the following May. The departure of Lennox made it desirable to reconsider the whole state of affairs, and a delay took place. While the plot stood thus suspended, a startling incident happened.

On the 2nd of May, 1583, the Papal nuncio at Paris wrote to the Pope's secretary :—" The Duke of Guise and the Duke of Mayenne have told me, that they have a plan for killing the Queen of England by the hand of a Catholic, though not one outwardly, who is near her person, and is ill-

[1] *Ib.* 39.   [2] *Ib.* 43.

affected towards her for having put to death some of his Catholic relations. . . . They have agreed to give him if he escapes, or else his sons, 100,000 francs. . . . The duke asks for no assistance from our lord for this affair ; but when the time comes, he will go to a place of his near the sea to await the event, and then cross over on a sudden to England. As to putting to death that wicked woman, I told the duke that I would not write about it to our lord the Pope, nor do I, nor tell your lordship to inform him of it, because, though I believe our lord the Pope would be glad that God should punish in any way whatever that enemy of his, still it would be unfitting that his Vicar should procure it by these means." The nuncio proceeds to say that he had informed the Duke of Guise of the agreement, which the Pope and Philip had made, to further his plan of invasion, viz. that 80,000 crowns were to be got ready, of which sum the Pope was to pay a fourth and Philip three-fourths.[1]

The Papal secretary answered this despatch on the 23rd of May, 1583 :—" I have reported to our lord the Pope what you have written to me in cipher about the affairs of England, and since his Holiness cannot but think it good that this kingdom should be, in some way or other, relieved from oppression, and restored to God and our holy religion, his Holiness says that in the event of the matter being effected, there is no doubt that the 80,000 crowns will be very well employed. His Holiness will, therefore, make no difficulty about paying his fourth."[2] Referring to the project of assassinating the Queen of England, the editors of Allen's Correspondence, themselves Roman Catholic priests, remark:—" Such is the history, now for the first time published, of this remarkable incident, related in the words of those who were personally cognisant of the facts. . . . What it comes to then is this: the Dukes of Guise and

[1] *Ib.* 46.   [2] *Ib.* 47.

Mayenne agreed to secure the payment of a large sum of money to a person who engaged in return to kill Queen Elizabeth. The Archbishop of Glasgow, the nuncio to the French Court, himself a bishop, the Cardinal of Como, the Spanish agent, J. B. Tassis, Philip II. of Spain, and perhaps the Pope himself, when they were made aware of the project, did not express the slightest disapprobation of it, but spoke only of the manifest advantage it would be to religion, if in some way or other the wicked woman were removed by death."[1]

Another change in Scottish affairs, and the urgent solicitations of Mary Stuart, revived the resolution of the parties to proceed with their design of an invasion. On the 30th of May the Papal nuncio wrote to the Pope's secretary:— "I think four thousand footmen will suffice for Scotland, and as to England, he [Guise] will act according to circumstances." In another letter of the same date, the nuncio announces the return of Parsons with the opinion of Philip that the invasion should be carried out in that year. "Whenever it is ready," continues the nuncio, "a report, explaining how the invasion is to be conducted, will be sent to our lord the Pope and the King of Spain, and then his Holiness and the Catholic King will take whatever resolution God may inspire them with."[2]

After long consideration, a definite plan for the invasion of the three kingdoms was forwarded by the nuncio to the Papal secretary on the 20th of June. The principal points in it were:—Three expeditions were to be got ready; one in Spain to invade Scotland, or England near the frontiers of Scotland. This expedition was to consist of ten thousand or twelve thousand men, or more if possible, and was to be victualled for twenty days after landing. It was to take with it money, to raise twenty thousand native troops, and

[1] *Ib.* 49.   [2] *Ib.* 52.

arms for these recruits, and was to be commanded by a leader chosen by the Pope and the Spanish King. The second expedition was to start from France under the command of one of the Guise brothers. Further, two thousand men were to be despatched to Ireland from Spain, and, to strengthen this force, money was to be sent to the Earl of Argyle and the Lord of the Isles, that they also might despatch troops to Ireland against the English.[1]

About this period of the conspiracy, a change in the plan of invasion appears to have been suddenly adopted, and a landing in Scotland given up. Unfavourable reports had come in from that country, the Kirk was too strong, and Protestantism had taken too firm a hold on its people.[2] Guise resolved to proceed with the enterprise without waiting to commence operations in Scotland. In August, he sent Parsons to Rome to give an account to the Pope of the proposed alteration, and to inform him that the invading army would embark from Flanders, and land upon the northern coasts of England, where the Catholics would receive it joyfully. "These," he said, "are so numerous, that in a few days twenty thousand of them will join the invading army on horseback." To facilitate the success of the expedition, Parsons was instructed to request the Pope to renew the bull of Pius against Elizabeth and all who should aid or favour her, to grant indulgences to those who should take part in the "holy work," and to declare that the Spanish King and Guise had undertaken the enterprise

[1] *Ib.* 53.
[2] "The report brought by M. de Menainville is, that Scotland is not at present in such a state as that our expedition can go thither and begin the enterprise on that side ... for the King is what he always has been in matters of religion. ... In fine, it is clear from de Menainville's report that neither on the side of the King, nor by the help of any particular party, nor by fortresses, or ports, is there any basis in Scotland for attempting the enterprise."—*From Tassis to Philip*, 24 June, 1583, *Ib.* 55.

at his instigation.[1] The Pope entered with ardour into the project as altered, though he himself had been of opinion that the attack on England should commence from Scotland. He wrote to Philip urging him to join the enterprise without delay. Philip replied that he would like nothing better, but that the expedition was not ready yet. Moreover, he assured Gregory, that he intended immediately to transport to Flanders the troops that had lately returned from Terceira, in order to send four thousand of them into England, when the necessary arrangements for a combined attack had been completed.[2] Whilst waiting for the Spanish ships, without which nothing could be done, Guise sent Charles Paget under an assumed name into England to obtain information, to arrange the place of landing, and to consult with the English confederates.

In the autumn of this year the project was discovered by the English government. Walsingham found out that Paget had come into the kingdom under a false name, that he had had interviews with the leading Roman Catholics, and that he had concerted plans with Francis Throckmorton. Throckmorton was arrested in November, and on being put to the rack revealed all. In the preceding September Creighton had been captured in the Channel with the full particulars of the scheme, as agreed upon when Lennox was in power, in his possession. All was now known; the confessions of Throckmorton and Creighton, and the document found in the possession of the latter, disclosed plans which were identical and removed all doubt.

Notwithstanding the arrest of Throckmorton and others, Allen and Parsons persuaded themselves that the English government was still unacquainted with the intended invasion. Fearing that the Pope and Philip might be deterred by the knowledge of what had taken place in

---

[1] *Ib.* 57.   [2] Mignet, *Marie Stuart*, from the Simancas records.

England from prosecuting the enterprise, they drew up in January, 1584, a joint report on the state of affairs in that country, copies of which they sent to the Pope and the Spanish King. In this they give reasons for believing that the "heretics" knew nothing of the "dealings between his Holiness and his Catholic Majesty." They express themselves satisfied that their adversaries had not found out " any detail of our affairs," and in conclusion they entreat the Pope and the King "with all possible earnestness not to defer the execution longer than is necessary, a prayer which we have been commanded by the Duke of Guise to offer in the duke's name."[1]

The project of a combined invasion of the three kingdoms was not abandoned until the death of the Duke of Anjou, formerly Alençon, in June, 1584. The death of this prince left Henry of Navarre, a Huguenot, presumptive heir to the French throne, and called off the attention of Guise from plans of foreign expeditions to the affairs of his own country. The League was formed, and in April, 1585, civil war broke out in France.

The discovery of a fresh project of invasion, the conspiracy of Throckmorton, and the plot of Somerville, in 1583, to assassinate the Queen,[2] renewed the apprehensions of the nation. Notwithstanding the proclamations issued against them, the disciples and missionaries of the arch-traitors, Allen and Parsons, continued to flock into the country. On the meeting of a new parliament in November, 1584, the

[1] *Letters, &c., of Cardinal Allen*, 61–3.

[2] The secular priests, differing from Dr. Lingard, entertained no doubt of the reality of Somerville's plot. "Anno 1583, Master Arden and Master Somerville were convicted by the laws of the realm to have purposed and contrived how they might have laid violent hands upon her Majesty's sacred person. Master Somerville's confession therein was so notorious as it may not be either qualified or denied. And Dr. Parry the very same year was plotting beyond the seas how he might have effected the like villainy."—*Important Considerations*.

famous bond of association in defence of the Queen was entered into by all classes, and its provisions were enacted in the first statute of the session.[1] The second was an Act against Jesuits and seminary priests, the principal provisions of which were:[2] that all Jesuits and seminary priests should depart the realm within forty days after the end of the session; that those who should remain in the kingdom beyond that time, or return into it, should be guilty of high treason; that they who should knowingly harbour or maintain such should be guilty of felony; and that all lay students in the seminaries, neglecting to return and take the oath of supremacy within six months after proclamation made in that behalf, should be adjudged traitors, and suffer as in cases of high treason. This was the second penal law, if we except that against the importation of Papal bulls in the thirteenth year of the Queen; it was also the last before the year of the Armada. The Act of the twenty-ninth of Elizabeth, 1587,[3] is not a penal statute; it merely provided that conveyances of land, made for the purpose of defeating the payment of the fines for non-attendance at church, should be void, and applied to all dissenters, Roman Catholic as well as Protestant.

Gregory XIII. died in April, 1585, and a fortnight later was succeeded by Sixtus V., who ascended the Papal throne full of vast designs. This Pontiff declared openly his intentions of assisting the King of Spain in an attack on England with far different zeal and efficiency from those with which Charles V. had been supported by former Popes.[4]

[1] 27 Eliz. c. 1.—The Association bond was signed by men of all ranks, and the engagement in it was to pursue to death all who should compass or attempt anything against the Queen's person.

[2] 27 Eliz. c. 2.—*An Act against Jesuits, seminary priests, and other such like disobedient persons.*

[3] 29 Eliz. c. 6.

[4] Ranke, 1, 472.

He complained loudly of the Spanish delays, and reminded Philip of the advantages which would accrue to him from a victory in England with a view to the reconquest of the Netherlands. Philip was already busy with his vast preparations for the grand attempt of the Armada. Notwithstanding the wealth of the Indies, Philip was always in want of money, and the expenses of an invasion of England were estimated to be enormous. Sixtus promised the King half a million of crowns, to be paid as follows: 200,000 when the Armada sailed; 100,000 when the troops disembarked; 100,000 at the end of six months; and 100,000 at the end of six months more. Besides, he agreed to contribute 200,000 each year that the war should last.[1] The Pope also renewed the bull of Pius against Elizabeth, excommunicated and deposed her afresh. In this new bull, he withdrew the temporary indulgence granted by Gregory to her subjects for obeying her, and did "straitly command under the indignation of Almighty God and pain of excommunication and the corporal punishment appointed by the laws, that none, of whatsoever condition or estate, presume to yield unto her obedience, favour, or other succurse; but that they and every of them concur by all means possible to her chastisement." In addition, he granted "a plenary indulgence and pardon of all their sins" to all such as, being truly contrite and confessed, should "assist, concur, or help in anywise" the deposition of Elizabeth and the punishment of her adherents.[2] Allen was raised to the cardinalate, as it was proposed to make him legate for England and Archbishop of Canterbury. He and Olivares, the Spanish ambassador at Rome, agreed upon a scheme for transferring the English bishoprics and the principal offices of the state to creatures of their own, should

---

[1] *Letters, &c., of Cardinal Allen*, 78.
[2] *A Declaration of the sentence and deposition of Elizabeth, the usurper, and pretended Queen of England.*—Tierney's *Dodd*, 3, Appd. 45.

the invasion be successful. Allen was willing to accept the Chancellorship too, " since," as a paper drawn up by himself and Olivares tells us, " for the purpose of putting things in order at the beginning, and promoting the service of God and that of His Majesty, no one can be found better informed and under greater obligations to His Majesty."[1] Allen, also as "cardinal of England," drew up his disgraceful *Admonition to the Nobility and People of the Kingdom*, from which some extracts have been given in a former page.

The defeat of the Armada, and the wonderful deliverance of England are known to all. Contrary to the expectations of the Pope and the King of Spain, and of Philip's hirelings, Parsons and Allen, the Roman Catholics of the Kingdom, as distinguished from the Papists, behaved well in the great emergency of their country. Two things contributed especially to this. The teaching of the Jesuits and seminary priests had not obliterated the old national feeling against the Papal claims to temporal power, or the patriotic hatred of a foreign invader. The fear, that the Spaniards would make no nice discrimination between English Protestants and Roman Catholics, worked to the same effect. Of this apprehension we have evidence from one of Allen's seminary priests,[2] and also from the circular letter of the Seculars. The priest wrote a letter to Mendoza, the Spanish ambassador in Paris, explaining the causes of the Armada's failure. One of these was, he says, the general alarm caused by the " foul, vile, irreverent, and violent speeches, such ireful and bloody threatenings of a Queen, of a nobility, yea, of the whole people of his own nation," in Allen's *Admonition*, and the belief that the numerous adventurers in the Armada

[1] *Letters, &c., of Cardinal Allen*, 106.
[2] " How each one of Dr. Allen's anticipations was falsified . . . is shown by a letter of one of Allen's own priests to Mendoza ; a translation of which is printed in the *Harleian Miscellany*, 1, 142."—Simpson's *Campion*, 341.

were coming " to have possessed the rooms of all the noblemen in England and Scotland." The secular priests inform us : " It is well known that the Duke of Medina Sidonia had given it out directly that, if once he might land in England, both Catholics and heretics that came in his way should be all one to him, his sword could not discern them ; so he might make way for his master, all was one to him."[1] Whether or not the duke made this threat is nothing to the purpose; the belief that he had done so was enough.

Although the conduct of the Roman Catholics was admirable, there is no doubt that there was an active Papistic party in the country, particularly among the priests, which favoured the invasion and was ready to assist it. The seminary priest already alluded to, addressing Mendoza, as the person who "had the principal managing hitherto of all causes . . . betwixt the King Catholic assisted with the potentates of the Holy League and all our countrymen which have professed obedience to the Church of Rome," deplores the failure of the Armada, and the despair into which that party had fallen. " With the hope of the landing of these great armies and our assistance in taking part, we here continued all this year past in assured hope of a full victory until the last month. But, alas, and with a deadly sorrow, we must all at home and abroad lament our sudden fall from an unmeasurable high joy to an unmeasurable deep despair." Parsons and Allen, who had the best means of knowing the sentiments of the Roman Catholic clergy, always relied upon the priests to further their treasonable designs through their spiritual influence. Parsons, in a memorandum to the Papal secretary in 1582, advised the Pope to create Allen Bishop of Durham for the purpose of helping the invasion, then projected, by the prestige which that dignity would give him. "It will be necessary," he tells the Pope, "that

[1] *Important Considerations.*

Mr. Allen be speedily apprised of the intention of his Holiness, that he may dispose of certain persons so as to have them in readiness against that time, and that he may also write and print secretly certain books which we are writing at this moment, with the view of satisfying the people of England. Moreover, at the proper time the principal Catholics of England will receive information of the affair by means of the priests."[1] In 1583 Allen addressed to the Pope a report on the state of England, entitled "A short note of the standing condition of affairs in England to show the easiness and opportuneness of the *sacred expedition.*" "The Catholics," says Allen, "are now much more numerous than they then [1569] were, and better instructed by our men and priests' daily exhortations. . . . So much so, that of all the orthodox in the whole realm, there is not one who any longer thinks himself bound in conscience to obey the Queen, though fear leads them to think that they may obey her, which fear will be removed when they see the foreign force; and we have lately published a book specially to prove that it is not only lawful, but even our bounden duty, to take up arms at the Pope's bidding, and to fight for the Catholic faith against the Queen and other heretics. And as the book is greedily read by all Catholics, it is impossible but that, when occasion serves, they should enroll themselves in the Catholic army. Because we still have, in spite of the numbers banished, nearly three hundred priests in various noblemen's and gentlemen's houses, and we are almost daily sending fresh ones who, when it is necessary, will direct the Catholics' consciences and actions in this matter."[2] The secular priests thirteen years later, after speaking of the numerous intrigues and attempts against England, confess that "in all these

---

[1] *Letters, &c., of Cardinal Allen,* 41.
[2] Simpson's *Campion,* 337.

plots none were more forward than many of us that were priests."[1] At the very end of Elizabeth's reign we have further proof of the strength of the Papistic party. On the day she was seized with her last illness, a "Protestation of allegiance"[2] was signed and presented to her Council by some priests, reciting that "for these many years past divers conspiracies against her Majesty's person and estate, and sundry forcible attempts for invading and conquering her dominions had been made, under we know not what pretences and inducements of restoring Catholic religion by the sword, a course most strange in the world, and undertaken peculiarly and solely against her Majesty ... by reason of which violent enterprises her Majesty, otherwise of singular clemency towards her subjects, hath been greatly moved to ordain and execute severer laws against Catholics ... than perhaps had ever been enacted, or thought upon, if such hostilities and wars had never been undertaken." It then goes on to declare, that if " the Pope should excommunicate every one born within her Majesty's dominions that would not forsake the defence of her Majesty and realms, and take part with such conspirators or invaders; in these and all other such-like cases we do think ourselves and all the lay Catholics ... bound in conscience not to obey this or any such censure, but will defend our prince and country, accounting it our duty so to do, and, notwithstanding any authority or any excommunication whatsoever, either denounced or to be denounced as is aforesaid, to yield unto her Majesty all obedience in temporal causes." Of the many hundred priests then in England, only thirteen could be induced to sign the protestation, "a lamentable proof," says Sir John Throckmorton, "of the prevalence of

[1] *Important Considerations.*
[2] The protestation is given in Tierney's *Dodd*, 3, Appd. 188, and in Butler's *English Catholics*, 1, 233.

the Papistic party."[1] And Charles Butler writes, "Much indeed is it to be lamented that it [the Protestation] was not generally signed by all the Catholic clergy and laity of England. But it was opposed by a powerful party."[2]

With these facts before us, is there any room for doubting that there was a strong party at home working for the destruction of England, and her conquest by the Spanish King? Parsons tells us that the priests were ready to give immediate information of an invasion to the principal Catholics, and Allen informs us that he was sending " almost daily " seminary priests into the country to direct "the consciences and actions" of the Roman Catholics in favour of the easiness and opportuneness of the sacred expedition which was to enslave England. When we remember the untiring hostility of the Roman Pontiffs, who for a period of thirty-three years never rested an instant from their intrigues, the excommunication and deposition of Elizabeth, the attacks on Ireland, and the confederacies of the Catholic powers, can we affect surprise that the English government enacted severe laws to prevent the entrance into the country of the missionaries of treason despatched by Parsons and Allen, or that it took the same view of affairs which these two took, and that it acted upon that view? With the world against England abroad, and internal treason, under the colour of religion, sapping her foundations at home, the wonder is, not that three or, at the most, four penal statutes, were passed in this reign, but that more numerous and more severe laws were not enacted; for the government had no means of distinguishing between the loyal Roman Catholics and the Papistic adherents of Philip. Such was the opinion of men

[1] "But . . . it only affords a lamentable proof of the prevalence of the *Papistic* party, when so few could be induced to sign it, and the promoters of it were treated at Rome as rebels to the See Apostolic."—Throckmorton, 131.

[2] *English Catholics*, 2, 63.

who themselves laboured under the rigours of these laws. William Watson, a seminary priest, affirmed that it was a marvel, considering the conduct of the Roman Catholics to the State, that a single one of them had been left alive in England. The Seculars, after enumerating the errors of which many of their body had been guilty, say: " In which case, the premises discreetly considered, there is no King or Prince in the world . . . having either force or metal in him, that would have endured us if possibly he could have been revenged, but rather, as we think, have utterly rooted us out of his territories as traitors and rebels both to him and his country. And, therefore, we may rejoice unfeignedly that God hath blessed this kingdom with so gracious and merciful a sovereign, who hath not dealt in this sort with us." These words were written in the forty-third year of Elizabeth's reign, and eight years after the last penal statute enacted during her life.

The defeat of the Armada did not put an end to Papal intrigues against England, or to Papal encouragement given to rebels against her government. A year before the sailing of the Armada, Parsons and Allen had drawn up for Philip II. a memorandum concerning the succession to the English crown. In this they asserted that there was no one, either in England or Scotland, entitled to succeed Elizabeth in right of the house of Lancaster; that all who claimed through the house of York were disqualified by heresy or other defects; and that no one outside the kingdom claimed through the house of Lancaster except the Spanish King. But as his claim to succeed by descent alone might give rise to opposition, they said that all difficulties would disappear if the intended invasion were successful;—for in that case, as the decree of the Lateran Council gives to Catholic princes the kingdoms which they conquer from heretics, and as the Catholics of England would gladly elect Philip for their

King, his title would then be assured.¹ In 1593 Parsons published his *Conference about the next succession to the Crown of England*, under the name of Doleman. This book, Cardinal D'Ossat informs us, was written at the instigation of Philip, and was circulated by the Spaniards throughout England, the Low Countries, and wherever else they thought it would further their designs.² In this treatise, Parsons maintained the right of the people to regulate the descent of the crown, and asserted that the profession of a false religion was sufficient to justify the exclusion of an heir entitled by blood.³ After stating that there had been no lawful Kings in England for many years on account of their illegitimacy, heresy, or other disqualications, he excluded from the succession all who were in any way connected with the royal family of England, including James of Scotland, and implied that Isabella, daughter of Philip II., was entitled to the crown on the death of Queen Elizabeth. The publication of this book was followed by another attempt at invasion on the part of the Spanish King in 1597, as Philip believed that, if the enterprise were successful his daughter might be placed upon the English throne. The expedition was a disastrous failure. The Spanish fleet set sail from Ferrol, with the design of seizing some strong post in the south of England, which might be held till the following spring, the season selected for the grand attempt. When the fleet was off the Scilly Isles, a storm arose and scattered it. The leader of the expedition, having collected his vessels, returned

---

[1] *Letters, &c., of Cardinal Allen*, 96.
[2] *Lettres du Cardinal D'Ossat*, 5, 48.
[3] On account of the principles contained in this book, portions of it were reprinted in 1648 under the title of *Speeches delivered at a conference concerning the power of parliaments to proceed against their Kings for misgovernment*. The book itself was re-published in 1680, when it was proposed to exclude the Duke of York from the succession on account of his religion. See *The Apostate Protestant*, a pamphlet published in 1682.

to Spain, and on the passage home sixteen sail were lost in a second storm.

Another scheme for giving a Roman Catholic successor to Elizabeth was planned at Rome about the year 1600. Clement VIII., who ascended the Papal throne in 1592, undervalued the character of the English Queen and the resources of her kingdom. At an audience granted by him to Cardinal D'Ossat, in 1597, the Pope said, " England has been conquered before, and may be again, especially now that she is disunited in religion, and governed by an old woman without a husband and without a certain successor. Neither you nor I are so old but that we may yet see her subdued."[1] Clement was resolved that no prince should succeed Elizabeth but one that would undertake to live in the bosom of his Church, and pay him the same obedience which other Catholic princes paid. With this view, he cast his eyes on the family of Parma, which made some pretensions to the English Crown through the royal house of Portugal. There were then two princes of this family living, Ranuccio, the reigning Duke, and his brother, the Cardinal Farnese. The Pope wished, in the first instance, to make the Duke King of England, but if it turned out that there was a strong party in that kingdom in favour of Arabella Stuart, then, as the Duke was already married, his brother the Cardinal was to be secularized, and to give her his hand. Clement endeavoured to unite the Kings of Spain and of France to effect this project of establishing a Roman Catholic successor on the English throne. He also sent three briefs to his nuncio in the Netherlands, to be published in England as soon as that ecclesiastic should be informed of the death of Elizabeth.[2] One brief was addressed to the clergy, one to

[1] *Lettres du Cardinal D'Ossat*, 2, 364.
[2] "S. S. a envoyé depuis peu de temps au Nonce qu'elle tient aux Pajs-bas, trois brefs, pour les guarder jusques à ce que le dit Nonce

the nobility, and the third to the people. By these briefs, the three estates of the realm were admonished and exhorted to bind themselves to receive as their King a Catholic named by the Pope, and were forbidden to aid any competitor who should not promise to restore the Roman Catholic religion, and to pay due obedience to the Papal See. Two of these briefs, those directed to the clergy and the nobility, together with the Pope's letter to the nuncio, were actually sent to Garnet, the Superior of the Jesuits in England. The Papal letter ordered the nuncio, "whenever that miserable woman should die,"[1] to spare no labour to certify the event to the Pope, and "to divulge the briefs in England by his authority and in the Pope's name, whose assistance should not want." Garnet subsequently stated that he destroyed these briefs after the peaceful accession of James; but not until he had shown them to Catesby, Winter, Tresham, Percy, and Oldcorne or Hall, who afterwards became notorious for their connexion with the Gunpowder Plot.[2]

The transmission of these briefs or bulls to England, and the desire of the Pope, expressed in them, to exclude a Protestant successor,[3] were followed by fatal consequences. The immediate effect of them was to give rise to the last conspiracy in the reign of Elizabeth, which was undertaken for the purpose of securing the transfer of the succession to the Spanish King, by an invasion and by an insurrection of the Roman

saura que la Reine d'Angleterre soit morte, et lors les envoyer en Angleterre, l'un aux ecclesiastiques, le second à la noblesse, et le troisième au tiers etat."—*Ib.* 5, 55.

[1] Quandocunque contingeret miseram illam fœminam ex hac vita excedere.—Garnet's Confession, Jardine's *Gunpowder Plot*, Append.

[2] Garnet's Confession.—*Ib.* Examination of Oldcorne and Garnet.—*State Papers, Domestic*, 1603-10, p. 300.

[3] "The main point of the two Breves was for to exclude all successors from the crown, *quantumcunque propinquitate sanguinis niterentur, nisi ejusmodi essent qui non modo fidem Catholicam tolerarent, sed eam etiam omni ope ac studio promoverent, ac more majorum id se jurejurando prestituros susciperent.*"—Garnet's Confession.

Catholics in England. The ultimate result of these bulls was the Gunpowder Plot. The principal persons engaged in the plan of invasion were Garnet, Greenway or Greenwell also a Jesuit, Catesby, Tresham, Thomas Winter, and Guido Faukes. About the latter end of 1601, the conspirators resolved to send two of their number to induce Philip to attempt another invasion of England. Winter and Greenway were despatched to Spain, and Garnet gave them a letter of recommendation to one Creswell, a Jesuit, who resided at the Spanish Court. The envoys arranged with Philip the plan of attack. Spain was to advance a sum of 100,000 crowns to secure a party in England in favour of the invasion; an army was to land in the spring of 1603, if numerous, on the coast of Essex or Kent—if deficient in numbers, at Milford Haven; while the English Roman Catholics were to be ready to join the Spanish force, and to furnish horses for their cavalry. On the return of Winter and Greenway to England, the particulars of the negotiation were made known to Garnet, and were carefully concealed by him within his own breast, though the time for their execution was fast approaching.[1] Prior to the departure of the envoys from Spain, it had been agreed between them and Philip that if Elizabeth should die before the time appointed for the invasion, intelligence of the event should be at once given to the Spanish King. Accordingly, on the Queen's decease in March, 1603, Christopher Wright was sent to Spain with instructions to ask Philip to renew the engagements previously made with Winter and Greenway. Like his predecessors, Wright was furnished with letters of recommendation from Garnet to Creswell. Wright was followed in June by Guido Faukes, who had been sent from Brussels to aid the negotiations, and who also carried letters to Creswell from Baldwin, a Jesuit residing in Flanders. Faukes was

[1] Tierney's *Dodd*, 4, 8.

authorized by Baldwin to inform Creswell that "about two thousand horses would be provided by the Catholics of England to join with the Spanish forces, horses being, of all other things, those necessaries that the Spanish force should stand in greatest need."[1] But the universal acquiescence in the title of James, and the union of the two countries, put an end to all hopes of an interference from abroad. That the Papal bulls were instrumental in bringing about the Gunpowder treason is shown by two circumstances: all who were engaged in the conspiracy for a Spanish invasion afterwards took part in the Gunpowder attempt. Catesby was the first mover and designer of that treason. Whenever an attempt was made to dissuade him from plots against James, he replied, "he was sure they were lawful, and used this argument—that it being lawful by the force of the said briefs of the Pope to have kept the King out, it was as lawful now to put him out."[2]

The mischievous proposal of the Pope to prevent the succession of James to the English crown received no support from the French King. Henry considered the plan of the Pope to be a mere chimera. In his answer to Cardinal D'Ossat he says: "As for the party of Arabella it is very weak. . . . I am afraid that the project of the Pope will be attended with very different results from those which he expects, and that it will render the condition of the Catholics more miserable than ever by inducing them to take up arms against the laws of the kingdom, and the legitimate successor. . . . The King of Scotland is the lawful heir, and is on the spot to secure his rights. . . . His Holiness need not think that his briefs will be sufficient to raise up a party

---

[1] Examination of Guido Faukes.—Tierney's *Dodd*, 4 App. 54.
[2] Examination of Henry Garnet.—Jardine, App. "The breves I thought necessary to acknowledge for many causes, especially Mr. Catesby having grounded himself thereon, and not on my advice."— Letter of Garnet to Mrs. Anne Vaux.

strong enough to stand against that of the King. As for myself, I desire as much as his Holiness that England should fall to the lot of a Catholic prince, nor am I ignorant of the reasons which should make me wish that the crown of England should remain separate from that of Scotland. . . . But it is an injustice to fight against what is just, and an imprudence to engage in an enterprise which has no chance of success, like the one proposed by the Pope."[1] The good sense of Henry was shown in these words. James succeeded to the English throne as quietly as a son succeeds to the private estate of his father. The only effects of the successive intrigues of Parsons,[2] of the Pope, and of the Papist faction, were to intensify among the people of England their suspicions of their Roman Catholic brethren, and to implant in the mind of James a distrust of that communion.

At the very time the Pope was thus labouring secretly to provide a Roman Catholic successor in England, he was acting more openly in Ireland. In 1598 Hugh O'Neil, Earl of Tyrone, broke out into a fresh rebellion. To encourage him, Clement sent him by the hand of Oviedo, a Spanish ecclesiastic whom he had created Archbishop of Dublin, a plume hallowed by his own apostolical benediction, and which, he gravely declared, was formed out of the feathers of a genuine phœnix. To this gift, O'Neil replied by a submissive letter in which "he prostrated himself before the father of spirits on earth," and requested the Pope to renew the excommunication of Elizabeth, which would enable the Pontiff's faithful subjects to act with success in the defence of *his* kingdom of Ireland.[3] In answer to this request Clement addressed a letter to O'Neil dated 20th January, 1601, in which he designated him "Captain-General of the

[1] *Lettres du Cardinal D'Ossat*, at the end of vol. 5.
[2] Allen had died in October, 1594.
[3] "Regnum hoc vestrum a te solo post Deum dependens, nosque humiles tuos subditos."—*Pacata Hibernia*, 1, 312.

Catholic army in Ireland." "We have been informed by your letter," writes the Pope, "and by the report of our dear son, Peter Lombard,[1] that the holy alliance, which you and many other princes and nobles of Ireland have formed, is by the mercy of God maintained and strengthened; and that by the aid of the same Lord of Hosts you have often combatted successfully against the English, the apostates from the Church and faith. . . . We commend, dear son, your pious magnanimity, and also that of the princes and all others who in league with you decline no danger for the glory of God, and prove themselves worthy successors of their ancestors, men renowned for martial exploits, and for zeal in the Catholic cause. Preserve, children, this excellent spirit, preserve your mutual concord, and the God of Peace will be with you, and will prostrate your enemies before your face . . . When opportunity offers, we shall write to our children the Catholic Kings and princes that they give you and your cause all possible assistance."[2] The Pope also sent a bull of indulgence in the form usually granted to Irish insurgents. In this he reminds them how honourably they had formerly engaged with James Fitzmaurice, afterwards with John and James Geraldine, and lately with O'Neil. He then bestows to such as will assist O'Neil with supplies, arms, munitions, or in any other way, a plenary indulgence, and remission of sins, such as were given to those warring against the Turks or for the recovery of the Holy Land.[3]

Contemporaneously with these proceedings of the Pope,

[1] Lombard, afterwards titular Archbishop of Armagh, wrote a history of Ireland in which he maintained that Ireland was an ancient fief of the Papacy, and that, although the Kings of England were for the present in possession, the island belonged to Rome by divine right; for which he quoted the prophet Isaiah.—Phelan's *Remains*, 2, 237; O'Conor's *Hist. Address*, 1, 91.

[2] *Pacata Hibernia*, 2, 667.

[3] *Ib.* 2, 605; Wilkins' *Concilia*, 4, 362. The date of the bull is 18th April, 1600.

Philip III., who had succeeded his father in 1859, had prepared an expedition against Ireland. In September, 1601, his fleet, consisting of forty-five ships, arrived at Kinsale, and Don Juan de Aquila, the commander, landed his army of 4000 men, most of them veteran soldiers, and took possession of the town. The Spanish general at once issued a proclamation, calling on the Irish to rise in the name of the Pope. He denied that he was anxious to withdraw the Irish from the allegiance of their lawful prince, for Elizabeth was not their sovereign. "Ye know well," he says, "that for many years since Elizabeth was deprived of her kingdom, and all her subjects absolved from their fidelity by the Pope, unto whom He that reigneth in the heavens, the King of Kings, hath committed all power that he should root up, destroy, plant, and build in such sort that he may punish temporal Kings if it shall be good for the spiritual edifice, even to their deposing, which thing has been done in the kingdoms of England and Ireland by many Popes, viz. by Pius Quintus, Gregory XIII., and now by Clement VIII., as it is well known, whose bulls are extant among us. I speak to Catholics, not to froward heretics. . . . Therefore it remaineth, that the Irish who adhere to us do work with us nothing that is against God's laws or their due obedience, nay, that which they do is according to God's word and the obedience which they owe to the Pope. . . . I admonish, exhort, and beseech you all, all I say unto whom these letters shall come, that as soon as possibly you can, you come to us with your friends and weapons; whoever shall do this shall find us prepared, and we will communicate unto them those things which we possess, and whoever shall, despising our wholesome counsel, do otherwise and remain in obedience to the English, we will persecute him as a heretic and a hateful enemy of the Church even unto death."[1]

[1] *Pacata Hibernia*, 2, 357.

The English at once drew all their forces together, and besieged Kinsale. O'Neil hastened to relieve the town, and enclosed them between his army and Kinsale. He and O'Donnell, Earl of Tyrconnell, with seven hundred Spaniards who had landed at Castlehaven, advanced to within six miles of the English camp. Leaving the President of Munster to watch the town, the Lord Deputy marched with twelve hundred foot and four hundred horse against the two Earls. The battle of Kinsale and its results are best described in the words of the Spanish commander when treating for the surrender of the town. "The King, my master," said Don Juan, "sent me to assist the Condes O'Neil and O'Donnell, presuming on their promise that I should have joined with them within a few days of the arrival of his forces. I expected long in vain, sustained the Viceroy's arms, saw them drawn to the greatest head they could possibly make, lodged within two miles of Kinsale, reinforced with certain companies of Spaniards, every hour promising to relieve us, and being joined together to force your camp; saw them at last broken with a handful of men, blown asunder into divers parts of the world, O'Donnell into Spain, O'Neil to the farthest parts of the North, so as I now find no such Condes in *Rerum Natura*[1] as I came to join withall; and therefore have moved this accord the rather to disengage the King, my master, from assisting a people so unable in themselves that the whole burden of the war must lie upon him, and so perfidious as perhaps might be induced in requital of his favour at last to betray him." This rebellion was ended by the submission of O'Neil in the last month of Elizabeth's reign.

The great Queen whom heaven vouchsafed to England at a time when even the existence of the kingdom as an inde-

[1] "Those were the very words he used," says the author of *Pacata Hibernia*, 2, 436.

pendent power was at stake, and when it was engaged in a struggle of life and death, died as she had lived victorious. At her accession she was met by dangers such as no English sovereign had ever faced before. The finances were disordered. The exhausted kingdom was at war with France and Scotland. Her title to the crown was contested by the Dauphiness of France. Above all, her people were divided. More than half of them believed that she was illegitimate, and therefore not the true heir. But by her rare prudence and courage she surmounted all her difficulties and left her people prosperous and triumphant. During her life she enjoyed not merely the love but the adoration of her subjects, for they saw in her the embodiment of the hopes and of the safety of England. When she appeared in public whole crowds threw themselves upon their knees, imploring blessings on her head and praying for her success against her enemies. Those who wish to comprehend the passion of loyalty and reverence which she was able to evoke from her people may turn to the journals of D'Ewes or Townsend, and read the scenes which took place in parliament when she put an end to monopolies, or they may consult the letter which one of Allen's seminary priests wrote in 1588 to the Spanish ambassador in Paris.[1] She lived long enough to witness the quarrels and dissensions which broke out between the secular priests and the Papistic faction, and to see that a national party, small indeed as yet, was growing up among the

[1] "There, she was generally saluted with cries, with shouts, with all tokens of love, of obedience, of readiness and willingness to fight for her, as seldom has been seen in a camp and army . . . and all tended to show a marvellous concord in a mutual love betwixt a Queen and her subjects, and of reverence and obedience of subjects to a sovereign; and all that day, wandering from place to place, I never heard any word spoken of her but in praising her for her stately person and princely behaviour, and in praying for her life and safety, and cursing of all her enemies, both traitors and all Papists, with earnest desire to venture their lives for her safety."—Somers' *Tracts*, 1, 442.

Roman Catholic clergy of England. When she came to the throne, by far the larger portion of the nation still clung to the old unreformed faith; before the end of her reign England was practically Protestant. But this was not her doing. The conversion of a minority of the English people into a Protestant majority was effected by the Popes of Rome and their emissaries. The four Pontiffs Pius V., Gregory XIII., Sixtus V., and Clement VIII., by their bulls of depositions, their instigations of rebellions, their invasions and plans of crusades, wrought the change, and sacrificed the Roman Catholic Church in England to the maintenance of their supremacy in temporal matters. Instead of the healing waters of the Gospel, they proffered an impure mixture of religion and treason, and multitudes of the Faithful turned from the cup with loathing. Though these Popes identified sedition with faith, and rebellion with religion, and though they by the last and most awful sanction of the Church, cut off all the loyal Roman Catholics of England from the unity of the body of Christ,[1] their teaching was neglected. Patriotism, aided by the conviction that the kingly office also was of God, and that a reformation by blood and violence was contrary to the injunctions of the Prince of Peace, gained the day. "Jesuitical plots," say the secular priests, "for the restoring of religion in this land by treasons or invasions are not sanctified or blessed by the hand of God . . . . the old approved paths of our forefathers . . . . will always prove the best. The ancient manner of planting the Catholic faith has been by preaching, prayers, private instructions, confessions, absolutions, and by the exercising of other priestly functions, given *ad edificationem non ad destructionem*, to teach

---

[1] "Declaramus prædictam Elizabetham . . . eique adhærentes a Christi corporis unitate præcisos."—The words of the bull of Pius, renewed by Gregory and Sixtus.

obedience, not rebellion, to fill men's hearts with joy and peace by the inward working of the Holy Ghost, and not to feed them with hopes of invasions and treacheries."[1] Allen's seminary priest declares: "I do find and know that many good and wise men, which of long time have secretly continued in most earnest devotion to the Pope's authority, begin now to stagger in their minds, and to conceive that this way of reformation intended by the Pope's Holiness is not allowable in the sight of God, by leaving the ancient course of the Church by excommunication, which was the exercise of the spiritual sword, and in place thereof to take the temporal sword and put it into a monarch's hand to invade this realm with force and arms, yea to destroy the Queen thereof and all her people addicted to her, which are in very truth now seen by great proof this year to be in a sort infinite and invincible, so as some begin to say that this purpose by violence, by blood, by slaughter, and by conquest, agreeth not with Christ's doctrine, nor the doctrine of St. Peter or St. Paul." And in another part of their circular letter the secular priests declare, that if the conspiracies, invasions, depositions, &c., had never taken place, the number of Roman Catholics in England would have been ten times as great as it was then, that is in 1601.

Some learned Roman Catholics,[2] historians and others, have asserted that the penal laws were not the result of a persecuting spirit, and that if the seditious doctrines connected

[1] "When the Catholic found not only that the Protestant government, but also that the Pope and the King of Spain, and the wiser and more politic sort of his priests, considered that he, as Catholic, was a probable rebel, he must have grown by degrees convinced that his religion was in a manner rebellion, and so have become with time either a confirmed conspirator or a wavering Catholic, and in either way have both weakened if not lost his own faith, and become a scandal to those who might have occasion to judge of Catholicism by his conduct."—Simpson's *Campion*, 336.

[2] Rev. Joseph Berington, Father Walsh, Rev. Charles O'Conor, Sir John Throckmorton. Even Dodd says: "They [the Roman Catholics]

with the Papal claims to depose monarchs, had never been propagated in England, no such laws would ever have been enacted against their communion. This opinion is certainly correct. Modern England and her reformed government were not ushered into existence with a religious persecution. Two facts alone are sufficient to prove this: one is, that for the first twenty-five years of that government—six years in the reign of Edward VI. and nineteen in that of Elizabeth —not a single Roman Catholic was put to death for any matter relating to religion ; the other is, that as the English government recognized the Church of Rome to be a true Church, it could not possibly have instituted a persecution against its members. The opinion of these learned writers is also borne out by a consideration of the course of events in Elizabeth's reign ; and of the occasions upon which the penal laws were enacted. From the list of these laws we may exclude all those passed in the first twelve years of her reign. Further, if we consider, as we ought, the act against the importation of Papal bulls as a general one and a revival of the old law, we may extend this period to her twenty-third year, that is, up to 1581.[1] The oath of supremacy, as explained by Elizabeth, by Convocation, and by Parliament, was a political test, and was freely taken by her Roman Catholic subjects until the publication of the bull of Pius. A much stricter one had been taken by all, without a murmur, during the reigns of Henry and Edward, and at the accession of Mary. Elizabeth's Act of Uniformity was the mildest form of religious coercion which the world had ever seen, and

were entertained by her [Elizabeth] in the army, and now and then in the cabinet, till such times as the misbehaviour of some particular persons drew a persecution upon the whole body, and occasioned those penal and sanguinary laws."—Tierney's *Dodd*, 3, 5.

[1] This is the date fixed on by the Roman Catholic clergy in their *Declaratio Motuum, &c.*, addressed in their name to the Pope in 1601.— Berington, *Panzani*, 28.

pressed equally on all dissenters of whatever kind. Twelve happy, quiet, and prosperous years followed her accession to the throne, during which the condition of the Roman Catholics was, according to their own testimony, one of peace and security. This cannot be gainsaid, that their state was one of perfect comfort, if we compare it with that of nonconformists in the other kingdoms of Europe, and if we think of the scenes of torture and death through which those unfortunates were then passing. But the gleam of tranquillity was soon overclouded. The disturbance came from the Pope. The spiritual father of the English Roman Catholics, violating the duties of a supreme priest, and neglecting the ancient ways of spreading the faith, sent, in 1569, an apostolical penitentiary to teach Englishmen that their Queen was a heretic and pagan, whose laws ought not to be obeyed. In the following year, by his bull of excommunication and deposition, he loosened, so far as he could effect it, every bond between them and her, and compelled her government to regard allegiance to himself as disloyalty to the State. Yet such was the forbearance of that government, that neither the rebellion in the north, nor the Papal bull, was followed by any restrictive legislation save that against the introduction of Papal bulls, which the treason of Felton had extorted. For the ten years which succeeded the publication of the bull of deposition, Rome was the centre of attempted and actual invasions of English territories, of confederacies against her, and of intrigues with her rebels and external enemies. Notwithstanding these provocations no fresh legislation ensued; even the Act against the introduction of Papal bulls was allowed to sleep on the statute book for six years. At last, in 1581, after three Papal expeditions for the invasion of Ireland, and after the kingdom had escaped a supreme crisis by the accident of the Portuguese King's death, England awoke to a sense of her peril. Rome, and the writings of Parsons and Allen, had taught her that there was a great difference between the old Roman Catholics and the converts to a new faith compounded of religion and treason. She knew that the Pope had sent his Jesuits and missionary priests to teach the new religion secretly in England, while at the same time he had despatched his legate to Ireland to declare open war. The consequence was that the Acts of 1581 and 1585, against reconciliation with the Roman Church, and against Jesuits and seminary priests, were passed. Lord Burghley tells us that the reason of the enactment of the former was, because the whole scope of these conversions was to preach the temporal authority of the Pope, and to discharge the English subjects from their allegiance. We know now, from the writings of Parsons and Allen, that Burghley was right; that Parsons lost no opportunity, either personally or by his treatises, of spreading the doctrine of the deposing power as *of faith*, that is, as necessary to salvation, and that Allen, by his " three hundred priests in noblemen's and gentlemen's houses," and by the " fresh ones " whom he was " almost daily " sending into England, was " directing the Catholics' consciences and actions " in favour of an invasion which he justified by the same doctrine.[1] The Act against Jesuits and seminary priests was passed, after repeated warnings, to prevent the promulgation of the most demoralising gospel ever preached to a people, viz. that they ought to disarm their sovereign by a show of devotion, while they nourished treason in their hearts. The last Act,[2] that of 1593, to restrain Roman

---

[1] " Allen wished to make every Catholic a conspirator."—Simpson's *Campion*, 342.

[2] 35 Eliz. c. 2.—*An Act for restraining Popish Recusants to some certain places of abode*. Contemporaneously with this Act another was passed [35 Eliz. c. 1], which Hallam says affected Roman Catholics as well as other dissenters. It appears from the use of the word "conventicles" in it, and from the form of " submission," that it was directed

Catholic recusants to within five miles of their abode, was passed in consequence of the numerous conspiracies, following each other in rapid succession against the person of the Queen. In judging these laws, it must be remembered that they were enacted at a time when the very existence of England was at stake. It may be argued that they were too severe, or that they were the result of panic at a time when the country was engaged in a life and death struggle with the Papacy and the power of Spain; but to attribute them to a persecuting spirit is against all the evidence. One question perpetually suggests itself to the student of this period, as he reads of the continued attempts of the Roman Pontiffs to subjugate England to a foreign conqueror, and to subvert her freedom. Are we to be for ever deafened with complaints of the severity of these Acts, without an allusion to the provocations which produced them, and without a single word of censure for the crimes of the Popes, who, with the temporal sword in their hands, and in violation of the laws of God and man, plotted the destruction of a country with which they were at peace, invaded its territories, excited a war of religion among its inhabitants, and corrupted the fidelity of its subjects?

Lord Burghley declared, in 1583, that the prosecutions of Roman Catholics were in no way connected with religious tenets. In 1607 James I. asserted that the late Queen had "never punished any Papist for religion."[1] By some this

against the Puritans. Sir W. Raleigh, speaking in parliament, evidently thought it was aimed at the Brownists.—Townsend's *Proceedings*, 76. The only mention of Roman Catholics in the Act is an exception in their favour. Upon this exception the editor of Neal's *Puritans* observes :— "It is remarkable that there is a proviso in this statute that no Popish recusant shall be compelled or bound to abjure [the realm] by virtue of this Act. Such was her Majesty's tenderness for the Papists while she was crushing Protestant dissenters."—Neal's *Puritans*, 1, 427, ed. 1822.

[1] *Apology for the oath of allegiance.*

testimony may be questioned as Protestant. We have, however, the evidence of men who lived throughout the reign of Elizabeth, and were themselves sufferers from the restrictions of the penal laws. In 1601 a circular letter or treatise was addressed to the members of their communion by some priests, who style themselves "we your ancient teachers and spiritual fathers, the secular priests in England." This letter or treatise is really a review of the treatment which the Roman Catholics received from Elizabeth during her life, and of their conduct to her and her government. These priests are of opinion that the penal laws were brought upon their community by the numerous attempts against England from without, and by the support which was given to them by Roman Catholics at home. Here is the conclusion at which they arrive. It is long, but every word of it deserves the careful attention of those who believe that the penal laws were the result of a persecuting spirit and not of political necessities. In reading it we should also remember that their statements are amply corroborated by the extracts from the letters and books of Parsons and Allen, which have been already given. "We are fully persuaded in our consciences and as men besides our learning who have some experience, that if the Catholics had never sought by indirect means to have vexed her Majesty with their designments against her Crown: if the Pope and King of Spain had never plotted with the Duke of Norfolk; if the rebels in the north had never been heard of; if the bull of Pius Quintus had never been known; if the said rebellion had never been justified; if neither Stukely nor the Pope had attempted anything against Ireland; if Gregory XIII. had not renewed the said excommunication; if the Jesuits had never come into England; if the Pope and King of Spain had not practised with the Duke of Guise for his attempt against her Majesty; if Parsons and the rest of the Jesuits, with other our

countrymen beyond the seas had never been agents in those
traitorous and bloody designments of Throckmorton, Parry,
Collen, York, Williams, Squire, and such like; if they had
not by their treatises and writings endeavoured to defame
their sovereign and their own country, labouring to have
many of their books to be translated into divers languages,
thereby to show more their own disloyalty; if Cardinal Allen
and Parsons had not published the renovation of the said
bull by Sixtus Quintus; if thereunto they had not added
their scurrilous and unmanly admonition, or rather most
profane libel against her Majesty; if they had not sought by
false persuasions and unghostly arguments to have allured
the hearts of all Catholics from their allegiance; if the Pope
had never been urged by them to have thrust the King of
Spain into that barbarous action against the realm; if they
themselves, with all the rest of that generation, had not
laboured greatly with the said King for the conquest and
invasion of this land by the Spaniards . . . if in all their
whole proceedings they had not from time to time depraved,
irritated, and provoked both her Majesty and the State with
these and many other such like their most ungodly and
unchristian practices; but on the contrary, if the Popes from
time to time had sought her Majesty by kind offices and
gentle persuasions, never ceasing the prosecution of those
and such like courses of humanity and gentleness; if the
Catholics and priests beyond the seas had laboured continually
for the furtherance of those most priest-like and divine
allurements, and had framed their own proceedings in all
their works and writings accordingly; if we at home, all of
us, both priests and people, had possessed our souls in meekness and humility, honoured her Majesty, borne with the
infirmities of the State, suffered all things and dealt as true
Catholic priests; if all of us, we say, had thus done, most
assuredly the State would have loved us or at least borne

Y

with us; where there is one Catholic, there would have been ten; there had been no speeches amongst us of racks and tortures, nor any cause to have used them, for none were ever vexed that way simply for that he was either priest or Catholic, but because they were suspected to have had their hands in some of the said most traitorous designments . . . and therefore let us all turn over the leaf and take another course than hitherto we have done."[1]

Were the Jesuits and seminary priests who were executed during the reign of Elizabeth martyrs for their religion? Their title to this name has been denied by some of their own communion on the ground that they died, not in defence of their faith, but in support of the dogma of the deposing power.[2] Gregory the Great declared that no one suffering for a specious or unreasonable cause, or for one which was not a part of the Catholic faith, was entitled to the denomination of confessors. "Ye ought to know," writes that Pope to the bishops of Hibernia or Iberia, who had complained of being under a persecution, "that, as St. Cyprian has said, it is the cause and not the punishment—*non pœna sed causa*—which makes the martyr."[3] It is certain that these men were put to death, not for any religious tenet, but for the political doctrine of the deposing power, and that that doctrine is not one of the verities of religion for which men are bound if necessary to suffer. "This then I infer," says the Rev. Joseph Berington, "and I have ample grounds for the inference, that as none of the old clergy suffered, and none

---

[1] There is no doubt that these *Important Considerations* were published in 1601. Camden quotes from them under the year 1602. Caron also quotes from them in his *Remonstrantia Hibernorum*, and calls the treatise *Epistola generalis Cleri Anglicani*. The Rev. Joseph Berington and Sir John Throckmorton give extracts from them.

[2] "They were martyrs to the deposing power, not to their religion."—Throckmorton. "It was not for any *tenet of the Catholic faith* that they were exposed to persecution."—Rev. Joseph Berington.

[3] Walsh, *Hist. of the Irish Remonstrance*, introd. 21.

of the new who roundly renounced the assumed prerogative of Papal despotism, it was not for any *tenet of the Catholic faith* that they were exposed to persecution.¹ The illustrious Bossuet asserted that the Catholics in England were not punished as Catholics, but "as public enemies, as men ever disposed, when the Pope should order, to revolt against the King."² Though the dogma for which these men suffered was no part of the Catholic faith, and though it was directly opposed to the teachings and traditions of the old Anglo-Catholic Church, we should not lightly disturb the crown of martyrdom which hangs above the graves of those who sacrificed themselves to it. No one can read their story without emotion. Their meek endurance, their heroic constancy, and their obedience to commands which they considered divine, are lessons to us all. Still, while we lament their fate, we must ever keep in mind one truth; that it is perfectly consistent to say that these men were martyrs, and yet to hold that it was the duty of the English government to put them to death. No plea of individual conscience or obligation should be allowed to arrest the sword which is drawn in defence of the State. An example which has been given before may be again adduced. If he, whom fifty millions of our fellow-subjects regard as the vice-gerent of God, were to send his moulvies and priests to teach that the

¹ Berington, *Panzani*, 34.

² "Interim id hæretici lucrifecerunt, id ecclesiæ Catholicæ detrimento fuit, quod Catholici, non ut Catholici, pœnas darent, sed ut publici hostes, prompti scilicet in regem insurgere, ubi Romano pontifici placuisset." See also a previous remark in the same chapter that "the bull of Pius V., by exciting the English Catholics to revolt, had only the effect of exposing them to a more certain death without a pretence on any solid grounds to the glory of martyrdom, as they would have been punished not as Catholics but as rebels." Neque quidquam aliud pontifex consequutus, quam ut Anglos Catholicos certius perituros ad arma impulisse videretur, nullo aut ambiguo martyrii titulo, quum ut perduelles diris modis necarentur.—*Defensio*, pars 1, lib. 4, c. 23.

Empress of India was an infidel, and ought to be deposed, her government would be bound to prevent their entrance into the country, and, if those missionaries violated the law enacted against their teaching, to execute them. Such was the course pursued by Elizabeth. By warning after warning she forbade the Jesuits and seminary priests to remain in or to return to England, and when these warnings were rejected, a law was enacted to punish future transgressions.

Secured from external attack by union amongst themselves, Englishmen look back, almost with indifference, upon the struggles and anxieties of their forefathers when their country was assailed by him who wielded the moral influence of Europe, in conjunction with the monarch, who, in possession of the wealth of the Indies and master of the finest infantry on earth, reigned at Naples, Milan, Brussels, and Madrid. Yet what futurities for England, for the kindred nation which was so soon to be united to her, and through them for the world, then trembled in the balance, and depended on the indomitable valour of the English people and the romantic daring of their "sea-dogs." Possibilities have no place in history. But as in those matters which lie beyond and above human knowledge man is for ever peering into the unknown, and asking questions which never can be answered, so also the historical student is obliged by the law of his nature to speculate on what might have been if the course of events had been different from what it has been,— if, for example, the Athenians had been defeated in the sea fight at Salamis, or if the Cross had gone down before the Crescent at the battle of Tours. If the Pope—for the continuity of policy counterbalances the change in the individual—and the King of Spain had succeeded in their attempts against England, small indeed had been our heritage in comparison with the wide and fair succession which is now our birth-right. That which we, in the imperfection of our generalisations, call the "Elizabethan Era" would never have existed. The awakening of England to a consciousness of her infinite capacities, the wonderful outburst of activity in every department of life, the spectacle of "a noble and puissant nation rousing herself like a strong man after sleep and shaking her invincible locks" would never have been witnessed. The tree of English literature, under the branches of which the various peoples of the Anglo-Saxon race shelter themselves, and on the fruits of which they are nurtured, being sapped at its roots, would never have blossomed into manifold luxuriance. The farthest West would have felt the effects of the subjugation of England. No pilgrim fathers would have carried to her shores the language, laws, institutions, and morals of the mother country. The forty-four States of the American Union might now be Spanish viceroyalties, inhabited by tribes of wandering savages and oppressed to swell the wealth of a distant court. In the East, the guiding hand of Great Britain would be unknown, and swarms of adventurers, Hindoo, Mogul, and Sikh, might still be tearing at the entrails of that India where now two hundred and fifty millions of our fellow-subjects enjoy a universal peace. To the genius of Elizabeth and the unconquerable will of her people, we owe our present position among the nations and our world-wide Empire.

CHAPTER V

THE REIGN OF JAMES I

CHAPTER V

THE Thirty Years' War waged against England by the Popes and their allies the Kings of Spain came to an end with the accession of James I. to the English Crown. This cessation was not the result of any change in the Papal policy, for more than twenty years later, in 1627, we find Urban VIII. urging the French and Spanish monarchs to make a joint attack upon England, and bargaining with them for a cession of Ireland to the Roman See should the attack be successful.[1] The suspension of hostilities was due to two circumstances, the exhaustion of Spain and the new strength which England had acquired in the eyes of Europe by her union with Scotland. Elizabeth in the beginning of her reign had extinguished for ever French influence in the northern kingdom; the united power of the whole island forbade for the present all hopes of any foreign interference whatever. Far from desiring a continuance of the war with England the King of Spain was only too glad to conclude a peace with James, and without Spanish co-operation the Popes could effect but little.[2]

---

[1] See the commencement of the next chapter.

[2] "I knew also the state of Spain well, his weakness, and poorness, and humbleness . . . that six times we had repulsed his forces, thrice in Ireland, thrice at sea, and once at Cadiz on his own coast. . . . I knew that where before time he was wont to have forty great sails at the least in his ports, now he hath not past six or seven . . . his pride so abated

For some time after the accession of James, though the Pope had attempted to prevent it, a persuasion prevailed at Rome that the King was inclined to the Roman Catholic faith, and hopes of his conversion were entertained.[1] This expectation led to some friendly advances on the side of the Pope in the first year of James's reign. Dr. Gifford, Dean of Lisle, arrived in England in August, 1603, with instructions from the Papal nuncio at Brussels to the effect that the Pope desired to repress insurrections on the part of the Roman Catholics, that there was nothing he wished more than to see the King a member of his Church, and that he was prepared to summon from England all such as his Majesty should reasonably consider as disaffected to himself and his government.[2] About the same time, the Papal nuncio at Paris informed the English ambassador that he had received authority from the Pope to recall from England all turbulent priests. A negotiation with the latter nuncio followed. James proposed that power should be given by the Pontiff to some person to excommunicate those Roman Catholics who should disturb the peace of the country, and also that a layman should be sent from Rome to England with whom the King might informally communicate. The former proposal was warmly supported by the nuncio at Paris. The Pope, however, refused his assent to both the proposals of the King. No doubt he had learned in the interval that James was attached to the Protestant faith, and had no intention of changing his religion. In truth, there could be no lasting and friendly connexion between a

us, notwithstanding his former high terms, he was glad to congratulate the King my master on his accession, and now cometh creeping unto him for peace."—Raleigh's words at his trial; Jardine, *Crim. Trials*, 1, 413. *State Trials*, 2, 11.

[1] Jardine, *Gunpowder Plot*, 17, note. *King James's Works*, 295.

[2] Instructions from the nuncio at Brussels, Tierney's *Dodd*, 4, Appendix, 60.

Protestant sovereign and a foreign Pontiff who claimed a right to interfere in the civil government of his kingdom. As James himself said in a proclamation issued in the first year of his reign : "Although we acknowledge ourselves so much beholden to the now Bishop of Rome for his kind offices and private temporal carriage towards us in many things . . . as Bishop of Rome, in state and condition of a secular prince, yet, when we consider and observe the course and claim of that see, we have no reason to imagine that princes of our religion and profession can expect any assurance long to continue, unless it might be assented, by mediation of other princes Christian, that some good course might be taken . . . to pluck up those roots of dangers and jealousies which arise for cause of religion as well between princes and princes as between them and their subjects, and to make it manifest that no state or potentate either hath or can challenge power to dispose of earthly things or monarchies, or to dispense with subjects' obedience to their natural sovereign."[1]

It has been urged by some writers that the accession of James offered a favourable opportunity for granting to the Roman Catholics of England a repeal of the penal laws. But, it may be asked, was such a course practicable ? These laws had been enacted from a belief that they were a political necessity. Had any change taken place since the enactment of the last of them to weaken that belief ? Was there any alteration either in the policy of the Popes, or in the behaviour of the Papistic faction, which in the eyes of the government and of the English people represented the whole body of Roman Catholics ? Until such a change was observable, the remembrance of thirty-three years of aggression on the part of the Roman Pontiffs, and of the innumerable treasons of the Papistic party at home for the same period,

[1] Proclamation of February 22, 1604.

could not be blotted out in a moment from the mind of a nation. But no change whatever had taken place. The Popes of Rome still claimed to be the suzerains of England, and, in the exercise of their supreme temporal power, to be entitled to set aside her lawful King, to dispose of her crown, and to absolve her subjects from their allegiance. Shortly before the accession of James, Clement VIII. had sent his bulls to England, exhorting the Roman Catholics to oppose his succession to the crown. Contemporaneously with these documents, Clement had despatched to Ireland a bull of indulgence to all such as should aid Tyrone in his rebellion against the English Government, and promised, in a letter admonishing him and his adherents to persevere in their rebellion, that he would endeavour to obtain help for them from the Catholic kings and princes. The Papistic party, which was labouring for the exclusion of a Protestant successor and for the forcible intervention of the Spanish King, was unchanged, and was as busy as ever both at home and abroad. Immediately after the accession of James, that party had sent an agent to Philip III. to request him to fulfil the engagement of invading England made by him in 1602. The Papists were active and enterprising, and naturally brought distrust upon the general body of Roman Catholics, with whom they were confounded, as the government and the English people had no means of distinguishing between them. Further, on a late occasion even the Roman Catholics, in contradistinction to the Papists, had appeared to favour the doctrine of the temporal power of the Popes. On the day when Elizabeth was seized with her last illness, certain priests, as has been said, had drawn up and presented to her Council a protestation of allegiance, in which they declared that in case of invasion by any foreign prelate, prince, or potentate, they would defend her Majesty and the realm, and that they were bound in conscience not to obey any Papal excommunication or censure issued against their prince. Unhappily this protestation was signed by thirteen secular priests only. If this document had been signed generally by the Roman Catholic clergy and laity, the distrust of the government and of the nation would at least have been greatly lessened, and a few years of domestic quiet would have entirely dissipated their suspicions and jealousies. "Had the Catholics," says the Rev. Joseph Berington, "in a body, on the accession of King James, waited on him with the *Protestation of allegiance* I have just stated, as containing their true and loyal sentiments, we should probably have heard no more of recusancy or penal prosecution."[1] This was not done, and their abstention was naturally interpreted as indicating that all Roman Catholics accepted the doctrines, that Papal excommunication justified an invasion, and that the Pope could dispense with the allegiance of English subjects. Until these doctrines were repudiated, and an unconditional allegiance towards the secular sovereign was professed, a reconciliation between that body and the government was impossible, as is shown by its subsequent history. No relief was extended to its members until they had disclaimed the doctrine of the deposing power and the belief "that the Pope of Rome, or any other foreign prince, prelate, state, or potentate, hath or ought to have any temporal or civil jurisdiction, power, superiority, or pre-eminence, directly or indirectly, within this realm."[2]

There can be no doubt that James was well-disposed towards the Roman Catholics, and sincerely desirous of alleviating their condition.[3] He arrived in the neighbour-

[1] Berington, *Memoirs of Panzani*, 73.
[2] The words of the oath imposed by 18 Geo. III., the first relief Act. It was stated in the Memorial of the Roman Catholics, presented ten years later to Pitt, "that the English Catholics have universally taken this oath."—Butler, *English Catholics*, 4, 9.
[3] " His [James's] good will to the professors of that religion from the

hood of London in the early part of May, 1603. In the preceding month, a petition had been presented to him by that body asking for a toleration of their religion. The petitioners assured him of their devoted allegiance, and reminded him of their services in behalf of his mother's cause and of his own, but there was no repudiation of the deposing power, nor any renunciation of the Pope's temporal claims.[1] An answer to this petition was given in the following July. Sir Thomas Tresham and a considerable body of distinguished Roman Catholics were summoned to Hampton Court to meet the Lords of the Privy Council. The representatives were received with every mark of respect,[2] and were informed by the Lords that it was the King's intention to exonerate thenceforth the Roman Catholics from the fines of £20 a-month for recusancy, and that they should enjoy this favour so long as "they kept themselves upright in all civil and true carriage towards his Majesty and the State without contempt." The representatives objected that recusancy alone might be held to be an act of contempt. To this objection it was answered by the Lords that the King would not account recusancy as contempt. In confirmation of this official assurance the fines for recusancy were remitted for the first two years of James's reign.[3] Other demonstrations of favour to the Roman Catholics were made at the same time. Titles of honour and

earliest impressions was deeply marked on his heart."—Berington's *Panzani*, 73.

[1] The Petition is to be found in Tierney's *Dodd*, 4, Appd. 72.

[2] *Petition Apologetical of the Lay Catholics*, 1604, p. 8.

[3] "It appears from some notes of Sir Julius Cæsar, who was Chancellor of the Exchequer in 1607, that in the last year of Queen Elizabeth's reign, the sums paid into the Exchequer . . . for recusants' fines and forfeitures was £10,333 9s. 7d. In the next year little more than £300 was paid . . . on this account. In the following year, being the second of James's reign, the sum hardly exceeded £200."—Jardine, *Gunpowder Plot*, 19.

THE REIGN OF JAMES I

lucrative employments were bestowed upon members of that persuasion, and one of them, Lord Henry Howard, was advanced to a seat in the Privy Council. The King himself, speaking of his disposition at this time towards the Roman Catholics, says: "How many did I honour with knighthood of known and open recusants? How indifferently did I give audience and access to both sides, bestowing equally all favours and honours on both professions? How free and continual access had all ranks and degrees of Papists in my court and company? And above all, how frankly and freely did I free recusants of their ordinary payments? Besides, it is evident what strait order was given out of my own mouth to the judges to spare the execution of all priests notwithstanding their conviction, joining thereto a gracious proclamation, whereby all priests, that were at liberty and not taken, might go out of the country by such a day, my general pardon having been extended to all convicted priests in prison; whereupon they were set at liberty as good subjects, and all priests that were taken after sent over and set at liberty there."[1] The interview between the deputies of the Roman Catholics and the Lords of the Privy Council took place before the King's coronation.

But the good intentions of the King were frustrated by the conduct of the Papistic faction. At the very moment when James was showing favour to the Roman Catholics there were two conspiracies of members of that party in existence against him—the one to dethrone him and support a Spanish invasion, the other to seize his person and extort from him a toleration for their body, and other concessions. Immediately after the death of Elizabeth in March, 1603, Christopher Wright was despatched to Madrid by Catesby, Francis Tresham, Garnet, and others, to call on Philip III. to invade England, according to his promise. Two months

[1] *King James's Works*, 253.

later, Guido Faukes followed Wright with instructions from Baldwin, a Jesuit who lived in Brussels, to aid the negotiations, and to offer two thousand horses, to be furnished by the Roman Catholics of England, for the assistance of the invading army. But the exhaustion of the Spanish monarchy forbade Philip from undertaking the enterprise; and, though he received the messengers kindly, he refused to adopt their proposals. The other conspiracy is known in our histories under the name of the "Surprise," or the "Bye." The intention of the conspirators in this plot was, to get possession of the person of the King, to convey him to the Tower, or to Dover Castle, and, when James was in their power, to keep him a close prisoner until he had granted a pardon to the confederates, ensured them a toleration of their religion, and agreed to remodel his ministry according to their advice. The plot was conceived by two priests, Watson and Clarke, and a Roman Catholic gentleman called Sir Griffin Markham. The exclusively religious character of the conspiracy is shown by the oath which was drawn up by its members:—"I, N. N., do here before God, our Blessed Lady, and all the holy angels and saints, attest in the faith of a Catholic Christian man, that from henceforth I will do my best endeavour by word, writing, action, or any other lawful means, to restore the Catholic faith in our country, to conserve the life of our sovereign in safety, and to preserve the laws of our land from all enemies of what sort, title, or condition soever they be, or may be."[1] All but a few, to whom the real object was disclosed, were left under the impression that they were to join only in the presentation of a petition to the King; and it was hoped that, when the opportunity of action arrived, the petitioners would follow the directions of their leaders. Lord Grey of Wilton, a Puritan, and Brooke, the brother of Lord Cobham, who were both discontented with the Government,

[1] Tierney's *Dodd*, 4, Appd. 38.

coquetted for some time with the conspirators—so far, at least, as concerned the presentation of a petition; but they appear to have drawn off as the period of executing the plan approached, deterred by the religious complexion of the plot. Watson and Clarke were arrested; and from the statements and confessions of the conspirators the King learned that other movements were on foot against him. Watson declared that the Jesuits were engaged in a plan in favour of a Spanish invasion; that they had collected large sums of money and horses to aid the invaders; and that he himself had entered into the project of the "Surprise" merely to defeat their designs. These were not unfounded assertions. Catesby and his associates were then making preparations to receive a Spanish army if Philip should send a favourable answer to their proposals; and Guido Faukes was offering him, on behalf of the English Roman Catholics, two thousand horses to join with the Spanish forces. What is strangest of all about this conspiracy is, that it was revealed to the government by the Jesuits. If we may believe Watson, this was done "for clearing of themselves by laying their own treasons and conspiracies to our charge." Watson and Markham had opened a correspondence with two Jesuits, Darcy and Gerard, for the purpose of a reconciliation between themselves and the members of the Society. Gerard declined their advances, and, having become acquainted with the conspiracy, wrote to his superior Garnet, and requested him to inform the archpriest of the plot. After some delay, Garnet and the archpriest revealed the conspiracy to the Bishop of London and other members of the Council. It is certain that Gerard was at this time engaged with Garnet, the superior of the Jesuits in England, in the other conspiracy for a Spanish invasion, and that he afterwards fled the country, being accused of participation in the Gunpowder Plot.

In consequence of these conspiracies, a proclamation was

issued in February, 1604, commanding all Jesuits and seminary priests to leave the kingdom before the 19th of the following month, and warning them that all who should remain in the country, or return to it, would be left to the penalties of the law, without hope of favour or remission of punishment. At the same time, a statute[1] was passed ordering the laws framed during the late reign against Jesuits, seminary priests, and recusants, to be enforced. It also provided that no one should send a child or other person under his obedience to a foreign seminary, under a penalty of a hundred pounds: every person going to such a seminary to be disabled from inheriting lands or goods; all those in schools abroad to return home within a year, or to be equally disabled; no person, unless licensed by the ordinary, to keep a school or act as schoolmaster in the house of a recusant, under a penalty of forty shillings a-day for the schoolmaster himself, and also for his employer.

The next year, 1605, was the year of the Gunpowder Plot, which, commencing with a few individuals, widened into a formidable conspiracy. No event—not even the St. Bartholomew massacre—ever made a stronger impression upon the imagination of a people. The atrocity of the design, and the extent of the mischief intended, produced a frenzy of horror and dread among all Englishmen. The universal horror was enhanced, if that were possible, by the fact that no mercy was to have been shown by the conspirators, even to those members of their own communion who sat in Parliament. There were then more than twenty Roman Catholic peers entitled to seats in the upper house; yet all these, together with the King and his family, the lords and the commons, were to have been involved in a common destruction, and a general anarchy was to have been let loose.

We cannot understand the past without placing ourselves,

[1] 1 James I., c. 4.

as it were, in it, and endeavouring to comprehend the feelings with which contemporaries regarded what was passing around them. The convictions and opinions of the times are the real objects of history, for they are the only sources from which policies and events arise. The former are causes, the latter but their effects, since thought determines action. Let us for a moment try to conceive what the sentiments of the English people must have been on the discovery of the Gunpowder Plot. At this period thirty-five years had elapsed since Pius V. had issued his bull, declaring that there was no lawful government in England, and commanding all English Roman Catholics to offer a perpetual hostility to their native sovereign. For upwards of thirty-three years, the Popes of Rome had directed all the moral and material resources at their disposal to effect the destruction of the country, and its conquest by a foreign invader. During the whole of that long time, a powerful and active party in the kingdom, calling itself Roman Catholic, had played into the hands of the Popes and the Spanish Kings, plotted rebellions, invited invasions, and conspired for the subjugation of England in the name and for the advancement of their religion. A new generation had arisen which was well aware of the agony of distress and danger through which the kingdom had passed. The manhood of England had grown up surrounded by the gravest perils from the machinations of the Popes, the hostility of Spain, and the conspiracies of their domestic foes. The struggle of life or death had ceased for a time, but there was no security that it would not be renewed. The whole strength of the kingdom might at any moment be called on to resist an attack. While England was thus watching and waiting with her hand on the sword, the general body of the Roman Catholics declined to offer guarantees of their fidelity, and by so doing gave just grounds for believing that their allegiance was doubtful. A party among them, which it was impossible to discriminate from the majority, had lately been guilty of two fresh conspiracies, and now had crowned the long series of its misdeeds by a crime which has been well described as an attempt to murder the nation in its representatives. What conclusion could the English people come to, but that there were no terms to be kept with men who tolerated such a party among them, and refused to separate themselves from it by a proffer of thorough allegiance to their sovereign, and of unconditional devotion to their country?

There is no reason to believe that the Gunpowder conspiracy was known at Rome before it was officially made public by the English government. The plot was not openly adopted by the Papal Court as the St. Bartholomew massacre had been, nor was it celebrated by religious processions, or by medals struck in its remembrance. But on the other hand, the Pope never issued any formal condemnation of it. No public censure of a crime so black proceeded from the Papal See. It was left to Blackwell, the arch-priest, to stigmatize the attempt as " an intolerable, uncharitable, scandalous, and desperate fact." Blackwell informed his flock that the Pope had written to him " in general " prohibiting all such unlawful attempts, and that he felt assured that his Holiness would, when notice should come to him, " by his public instruments manifest and declare to the world his utter dislike and detestation " of the plot.[1] But the Pope made no sign, nor did he ever declare to the world his detestation of the attempt. An enormous wickedness, which had shocked the conscience of Europe, and which had been exclusively designed by Roman Catholics for the promotion of their religion, was passed over in silence by the head of that communion. The First Bishop of the

[1] Blackwell's *Letters to the Catholic Clergy and Laity of England;* Tierney's *Dodd,* 4, App. 111–113.

Christian world manifested no public indignation for a crime which aimed at the destruction of the King of England and his family, the hierarchy, the whole nobility, and the knights and burgesses of the realm. The Pontiff, who claimed to be the Vicar of the Prince of Peace, uttered no denunciation against an attempt to restore in England what he considered the Church of God by wholesale murder. No priest or Jesuit engaged in the conspiracy was ever punished by the Pope for complicity in it. " Neither these that fled out of the country for it," says King James, " nor yet Baldwin, who, though he then remained in the Low Countries, was of counsel in it, were ever called to account for it by the Pope, much less punished, for meddling in so scandalous and enormous business."[1]

The arch-priest was not the only member of his communion who wished the Pope to condemn publicly the wickedness of the Gunpowder Plot. Twenty-five years later, a Papal agent, then resident in England, expressed his regret that the Pontiff had not declared his detestation of it. If he had done so, said the latter, the English people would have thought that the plot arose from the criminality of individuals, and not from the doctrines of Catholic teachers.[2] But these respectable ecclesiastics did not see that the Pope could not condemn the principles which inspired the conspirators without also condemning those upon which the Papacy had acted during the thirty years' war against England, and that her people were right in concluding that the principles were identical in both cases. These principles were, that all means were lawful to effect the restoration of the Roman Catholic Church, and that actions otherwise criminal changed their moral character when done in pursuance of this great object. To carry these into practice, the gunpowder traitors chose the short and simple method of

[1] *King James's Works*, 274.   [2] See next chapter.

explosion; the Popes preferred the more lengthened processes of invasions, conspiracies, and civil wars. But what difference is there between blowing up a town, and after a storm putting its inhabitants to the sword? The attempt against the houses of parliament, and the long continued endeavour of the Roman Pontiffs to restore their religion by blood and violence, stood on precisely similar grounds, and were equally opposed to the laws of God. We may, therefore, neglect any difference in the means adopted to carry them into execution. The Pope did not issue a condemnation of the gunpowder conspiracy simply because it would have been illogical and absurd for him to censure conduct which sprang from the same motives and principles upon which the Papacy itself had acted for upwards of a generation.

It was a consciousness of its own crimes against England and that those crimes proceeded from the same principles which actuated the powder conspirators, that prevented the Papacy from denouncing the plot, and paralyzed it in the performance of its moral duties. If we now turn to the effects produced by these principles on the minds of those Englishmen who accepted them, and whose conduct was guided by them, we shall be amazed at the depraved morality which prevailed among them. Of all the circumstances connected with the gunpowder conspiracy, nothing is more shocking than the fact that all sense of right and wrong appears to have been obscured in the consciences of the men who planned it. Patriotism, pity, humanity, neighbourly affection, all the social virtues, had disappeared before the tenet that all means of restoring the Roman Catholic religion were justifiable. The associates in the conspiracy were gentlemen of rank and education, yet they believed that, in undertaking the enterprise, they were promoting the cause of God, and many of them maintained to the last that it was meritorious in the sight of heaven. It is not often that we can look into the souls of criminals and discover the real motives upon which they acted, but the latest sayings of the gunpowder conspirators furnish us with such an opportunity. In a letter to his wife, Sir Everard Digby expressed his surprise that his conduct was disapproved of by some members of his communion. "If I had thought there had been the least sin in it, I would not have been of it for all the world, and no other cause drew me to hazard my fortune and life but zeal to God's religion. But when I heard that Catholics and priests thought that it should be a great sin that should be the cause of my end, it called my conscience in doubt of my very best actions and intentions." "Nothing grieves me," said Robert Winter to Faukes in the Tower, " but that there is not an apology made by some to justify our doings in this business; but our deaths will be a sufficient justification of it, and it is for God's cause." He also expressed his regret that " the business having been brought within a day or two of its execution should be so unhappily thwarted."[1] John Grant, another of the conspirators, on the day of his execution, was exhorted by the clergyman who attended him to entertain a proper sense of his situation and to ask pardon for his crime from heaven. Grant replied, with a cheerful countenance : " I am convinced that our project was so far from being sinful, that I entirely rely upon my merits in bearing a part of that noble action, as an abundant satisfaction and expiation for all sins committed by me during the rest of my life."[2] What a commentary do these facts supply on the Act of Elizabeth which forbade conversions to the new edition of the Christian religion imported into England by the Jesuits and seminary priests from Italian and Spanish schools.

The parliament met immediately after the discovery of the plot, and James addressed both houses in words of great

[1] Jardine, *Gunpowder Plot*, 152.   [2] *Ib.* 153.

moderation. He told them that though religion had engaged the conspirators in the late attempt, yet that they ought not to involve all Roman Catholics in the same guilt or to suppose that they were capable of similar crimes. He would be sorry that any who were innocent should receive blame or harm. That, though many Roman Catholics might remain good and faithful subjects, none of those that truly knew and believed the whole grounds and school conclusions of their doctrine could prove either good Christians or faithful subjects. For his part, they should see no alteration in his conduct arising from this cause save caution and wariness in discovering the mysteries of the wickedness, and severity in punishing those that should be found guilty. This speech was delivered on the 9th of November, and at its conclusion James adjourned the parliament until the 21st of the following January.

The King's moderation had but little effect amidst the perturbation of the public mind. On the reassembling of parliament, all men were thinking of the great deliverance vouchsafed to them, and of the means of preventing similar dangers in future. Two Acts, of great severity, were at once passed against recusants.[1] They were forbidden to appear at Court, or to remain within ten miles of London unless engaged in trade or employment in the city, or unless their only dwelling was in it or within ten miles of it. They were made incapable of any public office or charge, of practising medicine or the law, of acting as judges or officers in any court or corporation, or of being executors, administrators, or guardians. Pecuniary penalties were imposed if they were married or suffered their children to be baptized with any other rites than those of the Established Church, and, if they were not buried in a Protestant cemetery, their executors were liable to a penalty of twenty pounds. Every

[1] 3 James I. cc. 4 and 5.

child sent abroad for education was disqualified from taking any benefit by devise, descent, or gift, until he returned and conformed. Power was given to the King to refuse the penalty of £20 a-month, and in lieu thereof to take into his hands two-thirds of the lands of recusants. Every person retaining a recusant in his service was liable to a fine of £10 a-month.

But even at this juncture a way of safety was opened to the Roman Catholics by the King, by which, if they had availed themselves of it, they would soon have obtained peace and security. An opportunity was afforded them of showing that they were not disaffected to the government, and that, though their spiritual head claimed the right of allowing or disallowing the performance of their civil duties, their religion was not inconsistent with the safety of the State. Elizabeth's oath of supremacy, as explained by her Admonition, declared that the sovereign of England was the supreme governor of the realm in all ecclesiastical and temporal matters, and abolished all foreign powers repugnant to this right. James now called upon his Roman Catholic subjects merely to abjure the claim of the Pope to depose him, and to absolve them from their natural obedience. He was anxious to relieve the loyal portion from the burden of the penal laws, but the first step was to separate them from the disloyal. For this purpose he caused to be inserted in the first of the two statutes just mentioned, an oath which has always been known as the oath of allegiance, to distinguish it from that of supremacy. The oath was intended, as James informs us, " to make a separation between so many of my subjects, who, although they were otherwise Popishly affected, yet retained in their hearts the print of their natural duty to their sovereign, and those who, being carried away with the like fanatical zeal that the Powder traitors were, could not contain themselves within the bounds of their natural allegiance, but thought diversity of religion a safe pretext for all kind of treasons and rebellions against their sovereign."[1] In framing the oath of allegiance, the greatest care was taken that it should contain nothing but matters of civil obedience due by subjects to their Government. As a proof of this, James mentions the following remarkable fact: " The lower house of parliament, at the first framing of this oath, made it to contain that the Pope had no power to excommunicate me, which I caused them to reform, only making it to conclude, that no excommunication of the Pope can warrant my subjects to practise against my person or State, denying the deposition of Kings to be in the Pope's lawful powers, as, indeed, I take any such temporal violence to be far without the limits of such a spiritual censure as excommunication is. So careful was I that nothing should be contained in this oath except the profession of natural allegiance and civil and temporal obedience, with a promise to resist to all contrary uncivil violence."[2] It is now admitted by all Roman Catholics that the oath of allegiance proposed by James was perfectly free from any objection, and that it contained nothing inconsistent with their religion or their duty to the head of their Church. When James II. was Duke of York, he himself took the oath of allegiance, and intimated his intention of enforcing it when he should be King.[3] Every affirmative proposition in the oath respecting the rights of an English sovereign, and every denial of the Pope's deposing and absolving power have since been accepted by Roman Catholics over and over again in their oaths and petitions. The oath was as follows:—

1. I do truly and sincerely acknowledge, profess, testify, and declare in my conscience before God and the world, that

[1] *King James's Works*, 248.
[2] *Premonition to all Christian Monarchs.—Ib.* 292.
[3] Butler, *English Catholics*, 2, 220 ; Lingard, 9, 245.

our sovereign lord King James is lawful and rightful King
of this realm, and of all other his Majesty's dominions and
countries; and that the Pope, neither of himself nor by any
authority of the Church or See of Rome, or by any other
means with any other, hath any power or authority to depose
the King or to dispose any of his Majesty's kingdoms or
dominions, or to authorize any foreign prince to invade or
annoy him or his countries, or to discharge any of his subjects
of their allegiance and obedience to his Majesty, or to give
license or leave to any of them to bear arms, raise tumults,
or to offer any violence or hurt to his Majesty's royal
person, state, or government, or to any of his Majesty's
subjects within his Majesty's dominions.

2. Also, I do swear from my heart, that notwithstanding
any declaration or sentence of excommunication or deprivation
made or granted or to be made or granted by the Pope or
his successors, or by any authority derived, or pretended to
be derived, from him or his See against the said King, his
heirs, or successors, or any absolution of the said subjects
from their obedience, I will bear faith and true allegiance to
his Majesty, his heirs and successors, and him and them will
defend to the uttermost of my power against all conspiracies
and attempts whatsoever which shall be made against his or
their persons, their crowns and dignity, by reason or colour
of any such sentence or declaration, or otherwise, and will do
my best endeavour to disclose and make known unto his
Majesty, his heirs and successors, all treasons and traitorous
conspiracies which I shall know or hear of to be against him
or any of them.

3. And I do further swear that I do from my heart
abhor, detest, and abjure as impious and heretical, this
damnable doctrine, that princes, which be excommunicated or
deprived by the Pope, may be deposed or murdered by their
subjects or any other whatsoever.

4. And I do believe and in my conscience am resolved, that neither the Pope nor any other person whatsoever hath power to absolve me of this oath or any part thereof, which I acknowledge by good and full authority to be lawfully ministered unto me, and do renounce all pardons and dispensations to the contrary.

5. And all these things I do plainly and sincerely acknowledge and swear according to these express words by me spoken, and according to the plain and common sense and understanding of the same words, without any equivocation or mental evasion or secret reservation whatsoever. And I do make this recognition and acknowledgment heartily, willingly, and truly upon the true faith of a Christian.

The general effect of the oath was: it demanded an acknowledgment of the King's title, a renunciation of the deposing power, a promise of true allegiance in spite of any excommunication or Papal sentence of deposition, and a denial of the doctrine that excommunicated princes might be deposed or murdered by their subjects. It is plain that a refusal to take the oath was equivalent to an acceptance of the opinions which it called upon the deponent to disclaim, and to a denial that James was the lawful King of England, and as such entitled to true allegiance in case of his being excommunicated or deposed by the Pope. The subject who declined to take the oath must have believed all or some of the following propositions: that James was not the lawful King of England; that the Pope might depose him and give his kingdom to another; that the same authority might discharge his subjects from their allegiance; and that excommunicated princes might be deposed or murdered by their subjects. Each and all of these opinions were directly opposed to the safety of the government and the tranquillity of the nation. It is not too much to say—that the maintenance of any of these opinions—at a time when a foreign authority claimed the right by divine institution to depose monarchs, and to discharge their subjects from their obedience, unfitted those who held them for citizenship and justly excluded them from the enjoyment of its full benefits. For the subject who entertains opinions inconsistent with the security of the State is justly suspected and justly condemned to civil disabilities. It is the unquestionable duty of every man when called upon by the supreme power in the State to give such assurance of his loyalty as that power may require, provided there is nothing required from him contrary to his faith or conscience, and the Roman Catholics violated this clear duty in refusing the oath of allegiance.[1] How far the subject is bound to go in his obedience, and how far he should even stretch his conscience in his endeavour to give full satisfaction to his sovereign, is well shown by the example of Pope Gregory the Great. The Emperor Maurice made a law that no soldier should be allowed to become a monk until he had accomplished his term of military service, and directed Gregory to publish the ordinance. To this order Gregory replied: "I, being subject to your commands, have transmitted your law to be published through divers parts of the world; and because the law itself is not pleasing to Almighty God, I have represented my opinion thereof to my lord. Wherefore I have performed my duty on both sides, in yielding obedience to the Emperor and not concealing what I thought for God." Here the

[1] "The duty we owe to our sovereign doth not consist in taciturnity or keeping close within ourselves such allegiance as we think sufficient to afford them; but we are, especially when we are required thereunto, to make open profession of it, that we may appear unto them to be such subjects as we ought to be, and as they may rely upon, if either their kingdoms or safeties be in hazard or danger."—*Important Considerations.* "There is nothing in it [James's oath] which every Catholic is not *bound in conscience* to swear to, whenever it is proposed by the legitimate authority of the State."—O'Conor, *Hist. Address,* 2, 202.

Pope submitted to the secular sovereign even in a matter which he thought not pleasing to God, and subordinated his own opinion to the duty of obedience. Gregory's successor, in a purely indifferent matter which had nothing to do with religion, forbade the Roman Catholics of England to obey the laws of their country and to testify their submission to their sovereign's will. In doing so, he contravened the clear command of Scripture,[1] and was therefore guilty of disobedience to the divine injunctions.

When the statute was passed and the oath tendered, it was eagerly taken by many Roman Catholics, both of the clergy and laity.[2] But the Papistic party was still strong. A copy of the oath was conveyed to Robert Parsons, their agent at Rome. He and other Jesuits obtained a condemnation of it from the Pope. In September, 1606, Paul V. issued a bull, directed to the English Catholics, pronouncing the oath to be unlawful, and declaring that it contained "many things clearly contrary to faith and salvation."[3] He also admonished the members of his communion to refuse it, and advised them rather to suffer martyrdom. This the Pope did without any reference to or consultation with James, and without particularizing what was objectionable in the oath. Though the Pontiff was at that time in communication with James by means of secret

[1] "Let every soul be subject unto the higher powers . . . the powers that be are ordained of God."—Romans xiii. 1. "Submit yourselves to every ordinance of man for the Lord's sake; whether it be to the King, as supreme, or unto governors, as unto them that are sent by him for the punishment of evil-doers."—1 Peter ii. 13, 14.

[2] Of James's oath Bossuet said in 1730: "In the year 1606 King James proposed to the Roman Catholics an oath which, if they had taken, they might now be living in peace and security, under certain conditions." An. vero 1606, Jacobus rex juramentum præstari jussit a Romanis Catholicis, quod si præstitissent, libere ac tuto certis conditionibus in sua religione viverent.—*Defensio, pars* 1, *lib.* 4, *c.* 23.

[3] "Cum multa contineat quæ fidei atque saluti aperte adversantur."

agents,[1] and though the King was prepared to make alterations in the form of the oath,[2] Paul, urged on by the Jesuits, took a step which closed the door on a reconciliation between the English Roman Catholics and the government under which they lived, and necessitated a continuance of the penal laws.

As has been said, the Papal bull declared that the oath of allegiance contained many things clearly contrary to faith and salvation. This statement was untrue. There was not a word in it touching any point of religion. "As for the Catholic faith," asks King James, "can there be one word found in all that oath tending or sounding to matter of religion? Doth he that taketh it promise there to believe or not to believe any article of religion, or doth he so much as name a true or false Church there? . . . Neither is there any mention at all made therein, either *disertis verbis* or by any other indirect means, either of the hierarchy of the Church, of St. Peter's succession, of the See apostolic, or of any such matter."[3] That the Pope himself could not point out a single expression in the oath to which objection could be taken, is manifest from the way in which a petition of certain English priests was shortly afterwards treated by him. Thirteen[4] priests were confined in Newgate for not taking the oath. These unfortunate men forwarded a supplication to Paul, entreating him to point out those things in the oath which were contrary to faith and sal-

[1] "J'ai sçu depuis peu que le dit Baron de Magdaléne . . . a fait le voyage par commandement du Pape dont il est camerier . . . pour recommander au roi d'Angleterre les Catholiques au pays, l'assurer de leur obéissance, comme de la bonne volonté de sa Sainteté, &c." 20 April, 1606.—*Ambassades de M. de la Boderie*, 1, 284.

[2] *King James's Works*, 249.

[3] *Ib.* 269.

[4] The number is sometimes given as eight. But see Tierney's *Dodd*, 1, App. 205.

vation. In the most affecting terms they implored him, by the blood of the martyrs and by the bowels of the divine mercy, to take pity on them and on the afflicted Roman Catholics of England, and to specify those parts of the oath which rendered it unlawful to be taken.[1] To this touching appeal no answer was returned. The Court of Rome was well aware that the only objection to the oath, apparent on its face, was its denial of the Pope's temporal jurisdiction, and was afraid that any explanation would weaken its claims. Forty years later, the Papal See itself avowed a second objection to it, which will be mentioned in the next chapter.

When the bull condemning the oath was conveyed to England, the Roman Catholics were thrown into the utmost confusion, for they wished and felt it to be their duty to take the oath. Suspecting the agency of Parsons and the Jesuits, they questioned the authenticity of the bull, or asserted that it had been obtained on false pretences. To remove all doubts on this head, a second bull was issued in the August of the following year. "It has been reported unto us," says the Pope, "that certain among you dare to affirm, that the letter concerning the forbidding of the oath was not written of our own accord or of our own proper will, but rather for the respect and at the instigation of other men. And for that cause, the same do go about to persuade you that our commands in the said letter are not to be regarded. . . . Therefore we have thought good to write the second time to you and to signify unto you again, that our apostolic letter, dated the last

[1] "Per horum te martyrum sanguinem, per labores et ærumnas, per vincula, carceres, tormenta, cruciatus, per invictam patientiam. Si minus ista movent, per viscera misericordiæ Dei nostri, partem solicitudinis tuæ afflictissimis Angliæ rebus impende. . . . Saltem ut veritas magis elucescat, altiusque omnium mentibus inseratur, dignetur sanctitas tua palam omnibus facere, quænam illa sint in hoc religionis sacramento quæ aperte fidei et saluti adversantur."

year on the tenth of the calends of October concerning a prohibition of the oath, was written not only upon our proper motion and of our certain knowledge, but also after long and weighty deliberation concerning all those things which are contained in it, and that for that cause you are bound fully to observe them, rejecting all interpretations persuading to the contrary." This second bull also omitted to specify the passages which were contrary to faith and salvation.

On the publication of the oath of allegiance, Blackwell, the arch-priest and apostolic delegate in England, took it himself and advised the Roman Catholics to take it. Cardinal Bellarmine hastened to remonstrate with him on the grievousness of his backsliding, but the Cardinal's exhortations were ineffectual. Blackwell replied that, in taking the oath, he had denied, not the spiritual authority, but the temporal pretensions of the Pope, and that he was justified in so doing both by the opinions of divines and by the necessity of alleviating the sufferings of his flock. For this offence against the Papal claims Blackwell was deposed from his office of arch-priest, and George Birkhead was appointed in his stead. On the 1st of February, 1608, a third bull was issued removing Blackwell, repeating the condemnation of the oath, and ordering all priests, who had taken it and did not retract within a limited time, to be deprived of their faculties. For this purpose, a period of two months was prescribed by Birkhead, after which, all those priests who persisted in their error were to be deprived. Birkhead, however, shrank from taking a step which was certain to aggravate the miseries of his communion. He wrote to Rome requesting the Pope to pronounce the sentence of deprivation in that city, as it was not safe to pronounce it in England.[1] He also besought the Pontiff at least to issue, for the satisfaction of the government and the

[1] Tierney's *Dodd*, 4, 77; App. 141.

country, a bull enjoining the Roman Catholics under censure of excommunication, to abstain from all treasonable attempts against the King, and to act as good and obedient subjects. "If such a breve would be procured from his Holiness," he urges, "there is great hope, and not ungrounded, conceived of much ease and mitigation of pressures to follow to the body of Catholics thereby."[1] But a reconciliation between the English Roman Catholics and their government was the last thing desired at Rome. No notice was taken at the Papal Court of Birkhead's requests.[2] After three years' delay, Birkhead was at last compelled to notify to his assistants and to the Roman Catholic body, that those priests who had taken the oath and had not retracted were deprived of their faculties. These repeated denunciations of the Pope were effectual, and the oath was rejected by his communion in England.

In 1626, a fourth condemnation of the oath was issued by Urban VIII. "If violence should proceed so far," says Urban, "as to compel you to take that pernicious and unlawful oath of allegiance of England, remember that what you utter is heard by all the assembly of angels who are beholding you. And let your tongue cleave to your mouth rather than diminish by this form of oath the authority of St. Peter, for in it not only is allegiance given to the King, but the sacred sceptre of the universal Church is wrested from the Vicar of Almighty God. That which our predecessor Paul V. of blessed memory decreed with such deliberation, that ought ye altogether to observe as a decree of truth."[3]

Roman Catholic writers, unable to defend the conduct of the Popes in this matter, and aware that the oath contained nothing concerning faith or morals, have fallen back on an

---

[1] *Ib.* and App. 167.   [2] *Ib.*
[3] Sir John Throckmorton, *First Letter to the Catholic Clergy of England*, 136; Wilkins' *Concilia*, 4, 471.

argument which will not bear a moment's examination. It was not to the oath, say these apologists, that the Popes objected, but to the terms made use of in it. They assert that the oath was condemned at Rome because it applied the word "heretical" to the doctrine of the deposing power. The excuse is childish, and is really a terrible accusation against the Popes, for it declares that they sacrificed the welfare of the English Roman Catholics to an expression. But the excuse is not even true. The word "heretical" was not applied to the dogma of the deposing power but to the position "that princes which be excommunicated by the Pope may be deposed or murdered by their subjects." That princes may be excommunicated or deposed by the Pope is not denied or affirmed in the oath, for they are already so of whom the proposition speaks. All that is abjured is, that they may be, when excommunicated, deposed or murdered by their subjects. This objection to the oath was not the one taken by the Popes themselves, nor could a single expression justify the declaration of Paul V. that it contained *many* things contrary to faith and salvation, or the assertion of Urban that it wrested the sacred sceptre from his hands. Further, the excuse is contradicted by the uniform line of argument adopted by those who combated the lawfulness of the oath. Cardinal Bellarmine maintained that "the assertion that the Pope, as Pope and by divine right, has no temporal power, and cannot in any manner command secular persons or deprive them of their kingdoms and sovereignty though they deserve to be deprived of them, is not so much an opinion as a heresy."[1] Parsons, the active agent in obtaining the condemnation of the oath, wrote about this time from Rome: "About four or five months past a consultation was held of seven or eight of the most learned divines who could be chosen, to give their judgment on it [the oath].

[1] Butler, *Eng. Catholics*, 2, 191.

Their reasons are many, but all reduced to this, that it is of faith that the Pope hath authority to chastise princes on just grounds, and consequently, when it is called in question, it cannot be denied without renouncing our faith."[1] On another occasion, Parsons also wrote two letters to the arch-priest, Birkhead, respecting a similar matter. After the oath of James had been condemned by Paul, the English Roman Catholics, being desirous of giving to their government satisfactory assurance of their fidelity, drew up three forms of an oath of allegiance and sent them to Rome, hoping that one of them at least would be approved by the Pope. All three were rejected. The first of these letters is dated in August, 1608. In this Parsons writes: "There is a form sent hither of a new oath set down in divers fashions . . . a certain particular form of oath which, as I have not had time to confer [respecting] it with any learned men much less with his Holiness because the post is presently to depart, so I do assure myself that it will be misliked by many and most of all by his Holiness, that any forwardness should be showed to such oaths wherein either *tacite* or *expresse* his authority is impugned. And for your own part I would give you this counsel, that you be always the last in these matters and urge still his Holiness for particular direction."[2] In the second letter, dated in the following September, he says: "His Holiness's answer to the three forms of a new oath is, that he dislikes them all, or any other whatsoever that directly or indirectly may concern the authority of the See apostolic."[3]

While Paul V. was interfering with the civil duties of the subject in England, he was receiving a lesson respecting the just limits between the spiritual and secular jurisdictions from a minor European state. The Republic of Venice knew how to vindicate its temporal authority, and to defend

[1] Throckmorton, *First Letter*, 138.
[2] Dodd, *Church Hist.* 2, 485.   [3] *Ib.*

its interests from Papal encroachments. The Pope had demanded that certain ecclesiastics imprisoned for civil offences should be given up to him, and that two laws lately renewed by the Venetians, forbidding the alienation of immoveable property to the clergy, and rendering the erection of new churches dependent on the consent of the State, should be repealed. Both demands were refused by the Republic. On the 17th of April, 1606, Paul pronounced sentence of excommunication on the Doge, the senate, and all the constituted authorities, and ordered the clergy to publish the excommunication to their congregations, and to affix it on the doors of their churches. The Doge immediately announced to the clergy the determination of the government to uphold its temporal authority, and exhorted them to continue the performance of their sacred functions undeterred by the excommunication. The clergy did not hesitate for an instant, and not a single copy of the Papal sentence was hung up. Divine service went on in its accustomed manner, and the regular clergy acted in perfect unison with the secular. The new orders, the Jesuits, the Theatines, and the Capuchins, were the only exceptions to the general obedience. For this act of disaffection to the State, the Jesuits, who had left Venice on its rupture with the Pope, were not allowed to return, and Paul had to acquiesce in the exile of his faithful adherents. By the influence of the French and Spanish Kings an understanding between the Pope and the Republic was arrived at, both parties making concessions. The imprisoned ecclesiastics were delivered up to the Pope, and the laws of which he complained were suspended. On the other hand, Paul was obliged to revoke his excommunication, and offered to grant his absolution, but the Venetians refused to accept it, and insisted that the Papal censures were null and void from the beginning, and that consequently they stood in no need of absolution. At length it was agreed that the absolution should be pronounced in private and without the customary publicity. In this way a truce, which was more a show of reconciliation than a settlement of the disputed questions, was patched up between the parties. The quarrel had been observed with the greatest interest by the whole of Europe, and the general opinion was, that it had ended to the disadvantage of the Papal claims, inasmuch as the national clergy had sided with the secular government against the Pope, and Paul had been compelled by the inflexible resolution of the Venetians to abandon the Jesuits, whose only fault was implicit obedience to his commands.[1]

Of all the mistakes made by the English Roman Catholics—and they were many—the rejection of the oath proposed to them by James was the greatest.[2] By refusing it they acknowledged as an article of faith—for Paul had condemned the oath as contrary to salvation—that the Pope possessed the right of deposing princes, and of absolving subjects from their allegiance. They confirmed the general opinion that the profession of the Roman Catholic religion was inconsistent with the safety of the State, for men whose civil conduct was subject to the control of a foreign court could not be regarded as citizens. To the charge that their obedience was given to another than their native King, and that their loyalty and duty were placed at the mercy of that other, they could make no reply. When they were asked to

[1] The Jesuits were allowed to return to Venice fifty years later, during the pontificate of Alexander VII.

[2] "Of all the transactions which have taken place amongst the Catholics of this kingdom none has been so fatal in its consequences as the opposition made to the oath proposed to them by James.... The oath was condemned; the condemnation was acceded to by a subservient clergy, and the idea of an English Catholic has, from that time till within a few years, been inseparably associated with that of an abettor of the most dangerous of Ultramontane prejudices."—Throckmorton, *Second Letter*, 69.

give assurances of their allegiance to the sovereign of England and her constitution, their answer to their countrymen virtually was, " We are amongst you but not of you; your King is not our King, nor are your laws our laws; we accept the principles of the Papistic party; we owe obedience to the crowned priest at Rome, whose dictation as to our civil duties we are bound to follow, and we decline to deny his right to depose your King, to authorize the invasion of your territories, and to break the ties between you and us." Their error was a lamentable one. They had wandered far from the Catholicism of the old national Church, which, while it listened to the spiritual teaching of the first Christian bishop, knew how to give to Cæsar what was his due, and in its stead had accepted Popery, the new religion—new and strange to English ears—imported by the Jesuits and seminary priests, which placed in the hands of the Roman Pontiffs the temporal sword, and conferred on them supreme temporal power. Still, grievous as was their transgression, it is impossible wholly to withhold our commiseration from them. They acted from a mistaken sense of duty, and under the guidance of a misdirected conscience they preferred obedience to their supreme pastor to worldly ease, and sacrificed themselves to a tenet recommended by his authority. They were deceived by him in whom they trusted, who, under the false pretence that the oath of allegiance contained things contrary to faith and salvation, commanded them to disobey the laws of their country, and to stand aloof from their fellow-citizens. The truth was concealed from them, viz. that the Pope could make no claim upon his adherents which impaired the integrity of their civil allegiance.[1] This

---

[1] " I answer, that neither in virtue of the Vatican decrees, nor of any other decrees, nor of his supreme authority as head of the Christian Church, can the Pope make any claim upon those who adhere to his communion of such a nature as can impair the integrity of their civil

was the doctrine of the old Anglo-Catholic Church, of Lee, of Tunstall, of Gardiner, of Fisher, and of More.¹ The contrary doctrine would never have been received in England if the government of the Roman Catholics had been entrusted to native ordinaries and to a clergy educated at home; nor would the truths of their religion have been made the vehicle of opinions subversive of the authority of the State. But, unfortunately, the Popes were opposed to the institution of an English episcopacy, and by their emissaries, reared in Italian or Spanish schools, taught their communion that there was an uncontrolled temporal authority vested in them by divine appointment. The direct ecclesiastical government of the Roman Catholics was kept exclusively in the management of the Papal Court, and care was taken that those only should be appointed to its head who would best support Ultramontane principles. Political expediency, and not regard for the Church, determined the Popes to concentrate the whole influence of the body in the hands of one man. Their object was to secure a Roman Catholic successor to Elizabeth, whose death could not be far off.² For this purpose the office of arch-priest was established in 1598, and the appointment of bishops refused.³ In consequence of this policy, there was

allegiance."—Cardinal Manning, *The Vatican Decrees in their bearing on Civil Allegiance*, p. 41.

¹ "Both More and Fisher were willing enough to bind themselves to obedience to the law of succession defined by the statute which gave the crown to the issue of the union of Henry with Anne Boleyn, though they refused to swear that the marriage of Catherine had been null and void. . . . That is to say, they recognized the right of the three estates to give the Crown of England to whom they chose, legitimate or not, but did not recognize the right to define the spiritual questions of the sacrament of marriage and of the ecclesiastical supremacy. They must have held the opinion that the Church had power only over spiritual things, and not over civil and temporal matters."—Simpson's *Campion*, 56.

² Lingard, 6, 640, ed. 1849; Tierney's *Dodd*, 3, 47; Law's *Conflicts between the Jesuits and Seculars*, 60.

³ The name of arch-priest, or rural dean, has been used in the Church

no authority among the Roman Catholics of England to resist the civil ascendency of Rome, no bishops, irremovable except for a canonical crime, to guard their flocks against Ultramontane doctrines and mischievous bulls, such as those of Pius V., Gregory XIII., and Paul V. Their communion was governed by Roman dependants, appointed *ad nostrum et sedis apostolicæ beneplacitum*, whose powers were revocable at the pleasure of the Popes, and who, unlike bishops ordained to govern the particular Church entrusted to their care, possessed no authority beyond that contained in their commission. If any one of these creatures of a breath ventured to question the deposing power, he was immediately removed, as Blackwell was, and a more subservient instrument was appointed to his office ; or if subordinate priests dared to remember their duty as Englishmen, they were deprived of their faculties and reduced to poverty and want. This condition of affairs accounts for the slow movements of the English Roman Catholics in repudiating all civil dependence on the Papal Court, for those who desired to testify their allegiance were obliged to act in opposition to their ecclesiastical superiors and the admonitions of the Popes. In taking the step of freeing themselves from the temporal domination of Rome they were far behind the clergy and laity of other countries in Europe. The Venetians, as we have seen, adhered to the secular government in its contest with the Roman See, and their theologians condemned, as " seditious and sacrilegious," the maxims that Kings and States were subordinate to the Pope in civil matters, and that their subjects could be absolved from their obedience.[1] In France, the people and the clergy, from the

from early times. It was a new and strange title for one to whom was entrusted the government of the English and Scotch Roman Catholics.

[1] " Theologi Venetiani has propositiones tanquam seditiosas ac sacrilegas damnarunt ; Reges Regnorumque leges Pontifici in civilibus

time of Boniface VIII. and Philip le Bel, never wavered in the support of the sovereign against the temporal pretensions of the Papal Court. In 1614, the Commons in the States General urged and pressed that an oath of allegiance, declaring that the King had no superior but God, and that no power on earth had the right of dispensing with the obedience of the subject, should be imposed on all classes. In 1626, the sacred faculty of the University of Paris censured a treatise of the Jesuit, Sanctarellus, in which it was laid down that the Pope could inflict temporal punishment on sovereigns, and free their subjects from their obedience, and declared that these doctrines were "new, false, erroneous, and contrary to the Word of God."[1] The other faculties, and the Universities of Toulouse, Valence, Bordeaux, Poitiers, Caen, Rheims, and Bourges, concurred in this censure. In 1680, sixty doctors of the same sacred faculty at Paris gave it as their opinion that the English oath of allegiance might be taken by English Catholics with a safe conscience.[2] In 1682, the Gallican clergy subscribed unanimously the four articles of their celebrated Declaration. The first article resolved " that the power which Jesus Christ had given to St. Peter and his successors related only to spiritual things, and to those which concern salvation, and not to things civil and temporal. Kings and princes, therefore, are not, in temporals, subject to any ecclesiastical power,

subesse, vassallos Regum ab obedientia civili certis casibus eximi posse, aut in suos principes concitari."—Caron, *Remonstrantia Hibernorum*, pars 1, c. 6. s. 1.

[1] " Facultas improbavit et damnavit doctrinam, his propositionibus ... contentam, tanquam novam, falsam, erroneam, verbo Dei contrariam, Pontificiæ dignitati odium conciliantem, schismati occasionem præbentem, supremæ Regum authoritati, a Deo solo dependenti, derogantem, &c."—*Ib.* 1, c. 6, s. 2.

[2] *Answer of the Sacred Faculty of Divinity at Paris to the Queries proposed by the English Catholics*, 1789. Butler, *English Catholics*, 1, Appd.

either directly or indirectly, neither by the authority of the Keys can they be deposed, or their subjects freed from their faith, obedience, or oath of allegiance." This doctrine is now universally received, and was solemnly recognized by the Universities of Louvain, Douay, Paris, Alcala, Valladolid, and Salamanca, in 1788 and 1789. A few years later, in the beginning of the present century, the Pope himself, Pius VII., in his negotiations with the first Napoleon, expressed his willingness to acquiesce in the subscription of this article by the French clergy.[1] The growth of opinion abroad, unfavourable to the Papal pretensions, had an effect, though late, on the English Roman Catholics. At last they also awoke to a sense of independence, and cast off for ever their temporal dependence on the Roman Court. They too claimed the right of disclaiming the deposing power, a disclaimer which the Popes had long tolerated in France, in Venice, and many parts of Germany. In 1780, by an oath which was universally taken by them, and which had been approved by the four English Vicars Apostolic,[2] they solemnly renounced both the deposing and the absolving power, "without even consulting Rome, or regarding its former vain pretensions and unchristian condemnation."[3] The oath which the whole body then took, for the Papistic party had long disappeared, contained in it the clause which had been three times condemned by Paul V., by Urban VIII., and, as we shall see, by Innocent X.

The refusal of the Roman Catholics to profess their adhesion to the established government of their country, irrespective of external dictation, and their resolution to stand apart from its constitution, drew the attention of the English people to two anti-social tenets which were attributed to them, and which increased the distrust which their political

[1] Butler, *English Catholics*, 2, 223. [2] *Ib.* 3, 294, 5.
[3] Throckmorton, *Second Letter*, 71.

action had inspired. It was well known before the discovery of the Gunpowder Plot that the Jesuits, and those who were under their influence, constantly practised equivocation and mental reservation when interrogated on charges of treason. Robert Southwell,[1] a Jesuit, at his trial during the late Queen's reign, had justified equivocation even upon oath. The practice was also acknowledged and justified by Gerard, Strange, Andrews, and others who were examined expressly on the subject.[2] To guard against this doctrine, the oath of allegiance contained in its concluding section a declaration that the deponent took it "without any equivocation or mental evasion or secret reservation whatsoever." Garnet, the superior of the English Jesuits, before his trial for complicity in the Gunpowder Plot, avowed his belief that, "in cases where it becomes necessary to an individual, for his defence, or for avoiding any injustice or loss, or for obtaining any important advantage, without danger or mischief to any other person, there equivocation is lawful."[3] After his trial, he declared: "that in all cases where simple equivocation was allowable, it was lawful, if necessary, to confirm it by an oath. This I acknowledge to be according to my opinion, and the opinion of the schoolmen; and our reason is, for that in cases of lawful equivocation, the speech by equivocation being saved from a lie, the same speech may be, without perjury, confirmed by an oath, or by any other usual way, though it were by receiving the sacrament, if just necessity so requires."[4] During the whole inquiry Garnet acted in strict consistency

[1] The poet.

[2] Jardine, in preface to *A Treatise of Equivocation*. Strange, in his examination, said that he had never seen a work on equivocation, but that he knew Catholics held it lawful. Andrews stated that equivocation was lawful where the right of the questioner was denied.—*State Papers, Domestic*, 1603-10, 270, 273.

[3] Jardine, *Gunpowder Plot*, 233.

[4] *Ib.* 234.

with these principles, " never confessing any fact until it was proved against him, and never hesitating to declare palpable falsehoods respecting matters which tended to inculpate himself, and to affirm them by the most solemn oaths and protestations."[1] Another of the conspirators, Francis Tresham, in whose desk was found a *Treatise of Equivocation*, with its title altered, in Garnet's handwriting, to *A Treatise against Lying and Dissimulation*,[2] and with the *imprimatur* of the arch-priest attached at the end,[3] died with a lie in his mouth. A few hours before his death, Tresham signed a paper declaring, among other things, upon his salvation, that he had not seen Garnet for sixteen years; though Garnet himself admitted that Tresham had been with him continually until a few days before the discovery of the plot. At Garnet's trial this document was produced; and he was asked, what interpretation he put on Tresham's dying declaration? Garnet answered:—"It may be, my lord, he meant to

---

[1] *Ib.* 237. Lingard says: " By seeking shelter under equivocation he had deprived himself of the protection which the truth might have afforded him."

[2] This copy is now in the Bodleian Library. Its original title was: "*A Treatise of Equivocation; wherein is largely discussed the question whether a Catholic or any other person, before a magistrate, being demanded upon his oath whether a priest were in such a place, may, notwithstanding his perfect knowledge to the contrary, without perjury and securely in conscience, answer 'No'; with this secret meaning reserved in his mind, that he was not there so that any man is bound to detect it.*" The title was altered by Garnet into: "*A Treatise against Lying and Fraudulent Dissimulation; newly overseen by the author, and published for the defence of Innocency and the Instruction of Ignorants.*" The treatise was reprinted by Mr. Jardine in 1851, with a preface and notes showing the interpolations and deletions of Garnet.

[3] "Tractatus iste valde doctus et vere pius et Catholicus est. Certe, S. Scripturarum, patrum, doctorum, scholasticorum, canonistarum, et optimarum rationum præsidiis plenissime firmat æquitatem æquivocationis. Ideoque dignissimus est qui typis propagetur ad consolationem afflictorum Catholicorum et omnium piorum instructionem. Ita censeo, Georgius Blackwellus, archi-presbyter Angliæ et Protonotarius Apostolicus."

equivocate."[1] These occurrences generated the suspicion that Roman Catholics approved the doctrine of equivocation and mental reservation, and that no reliance could be placed on their most solemn asseverations. This suspicion was converted into belief by the innumerable treatises published abroad by foreign Jesuits, who taught how to evade the laws of God by a cunning use of words whilst conduct remained unaltered, and, by their fantastic and flagitious interpretations, strove to overthrow the code of Christian ethics and to corrupt the morality of the world.[2]

The belief in the Papal power of deposing Kings was a political danger, but the doctrine of equivocation and mental reservation was more odious, and even more pernicious. It struck at the very foundations of social intercourse, and broke down and confounded the distinction between truth and falsehood. Instead of fair and open dealing between man and man, it instructed each to resort to a train of subtle reasoning, for the purpose of deceiving and getting the better of the other. Every individual was justified in violating truth where, in his own fallible judgment, he was not bound to speak it. No immutable standard of right and wrong existed, but each might, at his own time, and for his own benefit, invest the false with the colour of the true. On the most solemn occasions, even if sanctified by the reception of the sacrament, the speaker might give to his words an arbitrary meaning, framed at his own will, and contrary to that which the rest of the world attached to them. Among all the perversions of a debased ingenuity, there was not one more demoralizing or more mischievous, for it nullified the

[1] *State Trials*, 2, 257.
[2] " Lord, who shall dwell in thy tabernacle or who shall rest upon thy holy hill? Even he that . . . speaketh the truth from his heart . . . that hath used no deceit in his tongue . . . he that sweareth unto his neighbour and disappointeth him not, *though it were to his own hindrance.*"—Psalm xv.

commandment of God, and destroyed the mutual confidence upon which society rests, while at the same time it tended to paralyze and circumvent by stratagem the justice of man.

The second anti-social tenet imputed to the Roman Catholics was, that they held it to be lawful in itself, or, by the dispensation of the Pope, to violate promises and oaths made to heretics. We are informed by many writers that such a doctrine was never sanctioned by the Roman Catholic Church. But this statement, however true it may be, is really not pertinent to the matter. The true question is, whether the governors and ministers of that Church, who represented it to outsiders, put forward and acted on this maxim, and consequently, whether the English people had sufficient grounds for believing that it was generally held by Roman Catholics? The only answer to this question is, that they had ample grounds. The Popes claimed, and exercised continually, the right of absolving all persons, princes or private individuals, from their obligations, and of dispensing with vows, oaths, and promises. Gregory VII. released all those who were bound by fealty or oath to excommunicated princes. Innocent III. laid it down that the Apostolic See must be always understood to be excepted in every kind of oath. The same Pontiff asserted that "those are not to be called oaths but perjuries, which are taken against the advantage of the ecclesiastical body." It is easy to see how much such maxims might be abused, but direct facts and words are not wanting. Urban VI. issued a solemn and general declaration against keeping faith with heretics and schismatics, and pronounced compacts made with them to be null and void, although entered into with them before they had lapsed into heresy or schism.[1] " We have lately heard,"

[1] "Ligas cum Hæreticis, quacunque firmitate roboratas, esse nullas."—Rymer, 7, 352. "Papa ad Imperatorem contra ligas cum Hæretiois."—Ib. 392.

writes that Pope, " that the King of Bohemia and his deceased father the Emperor have, either together or successively, made confederations, connexions, leagues, and conventions, with divers kings, princes, dukes, nobles, and others, and that some of these latter were at the time, or afterwards became, schismatics or heretics. Seeing that such confederations, connexions, leagues, and conventions, are rash, illegal, and null and void by the law, even though strengthened by an oath, by pledged faith, by apostolical confirmation, or by any other means whatsoever,[1] the said King and others who may have joined with him in such compacts are absolutely discharged from their performance, and are bound not to observe them. Nay, the said King is obliged, by his imperial office, and by his duty to the Church, to persecute to the utmost of his power such heretics and schismatics, since all communion with them is dangerous, and there ought not to be any participation of light with darkness, or of Christ with Belial."[2]

In 1416 occurred the ever memorable case of John Huss. In the Council of Constance, the safe conduct granted by the Emperor Sigismund to Huss, was violated, on the ground that he was a heretic. After his execution, a decree was issued by the Council that no safe conduct should be available against the jurisdiction of the Church in cases of heretical pravity. The genuineness of this decree has been questioned, but the Tridentine fathers entertained no doubt of its existence. For they proclaimed, in their eighteenth session, 1562, a safe conduct to the Protestants, in which they promised

[1] " Etiam si forent juramento vel fide data firmatæ, aut confirmatione Apostolica vel quacunque firmitate alia roboratæ."

[2] " Quinimo ipse rex hujusmodi schismaticos et hæreticos, ratione imperii ad quod electus et per nos approbatus existit, in favorem Sanctæ Romanæ ac universalis ecclesiæ, cujus est advocatus, pro posse persequi tenetur, quodque omnis communio cum talibus hæreticis seu schismaticis nimis periculosa existit, cum nulla sit prorsus nec esse debeat participatio lucis ad tenebras aut Christi ad Belial."

not to avail themselves, for this time, of any law, statute, or canon of any Council, especially Constance, or that of Sens, for the violation of their pledge.[1] At the Diet of Worms, a party, approving that which was done at the Council of Constance in the case of John Huss, contended that faith ought not to be kept with Luther, who attended that assembly under the protection of the Emperor's safe conduct.[2] Cardinal Allen taught, that the heresy of a master dissolved the bonds of obedience on the part of a servant, and that that of a father loosed the ties of nature, and put an end to his authority over his children.[3] In 1647, the English Parliament proposed to repeal the penal laws and to grant liberty of conscience to the Roman Catholics, provided they showed "that there was no inconsistency in their religion with the civil government of the kingdom."[4] Accordingly, a number of Roman Catholic noblemen and gentlemen, with several of their clergy, signed the negative of a formulary containing three propositions. One of these propositions was, "that it is lawful in itself, or by the dispensation of the Pope, to violate a promise or oath made to a heretic." The subscription to the formulary was condemned at Rome, without specifying any particular article, so that it was

[1] The words of the Tridentine safe-conduct are :—" Insuper, omni fraude et dolo exclusis, vera et bona fide promittit [sancta synodus] ipsam synodum nullam vel manifeste vel occulte occasionem quæsituram, aut aliqua auctoritate, potentia, jure vel statuto, privilegio legum, vel canonum, aut quorumcunque conciliorum, præsertim Constantiensis et Senensis, quacunque forma verborum expressa, in aliquod hujus fidei publicæ et plenissimæ assecurationis, ac publicæ et liberæ audientiæ, ipsis per ipsam synodum concessæ, præjudicium quovis modo usuram aut quemquam uti permissuram, quibus in hac parte pro hac vice deroget." In a note is given a reference to " Concil. Constantien. sess. 19 in cap. Quod non obstantibus salvis conductibus."— *Canones et Decreta Concilii Tridentini*, Romæ, 1845.
[2] Sarpi, *Hist. of the Council of Trent*, book 1, sub ann. 1521.
[3] Throckmorton, *First Letter*, 113.
[4] This transaction will be related at length in the next chapter.

naturally concluded that every proposition in the formulary
was affirmed, and that each was a point of the Roman
Catholic creed. It is a mistake to say that the belief, that
Roman Catholics held this tenet, was a prejudice confined to
the vulgar. It was entertained by the wisest men and the
coolest heads in the country. Ninety years after the time
we are now speaking of, the Apostle of Toleration excluded
Roman Catholics from its benefits on account of two opinions
attributed to them: one was, "that excommunicated princes
might be deposed by the Pope"—an opinion which their
communion had adopted by their rejection of the oath of
allegiance. The other was, "that faith was not to be kept
with heretics." Locke's words are: "We cannot find any
sect that teaches expressly and openly that men are not
obliged to keep their promise; that princes may be dethroned
by those that differ from them in religion; or that the dominion of all things belongs only to themselves. For these
things, proposed thus nakedly and plainly, would soon draw
on them the eye and hand of the magistrate, and awaken all
the care of the commonwealth to a watchfulness against the
spreading of so dangerous an evil. But, nevertheless, we
find those that say the same things in other words. What
else do they mean who teach that 'faith is not to be kept
with heretics'? Their meaning forsooth is, that the
privilege of breaking faith belongs unto themselves, for
they declare all that are not of their communion to be
heretics, or at least may declare them so whensoever they
think fit. What can be the meaning of their asserting
'that Kings excommunicated forfeit their crowns and
kingdoms'? It is evident that they thereby arrogate
unto themselves the power of Kings, because they challenge the power of excommunication as the peculiar
right of their hierarchy. . . . These, therefore, and
the like, who attribute unto the faithful, the religious,

and orthodox, that is, in plain terms, unto themselves any peculiar privilege or power above other mortals in civil governments, or who, upon pretence of religion, do challenge any manner of authority over such as are not associated with them in their ecclesiastical communion; I say, these have no right to be tolerated by the magistrate, as neither those that will not own and teach the duty of tolerating all men in matters of mere religion. For what do all these and the like doctrines signify, but that they may, and are ready, upon any occasion, to seize the government and possess themselves of the estates and fortunes of their fellow-subjects, and they only ask leave to be tolerated by the magistrate so long, until they find themselves strong enough to effect it?"[1] By their oath of 1780, the Roman Catholics repudiated this tenet also : " I do swear that I do reject and detest . . . and also that unchristian and impious principle that no faith is to be kept with heretics."

The original causes of the enactment of the penal laws were three in number ; the long and terrible struggle against the Popes and the Kings of Spain, the introduction by the Jesuits and seminary priests of a new faith which mixed up the truths of religion with treasonable designs, and the perpetual plots and conspiracies of the Papistic party at home. In all these transactions the Popes were the predominant actors and disposers, for with a word they might have restrained the Jesuits and seminarists from preaching an impure mixture of religion and disaffection, and have put an end to domestic conspiracies in favour of invasion and assassination. Papal advocates have filled Europe with their cries against the barbarity of the penal laws, while they have maintained a judicious silence respecting the crimes of the Roman Pontiffs against England. The case between the Popes and the English Government has seldom been fairly

[1] Locke, *First Letter on Toleration.*

put. A simple statement will clear the ground and enable us to form an impartial judgment on the action of both parties. Let it be granted on the one hand—the admission is difficult in the case of the Vicars of Him who declared that His kingdom was not of this world—that the Popes were justified in using every means for the restoration of their religion in England; that for this purpose they were bound to bring into play all the material resources at their disposal, to draw the temporal sword, and to resort to invasions, to the preaching of crusades, the encouragement of conspiracies, and the fomentation of civil wars. On the other hand let us consider the position of England and of her government. It is almost impossible for us at the present day to conceive the universal dread with which the gigantic power of Philip II. was regarded by his contemporaries. His hand was everywhere, in Germany, Italy, France, Spain, Portugal, and the New World. The Popes still exercised an immense influence in the councils of Europe, and they were united with the Spanish King in an endeavour to extirpate the Protestant religion, to conquer England and to subject her to foreign dictation. The English people were under no mistake respecting the nature of the contest which had been forced upon them. They rightly regarded it as a struggle of life and death which involved the very existence of their country as an independent nation, and as a war in defence of their right to worship God according to their conscience. If the Popes were right all through the long series of their aggressions undertaken for the restoration of their faith, surely the English people were also right in preserving their own and in repelling those attacks, and were justified in defending their homes, their religion, and their freedom, by every means in their power, even by statutes directed against conversions to a political faith which was not the Catholic faith, and against the preaching by foreign emissaries of doctrines subversive of their constitution.

The rejection of the oath of allegiance by the Roman Catholics and their adoption of the politico-religious sentiments of the Papistic party, put the seal on the continuance of the penal statutes. For, as Bishop Stillingfleet observes, "laws originally made upon the account of acknowledged treasonable practices, do continue just upon all those who do not give sufficient security against the principles leading to those practices."[1] A hundred and seventy years were to elapse before any relaxation of these statutes was obtained. No details are required to teach us what the Roman Catholics of England must have suffered during this long interval from the severity of the laws themselves, the insolent contumely of the underlings engaged in carrying them out, and above all from the contemptuous dislike of their fellow-citizens. For undoubtedly the general belief that Roman Catholics held the two tenets—that equivocation and mental reservation were lawful, and that faith was not to be kept with heretics—aggravated greatly the miseries of their condition. Men began to think that they were unfit for human society and incapable of its duties, a judgment not too harsh if, in addition to their political sentiments, they had in reality entertained such opinions. During this period of a hundred and seventy years, three opportunities offered themselves to the Roman Catholics of obtaining a repeal of the penal laws. One was defeated by the obstinacy of Innocent X., who clung to the phantom of the deposing power; one was wrecked by dissensions among themselves; and the third was thrown away by the reckless folly of James II. Though the sufferings of the Roman Catholics during the long night of their depression were very great, they were mild in comparison with the afflictions of the

[1] *Answer to Cressy*, p. 344.

Reformed in Roman Catholic countries. The comparison of the treatment which the former experienced in England with the fate of the Protestants abroad illustrates well the difference between restrictions imposed from political motives and the cruelties inflicted in the name of religion. The penal laws in England had been enacted to guard against real dangers,[1] but no political crimes were urged against the Protestants in many of those kingdoms where they were persecuted with a ferocity which was aimed at their destruction. The Roman Catholics of England were not hunted and exterminated like wild beasts as the Protestants were in Spain and Italy. They were not burned and buried alive by thousands as the Reformed were in the Netherlands. They were not driven from their country in shoals as the Protestants were from many parts of Germany. In 1627 the Emperor Ferdinand II. proclaimed that he would tolerate no one of what rank soever in the kingdom of Bohemia who did not agree with himself and the apostolic Church in the true faith.[2] In Bavaria all persons adhering to the Reformed religion were compelled to sell their property and to quit the country.[3] As late as 1731, 30,000 Protestants—it is almost incredible that such an outrage on humanity should have occurred in the eighteenth century—were driven into exile from Salzburg. There were no massacres of Roman Catholics in England such as overtook the Protestants in France and Savoy. Their community was

[1] "For when we consider on the one side, what we know ourselves concerning the laws made of later years with the occasions of them . . . as well against us that are priests, as also against other Catholics of the laity, and do find on the other side, what practices, under the pretence of religion, have been set on foot for the utter subversion both of the Queen and of the kingdom, it may in our opinions be rather wondered, that so many Catholics of both sorts are left alive in the realm to speak of the Catholic faith, than that the State hath proceeded with us from time to time as it hath done."—*Important Considerations.*

[2] Ranke, 2, 110. [3] *Ibid.* 1, 385.

not delivered up to a cold-blooded military execution, as the Protestants were in France and Austria by the dragonnades, nor were their homes made the scenes of torture, rape, and death, as happened in the former country on the revocation of the Edict of Nantes.[1] There were no such sights witnessed in England as the long-continued butchery of Eperies in Hungary in 1687, where for nine months thirty executioners obeyed the orders of Antonio Caraffa, cousin of the Papal nuncio, and put to death crowds of the Reformed with such hideous atrocities that the historian, Michiels, is obliged to apologise for mentioning them.[2] If a comparison be instituted between the sufferings of the Roman Catholics in England and the tortures inflicted upon the Protestants in Roman Catholic kingdoms, the former, great as they were, sink almost into insignificance.

[1] "Tout était en fait permis aux soldats sauf le viol et le meurtre, et encore cette restriction ne fut-elle toujours respectée ; d'ailleurs beaucoup de malheureux moururent ou demeurèrent estropiés des suites des traitements qu'ils avaient subis, et les tortures obscenes infligées aux femmes ne différaient guère du dernier outrage, que par une perversité plus raffinée."—Martin, *Histoire de France.* "Mais le viol était defendu ; quelle moquerie ; on ne punit personne même quand il fut suivi de meurtre."—Michelet.

[2] "Grâce aux livres des exécuteurs, grâce aux lettres de Léopold, nous savons les petits moyens qui opèrent ces œuvres pieux. Des ministres brulés vif a feu lent, des femmes empalées au fer rouge, des troupeaux d'hommes vendus aux galères turques et venetiennes, voila ce qui fit le miracle. Les Hongrois trouvèrent ces arguments des Jesuites irresistibles. Tout ce qui ne s'enfuit pas du pays fut touché et sentit la grace."—Michelet, *Louis XIV. et la Revocation de l'Edit de Nantes.*

CHAPTER VI

FROM THE ACCESSION OF CHARLES I TO THE REVOLUTION OF 1688

CHAPTER VI

CHARLES succeeded to the throne in the early part of 1625. A few months after his accession he was married to Henrietta of France. By the treaty of marriage a large household of French servants was to be allowed to the Queen. Dissensions and domestic feuds arose between Charles and his wife which were encouraged by the Queen's foreign attendants. From the moment of her arrival in England, Henrietta had taken a dislike to the country and her surroundings. She wrote again and again to her mother, expressing her desire to return to France, or at least to be able to communicate personally to her circumstances which she did not dare to commit to writing or to mention to a third person.[1] Charles was persuaded that the discontent of his wife was fomented by her French servants, and that they were endeavouring to "steal away his wife," or secretly plotting with the dissatisfied portion of his subjects.[2] His patience was soon exhausted, and in July, 1626, he dismissed the whole of the French

---

[1] "La regina [Inglese] ogni dì scriveva di voler tornare in Francia, o per lo meno vedersi con sua madre, per communicarle delle particolarità non communicabili, nè alla penna nè a terza persona."—Extract from the *Life of Urban VIII., Barberini MS.*, given by Tierney in Appd., Dodd, 5.

[2] "I writ to you by Ned Clarke that I thought I would have cause enough in a short time to put away the Monsieurs, either by attempting to steal away my wife or by making plots with my own subjects.... Yet seeing daily the maliciousness of the Monsieurs by making and

attendants, both male and female. The dismissal was resented by the King of France who sent over an ambassador extraordinary to settle the matter. It was arranged that a new establishment should be formed for Henrietta, consisting partly of French and partly of English servants, and harmony was restored between Charles and his Queen.

The mischievous activity of the Papal Court was immediately awakened by this trifling dispute, and another instance of its perpetual and implacable hostility to England was exhibited. Urban VIII. thought that there was a favourable opportunity for making an attack upon that country. The occasion was well chosen. In March, 1626, a peace had been suddenly proclaimed between France and Spain. In Germany, the Protestants had just been defeated at the battle of Lutter by the Imperialists under Tilly, and the whole of that country lay at the mercy of the Emperor, Ferdinand II. The very existence of Protestantism in Germany was at stake, while the Emperor, the champion of Catholicism, was freed from fear of the Turk by the dispute of the latter with the King of Persia. Urban lost no time. Taking advantage of the differences between the English and French courts respecting the establishment of Henrietta, he wrote to the Kings of France and Spain, exhorting them to arm in defence of God, and to unite in chastising the insolence of England whose impiety called to heaven for vengeance.[1] He also wrote to the Queen Mother, Marie de Medicis, to Richélieu, and others in France, and by his nuncio, Spada, he opened communications with the Spanish Court. In consequence of these exhortations, a negotiation

fomenting the discontentements in my wife, I could tarry no longer from advertising of you that I mean to seek for no other grounds to cashier my Monsieurs."—The King to the Duke of Buckingham, *Hardwicke State Papers*, 2, 2.

[1] Tierney's *Dodd*, 5, 163.

for an offensive alliance between the two kingdoms was secretly opened, and a treaty, drawn up by Richélieu and approved by Olivares, was signed on the 20th of April, 1627. The Spaniards agreed to commence the attack in the same year, while the French, having but few vessels ready, engaged to begin their armaments at once, to open their ports to Spanish war-ships, and to join the Spaniards in the following spring. The Spanish ambassador also undertook, that towards the end of July or beginning of August the Spanish fleet should be ready to invest England and Ireland, the Pope having asserted that he possessed a just title to the latter country on the ground that it was under the direct dominion of the Roman See. It was also proposed to put an end to the naval superiority of England and Holland by means of a general combination and the formation of an armed company, under the protection of which a direct communication between the Baltic, Flanders, France, Spain, and Italy, might be maintained without the participation of the Protestant maritime Powers. While France and Spain were thus secretly devising an attack on England, they were themselves surprised by an attack from that country. In July, 1627, Buckingham appeared on the coast of France with a powerful fleet, and occupied the Island of Rhé.[1]

In the early part of the reign of Charles, the English Roman Catholics were divided on two questions, the necessity of having an episcopal government, and the lawfulness of taking the oath of allegiance. Dissensions had arisen respecting the former question between the secular and regular clergy which almost amounted to a schism, and many of the most learned of both the clergy and laity were in favour of taking the oath of allegiance. For the purpose

[1] The history of this transaction is to be found in Ranke, 2, 113-118, and in a long extract from the *Life of Urban VIII.*, Tierney's *Dodd*, Append. vol. 5.

of settling the disputes respecting an episcopacy, and obtaining information as to the condition of the Roman Catholics, Urban despatched an accredited agent, Father Leander, into England in the latter end of 1633. This ecclesiastic was an Englishman born, and, during his stay in this country, passed under the name of Jones, that of his family, and of Scudamore or Skidmore. He had been educated at Oxford, and had obtained a fellowship at St. John's College. Having been converted and entered the Benedictine order, he was appointed Professor of Hebrew at Douay, from which place he addressed a petition to the King asking permission to visit England in order to see his friends and kindred.[1] His request was granted, and he arrived in London in the spring of 1634. His letters from England to his superiors at Rome are full of good sense, moderation, and real piety. If the measures of conciliation which he recommended had been adopted by the Papal Court, the condition of the English Roman Catholics would soon have been changed for the better, at least he himself and the leading men among them had no doubt that such would have been the case. Father Leander's first letter is addressed to Cardinal Bentivoglio, and is dated the 22nd of July, 1634.

After pointing out the advantages he enjoyed as being a native of England and on the spot, he says, "Two matters are now much debated among the Catholics here, the oath of allegiance, and the appointment of one or more English bishops. Two books have lately been published by Catholics on the oath, one printed by permission of the King,[2] the other in manuscript, but passed from hand to hand in numerous copies.[3] The latter, being against the oath, has

---

[1] Clarendon, *State Papers*, 1, 72.

[2] The title of this book was *A Pattern of Christian Loyalty*, by William Howard.

[3] By Edward Courteney, a Jesuit. This treatise supported the

given great dissatisfaction to the King from some reprehensible passages in it, and appears to me to be a poor production.¹ It is to be feared that the appearance of these books will renew the controversy respecting the oath to the great injury of the Catholics. The King himself is most kindly disposed to that body and to our lord the Pope, but the powerful party of the Puritans is displeased with his clemency and that of his government towards us. Hence we may expect fresh tribulations from this dispute respecting the oath. I have taken counsel with some wise, prudent, and moderate noblemen of our persuasion, as to what should be suggested to his Holiness, and what action he should take to avert the tempest and confirm the King in his kind treatment. Here is what they advise. The King declares that the only demand he makes in the oath is a profession of that civil and natural obedience which is due from subjects, and that he does not wish the spiritual authority of his Holiness to be abjured. He is willing to admit any explanation of its words, however subtle, in order that its taking might be rendered easier to the conscience of the Catholics. All these considerations make it evident that the oath, as set forth and declared by the Legislature, is very different from what it was thought to be when the Pope first condemned it. We expect, therefore, that his Holiness will moderate in some respects the Papal prohibitions. This is due both to the English Catholics, who have suffered more in defence of the Papal authority than any other people, and also to the King, who regards the Pope with veneration, and deserves the first advances in kindness from him. The holy Pontiff writes to pagan Kings in India and to schismatic

deposing power, and the authority of the Pope to make war, invade countries, &c.—Clarendon, *State Papers*, 1, 258.
¹ " Idem scriptor videtur mihi, nam totum ejus opusculum diligenter expendi, causam imbecilliter pugnare."

sovereigns in Abyssinia, nor does he wait until they first write to him; why should not his Holiness address equally kind letters to our King? His Holiness tolerates the rejection of his deposing power, which is the only matter in the oath of allegiance, in the kingdom of France. For do not all the Gallican bishops, noblemen, and the whole people, hold it as an indisputable dogma, that their King cannot be deposed for any cause by any power under heaven? If his Holiness tolerates these things in France, why should he not tolerate the same belief in England, a country which requires her wounds to be touched with a very gentle hand? Why should his Holiness not write a letter to our King to the following effect:—That he thanked him for his benign treatment of the Catholics, and exhorted him to continue it; that he considered him, and should always consider him, as the true and legitimate sovereign of his kingdoms, and treat him with the same regard and affection with which he treated the Kings of France and of Spain; that henceforth our King should be as safe as those sovereigns from the censures and denunciations of the Papal See? His Holiness might also express his regret that certain books had been published respecting the oath, and his determination to prohibit them for the future. Finally, to show his wish for a reconciliation with his Majesty, he might suspend his own decree and those of his predecessors against the oath, leaving it as it stood before any condemnation of it had emanated from Rome. These are the suggestions of some of the wisest and most intelligent Englishmen with whom I have consulted, and I myself with great respect join in the suggestions, as I believe that if they were attended to, they would be followed by the happiest consequences.'"[1]

In November of the same year, Father Leander addressed

[1] Clarendon, *State Papers*, 1, 129. The rest of the letter is taken up with the appointment of an English episcopacy.

a letter to the Pope himself, in which he deprecated the circulation of books in England which extolled immoderately the authority of Rome, and contained seditious propositions. He recommended the Pope to forbid under the heaviest penalties the publication of such treatises before and until they were examined and approved at Rome.[1]

The next letter is in December, and is addressed to Cardinal Barberini, the " protector of England " at the Papal Court. In this Leander advises "the most eminent fathers " to have recourse to measures of kindness and conciliation. " Permit me to speak with all freedom. What have you hitherto obtained by following the counsels of those who have recommended violent proceedings, and have extorted prohibitory decrees against the oath, to the great exasperation of our Kings, who are lost in astonishment that what is allowed in the Catholic kingdom of France is condemned here? What conclusion can our governors here come to, but that such decrees countenance crime, and justify those who attempted, by the Gunpowder Plot, the destruction of the King and of the whole nobility, inasmuch as they prevent the condemnation of the principles upon which those wicked men acted?[2] I know this is not a just inference, but

[1] *Ib.* 169.

[2] Charles Butler translates these sentences as follows:—" What else have our nobility and leading men gained by these decrees, than its being believed, that the doctrines, on which they are founded, countenanced the wicked men engaged in the gunpowder conspiracy, and excuse their attempt to destroy the sovereign and all the nobility, inasmuch as such doctrines prohibit the condemnation of the principles on which those men relied to justify their attempt? I know that this cannot be justly inferred, but I also know that our countrymen make the inference. If they had seen, that the Pope had published any decree which condemned both that detestable attempt and the principles on which it was endeavoured to be justified, they would have passed a very different judgment on that most unfortunate deed—they would have thought that it proceeded wholly from the criminality of the persons engaged in it, and not from the doctrines of the Catholic teachers."—*English Catholics,* 2, 318.

I also know that it is the inference which the English draw. If his Holiness had issued a sentence condemning that detestable wickedness and the principles which gave rise to it, the opinion of Englishmen would have been very different. They would have concluded that it proceeded from the guilt of individuals and not from the doctrines of Catholic teachers. Heretofore, you have put yourselves in the hands of advisers who, unacquainted with the true spirit of religion, have invoked the thunders of excommunication and the lightnings of prohibitions against the kingdom of England. The only result of this is, that calamity after calamity has overwhelmed the Catholics. Give, at last, some credence to those who counsel the paths of peace, and who believe that the Lord manifests himself, not in the storm but in the gentle breeze, not in wrath but in the spirit of meekness. I am convinced that, if you do so, we shall obtain from the King and his government much more within the short space of a few months than the advocates of violence have obtained during many long years."[1]

Father Leander enclosed in this letter an elaborate examination of the oath of allegiance, and makes the remark, that the oath was understood in England in a very different sense from that which those who procured from the Popes its condemnation, attached to it; that nothing was required by it but a profession of that civil obedience which was due to the sovereign by the Word of God, the law of nature, and the ancient enactments of the realm. He concludes by again recommending the suggestion of "the many prudent and pious Catholics," viz. that the Pope should suspend the condemnation of the oath, and gives instances of such suspensions in other cases.

We have seen that it was the wish of the wisest and most

[1] Clarendon, *State Papers*, 185.

moderate of the English Roman Catholics that the Pope should open a friendly communication with the King respecting the oath of allegiance. Father Leander drew up a draft of a letter from the Pope to Charles, and appears to have sent it to Rome. Its effect was as follows: "Hearing of your Majesty's clemency to your Catholic subjects, and entertaining a fatherly regard for your safety and well-being, we have resolved to send you a gracious and loving letter, that you may be encouraged to proceed still farther in the way of charity, and continue to extend to the Catholics your royal protection. Inasmuch as we have heard that you are well-disposed to our person, we regret that you have received annoyance, in the matter of the oath of allegiance, from the books written for and against the same. For the future, we shall give strict orders that no such publications be issued, and we shall make it manifest that those things which justly displease you displease us also. Be not troubled that our predecessors have condemned the oath. That was not done through any disrespect to your royal authority, but because learned men were persuaded that it contained many things contrary to faith. Now that we know that your Majesty understands it in a different sense, which sense it may bear if its words be liberally interpreted, and that it refers, not to a denial of our spiritual power, but to the safety of your person and kingdom, we no longer condemn the oath in the sense given to it by your Majesty. We exhort you, in return for our indulgence, to declare by a public edict the sense of the oath which we have been informed you attach to it, in order that all men may understand that there is nothing in it contrary to faith, nothing disrespectful to ourselves or to our spiritual authority, and that it concerns only your security and honour against presumptuous or unfaithful subjects. We shall never cease to secure your safety by every means in our power, and whatever you require to that end we shall gladly perform. May heaven long preserve you in peace and prosperity."[1]

But the wise and conciliatory measures proposed by Father Leander gave great offence at Rome, where a renunciation of the deposing power would not be listened to. From his apologetical letters to Cardinal Barberini, and from communications addressed to himself from that city by Father Welford, a Benedictine monk, we learn, that he was accused of rejecting the deposing power, of advocating the oath of allegiance, and of writing against those who defended the Papal bulls condemning it. "Rome," wrote Father Welford, "having stood for her rights so many ages in the cause of deposing princes, will be very unwilling to permit the oath, as the words lie, although glossed with another intention. Look over the oath which usually is exhibited to Catholics in Ireland; examine other forms of oath in Catholic countries; add to them, augment them, and endeavour to form them in that kind and those words which may secure and content his Majesty, as is most just and reasonable to be done; yet take heed of meddling with deponibility of princes, for that article will never pass here."[2] "How greatly is it to be lamented," exclaims a Roman Catholic writer, "that this chimerical claim of the Papal See stood in the way of so many wise and promising exertions to relieve the English Catholics from the dreadful persecutions under which they groaned; of so many attempts to restore, if not a communion of religious belief, at least a communion of peace and goodwill between Protestants and Catholics."[3]

As for Father Leander himself, he was afraid to return to Rome and thus fall into the hands of his enemies. He dreaded, in all probability, the fate of the unfortunate Benedictine, John Barnes, who, having written against the

[1] *Ib.* 205.   [2] *Ib.* 272.
[3] Butler's *English Catholics*, 2, 330.

temporal power of the Pope, was decoyed abroad, and conveyed by force to Rome, where he was imprisoned in the Inquisition till the confinement and ill-usage deprived him of his senses.[1] In October, 1635, Leander wrote to Windebank, the Secretary of State, asking that he might be allowed to spend the remainder of his life in England; " By the last letter of our Procurator from Rome . . . you may well perceive the trouble I am like to fall into by my adversaries' opposition, for no other cause than for joining the duty of a loyal subject and a good Christian Catholic, which should in no sort—nay, can in no sort—be separated. Out of which, I humbly beseech your honour to intercede for me to his Majesty, that he would vouchsafe to continue his favourable protection to me, that I may subsist here under his royal wings so long as I shall behave myself loyally and quietly, which shall be, I hope, as long as I live upon earth."[2] At the time Father Leander wrote this letter he had been for a long period suffering from an illness which caused his death in 1636. He died in London, and was buried in the chapel of Somerset House.

The Pope, being dissatisfied with Father Leander, sent another agent to England, Gregory Panzani, a secular Italian priest, who arrived in London towards the end of 1634. In the following January, Panzani had an interview with Windebank. He informed the secretary that the occasion of his coming to England was to pay a compliment to the Queen, to make himself acquainted with matters relating to the appointment of a bishop, and "incidentally, as occasion served, he was at liberty to regulate the concerns of the oath of allegiance."[3] He added, that the Pope was disposed to give his Majesty all the content imaginable, and

[1] Berington, *Panzani*, 141; Throckmorton, *First Letter*, 165.
[2] Clarendon, *State Papers*, 1, 331.
[3] Berington, *Panzani*, 143.

that if his Catholic subjects did not behave themselves with the utmost respect to the King in all civil matters, it was contrary to the knowledge and desire of the Pontiff. Windebank replied that the King had always signified the great respect he had for Urban, and that both on his account, and for other considerations, he had seldom pressed the execution of the laws against Catholics to extremity, and only reminded them occasionally of their condition by pecuniary fines, and that, too, very sparingly. He added, that it would be prudent on the part of the Pope either to recall or to moderate the briefs that were in force against such as took the oath of allegiance. Panzani replied that he had no specific commission on that subject, but it was his opinion that nothing would be altered in the briefs unless the oath was framed in a manner more agreeable to the Roman See. Windebank insisted that many Roman Catholics admitted that the oath might be taken with the King's comment restraining its sense to civil allegiance. That, said Panzani, may be the opinion of some of the party, but in things of this nature men are to act in concert, and govern themselves by a uniform practice. All I can say is, that I know it is the Pope's pleasure that the Catholics should answer all the demands of civil obedience. If that is the case, answered Windebank, let the Pope draw up the form of an oath, and send it hither. Panzani promised to write to Rome, and hoped that the application would be followed by the framing of an oath which would be at the same time palatable to the most scrupulous conscience and satisfactory to the Papal Court. The King had lately proposed a new oath to the Irish Roman Catholics, but even this was objected to by the Pope "as bearing still too hard on the Pope's spiritual power."[1] Panzani, however, sent this Irish oath to Rome as a model for that of England.

[1] There was not a word in the Irish oath referring to the Pope's

But Panzani's expectations were doomed to be disappointed. He received a letter from Cardinal Barberini informing him that the Papal Court was very much displeased with the liberty he had taken in declaring himself on the subject of the oath. The cardinal acquainted him that Rome ought to be very cautious and rather passive in controversies respecting it, "for," said he, "should we undertake to draw up forms of an oath, the English would pretend to be judges of the qualities of them, whereas it is our business to act as judges where faith is attacked or endangered." He also advised him not to concern himself with Courteney's book which Windebank had endeavoured to have censured at Rome : " This was entering too far into a thorny matter where he might prick his fingers. To condemn Courteney was to appear too openly against the authority of the See of Rome, and to approve of what he had written was too disobliging on the other side." In the conclusion of this long letter the cardinal remarks: " I wish you had been cautious in relation to the oath. Father Leander's example might have deterred you. His meddling about the oath was very ill taken by all parties, but being a person of no extraordinary reach he was not likely to do much either way. . . . It might perhaps not have been amiss to have mentioned in general terms something concerning

authority, either spiritual or temporal. " I do truly acknowledge, &c., before God and the world that our Sovereign Lord King Charles is lawful and rightful King of this realm, and of all other his Majesty's dominions and countries. And I will bear faith and true allegiance to his Majesty, his heirs and successors, and him and them will defend to the uttermost of my power against all conspiracies and attempts, whatsoever, which shall be made against his or their crown and dignity, and do my best endeavour to disclose and make known unto his Majesty, &c., or to the Lord Deputy . . . for the time being, all treasons and traitorous conspiracies which I shall know or hear to be intended against his Majesty or any of them. And I do make this recognition and acknowledgment heartily, willingly, and truly, upon the true faith of a Christian. So help me God."—Cox, *History of Ireland*, 2, 47.

the oath to Secretary Windebank, but you went too far in making proposals. In things of that kind it is your business to see, hear, and observe. It is a piece of necessary policy to seem to be fully informed of matters. ... It is a comfort to hear the Catholics are not persecuted. ... The softening of the Pope's brief which Windebank mentioned was a dangerous subject. You entered unadvisedly on that subject, yet were in the right to reply that not repealing but softening was to be the thing insisted on. I wish, however, you had never mentioned anything of sending hither about the form of an oath, since you are not ignorant how much his Holiness suffered on such another proposal concerning the sovereignty of the Grisons over the Valaisins. Should we form an oath here and send it to the King, they would examine it and censure it in England. On the whole it is my advice that you disengage yourself as well as you can from this troublesome affair of the oath."[1] It is evident that Father Leander had not been, and that Panzani was not, acquainted with the real policy of Rome. The Papal Court had made up its mind not to recede from its claims, nor to co-operate with the English government in framing an oath of allegiance, and had come to the unalterable determination never to allow the Roman Catholics of England to profess their loyalty and obedience to a Protestant or heretical ruler. This will be proved subsequently by letters and secret instructions from the Pope himself to his legate or nuncio in Ireland.

Like Father Leander, Panzani thought that a friendly correspondence between the English Court and the See of Rome was desirable, and that it should begin with a letter from the Pope to his Majesty, expressing in general terms the respect of his Holiness for the King, his esteem for the English people, and his wishes for their prosperity.[2]

[1] Berington's *Panzani*, 157-9.   [2] Butler, *English Catholics*, 2, 334.

Windebank proposed to Panzani that Urban should write an obliging letter to the King. The same request was made by several of the Roman Catholic nobility who were of opinion that such a letter would be acceptable.[1] To this suggestion the Court of Rome immediately and positively objected. Cardinal Barberini informed Panzani of the Pope's resolution to forbear any such advances, as it was the uniform custom of the Papal See to expect the first step to be made to it. " I commend," says the cardinal, " your reservedness in not making any promises of the Pope's writing to the King. Such things are never done but when princes have drawn a letter from his Holiness by writing first. Besides, a letter to the King must be by way of exhortation on the subject of religion, of which perhaps his Majesty is not yet disposed to hear."

Queen Henrietta was desirous of having a representative of her own at the Papal Court. The King hoped to benefit his nephew, the Palatine, through the mediation of Urban with the Emperor and the Spanish sovereign. This consideration induced Charles to consent to the establishment of a reciprocal agency at Rome and in England. Captain Arthur Brett, a Roman Catholic, was chosen as resident in that city, and the King, in 1635, drew up instructions for his guidance. Brett was directed not to meddle with affairs of religion, to remember that he was sent to Rome "merely for matters of state and intelligence," and to consider himself as the Queen's servant only. The instructions referred to the restoration of the Palatinate and the marriage of the King of Poland, but the bulk of them was taken up with the subject of the oath of allegiance, as the King hoped that the Pope would co-operate with him in lightening the yoke on the Roman Catholics. " You shall earnestly labour to clear all misunderstandings concerning the oath of allegiance,

[1] Berington, 146.

and endeavour to settle in them there a better opinion of it; assuring them the only scope and intent thereof is civil, and refers merely to government, and was made to distinguish between loyal and disloyal Roman Catholics, and to secure us of their faith and allegiance after so many treasonable attempts upon the persons of our predecessors, especially that horrible and damnable conspiracy of the gunpowder treason. That, therefore, if the Pope expect the continuance of our clemency to that party, he must revoke or suspend such briefs and censures as he hath published against the oath and those that take it; we being confident that most of the Roman Catholic party in this our realm of England would take it cheerfully were they not in fear of those briefs and censures, many of them, and among those, some of the clergy having not only taken it, but written in defence of the lawfulness of it, which shows their good inclination were they not terrified by an overawing power. And, therefore, the Pope only must be guilty of torturing their consciences and forcing this their disobedience, and of exposing them as much as in them lies, to those punishments which our laws do justly inflict upon them in this case, namely, the loss of their estates. . . . In the meantime we have wherewithal to justify ourselves to God and to all the world, that we desire nothing more than to be assured of that fidelity of our subjects which is due to us by the laws of God and man, and, without which, we can neither be sure of them, nor of the safety of our person or state, but shall ever be in distrust and jealousy of them. And, therefore, you are to labour chiefly in this, to make them understand how the Roman Catholic party groan under the calamity, and what a happiness it would be for them to be eased of this grievous burden laid upon them by the Pope. . . . And you are to use your best diligencies not only in this, but you must likewise mediate with the Pope to carry a gentle hand toward such

Roman Catholics as are moderate and peaceable, and well affected to the oath, that they may not suffer for their obedience and conformity, to the great disservice of us and the discouragement of those that would follow their example were they not in fear of censure. This we shall take very well, whereas on the contrary, without satisfaction in this business of the oath, you must assure them there can be no good intelligence between us and that party."[1] When Charles signed and dated these instructions with his own hand,[2] he little thought that all his efforts to ameliorate the state of his Roman Catholic subjects were to be in vain, and that the lamentable condition of that communion did not weigh a feather in the councils of the Pope as against his old-world claims to temporal jurisdiction. Two principles of the Papal policy forbade any reconciliation between the English Roman Catholics and their native government. One was the fixed resolution of the Popes not to give up an iota of their claim to the deposing power, the other was their determination never to allow Roman Catholics to profess allegiance to a Protestant sovereign. Rather than yield on these two points, they were prepared to witness the sufferings of the English Roman Catholics, and by their conduct to justify the continuation of the penal laws. "With what face can it be asserted," says a Roman Catholic historian and clergyman, "that the Roman Bishop or his court have constantly promoted the best interests of the English Catholics, when, as we have just seen, their religion itself was exposed to danger, and themselves and their posterity involved in much misery, that an ambitious prerogative, for such surely is the power of deposing princes, might not be curtailed?"[3] The reverend historian did not know or forgot that the principal motive for the action of the Papal Court,

[1] Clarendon, *State Papers*, 1, 354.   [2] *Ib.* 357.
[3] Berington's *Panzani*, 78.

as avowed by itself, was its resolve not to allow its adherents to profess their loyalty and obedience to a Protestant or heretical King.

Shortly after his appointment Brett was seized with a fever and died. Sir William Hamilton, brother to Lord Abercorn, was appointed in his place, and instructions similar to those given to Brett were delivered to him. Mr. George Conn, a Scotch Roman Catholic clerygman, in high esteem at Rome, was received in England as successor to Panzani who had resided two years in this country. Conn remained in England three years, and was succeeded by Count Rosetti, a layman, who openly resided in London and frequented the court as vested with a commission from the Pope.[1] When Charles erected his standard at Nottingham in August, 1642, and the civil war commenced, it was considered advisable to discontinue altogether the intercourse with Rome.

In 1641, the great Irish rebellion broke out. To the eternal disgrace of their names, the vast majority of the Roman Catholic nobility and gentry joined hands with the blood-stained insurgents of the North. A general assembly, regularly formed into Lords and Commons, was convened at Kilkenny. The confederates raised armies and appointed generals, drew up a new oath of allegiance, coined money, and despatched envoys to foreign powers inviting their assistance. The Pope, Innocent X., sent a legate, Rinuccini, with money and arms, to aid the confederates. On one occasion, Rinuccini, in a speech to the Council at Kilkenny, professed his fidelity, " first to God and religion and next to the King." He was at once reprimanded from Rome for having used such an expression respecting the King. In May, 1646, Cardinal Pamphili, the Papal Secretary of State,

[1] Hume, 5, 25, ed. 1830. An account of these missions, at the end of Nugent's *Memorials of Hampden*, states that Rosetti was a Cardinal.

wrote to him, finding fault with his words: "The Holy See never can by any positive act approve of the civil allegiance of Catholic subjects to a heretical prince. From this maxim of the Holy See, have arisen the many difficulties and disputes in England about the oath of allegiance. And his Holiness's displeasure is the greater, because you have left the original of your speech in the hands of the Catholic confederates, which, if published, will furnish heretics with arguments against the Pope's power over heretical princes, seeing that his Minister exhorts the Catholics of Ireland to allegiance to a heretical King. You must, therefore, withdraw the original, and suppress all copies of the said speech, and never indulge in such sentiments again."[1] On another occasion, in the same year, the legate was the first to sign a protestation of the clergy that they would never consent to a peace unless secure conditions were made "for religion, the King, and country." Cardinal Pamphili again reproved Rinuccini for acting in violation of his instructions, and informed him "that it had been the constant and uninterrupted practice of the Holy See never to allow its ministers to make or to consent to any public declaration of Catholic subjects for the defence of the Crown and person of a heretical prince; that his conduct furnished pretences to the enemies of the Holy See to reflect upon her as deviating from the maxims of sound policy to which she had ever adhered; and that the Pope desired that he would not, by any public act, show that he knew or consented to any declaration of allegiance which the Irish Catholics might, for political reasons, be compelled, or be willing to make to the King."[2]

These statements of the Papal Secretary suggest some painful reflections respecting previous declarations of the

[1] Carte's *Ormond*, 1, 578; O'Conor's *Historical Address*, 2, 415, and the authorities there quoted.
[2] *Ib.* and Hutton's *Embassy of Rinuccini in Ireland*, 580.

Popes. According to the bulls issued against the English oath of allegiance, its condemnation was based on purely religious considerations. Paul V. forbade its being taken, on the ground that it contained "many things clearly contrary to faith and salvation." Urban VIII. declared that it wrested the sacred sceptre of the Universal Church from the hands of the vicar of God. It will be remembered that thirteen priests, confined in Newgate for not taking the oath, implored Paul in the most moving terms to point out the passages in it which were opposed to faith and salvation. Why was this not done? Were the objections to the oath really founded on religion, or was religion merely the pretext for its condemnation? The Pope answers the latter question in the affirmative. Here we have the Pontiff himself, by the hand of his Cardinal-Secretary, declaring in a secret despatch to his legate, that the true reason, which influenced the Popes in their opposition to the oath, was their fixed resolution never to allow a protestation of allegiance to be made by Roman Catholics to a heretical prince, and that from the observance of this maxim all the difficulties and disputes about the English oath had arisen.

Some time in the year 1641 or 1642, the English Roman Catholics ventured to speak the convictions of their souls, and made an attempt to free themselves from the civil ascendency of the Papal Court. They presented a petition to Parliament in which they explained their political sentiments.[1] After reciting that "whereas divers political reasons

[1] The petition is in Cressy's *Exomologesis*, 72, first ed. 1647. It was removed from the subsequent edition. Hugh Cressy, an Englishman, had been Dean of Leighlin in Ireland, and Prebendary of Windsor in England. He became a convert to the Roman Catholic religion, and entered the Benedictine order. In 1647 he published his *Exomologesis or Motives of his Conversion*. The petition of the English Roman Catholics given by him was the model from which Richard Belling drew up the "Loyal Remonstrance" of the Irish Roman Catholic clergy in the reign of Charles II.

and now dead motives of State not unknown to your wisdom, as also some rigorous proceedings of the Court of Rome, and several seditious combinations, being spoken to the grief of your petitioners, which heretofore some few unworthy Catholics have practised both at home and abroad against their late sovereign and this realm, have been the occasion of many severe laws and too, too, penal statutes against all professors of the Catholic faith in this kingdom," they made a full declaration of their loyalty and attachment to their King and country, disclaimed the deposing power, and repudiated the opinion that faith was not to be kept with heretics. "The Catholics of England do acknowledge and profess King Charles now reigning to be their true and lawful King, supreme lord and rightful sovereign of this realm and of all other his Majesty's dominions. And therefore they acknowledge themselves to be obliged under pain of sin to obey his Majesty in all civil and temporal affairs as much as any other of his Majesty's subjects and as the laws and rules of government in this kingdom do require at their hands. And that, notwithstanding any power or pretension of the Pope or See of Rome, or any sentence or declaration of what kind or quality soever, given or to be given by the Pope, his predecessors or successors, or by any authority spiritual or temporal proceeding or derived from him or his See, against their said King and country, they will still acknowledge and perform to the utmost of their abilities their faithful loyalty and true allegiance to their said King and country. And they do openly disclaim and renounce all foreign power, be it either Papal or princely, spiritual or temporal, inasmuch as it may seem able or shall pretend to free, discharge, or absolve them from this obligation, or shall any way give them leave or license to raise tumults, bear arms, or offer any violence, to his Majesty's royal person, to the High Court of Parliament, to the State, or Government. Being all of them ready, not only to discover and make known to his Majesty and to the High Court of Parliament all the treasons and conspiracies made against him or it which shall come to their hearing, but also to lose their lives in the defence of their King and country, and to resist with their best endeavours all conspiracies and attempts made against their said King or country, be they framed or sent under what pretence or patronised by what foreign authority soever. And further they profess that all absolute princes and supreme governors, of what religion soever they be, are God's lieutenants upon earth, and that obedience is due unto them according to the laws of each commonwealth respectively in all civil and temporal affairs, and therefore they do protest against all doctrines and authority to the contrary. And they do hold it impious and against the Word of God to maintain, that any private subject may kill and murder the Anointed of God his prince, though of a different belief and religion from his. And they abhor and detest the practice thereof as damnable and wicked. And, lastly, they offer themselves most willingly to accept and embrace the late Protestation of Union made by the High Court of Parliament excepting only the clause of religion,[1] professing that they cannot without sin infringe or violate any contract or break their words and promises made or

---

[1] In consequence of the discovery of a correspondence between the court and the army, Pym, in May, 1641, proposed a Protestation of union to be made by both houses. The clause objected to in the above petition was the first clause in the Protestation. "I A. B. do in the presence of Almighty God promise, vow, and protest to maintain and defend, as far as lawfully I may, with my life, power, and estate, the true reformed Protestant religion expressed in the doctrines of the Church of England against all Popery and Popish innovations within this realm, &c." The petition of the Roman Catholics was presented to parliament some time between May, 1641, and the commencement of hostilities in August, 1642. Cressy says the petition was "offered to parliament immediately before these commotions."

given to any man, though of a different faith and belief from the Church of Rome. All which they do freely and sincerely acknowledge and protest as in the presence of God without any equivocation or mental reservation whatsoever."

The almost simultaneous breaking out of the Irish rebellion of 1641 and of the great civil war in England prevented any steps being taken on this loyal declaration; nevertheless it appears to have had important consequences. In 1647, hopes were entertained of composing the differences between the King and the Parliament, and it was proposed to comprehend the Roman Catholics in the general settlement. The first civil war was at an end, and Charles was with and in the power of the army. This proposal may have been the result of a real desire for toleration which many in the army then professed, or it may have arisen from the wish of that body to put pressure on the King to come to terms with it by withdrawing the Roman Catholics from the side of Charles. Whatever may have been the reasons, it was agreed, Sir Thomas Fairfax, the commander-in-chief, being the proposer of the measure,[1] that the penal statutes in force against the Roman Catholics should be repealed and liberty of conscience granted to them, on condition that they showed their religion was not inconsistent with the safety of the civil government. For this purpose they were required to sign in the negative three propositions submitted to them to the following effect :

1. That the Pope or the Church hath power to absolve any person or persons whatsoever from his or their obedience to the civil government established in this nation.

2. That it is lawful by the Pope's or Church's command or dispensation to kill, destroy, or otherwise injure, any person or persons whatsoever, because he or they are accused, condemned, censured, or excommunicated, for error, schism, or heresy.

[1] Walsh, *Hist. of the Irish Remonstrance*, 522-4.

3. That it is lawful in itself, or by the Pope's dispensation, to break either word or oath with any persons abovesaid under pretence of their being heretics.[1]

Fifty Roman Catholic noblemen and gentlemen together with several of their clergy subscribed these articles in the negative as was desired. No sooner was it known at Rome that this subscription had taken place than the disastrous vigilance of the Vatican was awakened. Innocent X. called a congregation for the special purpose of taking it into consideration.[2] It was condemned as heretical, and further it was declared that the subscribers had incurred the penalties denounced in the sacred canons and apostolical constitutions against those who denied the power of the Pope in causes of faith.[3] It is also to be remarked, that the condemnation did not specify any particular article to which the Pope and congregation objected. All were condemned alike without distinction, and the English people were left under the impression, that the three propositions taken affirmatively were articles of the Roman Catholic faith, namely, that the Pope or his Church had power to absolve subjects from their civil obedience to their government; that it was lawful at the command or dispensation of the Pope or the Church to kill and destroy persons accused, censured, or excommunicated for error, schism, or heresy; and that it was lawful in itself, or by the Pope's dispensation, to break faith pledged to heretics.

Nothing more was heard of the abolition or relaxation of

[1] *Ib.* nad Butler, *Eng. Catholics*, 2, 414.

[2] *Letter of Hieronymus de Vecchiis*, Papal nuncio at Brussels. Walsh, 16.

[3] "Sacra Congregatio resolutionem illam negativam tanquam hæreticam mox condemnat; subscriptoresque in pœnas, in sacris canonibus et constitutionibus apostolicis contra negantes potestatem pontificiam in causis fidei, incidisse declarat."—Caron, *Remonstrantia Hibernorum*, pars 1, c. 4, s. 3.

the penal laws. The Roman Catholics of England were cowed by the condemnation and by the civil tyranny of the Papal Court. It is worth while to compare their submissive demeanour with the more generous spirit which prevailed among their communion in France. A priest, who had subscribed the three propositions, wrote to the well-known Dr. Holden, an Englishman who had taken his degree of Doctor in Divinity in the Sorbonne, desiring to have his opinion respecting what he had done. Dr. Holden's answer contains the following paragraphs:—" Having seriously considered the three articles you sent me . . . I cannot refuse, neither in charity nor friendship, to give you my opinion concerning your subscription thereunto. Yet, being unwilling you should rely upon my private and particular judgment in a matter of such moment, I have consulted with several great and learned men of our nation, but especially some of the most ancient and learned doctors of our faculty here, whose constant sentiments are, that not only in their opinion your act is lawful, just, and true, but that it is also the general and universal belief of all the learned men in this kingdom. So that I see not upon what grounds you need fear or apprehend the censures which the decree of the congregation in Rome pretends you have incurred. . . . In a word I see nothing capable to beget a scruple, nor that ought to hinder any Catholic from subscribing to the articles as you have done. Nor shall I easily persuade myself that any wise and experienced man will shrink from so just an act. If your State, King, or Parliament will suffer and tolerate you to live quietly under them, which I wonder such able men should boggle at, I shall quickly provide and help you with such advice from the most learned and most virtuous divines of Europe, as will make your ecclesiastical government an example to all other States and kingdoms, your neighbours. And still conserving all due respect and spiritual obedience to the See of Rome, you shall free yourselves from all unnecessary and unfit dependence of the Roman Court, wherein I shall furnish you with the resolutions of such questions as will open the eyes of all your unexperienced and tender-conscienced countrymen who have not had, perhaps, the means to discern and distinguish their due and necessary obedience from a superfluous and unjust obsequiousness; and which shall withal make appear to all the Christian world the now well near fourscore years hard and unfatherly dealing of the Court of Rome over the poor persecuted and distressed Catholics of England. Let it therefore be your constant endeavour to give to the King, State, or Parliament, full satisfaction and assurance of your fidelity to the civil and political government of your kingdom whatsoever it shall be, which may most certainly stand with the integrity of your religion and conscience. For the rest, fear nothing, trust to the justice of your cause, which you may assuredly believe will not want support."[1]

Thus, to use the words of a pious and learned Roman Catholic divine, by "the hard and unfatherly dealing" of the Court of Rome on the one hand, and "the superfluous and unjust obsequiousness" of the English Roman Catholics on the other, was this design of restoring the latter to full citizenship defeated. Miserable indeed was their condition. They were between the hammer and the anvil; in danger from the laws of their country if they disobeyed them, and threatened with the fire of eternal perdition if they vindicated the purity of their loyalty. From the Papal Court there was no hope for them, for Rome was resolved not to recede one step from her claim to the deposing power, and to keep that claim alive as a whip for heretical or Protestant princes. The only mitigation of their sufferings which they

[1] Walsh, *Irish Remonstrance*, 524; Throckmorton, *Second Letter*, Append., 99.

could henceforth expect was from the merciful consideration of their own government. Their single claim to compassion was, that they were bound to obey the directions of their supreme spiritual pastor, *Da veniam, Imperator, tu carcerem, ille gehennam minatur;*[1]—pardon us our disobedience, for the authority which keeps the keys of heaven and hell constrains us to transgress your statutes.[2]

How far Cromwell, if he had lived till more settled times, would have granted toleration to the Roman Catholics, is not quite certain. Indications, however, survive which lead to the belief that he would have relaxed, if not repealed, the laws against them. Up to the time of his return from his Irish expedition, he was willing to concede to them only the celebration of their worship in their houses though not in public, but time and its lessons appear to have ripened and widened his views. In 1649, when he offered terms to the Governor of Ross in Ireland, he wrote to that officer: "As for that which you mention concerning liberty of conscience, I meddle not with any man's conscience. But if by liberty of conscience you mean a liberty to exercise the Mass, I judge it best to use plain dealing and to let you know, where the

[1] "Si aliud Imperator et aliud Deus, quid judicatis? . . . Quis prohibet? Major potestas. Da veniam, Imperator, tu carcerem, ille gehennam minatur."—St. Augustine, *De verbis Domini, Sermo* 6.

[2] Charles Butler thus speaks of the conduct of Innocent X.: "In the dreadful state of persecution in which the English Catholics were then placed, and in which an absolute and unequivocal disclaimer of the Pope's deposing power might have served them so effectually—which disclaimer the Popes actually tolerated in France, Venice, and in many parts of Germany—and which disclaimer, we must add, the universal Catholic world now publicly and unreservedly professes—was it quite just or quite humane for any Pope to pronounce its formal condemnation? Did not the severe persecution under which the English Catholics then groaned, point out to the common father of the faithful, that duty called on him not only not to check, but even to facilitate and to encourage every measure, which might either diminish the horrors, or abridge the term of their sufferings?"—*Eng. Catholics*, 2, 417.

Parliament of England have power that will not be allowed." In the following year he issued his *Declaration in answer to certain declarations and acts framed by the Irish Popish prelates and clergy in a conventicle at Clonmacnoise*. In this he says : "I shall not, where I have power and the Lord is pleased to bless me, suffer the exercise of the Mass where I can take notice of it. . . . As for the people, what thoughts they have in matters of religion in their own breasts I cannot reach; but shall think it my duty, if they walk honestly and peaceably, not to cause them in the least to suffer for the same, and shall endeavour to walk patiently and in love towards them, to see if at any time it shall please God to give them another or a better mind. And all men under the power of England within this dominion are hereby required and enjoined strictly and religiously to do the same." In 1654, he declared in a speech to his first parliament, that liberty of conscience was one of those "fundamentals" in government which might not be examined or altered, but were to be taken as the basis upon which the new administration was founded. "Liberty of conscience," he exclaimed, "is a natural right. This I say is a fundamental. It ought to be so. It is for us and the generations to come." At the dissolution of the same parliament in 1656 he made use of the following words: "Those that were sound in the faith, how proper was it for them to labour for liberty, for a just liberty, that men might not be trampled upon for their conscience! Had not they themselves laboured but lately under the weight of persecution? And was it fit for them to sit heavy upon others? Is it ingenuous to ask liberty and not to give it?" These expressions of the Protector are general, without qualification or exclusion of any sect, and if naturally interpreted would include Roman Catholics. The Independents, to whose party Cromwell belonged and upon whose support he relied against the Presbyterians and

Royalists, were in favour of toleration to all. We are informed by Baxter that Cromwell and his friends declared publicly that they could not understand what magistrates had to do with matters of religion, and that all men should be left to their consciences.[1] The same divine tells us that in 1662 the Independents desired that liberty of worship should be extended to Roman Catholics.[2] Intolerance formed no part of Cromwell's character. When it was discussed whether the Jews should be allowed to return to England and to have synagogues and cemeteries of their own, he advocated a legal sanction being given to their re-admission into the kingdom.[3] It would seem that the Roman Catholics themselves during his protectorate looked to Cromwell for toleration, and that they were encouraged by his friends and confidants in their expectation of obtaining it. A movement towards a reconciliation with him took place in that body. Thomas White, an eminent and learned secular priest, published in 1655 his *Obedience and Government*. His object was to show that when the sovereign was once deposed, even unjustly, it was for the public good to acquiesce in his removal rather than attempt his restoration. This treatise was regarded by all at the time as an approval of Cromwell's assumption of power and as an advice to Roman Catholics to support his government.[4] John Sergeant, another secular priest of great celebrity, exhorted the members

[1] *Baxter's Life, by Himself*, part 2, 193. [2] *Ib.* 429.
[3] Cromwell's scheme for the admission of the Jews was defeated, but when in 1656 a Portuguese Synagogue was opened in London, no objection was made by him. In the first year of Charles II., a remonstrance addressed to the King stated, that the Jews had endeavoured to buy St. Paul's for a synagogue in Cromwell's time.—*State Papers, Domestic*, 1660-1, p. 366.
[4] In 1660 twenty-six ecclesiastics of Douay College declared "from their hearts they abominated and execrated the work written in the English language by White during Cromwell's protectorate on Obedience and Government."—Butler, *English Catholics*, 2, 431.

of his communion to acknowledge the Commonwealth and
the Protector, and further, he disclaimed the deposing power.[1]
Somewhat later, negotiations took place between some of
Cromwell's friends and the Roman Catholics. Several con-
sultations concerning "their lamentable condition and the
regal power which Cromwell meant to assume"[2] were held
amongst themselves. It was proposed to address the Protector and to inform him that they were prepared to tender
to him such an oath as would bind "not merely their
conscience but their affections; nay, that they would give
him a greater pledge of their fidelity in the person of one
man who shall be a bishop or superintendent over the clergy
of England, and consequently have power over the consciences
of the whole Catholic body; whose residence shall be in
London or where Cromwell shall appoint, and who will from
time to time impose the execution of his commands as a
matter of conscience on the Catholics." On the other hand,
that body received intimation from "a man in great credit
with Cromwell" that their proposal would be accepted.
This design alarmed the Royalists greatly, and Richard
Belling was authorized by Lord D'Aubigny to inform
Charles II. of it. Belling reported to that prince that the
proposal was ready to be made and that it was likely to be
accepted. He also advised Charles to strengthen the attachment of the Roman Catholics by some extraordinary mark of
his favour to them, and recommended that, for this purpose,
he should permit his youngest brother, the Duke of Gloucester,
to be educated in their religion. Charles rejected this
suggestion of Belling, and gave it as his opinion that the
Roman Catholics were deceiving themselves in thinking that
the English Government was favourably disposed towards

[1] *Ib.* 429.
[2] These words fix the time about which these transactions took place,
as the question of the Kingship first emerged in the early part of 1657.

them.[1] The negotiations between that body and Cromwell were interrupted by the death of the Protector in 1658.[2]

After the restoration of Charles II. opportunities of obtaining a repeal, or at least an important relaxation, of the penal laws, presented themselves to the Roman Catholics both of England and Ireland. One opportunity, that offered to the English body, was lost by the dissensions which arose amongst its members; the other was deliberately rejected at the command and under the direct instigation of the Papal See. The King's Declaration from Breda contained a promise of toleration to all, and the English Roman Catholics naturally expected to be included in any scheme to be adopted. "We do declare a liberty to tender consciences; and that no man shall be disquieted or called in question for differences of opinion in matters of religion." In the following year, petitions on their behalf were presented

[1] The account of these negotiations is to be found in Thurloe, *State Papers*, 1, 170-4. Charles Butler gives a short abstract of them, and mentions that they had been preceded by similar negotiations between the Roman Catholics and the Independent body. It is almost certain that Sir Kenelm Digby, a leading Roman Catholic, expected to obtain from Cromwell a full toleration for his religion, and that he freely discussed the matter with him.—*Dict. of National Biography*, Sir Kenelm Digby. See also a remarkable letter, dated March, 1656, from Digby to Cromwell's Secretary, in which he professed his "passionate" devotion to the "service, honour, and interests" of the Protector.— Thurloe, *State Papers*, 4, 591.

[2] Negotiations also took place during the protectorate between the Irish Roman Catholics and Cromwell's Secretary. Edmund Reilly, titular Archbishop of Armagh, was the principal agent in these transactions. On one occasion, at a public dinner in London, he boasted that he had never been a well-wisher of Charles or his brothers, and that to the connivance of his party Cromwell owed his speedy conquest of Ireland. He also issued orders to the clergy of Armagh to pray for the Protector's prosperity. Shortly before the Restoration, the Spanish ambassador in Holland wrote to Rome, that if Reilly did not make his escape he would suffer death as a traitor, his practices with Thurloe and in Ireland being well known.—Walsh, *History of the Irish Remonstrance*, 610; O'Connor, *Historical Address*, 2, 172-190; Carte, *Ormond*, 2, 204.

to the House of Lords, and Colonel Tuke was allowed to state their case at the bar of the house.[1] In consequence of these proceedings, a committee was appointed to examine and report on those statutes which reached to the taking away of life in affairs of religion, and the judges were ordered to bring in a list of them. If the Roman Catholics had manifested on this occasion ordinary discretion and good sense, the appointment of this committee, the first name on which was that of the Duke of York, would have been the commencement of their complete relief. It was known that the King was in favour of repealing those laws, and during his exile he had often declared "that he would do his best, if ever God restored him to his kingdom, that those bloody laws might be repealed."[2] The temper of the peers was also favourable to their abolition, for Clarendon informs us that there did not appear "one lord in the house who seemed to be unwilling that those laws should be repealed." The report was completed, and the lords appointed a second committee to prepare a bill repealing the following penal statutes or such parts of them as should appear good to its members,—the fifth of Elizabeth, the Acts which imposed death on seminary priests, or made those receiving them guilty of felony, and also the clause in the first of James I., c. 4, concerning putting former laws against recusants, priests, and Jesuits, into execution.[3] As soon as this second committee was appointed, the Roman Catholic peers and their friends were diligent in their attendance for some days, and discussed the several Acts from which they desired to be relieved. But on a sudden their attendance relaxed, and the committee was discontinued, no one showing any solicitude about it. The cause

[1] *House of Lords' Journals*, 11, 276, 286.
[2] Clarendon, *Life and Continuation of the History*, 2, 107, Oxford, 1827.
[3] *Lords' Journal*, 11, 310.

of this apathy was, that disputes and dissensions had broken out in the body. Some meetings of a general assembly, consisting of their principal lords and gentlemen, the superiors of orders, and representatives of the secular clergy, were held at Arundel House. The form of a subscription was debated among them, and difficulties were started respecting the oath which it was intended they should take as a security for their fidelity to the King and for the peace of the country. Some were of opinion that the oath should contain a disclaimer of the Pope's temporal authority, others objected to this.[1] A proposal was also made, that none but secular priests, under a bishop and a settled form of government, should be tolerated in England, and that all regulars, particularly the Jesuits, should be forbidden the kingdom under the severest penalties.[2] There had long been grave disputes and differences among the English Roman Catholics respecting their internal government and the oath of allegiance; these were revived on this occasion, and the general assembly was dissolved to meet no more.

[1] Clarendon says, that the Jesuits broke up the assembly by declaring that Catholics could not deprive the Pope of his temporal authority. Lingard remarks on this, "Clarendon as usual is incorrect," for, he adds, the Jesuits since 1618 had been enjoined by their General, under pain of damnation, not to teach the doctrine of the temporal power either in word, writing, or print. Dr. Lingard should have known:—(1) that Sanctarellus, a Jesuit, published his treatise upholding the temporal power eight years after 1616, the true date of the injunction and not 1618; (2) that the injunction was revocable at the will of the General, and that it must have been recalled, as the treatise of Sanctarellus was published with the approbation and special license of Mutius Vitelleseus, General of the Jesuits, bearing date at Rome, May 25, 1624. In this very reign, the Jesuits put forth a catechism teaching the unlawfulness of the oath of allegiance, and issued a decree ordering absolution to be refused to those who took the oath or taught it to be lawful; the decree is dated Ghent, July 5th, 1681.—Throckmorton, *First Letter to the Catholic Clergy*, 180. They also published in this reign three treatises against it.—See Stillingfleet's *The Jesuits' Loyalty*, 1677.

[2] Clarendon, *Life* and *Continuation*, 2, 111; Berington's *Panzani*, 311.

The movement in England and the known partiality of Charles encouraged the Irish Roman Catholic clergy to petition the King for a mitigation of the laws which affected them. They were advised by their friends to incorporate in their petition a declaration of their sentiments respecting the obedience due from them to the civil government. They were especially recommended to avail themselves of the opportunity to profess their unqualified allegiance to the sovereign and their rejection of the deposing power, in order to allay the suspicions raised against them by the proceedings of the Papal nuncio and their adherence to him during the rebellion of 1641. Some time was passed in discussing the matter, and towards the end of 1661, the framing of the petition was entrusted to Richard Belling, formerly secretary to the Kilkenny Confederation. For the purpose of drawing it up, Belling made use of the petition presented to parliament by the English Roman Catholics about 1641 which has been already referred to. From this document he extracted the protestation of allegiance " word by word without any other change but of the application to the King instead of the Parliament, and of Ireland instead of England,"[1] and inserted it in the Irish petition or Remonstrance as it came to be called from its title.[2] This Remonstrance acknowledged the King to be the supreme lord and rightful sovereign of Ireland; that the clergy were bound to obey him in all civil and temporal affairs, and to pay him loyalty and obedience notwithstanding any sentence or declaration of the Pope; it disclaimed all foreign power, Papal or princely, spiritual or temporal, that should pretend to free them from this obligation, and declared that all princes, of what religion soever they might be, were independent under God, and

[1] Walsh, *History of the Irish Remonstrance*, p. 7.
[2] *The humble Remonstrance, Acknowledgment, Protestation, and Petition of the Roman Catholic Clergy of Ireland.*

that it was impious and against the Word of God to maintain that any private subject might kill his prince, though of a different religion.

During the remainder of the year 1661 and throughout 1662, the Remonstrance was discussed both in public and private, and finally it was subscribed by seventy of the Irish clergy, and by a hundred and sixty-four " of the chiefest lay nobility, gentry, and proprietors."[1] A copy of it was sent to London, where many of the Irish nobility and gentry were then assembled, the Act of Settlement being under consideration. Several meetings were held by these laymen in consultation with eminent members of the English Roman Catholic nobility. Their English associates strongly advised the Irish to sign the Remonstrance, and declared " that were the case of the Irish theirs, they and all the rest of the English nobility and gentry of the Roman communion would willingly sign that Remonstrance *in terminis*, and even sign it with their blood, were this necessary."[2] After many meetings and eight weeks' debates, the Remonstrance, with a few trifling changes in its preamble and at its close, to make it suitable to laymen, was adopted, and, having been signed by ninety-seven Irish noblemen and gentlemen then residing in London, was presented to the King, by whom it was most graciously received. The effect of the presentation was instantaneous. The Irish Roman Catholics were at once allowed by the express directions of Charles to exercise their religion in freedom and peace. " Is it not further," say eighteen Irish priests in their Expostulation to the Dublin Synod in 1666, " as manifestly apparent how graciously that instrument [the Remonstrance] after the signature of it was received by his Majesty ? how immediately the persecution in this kingdom ceased by his Majesty's express command. Nay, how ever since both

[1] Walsh, p. 2.   [2] *Ib.* 697.

people and clergy of our communion have enjoyed the great tranquillity and freedom in point of exercising our religion and functions, which we have so gladly seen, and which we so thankfully acknowledge to be still continued to us, yea in a higher measure enjoyed by us at this present, than we could almost have not long since either believed or hoped we should live to see."[1]

The Remonstrance was also approved by the English Dean and Chapter, who represented the secular priests of that country. In a letter, addressed to the Bishop of Dromore, the Dean informed him that the Irish clergy had done well in framing it. "To free the holy Catholic faith on one side from obloquies and redeem yourselves from calumnies, and on the other to relieve the laity under your charge from heavy pressure, and further to open a door to your liberty of religion, we must needs judge you have performed the office of good pastors both in framing and subscribing your allegiance to the prince; to hold forth to the whole world your religion free and spotless, your allegiance built on a basis immoveable, and yourselves well resolved subjects. For our parts, we would be glad to run into those occasions even with the hazard of our lives or the loss of our last drop of blood, to work out our freedom from the severity of our penal laws; much more would we think it happy to gain it with the renounce of an opinion which justly brings a jealousy upon us from our prince and fellow-subjects."[2]

The Papal See, carrying out its fatal policy of maintaining its fantastic claims to the deposing power and of forbidding a protestation of allegiance to be made by Roman

---

[1] In 1666 eighteen priests addressed an *Expostulatory Letter* to the Irish Synod exhorting its members to sign the Remonstrance. Of these, fourteen were Franciscans, two Dominicans, and two secular priests.

[2] Walsh, p. 55.

Catholics to a Protestant sovereign, at once interfered to prevent the signature of the Remonstrance in Ireland. Hieronymus de Vecchiis, the Papal nuncio at Brussels, to whom the superintendence of the Irish clergy was entrusted, wrote to several of them in 1662 against the Remonstrance, and many copies of his letter were dispersed with much diligence throughout the kingdom. "Your paternity hath desired from me what hath been resolved at Rome concerning the Declaration or Protestation beginning 'Your Majesty's faithful subjects,' and ending 'prescribed by the law,'[1] presented to the most serene King of England and subscribed by some Irish ecclesiastics. Wherefore I thought I should very well satisfy your desires if I communicated to you what hath been written thereupon by command of our most holy Lord. To wit, that after diligent discussion in several meetings of the most eminent cardinals and divines, that protestation hath been found, like the returning Hydra, to contain propositions agreeing with others heretofore condemned by the see apostolic, particularly by Paul V. of happy memory by a constitution in form of a brief, and lately in the year 1648 in a congregation purposely held to that end by Innocent X. And hence it is, that the most holy Lord hath thought no more necessary now but that this very thing should be declared, and commanded us to testify unto all this his mind, to the end it may appear publicly, that the said protestation, and subscriptions added, have not only not been approved by his Holiness, but not as much as permitted or even by connivance tolerated : Yea, that he hath grievously resented, that by the example of ecclesiastics the secular nobles of the foresaid kingdom of Ireland have been drawn into the same error, whose protestation and subscriptions he doth in like manner condemn according to the above form, and this to deliver the consciences of Catholics from

[1] The first and last words of the *Remonstrance*.

the fraud and error wherewith they are circumvented."[1] In another letter of the same year the nuncio writes: "The Formulary of your profession was brought to Rome, maturely there discussed, and utterly disallowed. His Holiness writes it to displease himself most grievously, to be in itself intolerable, and such as cannot in any manner be allowed. And his pleasure is that this be made known to all. For it agrees with that profession which heretofore hath so much grieved and was condemned by Pope Paul V. and lately again by Innocent X. . . . His Holiness very exceedingly both resents and admires that from you, priests and regular persons, the very first offspring should proceed whence also the lay nobility and gentry have been induced to this profession."[2] About the same time, Cardinal Barberini wrote, in the name of the whole congregation *de propaganda fide*, to the noblemen of Ireland, condemning the Remonstrance as a violation of faith. "They are made masters of error who give themselves for disciples of truth, and to show their fidelity to the King they destroy faith. In which procedure of theirs, that is chiefly to be admired, that they published a protestation in such terms whereby they may be said to have violated the Catholic faith and gained nothing which they might not have obtained, that very faith remaining entire. What excuse can they pretend, who, to testify their allegiance to their prince, have subscribed their names to some propositions condemned heretofore by the apostolic see? . . . What shame is it to the ecclesiastical order to behold them the leaders into error by whom others should have been instructed. . . . Wherefore such as have kept themselves free from subscriptions or from this kind of infectious disease, let them by all means beware that they be not drawn into the pit by their blind leaders."[3]

As the prospect was held out to the Roman Catholics of

[1] Walsh, p. 16.   [2] *Ib.* 514.   [3] *Ib.* 17.

Ireland of obtaining relief from the penal laws, it became desirable to know whether the Remonstrance represented the real opinions of their clergy on the question of allegiance to the State. If it did not, all further discussion was at an end, and the Government could only come to the conclusion that the Roman Catholic clergy, and the laity, over whom they exercised a dominant influence, were unfitted to be admitted into the constitution. To give an opportunity for a free and public debate on the subject of civil obedience, the Duke of Ormond, then Lieutenant of Ireland, allowed a national synod of that persuasion to be convened in Dublin. To the meeting of this synod, the Court of Rome and its ministers offered every opposition. In April, 1666, Cardinal Barberini wrote to the "clergy and Catholics of Ireland": "Four years now are almost passed since our most holy Lord, out of his love to you, hath by my letters admonished you of dangers to your salvation which are impending from false brethren. And when he mightily desired to hear news of the snare broken and you delivered, behold the sad tidings come of your having agreed amongst yourselves that a congregation shall be held at Dublin on the third of the Ides of June for deliberating on the point of subscribing that protestation, which, making show of the title of fidelity, asserts things contrary to the Catholic faith. . . . To those, who having passed the bounds of modesty, after so many vain endeavours, peradventure glory to have had this last success of the designed assembly, his Holiness doth threaten sore divine vengeance, if they turning from wicked thoughts do not abstain from such enterprises."[1] In May of the same year, Rospigliosi, then the Papal nuncio at Brussels, wrote to the "Bishops and clergy of Ireland" that their nation was in danger of contaminating the Catholic faith. "To that indeed tends the oath to the subscribing of which

[1] *Ib.* 633.

Walsh and Caron by so many subtle arts labour to persuade the churchmen, and so make them instruments and causes of the damnation of others. That is the end for which they use such great endeavours to promote the Dublin assembly. . . . And if Walsh and Caron do attempt anything besides, it looks not towards strengthening the fidelity of the people to their prince, but towards exterminating the purity of the Catholic religion whereof the foresaid oath is destructive, and consequently towards forcing the faithful Irish to deplorable and ever to be lamented ruin."[1]

The synod met on the 11th of June, 1666, and continued its sittings till the 25th of the same month. Another instance of what Dr. Holden calls the "hard and unfatherly dealing" of the Papal See, and of the "superfluous and unjust obsequiousness" of its adherents was manifested. The synod, overawed by the ascendency of Rome even in purely civil matters, refused to sign the Remonstrance, and drew up, on the 16th of June, what they called "a Remonstrance and Protestation of their loyalty." This instrument contained no denial of the deposing power, nor any mention of the Pope, and when read by the light of the schoolmen's mode of interpretation, and of the rule of the canonists that the Pope is not referred to in any document in which he is not named,[2] was evasive and offered no guarantee of their allegiance.[3] The Duke of Ormond refused to receive any protestation which did not include an explicit disclaimer of the deposing power, and the synod was dissolved.

Before the synod met, and the Remonstrance had been submitted to it for consideration, the Papal nuncio at Brussels prevailed on the Theological Faculty of Louvain to condemn

[1] *Ib.* 633.
[2] Our lawyers have a similar rule, that the sovereign is not bound by an Act of Parliament unless specially named in it.
[3] Walsh in his second treatise shows how defective and evasive the Protestation of the synod was.

it. Their condemnation was published in 1662, and ran as follows: "Forasmuch as the aforesaid Form involves a promise of a more ample obedience than secular princes can exact from their Catholic subjects, or their subjects can make unto them; and that, moreover, it contains some things repugnant to the sincere profession of the Catholic religion, therefore it must be held to be wholly unlawful and detestable."[1] It was against this censure that Redmond Caron, a pious and learned Franciscan, wrote his celebrated *Remonstrantia Hibernorum contra Lovanenses*, which appeared in 1665. It is amusing to contrast this judgment of the Louvain Theological Faculty with the later opinion of that body in 1788, when interrogated by the English Roman Catholics respecting the nature of the allegiance due by them to their government, and also respecting the power claimed by the Popes of absolving subjects from their obedience: "No man, nor any assembly of men, however eminent in dignity or power, not even the whole body of the Catholic Church, though assembled in General Council can, upon any ground or pretence whatsoever, weaken the bond of union between the sovereign and the people; still less can they absolve or free the subjects from their oath of allegiance."[2]

Father Walsh asserted, in 1673, that the Roman Catholic

[1] "Quia tamen supradicta formula [Hibernorum] complectitur amplioris obedientiæ promissionem quam possent Principes sæculares a subditis suis sæcularibus exigere, aut subditi ipsis præstare; et nonnulla insuper continet sinceræ professioni Catholicæ Religionis repugnantia; idcirco pro illicita prorsus ac detestabili habenda est. Quapropter quicunque præfatam professionis formulam nondum signarunt, cohibere se a signatura obligantur sub Sacrilegii reatu: Quicunque autem signarunt, religere signaturas suas obstringuntur sub consimili reatu; incauta namque definitio salubriter dissolvenda est, nec ea dissolutio reputanda est prævaricatio, sed temeritatis emendatio."—Caron, *Remonstrantia Hibernorum*, c. 5, s. 1.

[2] *Answer of the University of Louvain to Questions submitted to it by the Roman Catholics of England.*—Butler, *English Catholics*, 1, Appendix.

clergy of Ireland, by their refusal to sign the Remonstrance, lost "a fair opportunity of being not only eased of all their pressure from the penal laws, but rendered as happy as they could in reason desire or even wish."[1] This statement of Walsh does not point out the parties who really brought about the failure. The Irish clergy and laity desired to make a profession of their obedience and loyalty, but they were restrained by the influence of Rome, which forbade a reconciliation between them and their government. What excuse can be offered for the abuses of ecclesiastical authority of which the Roman Pontiffs were guilty, both in England and Ireland? Where was the spirit of charity and wisdom to be looked for, if not in the Councils of the Popes, who were at the same time Kings and Spiritual Pastors, and had their agents and overseers in every corner of Europe to report on the necessities and afflictions of their flocks? Yet, those Pontiffs, forgetting the example of their saintly predecessor, who subordinated his own opinion to the duty of obeying his secular prince, interfered with the civil duties of the subject, and entailed innumerable evils on their people in both countries. In England, successive Popes, under the false pretence that the oath of allegiance contained many things contrary to faith and salvation, harassed the consciences of their adherents, closed the gates of the constitution against them, and involved them and their posterity in misery for many generations. By making their faith the vehicle of treasonable tenets, they rendered its toleration inconsistent with the safety of the State, and sacrificed their Church to the maintenance of their temporal claims. In Ireland the same policy was pursued. Though the Papal See was perfectly aware that the Remonstrance was unexceptionable, and did not contain one word referring to faith or morals,[2]

[1] Bishop Kennet's *Register*, *Eccles. and Civil*, 484.
[2] "The instrument [the Remonstrance] is now acknowledged by

every art and every misrepresentation were made use of to prevent its signature. It was denounced as a violation of the Catholic faith, as destructive to religion, as dangerous to salvation, and all the priests who signed it were persecuted by monitories, citations, exclusion from promotion, and even by excommunications.[1] The consciences of the faithful were alarmed, and the clergy were terrorized from giving such a guarantee of their loyalty as would have secured relief to themselves and to the laity. It is impossible to survey the unrighteous conduct of the Popes to the sovereigns of England from the commencement of the reign of Elizabeth, and particularly their proceedings in the matter of the English oath of allegiance and the Irish Remonstrance, without being reminded of the saying of a statesman,[2] who observed character with a discriminating eye,—that of all men who can read and write, ecclesiastics understand the least, and take the worst measure of human affairs. Once they depart from the sanctuary, and usurp the direction of civil duties outside the pale of their spiritual charge, Providence appears to strike them with a darkness more than Egyptian.

During the latter portion of the short and unhappy reign of James II. the intercourse between the courts of England and Rome was open and avowed. Immediately after his accession, the King sent as his agent to Rome John Caryll, who assumed no public character and avoided all display. But this modest representation did not satisfy the extreme party about James, and in December, 1686, Lord Castlemaine

Catholics to be perfectly free from objection."—Throckmorton, *First Letter*, 155.

[1] "We are," says Walsh, "for no other crime than this steady loyalty, labouring now above twenty years under a sentence of excommunication which deprives us of the sacraments, of our characters, of our promotion in the Church, of all our temporalities, of all benefits of the Christian religion during life and of Christian burial after death."— *Causa Vales.*, quoted by O'Conor, *Hist. Address*; 1, 112.

[2] Lord Clarendon.

was despatched on a splendid embassy to the Pope. A more unfortunate choice could not have been made. Castlemaine was only known as the husband of a shameless woman, who had been one of the late King's mistresses, and had been created Duchess of Cleveland. To send such a man as ambassador to the Papal Court was something very like an affront to the Pontiff. Innocent XI. was well aware of the indiscreet zeal of the King, and received Castlemaine with the utmost coldness. Subsequently, the Pope complained to James of the indecent vehemence of a memorial presented to him by the ambassador.[1] Castlemaine was so dissatisfied with his position at Rome that he threatened to leave. Thereupon he was politely dismissed by Innocent with the advice not to travel in the heat of the day. Upon the return of Castlemaine, Lord Thomas Howard was sent in his place, and remained in Rome until shortly before the revolution.[2] In return for the mission of Caryll, Monsignor d'Adda, a sensible and moderate ecclesiastic, had arrived in England in November, 1685, with the powers of a Papal nuncio, but without any official character. Having been appointed Archbishop of Amasia in 1687, James insisted on the ceremony of his consecration being performed in the chapel of St. James's Palace. In July of the same year, a public and solemn reception was accorded to the nuncio at Windsor, and a procession took place in his honour in which he appeared in one of the royal carriages robed in his ecclesiastical dress.

Before James came to the throne, he had experienced a remarkable change in public opinion in favour of himself. At one time he was the most detested man in England. The

---

[1] Dodd, *Church History*, 3, 511.

[2] Lord Thomas Howard was appointed, in 1688, Lord Lieutenant of the West Riding of Yorkshire in the place of Lord Burlington, who had resigned his commission.—*Reresby's Memoirs*, 391, 404.

well-founded belief that he and his brother were secretly conspiring with Louis XIV. against the constitution and the Church of the country, had driven the English people into the frenzy of the Popish plot, and had suggested the bold and premature expedient of excluding James from the throne. But the folly and extravagance of the Whig party gave birth to a reaction in favour of the court and, in particular, of the prince. The countenance which that party lent to the succession of the Duke of Monmouth, the illegal violence of the House of Commons in 1680 and 1681, the schemes of insurrection projected in 1682, and the Rye House conspiracy, disgusted the nation, in whose memory the troubles of the great civil war were still fresh. The old feeling respecting the sacredness of the hereditary right revived, and James was with general approbation restored to the office of Lord High Admiral which he had resigned on the passing of the Test Act.[1]

At his accession James was undoubtedly popular.[2] Strange to say, no alarm was felt on account of his religion. His steady adherence to it under many difficulties and temptations appears even to have gained the respect and confidence of the nation. He was regarded as pre-eminently a man of sincerity, whose word was his bond. A few hours after the death of his brother he addressed the Council in a short and unprepared speech. "I know," said he, "the principles of the Church of England are for monarchy, and the members of it have showed themselves good and loyal subjects; therefore I shall always take care to defend and support it." The words were caught up, and ran like fire through town and country. "We have now for our Church the word of a King

[1] Lingard, quoting Evelyn: "Every one was glad of this change, those in the late commission being utterly ignorant of their duty, to the great damage of the navy."

[2] Fox, Mackintosh, Hallam, &c. testify to this.

and a word never broken," said a Protestant preacher,[1] and the promise was regarded as a greater security than any laws could afford.[2]

The first and only Parliament of James's reign met on the 19th of May, 1685, three months after his accession. The King in his opening speech renewed the engagement he had made to his Council. "What I said to my privy council at my first coming there, I am desirous to renew to you, wherein I fully declare my opinion concerning the principles of the Church of England, whose members have showed themselves so eminently loyal in the worst of times in defence of my father and support of my brother of blessed memory, that I will always take care to defend and support it. I will make it my endeavour to preserve the Government both in Church and State as it is now by law established."[3] The Parliament was perfectly satisfied, and granted the King a permanent revenue of two millions, though a month before its meeting James had discharged from prison some thousands of Roman Catholics who were confined for refusing the oaths of supremacy and allegiance. Nor was this the only example of the perfect trust reposed in the King. The House of Commons had resolved itself into a grand committee of religion in order to provide for the security of the Established Church. On the 27th of May two resolutions of this Committee were reported to the House: the first expressed attachment to the Church; the second called upon the King to execute the laws against all "dissenters whatsoever." A few days later, the decision of the Committee was unanimously reversed, and it was resolved "that this House doth acquiesce,

---

[1] Dr. Sharp, afterwards Archbishop of York. He was the first of the clergy who fell under the displeasure of the King.—Neal, *History of the Puritans*, 5, 1, note.

[2] Burnet, *History of his own Times*, 620.

[3] *Parliamentary History*, 4, 1351.

entirely rely, and rest wholly satisfied, in His Majesty's gracious word and repeated declaration to support and defend the religion of the Church of England, as it is now by law established, which is dearer to us than our lives." The parliament was prorogued on the 2nd of July, in consequence of Monmouth's invasion.

The two objects in favour of his own communion which James had in view were, the repeal of the penal laws and the removal of religious tests as qualifications for office. These two objects have been confounded in the histories of this reign, but they ought to be kept perfectly distinct, as they were by the King and his contemporaries. The first was feasible ; the attempt to repeal the Test Act was altogether premature. That Act was regarded as the bulwark of the Established Church, and it was felt to be especially necessary during the reign of a Roman Catholic King to prevent him filling all the offices of the State with members of his own religion. There is not the slightest reason to doubt that, with patience and wisdom, James would have succeeded in obtaining a repeal of the penal laws. The Pope and his nuncio were of opinion that he should aim at the abolition of these laws and leave the tests alone for the present. The moderate Roman Catholics were also in favour of this policy, but James was hurried on by the counsels of the small cabal about him, and by his own headstrong rashness. To spread his religion and to tempt converts to his own communion with the sweets of office was his object, rather than to free that body from the laws under which it laboured. He told the French ambassador that the admissibility to office would make more converts than the right of celebrating Mass in public. He, therefore, directed his efforts principally to obtain a repeal of the tests, and when he found that this was impossible, he had recourse to dispensations both special and general. If James had kept his promise to protect the national Church—that is, as Bossuet puts it, if he had maintained the existing laws, and, as King, executed them[1]—the Roman Catholics would have obtained complete toleration, and that toleration would have led, at no very distant time, to their admission to office. Penal statutes would have gone first, those imposing civil disabilities would have followed. With a King, who was the chief Roman Catholic in the realm, performing the duties of the highest office to the satisfaction of his subjects, it would have been paradoxical to exclude from minor employments those who were of that King's religion.

The second and last session of Parliament began on the 9th of November, 1685, and lasted only eleven days. A great change in public opinion had taken place since the prorogation in July. Instead of confidence in the King, the Houses, particularly the Commons, manifested distrust and a spirit of suspicion. This feeling was not caused by the conduct of James during the recess, though it was greatly increased by his declaration at the opening of the session that he would not dismiss the unqualified officers from the army. It was the result of an event which had taken place abroad. Louis XIV. had often promised to maintain the privileges of his reformed subjects, yet, on the 17th of October in this year, he formally revoked the great charter which, though too often violated, was still a protection to the Protestants of France, and delivered up a peaceable and industrious community to the barbarities of a military execution. The effect on English opinion was immediate. The old fears of persecution were revived, and men asked what security was there that a similar policy would not be adopted in Eng-

---

[1] Bossuet was of opinion that it was the duty of James "to protect and defend the Church of England as by law established."—Mazure, *La Revolution de* 1688, 3, Appendix.

land. James had increased, and was steadily increasing, the army, and explicitly declared to parliament that he would retain its Roman Catholic officers, in violation of the law.[1] From this time commenced that general discontent which ended in the Revolution. Yet, in spite of the distrust with which the King began to be regarded, he might still have obtained a repeal of the penal laws. In 1687, Stewart, a Scotch lawyer, was authorized by James to write to Fagel, the Grand Pensionary of Holland, to gain the concurrence of the Prince and Princess of Orange to the abolition of the penal laws and of the tests. After some delay an answer was sent, in which the Pensionary declared that the Prince and Princess were ready to concur in granting a full liberty of conscience, and in repealing the penal laws, "provided always that those laws remain still in their full vigour, by which the Roman Catholics are shut out of both Houses of Parliament, and out of all employments, ecclesiastical, civil, and military."[2] The King ordered Stewart to reply that he would have all or nothing. It is clear that with the support of the Prince of Orange, who was the natural head of the English Opposition, and to whom the eyes of all were then directed, James might easily have effected the repeal of the penal laws. Though he was implored by the lay Roman Catholics to accept the offer,[3] and thus make them easy and secure for the future, he neglected the opportunity, and left them exposed to the severity of those laws.

This is not the place to recall the constitutional mistakes

[1] "Let no man take exception that there are some officers in the army not qualified according to the late Test for their employments. . . . I will deal plainly with you that, after having had the benefit of their service in such a time of need and danger, I will neither expose them to disgrace nor myself to the want of them, if there should be another rebellion to make them necessary to me."—*Parl. Hist.* 4, 1371.

[2] *State Tracts*, 2, 334, where Fagel's answer is given in full.

[3] Burnet, *History of the Reign of James II.* 246, Oxford, 1852.

of a King who seemed to be bent on his own destruction. It is only requisite to point out the fatal effects of James's proceedings on the hopes of a communion which he might so easily have benefited. A great experiment, as it were, was made by the English people in the case of the most prominent representative of that communion as to his trustworthiness, and in the trial he was found wanting. A Roman Catholic prince was saved from banishment and exclusion from the throne by the Church of England. On his accession, he acknowledged again and again the debt which he owed to that Church, and swore at his coronation to defend and maintain its rights and privileges. By the support of the same Church he was rendered the most powerful of English sovereigns since the reign of Elizabeth. If ever a man was bound to protect and support the English Church, James was that man. If he was false to his promises, what member of his faith could be expected to be true? Yet, forgetful of the ties of gratitude and honour, he attacked the great institution to which his very existence as a King was due, and broke engagements which he ought to have considered inviolable. By his faithlessness and violence he strengthened every prejudice and confirmed every suspicion against the members of his religion. "There was then no doubt," so men reasoned, " that to Roman Catholics nothing was sacred but their own Church. Every rule of morality might be violated, every claim of honour might be neglected, for its advancement. No faith was to be kept with heretics, nor were oaths and promises made to them to be observed. A persecution, similar to that now raging in France, awaits us." A certain conviction that Roman Catholics held the anti-social tenets attributed to them, and that they could not be trusted in any of the relations of life, was the result of James's treachery, and this conviction delayed for more than a hundred years the relief of that unfortunate body, which during that further period continued to expiate its own political errors and the sins and transgressions of its ecclesiastical and secular leaders.

A few words may be added here respecting the sentiments with which the Roman Catholics regarded the new government established by the Revolution. With their usual ill-luck or under bad guidance they refused to accede to it, and continued to look upon the Stuarts as their legitimate sovereigns. The disputes among them concerning the oath of allegiance ceased, for why dispute about oaths, when the right of him who demanded them was denied? Though the oath of allegiance and that of supremacy were both altered,[1] the former being cleared of all objectionable expressions, and the latter from the affirmative clause respecting the supreme governorship in all spiritual and ecclesiastical causes, they declined to take these tests of obedience to the successors of James, and, like the Protestant non-jurors, maintained their devotion to the abdicated family. Like them, too, they became a branch of the great and dangerous party of the Jacobites and were necessarily discountenanced and repressed. At length, when time had shown them the impossibility of a Stuart restoration, they transferred their affections to the line of Brunswick. In 1778, they presented an address to George III. in which they acknowledged his title to the crown, and declared that "their dissent from the

---

[1] The new oath of allegiance was:—"I do sincerely promise and swear, that I will be faithful and bear true allegiance to their Majesties King William and Queen Mary." That of supremacy was:—"I do swear that I do from my heart abhor, detest, and abjure as impious and heretical, that damnable doctrine and position that princes excommunicated or deprived by the Pope, or any authority of the See of Rome, may be deposed or murdered by their subjects or any other whatsoever. And I do declare that no foreign prince, person, prelate, state, or potentate, hath or ought to have any jurisdiction, power, superiority, pre-eminence, or authority, ecclesiastical or spiritual, within this realm."

legal establishment[1] was purely conscientious, and that they held no opinions adverse to his Majesty's government or repugnant to the duties of good citizens." The mists of prejudice and apprehension disappeared, and within fifty years,—a short time to allay the fears and suspicions of a nation,—they were admitted into the constitution.

[1] Upon this expression, Sir John Throckmorton remarks, "After this assertion by which the whole body of Catholics declare themselves *Dissenters from the establishment*, it is wonderful that any offence should have been taken at the appellation of *Catholic dissenters*. After all, this is no new appellation; our ancestors were called *Catholic dissenters* in the reign of James II. in publications which were printed by authority. It gave no offence at the time."—*First Letter*, 195.

THE END.

Printed by Ponsonby and Weldrick, Dublin.

IN

GENERAL LITERATURE

PUBLISHED BY

MESSRS. LONGMANS, GREEN, & CO.

39 PATERNOSTER ROW, LONDON, E.C.

MESSRS. LONGMANS, GREEN, & CO.

Issue the undermentioned Lists of their Publications, which may be had post free on application:—

1. MONTHLY LIST OF NEW WORKS AND NEW EDITIONS.

2. QUARTERLY LIST OF ANNOUNCEMENTS AND NEW WORKS.

3. NOTES ON BOOKS; BEING AN ANALYSIS OF THE WORKS PUBLISHED DURING EACH QUARTER.

4. CATALOGUE OF SCIENTIFIC WORKS.

5. CATALOGUE OF MEDICAL AND SURGICAL WORKS.

6. CATALOGUE OF SCHOOL BOOKS AND EDUCATIONAL WORKS.

7. CATALOGUE OF BOOKS FOR ELEMENTARY SCHOOLS AND PUPIL TEACHERS.

8. CATALOGUE OF THEOLOGICAL WORKS BY DIVINES AND MEMBERS OF THE CHURCH OF ENGLAND.

9. CATALOGUE OF WORKS IN GENERAL LITERATURE.

ABBEY and OVERTON.—**The English Church in the Eighteenth Century.** By CHARLES J. ABBEY and JOHN H. OVERTON. Cr. 8vo. 7s. 6d.

ABBOTT.—**Hellenica.** A Collection of Essays on Greek Poetry, Philosophy, History, and Religion. Edited by EVELYN ABBOTT, M.A., LL.D., Fellow and Tutor of Balliol College, Oxford. 8vo. 16s.

ABBOTT (Evelyn, M.A., LL.D.)—WORKS BY.

A Skeleton Outline of Greek History. Chronologically Arranged. Crown 8vo. 2s. 6d.

A History of Greece. In Two Parts.
Part I.—From the Earliest Times to the Ionian Revolt. Crown 8vo. 10s. 6d.
Part II. Vol. I.—500-445 B.C. [*In the Press.*
Vol. II.—[*In Preparation*].

ACLAND and RANSOME.—**A Handbook in Outline of the Political History of England to 1890.** Chronologically Arranged. By A. H. DYKE ACLAND, M.P., and CYRIL RANSOME, M.A. Crown 8vo. 6s.

ACTON.—**Modern Cookery.** By ELIZA ACTON. With 150 Woodcuts. Fcp. 8vo. 4s. 6d.

A. K. H. B.—THE ESSAYS AND CONTRIBUTIONS OF. Crown 8vo.

Autumn Holidays of a Country Parson. 3s. 6d.
Changed Aspects of Unchanged Truths. 3s. 6d.
Commonplace Philosopher. 3s. 6d.
Counsel and Comfort from a City Pulpit. 3s. 6d.
Critical Essays of a Country Parson. 3s. 6d.

[*Continued on next page.*

*A. K. H. B.—THE ESSAYS AND CONTRIBUTIONS OF—*continued.

East Coast Days and Memories. 3s. 6d.
Graver Thoughts of a Country Parson. Three Series. 3s. 6d. each.
Landscapes, Churches, and Moralities. 3s. 6d.
Leisure Hours in Town. 3s. 6d.
Lessons of Middle Age. 3s. 6d.
Our Little Life. Two Series. 3s. 6d. each.
Our Homely Comedy and Tragedy. 3s. 6d.
Present Day Thoughts. 3s. 6d.
Recreations of a Country Parson. Three Series. 3s. 6d. each.
Seaside Musings. 3s. 6d.
Sunday Afternoons in the Parish Church of a Scottish University City. 3s. 6d.
'To Meet the Day' through the Christian year: being a Text of Scripture, with an Original Meditation and a Short Selection in Verse for Every Day. 4s. 6d.

American Whist, Illustrated: containing the Laws and Principles of the Game, the Analysis of the New Play and American Leads, and a Series of Hands in Diagram, and combining Whist Universal and American Whist. By G. W. P. Fcp. 8vo. 6s. 6d.

*AMOS.—***A Primer of the English Constitution and Government.** By SHELDON AMOS. Crown 8vo. 6s.

Annual Register (The). A Review of Public Events at Home and Abroad, for the year 1890. 8vo. 18s.
*** Volumes of the 'Annual Register' for the years 1863-1889 can still be had.

ANSTEY (F.)—WORKS BY.

The Black Poodle, and other Stories. Crown 8vo. 2s. bds.; 2s. 6d. cl.

Voces Populi. Reprinted from *Punch.* With 20 Illustrations by J. BERNARD PARTRIDGE. Fcp. 4to. 5s.

ARISTOTLE.—THE WORKS OF.

The Politics: G. Bekker's Greek Text of Books I. III. IV. (VII.) with an English Translation by W. E. BOLLAND, M.A.; and short Introductory Essays by A. LANG, M.A. Crown 8vo. 7s. 6d.

The Politics: Introductory Essays. By ANDREW LANG. (From Bolland and Lang's 'Politics'.) Crown 8vo. 2s. 6d.

The Ethics: Greek Text, Illustrated with Essays and Notes. By Sir ALEXANDER GRANT, Bart., M.A., LL.D. 2 vols. 8vo. 32s.

The Nicomachean Ethics: Newly Translated into English. By ROBERT WILLIAMS, Barrister-at-Law. Crown 8vo. 7s. 6d.

ARMSTRONG (G. F. Savage-)—WORKS BY.

Poems: Lyrical and Dramatic. Fcp. 8vo. 6s.

King Saul. (The Tragedy of Israel, Part I.) Fcp. 8vo. 5s.

King David. (The Tragedy of Israel, Part II.) Fcp. 8vo. 6s.

King Solomon. (The Tragedy of Israel, Part III.) Fcp. 8vo. 6s.

Ugone: A Tragedy. Fcp. 8vo. 6s.

A Garland from Greece; Poems. Fcp. 8vo. 9s.

Stories of Wicklow; Poems. Fcp. 8vo. 9s.

Mephistopheles in Broadcloth: a Satire. Fcp. 8vo. 4s.

The Life and Letters of Edmund J. Armstrong. Fcp. 8vo. 7s. 6d.

ARMSTRONG (E. J.)—WORKS BY.

Poetical Works. Fcp. 8vo. 5s.

Essays and Sketches. Fcp. 8vo. 5s.

ARMSTRONG. — **Elizabeth Farnese:** the Termagant of Spain. By EDWARD ARMSTRONG, Queen's College, Oxford. [*In the press.*

ARNOLD (Sir Edwin, K.C.I.E.)—WORKS BY.

The Light of the World; or, the Great Consummation. A Poem. Crown 8vo. 7s. 6d. net.

Seas and Lands. Reprinted letters from the 'Daily Telegraph'. With numerous Illustrations. 8vo. 21s.

ARNOLD (Dr. T.)—WORKS BY.

Introductory Lectures on Modern History. 8vo. 7s. 6d.

Miscellaneous Works. 8vo. 7s. 6d.

*ASHLEY.—***English Economic History and Theory.** By W. J. ASHLEY, M.A. Part I. The Middle Ages. 5s.

Atelier (The) du Lys; or, An Art Student in the Reign of Terror. By the Author of 'Mademoiselle Mori'. Crown 8vo. 2s. 6d.

BY THE SAME AUTHOR.

Mademoiselle Mori: a Tale of Modern Rome. Crown 8vo. 2s. 6d.

That Child. Illustrated by GORDON BROWNE. Crown 8vo. 2s. 6d.

[*Continued on next page.*

PUBLISHED BY MESSRS. LONGMANS, GREEN, & CO. 3

Atelier (The) du Lys—*WORKS BY THE AUTHOR OF—continued.*

Under a Cloud. Cr. 8vo. 2s. 6d.

The Fiddler of Lugau. With Illustrations by W. RALSTON. Crown 8vo. 2s. 6d.

A Child of the Revolution. With Illustrations by C. J. STANILAND. Crown 8vo. 2s. 6d.

Hester's Venture: a Novel. Cr. 8vo. 2s. 6d.

In the Olden Time: a Tale of the Peasant War in Germany. Cr. 8vo. 2s. 6d.

BACON.—THE WORKS AND LIFE OF.

Complete Works. Edited by R. L. ELLIS, J. SPEDDING, and D. D. HEATH. 7 vols. 8vo. £3 13s. 6d.

Letters and Life, including all his Occasional Works. Edited by J. SPEDDING. 7 vols. 8vo. £4 4s.

The Essays; with Annotations. By RICHARD WHATELY, D.D., 8vo. 10s. 6d.

The Essays; with Introduction, Notes, and Index. By E. A. ABBOTT, D.D. 2 vols. fcp. 8vo. price 6s. Text and Index only, without Introduction and Notes, in 1 vol. Fcp. 8vo. 2s. 6d.

The BADMINTON LIBRARY, Edited by the DUKE OF BEAUFORT, K.G., assisted by ALFRED E. T. WATSON.

Hunting. By the DUKE OF BEAUFORT, K.G., and MOWBRAY MORRIS. With 53 Illus. by J. Sturgess, J. Charlton, and A. M. Biddulph. Cr. 8vo. 10s. 6d.

Fishing. By H. CHOLMONDELEY-PENNELL.
Vol. I. Salmon, Trout, and Grayling. With 158 Illustrations. Cr. 8vo. 10s. 6d.
Vol. II. Pike and other Coarse Fish. With 132 Illustrations. Cr. 8vo. 10s. 6d.

Racing and Steeplechasing. By the EARL OF SUFFOLK AND BERKSHIRE, W. G. CRAVEN, &c. With 56 Illustrations by J. Sturgess. Cr. 8vo. 10s. 6d.

Shooting. By LORD WALSINGHAM and Sir RALPH PAYNE-GALLWEY, Bart.
Vol. I. Field and Covert. With 105 Illustrations. Cr. 8vo. 10s. 6d.
Vol. II. Moor and Marsh. With 65 Illustrations. Cr. 8vo. 10s. 6d.

Cycling. By VISCOUNT BURY (Earl of Albemarle), K.C.M.G., and G. LACY HILLIER. With 19 Plates and 70 Woodcuts, &c., by Viscount Bury, Joseph Pennell, &c. Crown 8vo. 10s. 6d.

The BADMINTON LIBRARY—*continued.*

Athletics and Football. By MONTAGUE SHEARMAN. With 6 full-page Illustrations and 45 Woodcuts, &c., by Stanley Berkeley, and from Photographs by G. Mitchell. Crown 8vo. 10s. 6d.

Boating. By W. B. WOODGATE. With 10 full-page Illustrations and 39 woodcuts, &c., in the Text. Cr. 8vo. 10s. 6d.

Cricket. By A. G. STEEL and the Hon. R. H. LYTTELTON, With 11 full-page Illustrations and 52 Woodcuts, &c., in the Text, by Lucien Davis. Cr. 8vo. 10s. 6d.

Driving. By the DUKE OF BEAUFORT. With 11 Plates and 54 Woodcuts, &c., by J. Sturgess and G. D. Giles. Crown 8vo. 10s. 6d.

Fencing, Boxing, and Wrestling. By WALTER H. POLLOCK, F. C. GROVE, C. PREVOST, E. B. MICHELL, and WALTER ARMSTRONG. With 18 Plates and 24 Woodcuts, &c. Crown 8vo. 10s. 6d.

Golf. By HORACE HUTCHINSON, the Rt. Hon. A. J. BALFOUR, M.P., ANDREW LANG, Sir W. G. SIMPSON, Bart., &c. With 19 Plates and 69 Woodcuts, &c. Crown 8vo. 10s. 6d.

Tennis, Lawn Tennis, Rackets, and Fives. By J. M. and C. G. HEATHCOTE, E. O. PLEYDELL-BOUVERIE, and A. C. AINGER. With 12 Plates and 67 Woodcuts, &c. Crown 8vo. 10s. 6d.

Riding and Polo. By Captain ROBERT WEIR, Riding Master, R.H.G., and J. MORAY BROWN. With Contributions by the Duke of Beaufort, K.G., the Earl of Suffolk and Berkshire, the Earl of Onslow, E. L. Anderson, and Alfred E. T. Watson. With 18 Plates and 41 Woodcuts, &c. Crown 8vo. 10s. 6d.

BAGEHOT (Walter).—WORKS BY.

Biographical Studies. 8vo. 12s.

Economic Studies. 8vo. 10s. 6d.

Literary Studies. 2 vols. 8vo. 28s.

The Postulates of English Political Economy. Cr. 8vo. 2s. 6d.

A Practical Plan for Assimilating the English and American Money as a Step towards a Universal Money. Cr. 8vo. 2s. 6d.

BAGWELL.—**Ireland under the Tudors**, with a Succinct Account of the Earlier History. By RICHARD BAGWELL, M.A. (3 vols.) Vols. I. and II. From the first invasion of the Northmen to the year 1578. 8vo. 32s. Vol. III. 1578-1603. 8vo. 18s.

BAIN (Alexander).—*WORKS BY.*
Mental and Moral Science. Cr. 8vo. 10s. 6d.
Senses and the Intellect. 8vo. 15s.
Emotions and the Will. 8vo. 15s.
Logic, Deductive, and Inductive. PART I. *Deduction*, 4s. PART II. *Induction*, 6s. 6d.
Practical Essays. Cr. 8vo. 2s.

BAKER.—**By the Western Sea:** a Summer Idyll. By JAMES BAKER, F.R.G.S. Author of 'John Westacott'. Crown 8vo. 3s. 6d.

BAKER (Sir S. W.).—*WORKS BY.*
Eight Years in Ceylon. With 6 Illustrations. Crown 8vo. 3s. 6d.
The Rifle and the Hound in Ceylon. With 6 Illustrations. Crown 8vo. 3s. 6d.

BALL (The Rt. Hon. J. T.).—*WORKS BY.*
The Reformed Church of Ireland. (1537-1889). 8vo. 7s. 6d.
Historical Review of the Legislative Systems Operative in Ireland, from the Invasion of Henry the Second to the Union (1172-1800). 8vo. 6s.

BEACONSFIELD (The Earl of).—*WORKS BY.*
Novels and Tales. The Hughenden Edition. With 2 Portraits and 11 Vignettes. 11 vols. Crown 8vo. 42s.
Endymion.   Henrietta Temple.
Lothair.   Contarini, Fleming, &c.
Coningsby.   Alroy, Ixion, &c.
Tancred. Sybil.   The Young Duke, &c.
Venetia.   Vivian Grey.
Novels and Tales. Cheap Edition. Complete in 11 vols. Crown 8vo. 1s. each, boards; 1s. 6d. each, cloth.

BECKER (Professor).—*WORKS BY.*
Gallus; or, Roman Scenes in the Time of Augustus. Post 8vo. 7s. 6d.
Charicles; or, Illustrations of the Private Life of the Ancient Greeks. Post 8vo. 7s. 6d.

BELL (Mrs. Hugh).—*WORKS BY.*
Will o' the Wisp: a Story. Illustrated by E. L. SHUTE. Crown 8vo. 3s. 6d.
Chamber Comedies: a Collection of Plays and Monologues for the Drawing Room. Crown 8vo. 6s.

BLAKE.—**Tables for the Conversion of 5 per Cent. Interest from $\frac{1}{16}$ to 7 per Cent.** By J. BLAKE, of the London Joint Stock Bank, Limited. 8vo. 12s. 6d.

Book (The) of Wedding Days. Arranged on the Plan of a Birthday Book. With 96 Illustrated Borders, Frontispiece, and Title-page by WALTER CRANE; and Quotations for each Day. Compiled and Arranged by K. E. J. REID, MAY ROSS, and MABEL BAMFIELD. 4to. 21s.

BRASSEY (Lady).—*WORKS BY.*
A Voyage in the 'Sunbeam,' our Home on the Ocean for Eleven Months.
Library Edition. With 8 Maps and Charts, and 118 Illustrations, 8vo. 21s.
Cabinet Edition. With Map and 66 Illustrations, Crown 8vo. 7s. 6d.
'Silver Library' Edition. With 66 Illustrations. Crown 8vo. 3s. 6d.
Popular Edition. With 60 Illustrations, 4to. 6d. sewed, 1s. cloth.
School Edition. With 37 Illustrations, Fcp. 2s. cloth, or 3s. white parchment.
Sunshine and Storm in the East.
Library Edition. With 2 Maps and 114 Illustrations, 8vo. 21s.
Cabinet Edition. With 2 Maps and 114 Illustrations, Crown 8vo. 7s. 6d.
Popular Edition. With 103 Illustrations, 4to. 6d. sewed, 1s. cloth.
In the Trades, the Tropics, and the 'Roaring Forties'.
Cabinet Edition. With Map and 220 Illustrations, Crown 8vo. 7s. 6d.
Popular Edition. With 183 Illustrations, 4to. 6d. sewed, 1s. cloth.
The Last Voyage to India and Australia in the 'Sunbeam'. With Charts and Maps, and 40 Illustrations in Monotone (20 full-page), and nearly 200 Illustrations in the Text from Drawings by R. T. PRITCHETT. 8vo. 21s.
Three Voyages in the 'Sunbeam'. Popular Edition. With 346 Illustrations, 4to. 2s. 6d.

BRAY.—**The Philosophy of Necessity;** or, Law in Mind as in Matter. By CHARLES BRAY. Crown 8vo. 5s.

BRIGHT.—A History of England. By the Rev. J. FRANCK BRIGHT, D.D., Master of University College, Oxford. 4 vols. Crown 8vo.
Period I.—Mediæval Monarchy: The Departure of the Romans to Richard III. From A.D. 449 to 1485. 4s. 6d.
Period II.—Personal Monarchy: Henry VII. to James II. From 1485 to 1688. 5s.
Period III.—Constitutional Monarchy: William and Mary to William IV. From 1689 to 1837. 7s. 6d.
Period IV.—The Growth of Democracy: Victoria. From 1837 to 1880. 6s.

BROKE.—With Sack and Stock in Alaska. By GEORGE BROKE, A.C., F.R.G.S. With 2 Maps. Crown 8vo. 5s.

BRYDEN.—Kloof and Karroo: Sport, Legend, and Natural History in Cape Colony. By H. A. BRYDEN. With 17 Illustrations. 8vo. 10s. 6d.

BUCKLE.—History of Civilisation in England and France, Spain and Scotland. By HENRY THOMAS BUCKLE. 3 vols. Cr. 8vo. 24s.

BULL (Thomas).—WORKS BY.
Hints to Mothers on the Management of their Health during the Period of Pregnancy. Fcp. 8vo. 1s. 6d.
The Maternal Management of Children in Health and Disease. Fcp. 8vo. 1s. 6d.

BUTLER (Samuel).—WORKS BY.
Op. 1. Erewhon. Crown 8vo. 5s.
Op. 2. The Fair Haven. A Work in defence of the Miraculous Element in our Lord's Ministry. Crown 8vo. 7s. 6d.
Op. 3. Life and Habit. An Essay after a Completer View of Evolution. Crown 8vo. 7s. 6d.
Op. 4. Evolution, Old and New. Crown 8vo. 10s. 6d.
Op. 5. Unconscious Memory. Crown 8vo. 7s. 6d.
Op. 6. Alps and Sanctuaries of Piedmont and the Canton Ticino. Illustrated. Pott 4to. 10s. 6d.
Op. 7. Selections from Ops. 1-6. With Remarks on Mr. G. J. ROMANES' 'Mental Evolution in Animals'. Cr. 8vo. 7s. 6d.

BUTLER (Samuel).—WORKS BY.—continued.
Op. 8. Luck, or Cunning, as the Main Means of Organic Modification? Cr. 8vo. 7s. 6d.
Op. 9. Ex Voto. An Account of the Sacro Monte or New Jerusalem at Varallo-Sesia. 10s. 6d.
Holbein's 'La Danse'. A Note on a Drawing called 'La Danse'. 3s.

CARLYLE.—Thomas Carlyle: a History of His Life. By J. A. FROUDE. 1795-1835, 2 vols. Crown 8vo. 7s. 1834-1881, 2 vols. Crown 8vo. 7s.

CASE.—Physical Realism: being an Analytical Philosophy from the Physical Objects of Science to the Physical Data of Sense. By THOMAS CASE, M.A., Fellow and Senior Tutor, C.C.C. 8vo. 15s.

CHETWYND.—Racing Reminiscences and Experiences of the Turf. By Sir GEORGE CHETWYND, Bart. 2 vols. 8vo. 21s.

CHILD.—Church and State under the Tudors. By GILBERT W. CHILD, M.A. 8vo. 15s.

CHISHOLM.—Handbook of Commercial Geography. By G. G. CHISHOLM. With 29 Maps. 8vo. 16s.

CHURCH.—Sir Richard Church, C.B., G.C.H. Commander-in-Chief of the Greeks in the War of Independence: a Memoir. By STANLEY LANE-POOLE. With 2 Plans. 8vo. 5s.

CLIVE.—Poems. By V. (Mrs. ARCHER CLIVE), Author of 'Paul Ferroll'. Including the IX. Poems. Fcp. 8vo. 6s.

CLODD.—The Story of Creation: a Plain Account of Evolution. By EDWARD CLODD. With 77 Illustrations. Crown 8vo. 3s. 6d.

CLUTTERBUCK (W. J.).—WORKS BY.
The Skipper in Arctic Seas. With 39 Illustrations. Cr. 8vo. 10s. 6d.
About Ceylon and Borneo: being an Account of Two Visits to Ceylon, one to Borneo, and How we Fell Out on our Homeward Journey. With 47 Illustrations. Crown 8vo.

COLENSO.—The Pentateuch and Book of Joshua Critically Examined. By J. W. COLENSO, D.D., late Bishop of Natal. Cr. 8vo. 6s.

COMYN.—**Atherstone Priory:** a Tale. By L. N. COMYN. Cr. 8vo. 2s. 6d.

CONINGTON (John).— *WORKS BY.*
The Æneid of Virgil. Translated into English Verse. Crown 8vo. 6s.
The Poems of Virgil. Translated into English Prose. Crown 8vo. 6s.

COX.— **A General History of Greece,** from the Earliest Period to the Death of Alexander the Great; with a sketch of the subsequent History to the Present Time. By the Rev. Sir G. W. COX, Bart., M.A. With 11 Maps and Plans. Crown 8vo. 7s. 6d.

CRAKE (Rev. A. D.).— *WORKS BY.*
Historical Tales. Crown 8vo. 5 vols. 2s. 6d. each.
Edwy the Fair; or, The First Chronicle of Æscendune.
Alfgar the Dane; or, the Second Chronicle of Æscendune.
The Rival Heirs: being the Third and Last Chronicle of Æscendune.
The House of Walderne. A Tale of the Cloister and the Forest in the Days of the Barons' Wars.
Brian Fitz-Count. A Story of Wallingford Castle and Dorchester Abbey.
History of the Church under the Roman Empire, A.D. 30-476. Crown 8vo. 7s. 6d.

CREIGHTON.— **History of the Papacy during the Reformation.** By MANDELL CREIGHTON, D.D., LL.D., Bishop of Peterborough. 8vo. Vols. I. and II., 1378-1464, 32s.; Vols. III. and IV., 1464-1518, 24s.

CRUMP (A.).— *WORKS BY.*
A Short Enquiry into the Formation of Political Opinion, from the reign of the Great Families to the Advent of Democracy. 8vo. 7s. 6d.
An Investigation into the Causes of the Great Fall in Prices which took place coincidently with the Demonetisation of Silver by Germany. 8vo. 6s.

CUDWORTH.—**An Introduction to Cudworth's Treatise concerning Eternal and Immutable Morality.** By W. R. SCOTT. Crown 8vo. 3s.

CURZON.—**Russia in Central Asia in 1889, and the Anglo-Russian Question.** By the Hon. GEORGE N. CURZON, M.P. 8vo. 21s.

DANTE.—**La Commedia di Dante.** A New Text, carefully Revised with the aid of the most recent Editions and Collations. Small 8vo. 6s.

DAVIDSON (W. L.).— *WORKS BY.*
The Logic of Definition Explained and Applied. Cr. 8vo. 6s.
Leading and Important English Words Explained and Exemplified. Fcp. 8vo. 3s. 6d.

DELAND (Mrs.).— *WORKS BY.*
John Ward, Preacher: a Story. Crown 8vo. 2s. boards. 2s. 6d. cloth.
Sidney: a Novel. Crown 8vo. 6s.
The Old Garden, and other Verses. Fcp. 8vo. 5s.

DE LA SAUSSAYE.—**A Manual of the Science of Religion.** By Professor CHANTEPIE DE LA SAUSSAYE. Translated by Mrs. COLYER FERGUSSON (née MAX MULLER). Revised by the Author. Crown 8vo. 12s. 6d.

DE REDCLIFFE.—**The Life of the Right Hon. Stratford Canning: Viscount Stratford De Redcliffe.** By STANLEY LANE-POOLE. Cabinet Edition, abridged, with 3 Portraits, 1 vol. Crown 8vo. 7s. 6d.

DE SALIS (Mrs.).— *WORKS BY.*
Cakes and Confections à la Mode. Fcp. 8vo. 1s. 6d. boards.
Dressed Game and Poultry à la Mode. Fcp. 8vo. 1s. 6d. bds.
Dressed Vegetables à la Mode. Fcp. 8vo. 1s. 6d. boards.
Drinks à la Mode. Fcp. 8vo. 1s. 6d. boards.
Entrées à la Mode. Fcp. 8vo. 1s. 6d. boards.
Floral Decorations. Suggestions and Descriptions. Fcap. 8vo. 1s. 6d.
Oysters à la Mode. Fcp. 8vo. 1s. 6d. boards.

[*Continued on next page.*

DE SALIS (*Mrs.*).—*WORKS BY.—cont.*
Puddings and Pastry à la Mode. Fcp. 8vo. 1s. 6d. boards.
Savouries à la Mode. Fcp. 8vo. 1s. 6d. boards.
Soups and Dressed Fish à la Mode. Fcp. 8vo. 1s. 6d. boards.
Sweets and Supper Dishes à la Mode. Fcp. 8vo. 1s. 6d. boards.
Tempting Dishes for Small Incomes. Fcp. 8vo. 1s. 6d.
Wrinkles and Notions for every Household. Crown 8vo. 2s. 6d.

DE TOCQUEVILLE.—**Democracy in America.** By ALEXIS DE TOCQUEVILLE. 2 vols. Crown 8vo. 16s.

DOUGALL.—**Beggars All:** a Novel. By L. DOUGALL. Crown 8vo. 6s.

DOWELL.—**A History of Taxation and Taxes in England** from the Earliest Times to the Year 1885. By STEPHEN DOWELL. (4 vols. 8vo.) Vols. I. and II. The History of Taxation, 21s. Vols. III. and IV. The History of Taxes, 21s.

DOYLE (*A. Conan*).—*WORKS BY.*
Micah Clarke. A tale of Monmouth's Rebellion. With Frontispiece and Vignette. Crown 8vo. 3s. 6d.
The Captain of the Polestar; and other Tales. Crown 8vo. 6s.

DRANE.—**The History of St. Dominic.** By AUGUSTA THEODORA DRANE. 32 Illustrations. 8vo. 15s.

Dublin University Press Series (The): a Series of Works undertaken by the Provost and Senior Fellows of Trinity College, Dublin.
Abbott's (T. K.) Codex Rescriptus Dublinensis of St. Matthew. 4to. 21s.
—— Evangeliorum Versio Antehieronymiana ex Codice Usseriano (Dublinensi). 2 vols. Crown 8vo. 21s.
Allman's (G. J.) Greek Geometry from Thales to Euclid. 8vo. 10s. 6d.
Burnside (W. S.) and Panton's (A. W.) Theory of Equations. 8vo. 12s. 6d.
Casey's (John) Sequel to Euclid's Elements. Crown 8vo. 3s. 6d.
—— Analytical Geometry of the Conic Sections. Crown 8vo. 7s. 6d.

Dublin University Press Series (The).—*continued.*
Davies' (J. F.) Eumenides of Æschylus. With Metrical English Translation. 8vo. 7s.
Dublin Translations into Greek and Latin Verse. Edited by R. Y. Tyrrell. 8vo. 6s.
Graves' (R. P.) Life of Sir William Hamilton. 3 vols. 15s. each.
Griffin (R. W.) on Parabola, Ellipse, and Hyperbola. Crown 8vo. 6s.
Hobart's (W. K.) Medical Language of St. Luke. 8vo. 16s.
Leslie's (T. E. Cliffe) Essays in Political Economy. 8vo. 10s. 6d.
Macalister's (A.) Zoology and Morphology of Vertebrata. 8vo. 10s. 6d.
MacCullagh's (James) Mathematical and other Tracts. 8vo. 15s.
Maguire's (T.) Parmenides of Plato, Text, with Introduction, Analysis, &c. 8vo. 7s. 6d.
Monck's (W. H. S.) Introduction to Logic. Crown 8vo. 5s.
Roberts' (R. A.) Examples on the Analytic Geometry of Plane Conics. Cr. 8vo. 5s.
Southey's (R.) Correspondence with Caroline Bowles. Edited by E. Dowden. 8vo. 14s.
Stubbs' (J. W.) History of the University of Dublin, from its Foundation to the End of the Eighteenth Century. 8vo. 12s. 6d.
Thornhill's (W. J.) The Æneid of Virgil, freely translated into English Blank Verse. Crown 8vo. 7s. 6d.
Tyrrell's (R. Y.) Cicero's Correspondence. Vols. I. II. III. 8vo. each 12s.
—— The Acharnians of Aristophanes, translated into English Verse. Crown 8vo. 1s.
Webb's (T. E.) Goethe's Faust, Translation and Notes. 8vo. 12s. 6d.
—— The Veil of Isis: a Series of Essays on Idealism. 8vo. 10s. 6d.
Wilkins' (G.) The Growth of the Homeric Poems. 8vo. 6s.

Epochs of Modern History. Edited by C. COLBECK, M.A. 19 vols. Fcp. 8vo. with Maps, 2s. 6d. each.
Airy's (O.) The English Restoration and Louis XIV. (1648-1678).
Church's (Very Rev. R. W.) The Beginning of the Middle Ages. With 3 Maps.

[*Continued on next page.*

Epochs of Modern History.—*cont.*

Cox's (Rev. Sir G. W.) The Crusades. With a Map.

Creighton's (Rev. M.) The Age of Elizabeth. With 5 Maps.

Gairdner's (J.) The Houses of Lancaster and York; with the Conquest and Loss of France. With 5 Maps.

Gardiner's (S. R.) The First Two Stuarts and the Puritan Revolution (1603-1660). With 4 Maps.

—— The Thirty Years' War (1618-1648). With a Map.

Gardiner's (Mrs. S. R.) The French Revolution (1789-1795). With 7 Maps.

Hale's 'Rev. E.) The Fall of the Stuarts; and Western Europe (1678-1697). With 11 Maps and Plans.

Johnson's (Rev. A. H.) The Normans in Europe. With 3 Maps.

Longman's (F. W.) Frederick the Great and the Seven Years' War. With 2 Maps.

Ludlow's (J. M.) The War of American Independence (1775-1783). With 4 Maps.

McCarthy's (Justin) The Epoch of Reform (1830-1850).

Moberly's (Rev. C. E.) The Early Tudors.

Morris's (E. E.) The Age of Anne. With 7 Maps and Plans.

—— The Early Hanoverians. With 9 Maps and Plans.

Seebohm's (F.) The Era of the Protestant Revolution. With 4 Maps.

Stubbs' (Right Rev. W.) The Early Plantagenets. With 2 Maps.

Warburton's (Rev. W.) Edward the Third. With 3 Maps.

Epochs of Church History. Edited by MANDELL CREIGHTON, D.D., Bishop of Peterborough. Fcp. 8vo. 2s. 6d. each.

Balzani's (U.) The Popes and the Hohenstaufen.

Brodrick's (Hon. G. C.) A History of the University of Oxford.

Carr's (Rev. A.) The Church and the Roman Empire.

Gwatkin's (H. M.) The Arian Controversy.

Hunt's (Rev. W.) The English Church in the Middle Ages.

Mullinger's (J. B.) A History of the University of Cambridge.

Overton's (Rev. J. H.) The Evangelical Revival in the Eighteenth Century.

Epochs of Church History.—*cont.*

Perry's (Rev. G. G.) The History of the Reformation in England.

Plummer's (A.) The Church of the Early Fathers.

Poole's (R. L.) Wycliffe and Early Movements of Reform.

Stephen's (Rev. W. R. W.) Hildebrand and his Times.

Tozer's (Rev. H. F.) The Church and the Eastern Empire.

Tucker's (Rev. H. W.) The English Church in other Lands.

Wakeman's (H. O.) The Church and the Puritans (1570-1660.)

Ward's (A. W.) The Counter-Reformation.

Epochs of Ancient History.

Edited by the Rev. Sir G. W. COX, Bart., M.A., and by C. SANKEY, M.A. 10 volumes, Fcp. 8vo. with Maps, 2s. 6d. each.

Beesly's (A. H.) The Gracchi, Marius, and Sulla. With 2 Maps.

Capes' (Rev. W. W.) The Early Roman Empire. From the Assassination of Julius Cæsar to the Assassination of Domitian. With 2 Maps.

—— The Roman Empire of the Second Century, or the Age of the Antonines. With 2 Maps.

Cox's (Rev. Sir G. W.) The Athenian Empire from the Flight of Xerxes to the Fall of Athens. With 5 Maps.

—— The Greeks and the Persians. With 4 Maps.

Curteis's (A. M.) The Rise of the Macedonian Empire. With 8 Maps.

Ihne's (W.) Rome to its Capture by the Gauls. With a Map.

Merivale's (Very Rev. C.) The Roman Triumvirates. With a Map.

Sankey's (C.) The Spartan and Theban Supremacies. With 5 Maps.

Smith's (R. B.) Rome and Carthage, the Punic Wars. With 9 Maps and Plans.

Epochs of American History.

Edited by Dr. ALBERT BUSHNELL HART, Assistant Professor of History in Harvard College.

Hart's (A. B.) Formation of the Union (1763-1829). Fcp. 8vo. [*In preparation.*

Thwaites's (R. G.) The Colonies (1492-1763). Fcp. 8vo. 3s. 6d. [*Ready.*

Wilson's (W.) Division and Re-union (1829-1889). Fcp. 8vo. [*In preparation.*

Epochs of English History. Complete in One Volume, with 27 Tables and Pedigrees, and 23 Maps. Fcp. 8vo, 5s.

₊ For details of Parts *see* Longmans & Co.'s Catalogue of School Books.

EWALD (Heinrich).—WORKS BY.

The Antiquities of Israel. Translated from the German by H. S. SOLLY, M.A. 8vo. 12s. 6d.

The History of Israel. Translated from the German. 8 vols. 8vo. Vols. I. and II. 24s. Vols. III. and IV. 21s. Vol. V. 18s. Vol. VI. 16s. Vol. VII. 21s. Vol. VIII., with Index to the Complete Work, 18s.

FARNELL.—**Greek Lyric Poetry:** a Complete Collection of the Surviving Passages from the Greek Song-Writers. Arranged with Prefatory Articles, Introductory Matter, and Commentary. By GEORGE S. FARNELL, M.A. With 5 Plates. 8vo. 16s.

FARRAR (Ven. Archdeacon).—WORKS BY.

Darkness and Dawn; or, Scenes in the Days of Nero. An Historic Tale. 2 vols. 8vo. 28s.

Language and Languages. A Revised Edition of *Chapters on Language and Families of Speech*. Crown 8vo. 6s.

FITZWYGRAM. — **Horses and Stables.** By Major-General Sir F. FITZWYGRAM, Bart. With 19 pages of Illustrations. 8vo. 5s.

FORD.—**The Theory and Practice of Archery.** By the late HORACE FORD. New Edition, thoroughly Revised and Re-written by W. BUTT, M.A. With a Preface by C. J. LONGMAN, M.A., F.S.A. 8vo. 14s.

FOUARD.—**The Christ the Son of God:** a Life of our Lord and Saviour Jesus Christ. By the Abbé CONSTANT FOUARD. With an Introduction by Cardinal MANNING. 2 vols. Crown 8vo. 14s.

FOX. — **The Early History of Charles James Fox.** By the Right Hon. Sir G. O. TREVELYAN, Bart. Library Edition, 8vo. 18s. Cabinet Edition, Crown 8vo. 6s.

FRANCIS.—**A Book on Angling**; or, Treatise on the Art of Fishing in every branch; including full Illustrated List of Salmon Flies. By FRANCIS FRANCIS. With Portrait and Coloured Plates. Crown 8vo. 15s.

FREEMAN.—**The Historical Geography of Europe.** By E. A. FREEMAN. With 65 Maps. 2 vols. 8vo. 31s. 6d.

FROUDE (James A.).—WORKS BY.

The History of England, from the Fall of Wolsey to the Defeat of the Spanish Armada. 12 vols. Crown 8vo. 3s. 6d. each.

The Divorce of Catherine of Aragon; the Story as told by the Imperial Ambassadors resident at the Court of Henry VIII. *In usum Laicorum.* 8vo. 16s.

Short Studies on Great Subjects. Cabinet Edition, 4 vols. Crown 8vo. 24s. Cheap Edition, 4 vols. Crown 8vo. 3s. 6d. each.

Cæsar: a Sketch. Crown 8vo. 3s. 6d.

The English in Ireland in the Eighteenth Century. 3 vols. Crown 8vo. 18s.

Oceana; or, England and her Colonies. With 9 Illustrations. Crown 8vo. 2s. boards, 2s. 6d. cloth.

The English in the West Indies; or, the Bow of Ulysses. With 9 Illustrations. Crown 8vo. 2s. boards, 2s. 6d. cloth.

The Two Chiefs of Dunboy; an Irish Romance of the Last Century. Crown 8vo. 3s. 6d.

Thomas Carlyle, a History of his Life. 1795 to 1835. 2 vols. Crown 8vo. 7s. 1834 to 1881. 2 vols. Crown 8vo. 7s.

GALLWEY.—**Letters to Young Shooters.** (First Series.) On the Choice and Use of a Gun. By Sir RALPH PAYNE-GALLWEY, Bart. With Illustrations. Crown 8vo. 7s. 6d.

GARDINER (Samuel Rawson).—WORKS BY.

History of England, from the Accession of James I. to the Outbreak of the Civil War, 1603-1642. 10 vols. Crown 8vo. price 6s. each.

A History of the Great Civil War, 1642-1649. (3 vols.) Vol. I. 1642-1644. With 24 Maps. 8vo. 21s. (*out of print*). Vol. II. 1644-1647. With 21 Maps. 8vo. 24s. Vol. III. 1647-1649. 8vo.

GARDINER (Samuel Rawson).—*WORKS BY.—continued.*

The Student's History of England. Vol. I. B.C. 55—A.D. 1509, with 173 Illustrations. Crown 8vo. 4s. Vol. II. 1509-1689, with 96 Illustrations. Crown 8vo. 4s. Vol. III. (1689-1865). Crown 8vo. 4s. Complete in 1 vol. Crown 8vo. 12s.

A School Atlas of English History. A Companion Atlas to the 'Student's History of England'. With 66 Maps and 22 Plans of Battles, &c. Fcap. 4to. 5s.

GIBERNE.—WORKS BY.

Nigel Browning. Crown 8vo. 5s.

Miss Devereux, Spinster. A Novel. 2 vols. Crown 8vo. 17s.

*GOETHE.—***Faust.** A New Translation chiefly in Blank Verse; with Introduction and Notes. By JAMES ADEY BIRDS. Crown 8vo. 6s.

Faust. The Second Part. A New Translation in Verse. By JAMES ADEY BIRDS. Crown 8vo. 6s.

*GREEN.—***The Works of Thomas Hill Green.** Edited by R. L. NETTLESHIP. (3 vols.) Vols. I. and II.—Philosophical Works. 8vo. 16s. each. Vol. III.—Miscellanies. With Index to the three Volumes and Memoir. 8vo. 21s.

The Witness of God and Faith: Two Lay Sermons. By T. H. GREEN. Fcp. 8vo. 2s.

*GREVILLE.—***A Journal of the Reigns of King George IV., King William IV., and Queen Victoria.** By C. C. F. GREVILLE. Edited by H. REEVE. 8 vols. Crown 8vo. 6s. each.

GWILT. — **An Encyclopædia of Architecture.** By JOSEPH GWILT, F.S.A. Illustrated with more than 1700 Engravings on Wood. 8vo. 52s. 6d.

*HAGGARD.—***Life and its Author:** an Essay in Verse. By ELLA HAGGARD. With a Memoir by H. RIDER HAGGARD, and Portrait. Fcp. 8vo. 3s. 6d.

HAGGARD (H. Rider).—WORKS BY.

She. With 32 Illustrations by M. GREIFFENHAGEN and C. H. M. KERR. Crown 8vo. 3s. 6d.

Allan Quatermain. With 31 Illustrations by C. H. M. KERR. Crown 8vo. 3s. 6d.

HAGGARD (H. Rider.)—WORKS BY.—continued.

Maiwa's Revenge; or, The War of the Little Hand. Crown 8vo. 1s. boards; 1s. 6d. cloth.

Colonel Quaritch, V.C. A Novel. Crown 8vo. 3s. 6d.

Cleopatra: being an Account of the Fall and Vengeance of Harmachis, the Royal Egyptian. With 29 Full-page Illustrations by M. Greiffenhagen and R. Caton Woodville. Crown 8vo. 3s. 6d.

Beatrice. A Novel. Cr. 8vo. 6s.

Eric Brighteyes. With 17 Plates and 34 Illustrations in the Text by LANCELOT SPEED. Crown 8vo. 6s.

HAGGARD and *LANG.* — **The World's Desire.** By H. RIDER HAGGARD and ANDREW LANG. Crown 8vo. 6s.

HALLIWELL-PHILLIPPS. — **A Calendar of the Halliwell-Phillipps' collection of Shakespearean Rarities formerly preserved at Hollingbury Copse, Brighton.** Second Edition. Enlarged by ERNEST E. BAKER, F.S.A. 8vo. 10s. 6d.

*HARRISON.—***Myths of the Odyssey in Art and Literature.** Illustrated with Outline Drawings. By JANE E. HARRISON. 8vo. 18s.

*HARRISON.—***The Contemporary History of the French Revolution,** compiled from the 'Annual Register'. By F. BAYFORD HARRISON. Crown 8vo. 3s. 6d.

HARTE (Bret).—WORKS BY.

In the Carquinez Woods. Fcp. 8vo. 1s. boards; 1s. 6d. cloth.

On the Frontier. 16mo. 1s.

By Shore and Sedge. 16mo. 1s.

HARTWIG (Dr.).—WORKS BY.

The Sea and its Living Wonders. With 12 Plates and 303 Woodcuts. 8vo. 10s. 6d.

The Tropical World. With 8 Plates and 172 Woodcuts. 8vo. 10s. 6d.

The Polar World. With 3 Maps, 8 Plates and 85 Woodcuts. 8vo. 10s. 6d.

The Subterranean World. With 3 Maps and 80 Woodcuts. 8vo. 10s. 6d.

The Aerial World. With Map, 8 Plates and 60 Woodcuts. 8vo. 10s. 6d.

HAVELOCK. — **Memoirs of Sir Henry Havelock, K.C.B.** By JOHN CLARK MARSHMAN. Crown 8vo. 3s. 6d.

HEARN (W. Edward). — *WORKS BY.*

The Government of England: its Structure and its Development. 8vo. 16s.

The Aryan Household: its Structure and its Development. An Introduction to Comparative Jurisprudence. 8vo. 16s.

HISTORIC TOWNS. Edited by E. A. FREEMAN, D.C.L., and Rev. WILLIAM HUNT, M.A. With Maps and Plans. Crown 8vo. 3s. 6d. each.

Bristol. By Rev. W. HUNT.

Carlisle. By Rev. MANDELL CREIGHTON.

Cinque Ports. By MONTAGU BURROWS.

Colchester. By Rev. E. L. CUTTS.

Exeter. By E. A. FREEMAN.

London. By Rev. W. J. LOFTIE.

Oxford. By Rev. C. W. BOASE.

Winchester. By Rev. G. W. KITCHIN, D.D.

New York. By THEODORE ROOSEVELT.

Boston (U.S.). By HENRY CABOT LODGE.

York. By Rev. JAMES RAINE.
[*In Preparation.*

HODGSON (Shadworth H.). — *WORKS BY.*

Time and Space: a Metaphysical Essay. 8vo. 16s.

The Theory of Practice: an Ethical Enquiry. 2 vols. 8vo. 24s.

The Philosophy of Reflection: 2 vols. 8vo. 21s.

Outcast Essays and Verse Translations. Essays: The Genius of De Quincey—De Quincey as Political Economist—The Supernatural in English Poetry; with Note on the True Symbol of Christian Union—English Verse. Verse Translations: Nineteen Passages from Lucretius, Horace, Homer, &c. Crown 8vo. 8s. 6d.

HOWITT. — **Visits to Remarkable Places,** Old Halls, Battle-Fields, Scenes, illustrative of Striking Passages in English History and Poetry. By WILLIAM HOWITT. With 80 Illustrations. Crown 8vo. 3s. 6d.

HULLAH (John). — *WORKS BY.*

Course of Lectures on the History of Modern Music. 8vo. 8s. 6d.

Course of Lectures on the Transition Period of Musical History. 8vo. 10s. 6d.

HUME. — **The Philosophical Works of David Hume.** Edited by T. H. GREEN and T. H. GROSE. 4 vols. 8vo. 56s. Or Separately, Essays, 2 vols. 28s. Treatise of Human Nature. 2 vols. 28s.

HUTCHINSON (Horace). — *WORKS BY.*

Creatures of Circumstance: A Novel. 3 vols. Crown 8vo. 25s. 6d.

Famous Golf Links. By HORACE G. HUTCHINSON, ANDREW LANG, H. S. C. EVERARD, T. RUTHERFORD CLARK, &c. With numerous Illustrations by F. P. HOPKINS, T. HODGES, H. S. KING, and from Photographs. Crown 8vo. 6s.

HUTH. — **The Marriage of Near Kin,** considered with respect to the Law of Nations, the Result of Experience, and the Teachings of Biology. By ALFRED H. HUTH. Royal 8vo. 21s.

INGELOW (Jean). — *WORKS BY.*

Poetical Works. Vols. I. and II. Fcp. 8vo. 12s. Vol. III. Fcp. 8vo. 5s.

Lyrical and other Poems. Selected from the Writings of JEAN INGELOW. Fcp. 8vo. 2s. 6d. cloth plain; 3s. cloth gilt.

Very Young and Quite Another Story: Two Stories. Cr. 8vo. 6s.

JAMESON (Mrs.). — *WORKS BY.*

Sacred and Legendary Art. With 19 Etchings and 187 Woodcuts. 2 vols. 8vo. 20s. net.

Legends of the Madonna. The Virgin Mary as represented in Sacred and Legendary Art. With 27 Etchings and 165 Woodcuts. 1 vol. 8vo. 10s. net.
[*Continued on next page.*

JAMESON (Mrs.).—WORKS BY.—continued.

Legends of the Monastic Orders. With 11 Etchings and 88 Woodcuts. 1 vol. 8vo. 10s. net.

History of Our Lord. His Types and Precursors. Completed by Lady EASTLAKE. With 31 Etchings and 281 Woodcuts. 2 vols. 8vo. 20s. net.

JEFFERIES (Richard).—WORKS BY.

Field and Hedgerow: last Essays. With Portrait. Crown 8vo. 3s. 6d.

The Story of My Heart: my Autobiography. With Portrait and new Preface by C. J. LONGMAN. Crown 8vo. 3s. 6d.

*JENNINGS.—***Ecclesia Anglicana.** A History of the Church of Christ in England, from the Earliest to the Present Times. By the Rev. ARTHUR CHARLES JENNINGS, M.A. Crown 8vo. 7s. 6d.

*JOHNSON.—***The Patentee's Manual;** a Treatise on the Law and Practice of Letters Patent. By J. JOHNSON and J. H. JOHNSON. 8vo. 10s. 6d.

*JORDAN (William Leighton).—***The Standard of Value.** By WILLIAM LEIGHTON JORDAN. 8vo. 6s.

*JUSTINIAN.—***The Institutes of Justinian;** Latin Text, chiefly that of Huschke, with English Introduction. Translation, Notes, and Summary. By THOMAS C. SANDARS, M.A. 8vo. 18s.

KALISCH (M. M.).—WORKS BY.

Bible Studies. Part I. The Prophecies of Balaam. 8vo. 10s. 6d. Part II. The Book of Jonah. 8vo. 10s. 6d.

Commentary on the Old Testament; with a New Translation. Vol. I. Genesis, 8vo. 18s. or adapted for the General Reader, 12s. Vol. II. Exodus, 15s. or adapted for the General Reader, 12s. Vol. III. Leviticus, Part I. 15s. or adapted for the General Reader, 8s. Vol. IV. Leviticus, Part II. 15s. or adapted for the General Reader, 8s.

KANT (Immanuel).—WORKS BY.

Critique of Practical Reason, and other Works on the Theory of Ethics. Translated by T. K. Abbott, B.D. With Memoir. 8vo. 12s. 6d.

Introduction to Logic, and his Essay on the Mistaken Subtilty of the Four Figures. Translated by T. K. Abbott. Notes by S. T. Coleridge. 8vo. 6s.

*KENNEDY.—***Pictures in Rhyme.** By ARTHUR CLARK KENNEDY. With 4 Illustrations by MAURICE GREIFFENHAGEN. Crown 8vo. 6s.

*KILLICK.—***Handbook to Mill's System of Logic.** By the Rev. A. H. KILLICK, M.A. Crown 8vo. 3s. 6d.

KNIGHT (E. F.).—WORKS BY.

The Cruise of the 'Alerte'; the Narrative of a Search for Treasure on the Desert Island of Trinidad. With 2 Maps and 23 Illustrations. Crown 8vo. 10s. 6d.

Save Me from my Friends: a Novel. Crown 8vo. 6s.

LADD (George T.).—WORKS BY.

Elements of Physiological Psychology. 8vo. 21s.

Outlines of Physiological Psychology. A Text-book of Mental Science for Academies and Colleges. 8vo. 12s.

LANG (Andrew).—WORKS BY.

Custom and Myth: Studies of Early Usage and Belief. With 15 Illustrations. Crown 8vo. 7s. 6d.

Books and Bookmen. With 2 Coloured Plates and 17 Illustrations. Cr. 8vo. 6s. 6d.

Grass of Parnassus. A Volume of Selected Verses. Fcp. 8vo. 6s.

Angling Sketches. With Illustrations by W. G. Brown Murdoch. Crown 8vo. 7s 6d..

Ballads of Books. Edited by ANDREW LANG. Fcp. 8vo. 6s.

The Blue Fairy Book. Edited by ANDREW LANG. With 8 Plates and 130 Illustrations in the Text by H. J. Ford and G. P. Jacomb Hood. Cr. 8vo. 6s.

The Red Fairy Book. Edited by ANDREW LANG. With 4 Plates and 96 Illustrations in the Text by H. J. Ford and Lancelot Speed. Crown 8vo. 6s.

The Blue Poetry Book. Edited by ANDREW LANG. With 12 Plates and 88 Illustrations in the Text by H. J. Ford and Lancelot Speed. Crown 8vo. 6s.

*LAVISSE.—***General View of the Political History of Europe.** By ERNEST LAVISSE, Professor at the Sorbonne. Translated, with the Author's sanction, by CHARLES GROSS, Ph.D.

LAYARD.—Poems. By NINA F. LAYARD. Crown 8vo. 6s.

LECKY (W. E. H.).—WORKS BY.

History of England in the Eighteenth Century. 8vo. Vols. I. & II. 1700-1760. 36s. Vols. III. & IV. 1760-1784. 36s. Vols. V. & VI. 1784-1793. 36s. Vols. VII. & VIII. 1793-1800. 36s.

The History of European Morals from Augustus to Charlemagne. 2 vols. Crown 8vo. 16s.

History of the Rise and Influence of the Spirit of Rationalism in Europe. 2 vols. Crown 8vo. 16s.

Poems. Fcp. 8vo. 5s.

LEES and CLUTTERBUCK.—B. C. 1887, A Ramble in British Columbia. By J. A. LEES and W. J. CLUTTERBUCK. With Map and 75 Illustrations. Crown 8vo. 6s.

LEGER.—A History of Austro-Hungary. From the Earliest Time to the year 1889. By LOUIS LEGER. With a Preface by E. A. FREEMAN, D.C.L. Crown 8vo. 10s. 6d.

LEWES.—The History of Philosophy, from Thales to Comte. By GEORGE HENRY LEWES. 2 vols. 8vo. 32s.

LIDDELL.—The Memoirs of the Tenth Royal Hussars (Prince of Wales' Own): Historical and Social. Collected and Arranged by Colonel R. S. LIDDELL, late Commanding Tenth Royal Hussars. With Portraits and Coloured Illustration. Imperial 8vo. 63s.

LLOYD.—The Science of Agriculture. By F. J. LLOYD. 8vo. 12s.

LONGMAN (Frederick W.).—WORKS BY.

Chess Openings. Fcp. 8vo. 2s. 6d.

Frederick the Great and the Seven Years' War. Fcp. 8vo. 2s. 6d.

Longman's Magazine. Published Monthly. Price Sixpence. Vols, 1-17. 8vo. price 5s. each.

Longmans' New Atlas. Political and Physical. For the Use of Schools and Private Persons. Consisting of 40 Quarto and 16 Octavo Maps and Diagrams, and 16 Plates of Views. Edited by GEO. G. CHISHOLM, M.A., B.Sc. Imp. 4to. or Imp. 8vo. 12s. 6d.

LOUDON (J. C.).—WORKS BY.

Encyclopædia of Gardening. With 1000 Woodcuts. 8vo. 21s.

Encyclopædia of Agriculture; the Laying-out, Improvement, and Management of Landed Property. With 1100 Woodcuts. 8vo. 21s.

Encyclopædia of Plants; the Specific Character, &c., of all Plants found in Great Britain. With 12,000 Woodcuts. 8vo. 42s.

LUBBOCK.—The Origin of Civilisation and the Primitive Condition of Man. By Sir J. LUBBOCK, Bart., M.P. With 5 Plates and 20 Illustrations in the Text. 8vo. 18s.

LYALL.—The Autobiography of a Slander. By EDNA LYALL, Author of 'Donovan,' &c. Fcp. 8vo. 1s. sewed.

LYDE.—An Introduction to Ancient History: being a Sketch of the History of Egypt, Mesopotamia, Greece, and Rome. With a Chapter on the Development of the Roman Empire into the Powers of Modern Europe. By LIONEL W. LYDE, M.A. With 3 Coloured Maps. Crown 8vo. 3s.

MACAULAY (Lord).—WORKS OF.

Complete Works of Lord Macaulay:
Library Edition, 8 vols. 8vo. £5 5s.
Cabinet Edition, 16 vols. Post 8vo. £4 16s.

History of England from the Accession of James the Second:
Popular Edition, 2 vols. Crown 8vo. 5s.
Student's Edition, 2 vols. Crown 8vo. 12s.
People's Edition, 4 vols. Crown 8vo. 16s.
Cabinet Edition, 8 vols. Post 8vo. 48s.
Library Edition, 5 vols. 8vo. £4.

Critical and Historical Essays, with Lays of Ancient Rome, in 1 volume:
Popular Edition, Crown 8vo. 2s. 6d.
Authorised Edition, Crown 8vo. 2s. or 3s. 6d. gilt edges.

MACAULAY (Lord).—WORKS OF.—continued.

Critical and Historical Essays:
Student's Edition, 1 vol. Crown 8vo. 6s.
People's Edition, 2 vols. Crown 8vo. 8s.
Trevelyan Edition, 2 vols. Crown 8vo. 9s.
Cabinet Edition, 4 vols. Post 8vo. 24s.
Library Edition, 3 vols. 8vo. 36s.

Essays which may be had separately price 6d. each sewed, 1s. each cloth:
Addison and Walpole.
Frederick the Great.
Croker's Boswell's Johnson.
Hallam's Constitutional History.
Warren Hastings. (3d. sewed, 6d cloth.)
The Earl of Chatham (Two Essays).
Ranke and Gladstone.
Milton and Machiavelli.
Lord Bacon.
Lord Clive.
Lord Byron, and The Comic Dramatists of the Restoration.

The Essay on Warren Hastings annotated by S. HALES, 1s. 6d.
The Essay on Lord Clive annotated by H. COURTHOPE BOWEN, M.A., 2s. 6d.

Speeches:
People's Edition, Crown 8vo. 3s. 6d.

Lays of Ancient Rome, &c.:
Illustrated by G. Scharf, Fcp. 4to. 10s. 6d.

——————— Bijou Edition, 18mo. 2s. 6d. gilt top.

——————— Popular Edition, Fcp. 4to. 6d. sewed, 1s. cloth.

Illustrated by J. R. Weguelin, Crown 8vo. 3s. 6d. cloth extra, gilt edges.
Cabinet Edition, Post 8vo. 3s. 6d.
Annotated Edition. Fcp. 8vo. 1s. sewed, 1s. 6d. cloth.

Miscellaneous Writings:
People's Edition, 1 vol. Crown 8vo. 4s. 6d.
Library Edition, 2 vols. 8vo. 21s.

Miscellaneous Writings and Speeches:
Popular Edition, 1 vol. Crown 8vo. 2s. 6d.
Student's Edition, in 1 vol. Crown 8vo. 6s.
Cabinet Edition, including Indian Penal Code, Lays of Ancient Rome, and Miscellaneous Poems, 4 vols. Post 8vo. 24s.

Selections from the Writings of Lord Macaulay. Edited, with Occasional Notes, by the Right Hon. Sir G. O. TREVELYAN, Bart. Cr. 8vo. 6s.

MACAULAY (Lord).—WORKS OF.—continued.

The Life and Letters of Lord Macaulay. By the Right Hon. Sir G. O. TREVELYAN, Bart.:
Popular Edition, 1 vol. Crown 8vo. 2s. 6d.
Student's Edition, 1 vol. Crown 8vo. 6s.
Cabinet Edition, 2 vols. Post 8vo. 12s.
Library Edition, 2 vols. 8vo. 36s.

MACDONALD (Geo.).—WORKS BY.
Unspoken Sermons. Three Series. Crown 8vo. 3s. 6d. each.

The Miracles of Our Lord. Crown 8vo. 3s. 6d.

A Book of Strife, in the Form of the Diary of an Old Soul: Poems. 12mo. 6s.

MACFARREN (Sir G. A.).—WORKS BY.
Lectures on Harmony. 8vo. 12s.

Addresses and Lectures. Crown 8vo. 6s. 6d.

MACKAIL.—**Select Epigrams from the Greek Anthology.** Edited, with a Revised Text, Introduction, Translation, and Notes, by J. W. MACKAIL, M.A. 8vo. 16s.

MACLEOD (Henry D.).—WORKS BY.
The Elements of Banking. Crown 8vo. 3s. 6d.

The Theory and Practice of Banking. Vol. I. 8vo. 12s. Vol. II. 14s.

The Theory of Credit. 8vo. Vol. I. 7s. 6d.; Vol. II. Part I. 4s. 6d.; Vol. II. Part II. 10s. 6d.

MᶜCULLOCH.—**The Dictionary of Commerce** and Commercial Navigation of the late J. R. MCCULLOCH. 8vo. with 11 Maps and 30 Charts, 63s.

MACVINE.—**Sixty-Three Years' Angling,** from the Mountain Streamlet to the Mighty Tay. By JOHN MACVINE. Crown 8vo. 10s. 6d.

MALMESBURY.—**Memoirs of an Ex-Minister.** By the Earl of MALMESBURY. Crown 8vo. 7s. 6d.

MANNERING.—**With Axe and Rope in the New Zealand Alps.** By GEORGE EDWARD MANNERING, Member of the Alpine Club. 8vo. 12s. 6d.

MANUALS OF CATHOLIC PHILOSOPHY (*Stonyhurst Series*):

Logic. By RICHARD F. CLARKE, S.J. Crown 8vo. 5s.

First Principles of Knowledge. By JOHN RICKABY, S.J. Crown 8vo. 5s.

Moral Philosophy (Ethics and Natural Law). By JOSEPH RICKABY, S.J. Crown 8vo. 5s.

General Metaphysics. By JOHN RICKABY, S.J. Crown 8vo. 5s.

Psychology. By MICHAEL MAHER, S.J. Crown 8vo. 6s. 6d.

Natural Theology. By BERNARD BOEDDER, S.J. Crown 8vo. 6s. 6d.

MARTINEAU (James).—WORKS BY.

Hours of Thought on Sacred Things. Two Volumes of Sermons. 2 vols. Crown 8vo. 7s. 6d. each.

Endeavours after the Christian Life. Discourses. Cr. 8vo. 7s. 6d.

The Seat of Authority in Religion. 8vo. 14s.

Essays, Reviews, and Addresses. 4 vols. Cr.8vo. 7s. 6d. each.
I. Personal: Political.
II. Ecclesiastical: Historical.
III. Theological: Philosophical.
IV. Academical: Religious.

*MASON.—***The Steps of the Sun:** Daily Readings of Prose. Selected by AGNES MASON. 16mo. 3s. 6d.

MATTHEWS (Brander).—WORKS BY.

A Family Tree, and other Stories. Crown 8vo. 6s.

Pen and Ink: Papers on Subjects of more or less Importance. Cr. 8vo. 5s.

With My Friends: Tales told in Partnership. With an Introductory Essay on the Art and Mystery of Collaboration. Crown 8vo. 6s.

MAUNDER'S TREASURIES.

Biographical Treasury. With Supplement brought down to 1889, by Rev. JAS. WOOD. Fcp. 8vo. 6s.

Treasury of Natural History; or, Popular Dictionary of Zoology. Fcp. 8vo. with 900 Woodcuts, 6s.

Treasury of Geography, Physical, Historical, Descriptive, and Political. With 7 Maps and 16 Plates. Fcp. 8vo. 9s.
[*Continued.*

MAUNDER'S TREASURIES.—*continued.*

Scientific and Literary Treasury. Fcp. 8vo. 6s.

Historical Treasury: Outlines of Universal History, Separate Histories of all Nations. Fcp. 8vo. 6s.

Treasury of Knowledge and Library of Reference. Comprising an English Dictionary and Grammar, Universal Gazetteer, Classical Dictionary, Chronology, Law Dictionary, &c. Fcp. 8vo. 6s.

The Treasury of Bible Knowledge. By the Rev. J. AYRE, M.A. With 5 Maps, 15 Plates, and 300 Woodcuts. Fcp. 8vo. 6s.

The Treasury of Botany. Edited by J. LINDLEY, F.R.S., and T. MOORE, F.L.S. With 274 Woodcuts and 20 Steel Plates. 2 vols. Fcp. 8vo. 12s.

MAX MÜLLER (F.).—WORKS BY.

Selected Essays on Language, Mythology and Religion. 2 vols. Crown 8vo. 16s.

The Science of Language, Founded on Lectures delivered at the Royal Institution in 1861 and 1863. 2 vols. Crown 8vo. 21s.

Three Lectures on the Science of Language and its Place in General Education, delivered at the Oxford University Extension Meeting, 1889. Crown 8vo. 3s.

Hibbert Lectures on the Origin and Growth of Religion, as illustrated by the Religions of India. Crown 8vo. 7s. 6d.

Introduction to the Science of Religion; Four Lectures delivered at the Royal Institution. Crown 8vo. 7s. 6d.

Natural Religion. The Gifford Lectures, delivered before the University of Glasgow in 1888. Crown 8vo. 10s. 6d.

Physical Religion. The Gifford Lectures, delivered before the University of Glasgow in 1890. Crown 8vo. 10s. 6d.

The Science of Thought. 8vo. 21s.

Three Introductory Lectures on the Science of Thought. 8vo. 2s. 6d.

[*Continued on next page.*

MAX MÜLLER (F.).—WORKS BY.—continued.

Biographies of Words, and the Home of the Aryas. Crown 8vo. 7s. 6d.

A Sanskrit Grammar for Beginners. New and Abridged Edition. By A. A. MACDONELL. Cr. 8vo. 6s.

MAY.—**The Constitutional History of England** since the Accession of George III. 1760-1870. By the Right Hon. Sir THOMAS ERSKINE MAY, K.C.B. 3 vols. Crown 8vo. 18s.

MEADE (L. T.).—WORKS BY.

The O'Donnells of Inchfawn. With Frontispiece by A. CHASEMORE. Crown 8vo. 6s.

Daddy's Boy. With Illustrations. Crown 8vo. 5s.

Deb and the Duchess. With Illustrations by M. E. EDWARDS. Crown 8vo. 5s.

House of Surprises. With Illustrations by EDITH M. SCANNELL. Cr. 8vo. 3s. 6d.

The Beresford Prize. With Illustrations by M. E. EDWARDS. Crown 8vo. 5s.

MEATH (The Earl of).—WORKS BY.

Social Arrows: Reprinted Articles on various Social Subjects. Crown 8vo. 5s.

Prosperity or Pauperism? Physical, Industrial, and Technical Training. (Edited by the EARL OF MEATH.) 8vo. 5s.

MELVILLE (G. J. Whyte).—NOVELS BY. Crown 8vo. 1s. each, boards; 1s. 6d. each, cloth.

The Gladiators.	Holmby House.
The Interpreter.	Kate Coventry.
Good for Nothing.	Digby Grand.
The Queen's Maries.	General Bounce.

MENDELSSOHN.—**The Letters of Felix Mendelssohn.** Translated by Lady WALLACE. 2 vols. Crown 8vo. 10s.

MERIVALE (The Very Rev. Chas.).—WORKS BY.

History of the Romans under the Empire. Cabinet Edition, 8 vols. Crown 8vo. 48s.
Popular Edition, 8 vols. Cr. 8vo. 3s. 6d. each.

The Fall of the Roman Republic: a Short History of the Last Century of the Commonwealth. 12mo. 7s. 6d.

General History of Rome from B.C. 753 to A.D. 476. Cr. 8vo. 7s. 6d.

The Roman Triumvirates. With Maps. Fcp. 8vo. 2s. 6d.

MILES.—**The Correspondence of William Augustus Miles on the French Revolution, 1789-1817.** Edited by the Rev. CHARLES POPHAM MILES, M.A. 2 vols. 8vo. 32s.

MILL.—**Analysis of the Phenomena of the Human Mind.** By JAMES MILL. 2 vols. 8vo. 28s.

MILL (John Stuart).—WORKS BY.

Principles of Political Economy. Library Edition, 2 vols. 8vo. 30s.
People's Edition, 1 vols. Crown 8vo. 5s.

A System of Logic. Cr. 8vo. 5s.

On Liberty. Crown 8vo. 1s. 4d.

On Representative Government. Crown 8vo. 2s.

Utilitarianism. 8vo. 5s.

Examination of Sir William Hamilton's Philosophy. 8vo. 16s.

Nature, the Utility of Religion, and Theism. Three Essays. 8vo. 5s.

MOLESWORTH (Mrs.).—WORKS BY.

Marrying and Giving in Marriage: a Novel. Illustrated. Fcp. 8vo. 2s. 6d.

Silverthorns. Illustrated. Crown 8vo. 5s.

The Palace in the Garden. Illustrated. Crown 8vo. 5s.

The Third Miss St. Quentin. Crown 8vo. 6s.

Neighbours. Illustrated. Crown 8vo. 6s.

The Story of a Spring Morning, &c. Illustrated. Crown 8vo. 5s.

MOORE.—Dante and his Early Biographers. By EDWARD MOORE, D.D., Principal of St. Edmund Hall, Oxford. Crown 8vo. 4s. 6d.

MULHALL.—History of Prices since the Year 1850. By MICHAEL G. MULHALL. Cr. 8vo. 6s.

MURRAY.—A Dangerous Catspaw: a Story. By DAVID CHRISTIE MURRAY and HENRY MURRAY. Crown 8vo. 2s. 6d.

MURRAY and HERMAN.—Wild Darrie: a Story. By CHRISTIE MURRAY and HENRY HERMAN. Crown 8vo. 2s. boards; 2s. 6d. cloth.

NANSEN.—The First Crossing of Greenland. By Dr. FRIDTJOF NANSEN. With 5 Maps, 12 Plates, and 150 Illustrations in the Text. 2 vols. 8vo. 36s.

NAPIER.—The Life of Sir Joseph Napier, Bart., Ex-Lord Chancellor of Ireland. By ALEX. CHARLES EWALD, F.S.A. With Portrait. 8vo. 15s.

NAPIER.—The Lectures, Essays, and Letters of the Right Hon. Sir Joseph Napier, Bart., late Lord Chancellor of Ireland. 8vo. 12s. 6d.

NESBIT.—Leaves of Life: Verses. By E. NESBIT. Crown 8vo. 5s.

NEWMAN.—The Letters and Correspondence of John Henry Newman during his Life in the English Church. With a brief Autobiographical Memoir. Arranged and Edited by ANNE MOZLEY. With Portraits. 2 vols. 8vo. 30s. net.

NEWMAN (Cardinal).—WORKS BY.

Apologia pro Vitâ Sua. Cabinet Edition, Crown 8vo. 6s. Cheap Edition, Crown 8vo. 3s. 6d.

Sermons to Mixed Congregations. Crown 8vo. 6s.

Sermons on Various Occasions. Crown 8vo. 6s.

The Idea of a University defined and illustrated. Cabinet Edition, Crown 8vo. 7s. Cheap Edition, Crown 8vo. 3s. 6d.

NEWMAN (Cardinal).—WORKS BY.—*continued.*

Historical Sketches. 3 vols. Cr. 8vo. 6s. each.

The Arians of the Fourth Century. Cabinet Edition, Crown 8vo. 6s. Cheap Edition, Cr. 8vo. 3s. 6d.

Select Treatises of St. Athanasius in Controversy with the Arians. Freely Translated. 2 vols. Cr. 8vo. 15s.

Discussions and Arguments on Various Subjects. Cabinet Edition, Crown 8vo. 6s. Cheap Edition, Crown 8vo. 3s. 6d.

An Essay on the Development of Christian Doctrine. Cabinet Edition, Crown 8vo. 6s. Cheap Edition, Crown 8vo. 3s. 6d.

Certain Difficulties felt by Anglicans in Catholic Teaching Considered. Cabinet Edition, Vol. I., Crown 8vo. 7s. 6d.; Vol. II., Cr. 8vo. 5s. 6d. Cheap Edition, 2 vols. Cr. 8vo. 3s. 6d. each.

The Via Media of the Anglican Church, illustrated in Lectures, &c. 2 vols. Crown 8vo. 6s. each.

Essays, Critical and Historical. Cabinet Edition, 2 vols. Crown 8vo. 12s. Cheap Edition, 2 vols. Crown 8vo. 7s.

Essays on Biblical and on Ecclesiastical Miracles. Cabinet Edition, Crown 8vo. 6s. Cheap Edition, Crown 8vo. 3s. 6d.

Tracts. 1. Dissertatiunculæ. 2. On the Text of the Seven Epistles of St. Ignatius. 3. Doctrinal Causes of Arianism. 4. Apollinarianism. 5. St. Cyril's Formula. 6. Ordo de Tempore. 7. Douay Version of Scripture. Crown 8vo. 8s.

An Essay in Aid of a Grammar of Assent. Cabinet Edition, Crown 8vo. 7s. 6d. Cheap Edition, Crown 8vo. 3s. 6d.

Present Position of Catholics in England. Crown 8vo. 7s. 6d.

Callista: a Tale of the Third Century. Cabinet Edition, Crown 8vo. 6s. Cheap Edition, Crown 8vo. 3s. 6d.

[*Continued on next page.*

NEWMAN (Cardinal).—WORKS OF.— continued.

Loss and Gain: a Tale. Cabinet Edition, Crown 8vo. 6s. Cheap Edition, Crown 8vo. 3s. 6d.

The Dream of Gerontius. 16mo. 6d. sewed, 1s. cloth.

Verses on Various Occasions. Cabinet Edition, Crown 8vo. 6s. Cheap Edition, Crown 8vo. 3s. 6d.

⁎⁎ For Cardinal Newman's other Works see Messrs. Longmans & Co.'s *Catalogue of Theological Works.*

NORRIS.—**Mrs. Fenton:** a Sketch. By W. E. NORRIS. Crown 8vo. 6s.

NORTON (Charles L.).—WORKS BY.

Political Americanisms: a Glossary of Terms and Phrases Current at Different Periods in American Politics. Fcp. 8vo. 2s. 6d.

A Handbook of Florida. With 49 Maps and Plans. Fcp. 8vo. 5s.

O'BRIEN.—**When we were Boys:** a Novel. By WILLIAM O'BRIEN, M.P. Crown 8vo. 2s. 6d.

OLIPHANT (Mrs.).—NOVELS BY.

Madam. Cr. 8vo. 1s. bds.; 1s. 6d. cl.

In Trust. Cr. 8vo. 1s. bds.; 1s. 6d. cl.

Lady Car: the Sequel of a Life. Crown 8vo. 2s. 6d.

OMAN.—**A History of Greece from the Earliest Times to the Macedonian Conquest.** By C. W. C. OMAN, M.A., F.S.A. With Maps and Plans. Crown 8vo. 4s. 6d.

O'REILLY.—**Hurstleigh Dene:** a Tale. By Mrs. O'REILLY. Illustrated by M. ELLEN EDWARDS. Cr. 8vo. 5s.

PAUL.—**Principles of the History of Language.** By HERMANN PAUL. Translated by H. A. STRONG. 8vo. 10s. 6d.

PAYN (James).—NOVELS BY.

The Luck of the Darrells. Cr. 8vo. 1s. boards; 1s. 6d. cloth.

Thicker than Water. Crown 8vo. 1s. boards; 1s. 6d. cloth.

PERRING (Sir Philip).—WORKS BY.

Hard Knots in Shakespeare. 8vo. 7s. 6d.

The 'Works and Days' of Moses. Crown 8vo. 3s. 6d.

PHILLIPPS-WOLLEY.—**Snap:** a Legend of the Lone Mountain. By C. PHILLIPPS-WOLLEY. With 13 Illustrations by H. G. WILLINK. Cr. 8vo. 6s.

POLE.—**The Theory of the Modern Scientific Game of Whist.** By W. POLE, F.R.S. Fcp. 8vo. 2s. 6d.

POLLOCK.—**The Seal of Fate:** a Novel. By Lady POLLOCK and W. H. POLLOCK. Crown 8vo. 6s.

POOLE.—**Cookery for the Diabetic.** By W. H. and Mrs. POOLE. With Preface by Dr. PAVY. Fcp. 8vo. 2s. 6d.

PRENDERGAST. — **Ireland, from the Restoration to the Revolution,** 1660-1690. By JOHN P. PRENDERGAST. 8vo. 5s.

PRINSEP.—**Virginie:** a Tale of One Hundred Years Ago. By VAL PRINSEP, A.R.A. 3 vols. Crown 8vo. 25s. 6d.

PROCTOR (R. A.).—WORKS BY.

Old and New Astronomy. 12 Parts, 2s. 6d. each. Supplementary Section, 1s. Complete in 1 vol. 4to. 36s. [*In course of publication.*

The Orbs Around Us; a Series of Essays on the Moon and Planets, Meteors and Comets. With Chart and Diagrams. Crown 8vo. 5s.

Other Worlds than Ours; The Plurality of Worlds Studied under the Light of Recent Scientific Researches. With 14 Illustrations. Crown 8vo. 5s.

The Moon; her Motions, Aspects Scenery, and Physical Condition. With Plates, Charts, Woodcuts, &c. Cr. 8vo. 5s.

Universe of Stars; Presenting Researches into and New Views respecting the Constitution of the Heavens. With 22 Charts and 22 Diagrams. 8vo. 10s. 6d.

Larger Star Atlas for the Library, in 12 Circular Maps, with Introduction and 2 Index Pages. Folio, 15s. or Maps only, 12s. 6d.

PROCTOR (R. A.).—*WORKS BY.* —*continued.*

The Student's Atlas. In Twelve Circular Maps on a Uniform Projection and one Scale. 8vo. 5s.

New Star Atlas for the Library, the School, and the Observatory, in 12 Circular Maps. Crown 8vo. 5s.

Light Science for Leisure Hours. Familiar Essays on Scientific Subjects. 3 vols. Crown 8vo. 5s. each.

Chance and Luck; a Discussion of the Laws of Luck, Coincidences, Wagers, Lotteries, and the Fallacies of Gambling, &c. Crown 8vo. 2s. boards; 2s. 6d. cloth.

Studies of Venus-Transits. With 7 Diagrams and 10 Plates. 8vo. 5s.

How to Play Whist: with the Laws and Etiquette of Whist. Crown 8vo. 3s. 6d.

Home Whist: an Easy Guide to Correct Play. 16mo. 1s.

The Stars in their Seasons. An Easy Guide to a Knowledge of the Star Groups, in 12 Maps. Roy. 8vo. 5s.

Star Primer. Showing the Starry Sky Week by Week, in 24 Hourly Maps. Crown 4to. 2s. 6d.

The Seasons pictured in 48 Sun-Views of the Earth, and 24 Zodiacal Maps, &c. Demy 4to. 5s.

Strength and Happiness. With 9 Illustrations. Crown 8vo. 5s.

Strength: How to get Strong and keep Strong, with Chapters on Rowing and Swimming, Fat, Age, and the Waist. With 9 Illustrations. Crown 8vo. 2s.

Rough Ways Made Smooth. Familiar Essays on Scientific Subjects. Crown 8vo. 5s.

Our Place Among Infinities. A Series of Essays contrasting our Little Abode in Space and Time with the Infinities around us. Crown 8vo. 5s.

The Expanse of Heaven. Essays on the Wonders of the Firmament. Cr. 8vo. 5s.

PROCTOR (R. A.).—*WORKS BY.* —*continued.*

The Great Pyramid, Observatory, Tomb, and Temple. With Illustrations. Crown 8vo. 5s.

Pleasant Ways in Science. Cr. 8vo. 5s.

Myths and Marvels of Astronomy. Crown 8vo. 5s.

Nature Studies. By GRANT ALLEN, A. WILSON, T. FOSTER, E. CLODD, and R. A. PROCTOR. Crown 8vo. 5s.

Leisure Readings. By E. CLODD, A. WILSON, T. FOSTER, A. C. RANYARD, and R. A. PROCTOR. Crown 8vo. 5s.

PRYCE.—**The Ancient British Church**: an Historical Essay. By JOHN PRYCE, M.A. Crown 8vo. 6s.

RANSOME.—**The Rise of Constitutional Government in England**: being a Series of Twenty Lectures on the History of the English Constitution delivered to a Popular Audience. By CYRIL RANSOME, M.A. Crown 8vo. 6s.

RAWLINSON.—**The History of Phœnicia.** By GEORGE RAWLINSON, M.A., Canon of Canterbury, &c. With numerous Illustrations. 8vo. 24s.

READER.—**Echoes of Thought**: a Medley of Verse. By EMILY E. READER. Fcp. 8vo. 5s. cloth, gilt top.

RENDLE and NORMAN.—**The Inns of Old Southwark**, and their Associations. By WILLIAM RENDLE, F.R.C.S., and PHILIP NORMAN, F.S.A. With numerous Illustrations. Roy.8vo. 28s.

RIBOT.—**The Psychology of Attention.** By TH. RIBOT. Crown 8vo. 3s.

RICH.—**A Dictionary of Roman and Greek Antiquities.** With 2000 Woodcuts. By A. RICH. Crown 8vo. 7s. 6d.

RICHARDSON.—**National Health.** Abridged from 'The Health of Nations'. A Review of the Works of Sir Edwin Chadwick, K.C.B. By Dr. B. W. RICHARDSON. Crown, 4s. 6d.

RILEY.—**Athos**; or, the Mountain of the Monks. By ATHELSTAN RILEY, M.A., F.R.G.S. With Map and 29 Illustrations. 8vo. 21s.

RILEY.—**Old-Fashioned Roses**: Poems. By JAMES WHITCOMB RILEY. 12mo. 5s.

ROCKHILL.—**The Land of the Lamas**: Notes of a Journey through China, Mangolia and Tibet. With 2 Maps and 6 Illustrations. By WILLIAM WOODVILLE ROCKHILL. 8vo. 15s.

ROGET.—**A History of the 'Old Water-Colour' Society** (now the Royal Society of Painters in Water-Colours). With Biographical Notices of its Older and all its Deceased Members and Associates. By JOHN LEWIS ROGET, M.A. 2 vols. Royal 8vo. 42s.

ROGET.—**Thesaurus of English Words and Phrases.** Classified and Arranged so as to facilitate the Expression of Ideas. By PETER M. ROGET. Crown 8vo. 10s. 6d.

RONALDS. — **The Fly-Fisher's Entomology.** By ALFRED RONALDS. With 20 Coloured Plates. 8vo. 14s.

ROSSETTI.—**A Shadow of Dante**: being an Essay towards studying Himself, his World, and his Pilgrimage. By MARIA FRANCESCA ROSSETTI. With Illustrations. Crown 8vo. 10s. 6d.

RUSSELL.—**A Life of Lord John Russell (Earl Russell, K.G.).** By SPENCER WALPOLE. With 2 Portraits. 2 vols. 8vo. 36s. Cabinet Edition, 2 vols. Crown 8vo. 12s.

SEEBOHM (Frederic).—*WORKS BY.*

The Oxford Reformers—John Colet, Erasmus, and Thomas More; a History of their Fellow-Work. 8vo. 14s.

The English Village Community Examined in its Relations to the Manorial and Tribal Systems, &c. 13 Maps and Plates. 8vo. 16s.

The Era of the Protestant Revolution. With Map. Fcp. 8vo. 2s. 6d.

SEWELL.—**Stories and Tales.** By ELIZABETH M. SEWELL. Crown 8vo. 1s. 6d. each, cloth plain; 2s. 6d. each, cloth extra, gilt edges:—

Amy Herbert.	Laneton Parsonage.
The Earl's Daughter.	Ursula.
The Experience of Life.	Gertrude.
A Glimpse of the World.	Ivors.
Cleve Hall.	Home Life.
Katharine Ashton.	After Life.
Margaret Percival.	

SHAKESPEARE. — **Bowdler's Family Shakespeare.** 1 Vol. 8vo. With 36 Woodcuts, 14s. or in 6 vols. Fcp. 8vo. 21s.

Outline of the Life of Shakespeare. By J. O. HALLIWELL-PHILLIPPS. 2 vols. Royal 8vo. £1 1s.

A Calendar of the Halliwell-Phillipps' Collection of Shakespearean Rarities Formerly Preserved at Hollingbury Copse, Brighton. Enlarged by ERNEST E. BAKER, F.S.A. 8vo. 10s. 6d.

Shakespeare's True Life. By JAMES WALTER. With 500 Illustrations. Imp. 8vo. 21s.

The Shakespeare Birthday Book. By MARY F. DUNBAR. 32mo. 1s. 6d. cloth. With Photographs, 32mo. 5s. Drawing-Room Edition, with Photographs, Fcp. 8vo. 10s. 6d.

SHORT.—**Sketch of the History of the Church of England** to the Revolution of 1688. By T. V. SHORT, D.D. Crown 8vo. 7s. 6d.

SILVER LIBRARY (The).—Cr. 8vo. 3s. 6d. each volume.

Baker's (Sir S. W.) **Eight Years in Ceylon.** With 6 Illustrations. 3s. 6d.

Baker's (Sir S. W.) **Rifle and Hound in Ceylon.** With 6 Illustrations. 3s. 6d.

Brassey's (Lady) **A Voyage in the 'Sunbeam'.** With 66 Illustrations. 3s. 6d.

Clodd's (E.) **Story of Creation**: a Plain Account of Evolution. With 77 Illustrations. 3s. 6d.

Doyle's (A. Conan) **Micah Clarke.** A Tale of Monmouth's Rebellion. 3s. 6d.

Froude's (J. A.) **Short Studies on Great Subjects.** 4 vols. 3s. 6d. each.

Froude's (J. A.) **Cæsar**: a Sketch. 3s. 6d.

SILVER LIBRARY (The).—
continued.

Froude's (J. A.) Thomas Carlyle: a History of his Life. 1795-1835. 2 vols. 1834-1881. 2 vols. 7s. each.

Froude's (J. A.) The Two Chiefs of Dunboy: an Irish Romance of the Last Century. 3s. 6d.

Gleig's (Rev. G. R.) Life of the Duke of Wellington. With Portrait. 3s. 6d.

Haggard's (H. R.) She: A History of Adventure. 32 Illustrations. 3s. 6d.

Haggard's (H. R.) Allan Quatermain. With 20 Illustrations. 3s. 6d.

Haggard's (H. R.) Colonel Quaritch, V.C.: a Tale of Country Life. 3s. 6d.

Haggard's (H. R.) Cleopatra. With 29 Full-page Illustrations. 3s. 6d.

Howitt's (W.) Visits to Remarkable Places. 80 Illustrations. 3s. 6d.

Jefferies' (R.) The Story of My Heart: My Autobiography. With Portrait. 3s. 6d.

Jefferies' (R.) Field and Hedgerow. Last Essays of. With Portrait. 3s. 6d.

Macleod's (H. D.) The Elements of Banking. 3s. 6d.

Marshman's (J. C.) Memoirs of Sir Henry Havelock. 3s. 6d.

Merivale's (Dean) History of the Romans under the Empire. 8 vols. 3s. 6d. each.

Mill's (J. S.) Principles of Political Economy. 3s. 6d.

Mill's (J. S.) System of Logic. 3s. 6d.

Newman's (Cardinal) Historical Sketches. 3 vols. 3s. 6d. each.

Newman's (Cardinal) Apologia Pro Vitâ Sua. 3s. 6d.

Newman's (Cardinal) Callista: a Tale of the Third Century. 3s. 6d.

Newman's (Cardinal) Loss and Gain: a Tale. 3s. 6d.

Newman's (Cardinal) Essays, Critical and Historical. 2 vols. 7s.

Newman's (Cardinal) An Essay on the Development of Christian Doctrine. 3s. 6d.

Newman's (Cardinal) The Arians of the Fourth Century. 3s. 6d.

Newman's (Cardinal) Verses on Various Occasions. 3s. 6d.

Newman's (Cardinal) Parochial and Plain Sermons. 8 vols. 3s. 6d. each.

SILVER LIBRARY (The).—
continued.

Newman's (Cardinal) Selection, adapted to the Seasons of the Ecclesiastical Year, from the 'Parochial and Plain Sermons'. 3s. 6d.

Newman's (Cardinal) Sermons bearing upon Subjects of the Day. Edited by the Rev. W. J. Copeland, B.D., late Rector of Farnham, Essex. 3s. 6d.

Newman's (Cardinal) Difficulties felt by Anglicans in Catholic Teaching Considered. 2 vols. 3s. 6d. each.

Newman's (Cardinal) The Idea of a University Defined and Illustrated. 3s. 6d.

Newman's (Cardinal) Biblical and Ecclesiastical Miracles. 3s. 6d.

Newman's (Cardinal) Discussions and Arguments on Various Subjects. 3s. 6d.

Newman's (Cardinal) Grammar of Assent. 3s. 6d.

Newman's (Cardinal) The Via Media of the Anglican Church, illustrated in Lectures, &c. 2 vols. 3s. 6d. each.

Stanley's (Bishop) Familiar History of Birds. 160 Illustrations. 3s. 6d.

Wood's (Rev. J. G.) Petland Revisited. With 33 Illustrations. 3s. 6d.

Wood's (Rev. J. G.) Strange Dwellings: With 60 Illustrations. 3s. 6d.

Wood's (Rev. J. G.) Out of Doors. 11 Illustrations. 3s. 6d.

SMITH (Gregory).—**Fra Angelico,** and other Short Poems. By GREGORY SMITH. Crown 8vo. 4s. 6d.

SMITH (R. Bosworth).—**Carthage and the Carthagenians.** By R. BOSWORTH SMITH, M.A. Maps, Plans, &c. Crown 8vo. 6s.

Sophocles. Translated into English Verse. By ROBERT WHITELAW, M.A. Assistant-Master in Rugby School; late Fellow of Trinity College, Cambridge. Crown 8vo. 8s. 6d.

STANLEY.—**A Familiar History of Birds.** By E. STANLEY, D.D. With 160 Woodcuts. Crown 8vo. 3s. 6d.

STEEL (J. H.).—WORKS BY.

A Treatise on the Diseases of the Dog; being a Manual of Canine Pathology. Especially adapted for the Use of Veterinary Practitioners and Students. 88 Illustrations. 8vo. 10s. 6d.

STEEL (J. H.).—WORKS BY.—cont.

A Treatise on the Diseases of the Ox; being a Manual of Bovine Pathology. Especially adapted for the use of Veterinary Practitioners and Students. 2 Plates and 117 Woodcuts. 8vo. 15s.

A Treatise on the Diseases of the Sheep; being a Manual of Ovine Pathology. Especially adapted for the use of Veterinary Practitioners and Students. With Coloured Plate and 99 Woodcuts. 8vo. 12s.

STEPHEN.—**Essays in Ecclesiastical Biography.** By the Right Hon. Sir J. STEPHEN. Crown 8vo. 7s. 6d.

STEPHENS.—**A History of the French Revolution.** By H. MORSE STEPHENS, Balliol College, Oxford. 3 vols. 8vo. Vol. I. and II. 18s. each. [*Ready.*

STEVENSON (Robt. Louis).—WORKS BY.

A Child's Garden of Verses. Small Fcp. 8vo. 5s.

The Dynamiter. Fcp. 8vo. 1s. sewed; 1s. 6d. cloth.

Strange Case of Dr. Jekyll and Mr. Hyde. Fcp. 8vo. 1s. swd.; 1s. 6d. cloth.

STEVENSON and OSBOURNE.—**The Wrong Box.** By ROBERT LOUIS STEVENSON and LLOYD OSBOURNE. Crown 8vo. 5s.

STOCK.—**Deductive Logic.** By ST. GEORGE STOCK. Fcp. 8vo. 3s. 6d.

'*STONEHENGE*'.—**The Dog in Health and Disease.** By 'STONEHENGE'. With 84 Wood Engravings. Square Crown 8vo. 7s. 6d.

STRONG, LOGEMAN, and WHEELER.—**Introduction to the Study of the History of Language.** By HERBERT A. STRONG, M.A., LL.D.; WILLEM S. LOGEMAN; and BENJAMIN IDE WHEELER. 8vo. 10s. 6d.

STUTFIELD.—**The Brethren of Mount Atlas:** being the First Part of an African Theosophical Story. By HUGH E. M. STUTFIELD, F.R.G.S. Author of 'El Maghreb: 1200 Miles' Ride through Marocco'. Crown 8vo.

Supernatural Religion; an Inquiry into the Reality of Divine Revelation. 3 vols. 8vo. 36s.

Reply (A) to Dr. Lightfoot's Essays. By the Author of 'Supernatural Religion'. 8vo. 6s.

SWINBURNE.—**Picture Logic;** an Attempt to Popularise the Science of Reasoning. By A. J. SWINBURNE, B.A. Post 8vo. 5s.

SYMES (James).—WORKS BY.

Prelude to Modern History: being a Brief Sketch of the World's History from the Third to the Ninth Century. With 5 Maps. Crown 8vo. 2s. 6d.

A Companion to School Histories of England; being a Series of Short Essays on the most Important Movements, Social, Literary, and Political, in English History. Crown 8vo. 2s. 6d.

Political Economy: a Short Text-Book of Political Economy. With Problems for Solution, and Hints for Supplementary Reading. Crown 8vo. 2s. 6d.

TAYLOR.—**A Student's Manual of the History of India,** from the Earliest Period to the Present Time. By Colonel MEADOWS TAYLOR, C.S.I., &c. Crown 8vo. 7s. 6d.

THOMPSON (D. Greenleaf).—WORKS BY.

The Problem of Evil: an Introduction to the Practical Sciences. 8vo. 10s. 6d.

A System of Psychology. 2 vols. 8vo. 36s.

The Religious Sentiments of the Human Mind. 8vo. 7s. 6d.

Social Progress: an Essay. 8vo. 7s. 6d.

The Philosophy of Fiction in Literature: an Essay. Cr. 8vo. 6s.

Three in Norway. By Two of THEM. With a Map and 59 Illustrations. Cr. 8vo. 2s. boards; 2s. 6d. cloth.

TIREBUCK.—**Dorrie:** a Novel. By WILLIAM TIREBUCK. Author of 'Saint Margaret,' &c. Crown 8vo. 6s.

TOYNBEE.—**Lectures on the Industrial Revolution of the 18th Century in England.** By the late ARNOLD TOYNBEE, Tutor of Balliol College, Oxford. Together with a Short Memoir by B. JOWETT, Master of Balliol College, Oxford. 8vo. 10s. 6d.

TREVELYAN (Sir G. O., Bart.).—WORKS BY.

The Life and Letters of Lord Macaulay.
POPULAR EDITION, Crown 8vo. 2s. 6d.
STUDENT'S EDITION, Crown 8vo. 6s.
CABINET EDITION, 2 vols. Cr. 8vo. 12s.
LIBRARY EDITION, 2 vols. 8vo. 36s.

The Early History of Charles James Fox. Library Edition, 8vo. 18s. Cabinet Edition, Cr. 8vo. 6s.

TROLLOPE (Anthony).—NOVELS BY.

The Warden. Crown 8vo. 1s. boards; 1s. 6d. cloth.

Barchester Towers. Crown 8vo. 1s. boards; 1s. 6d. cloth.

VILLE.—**The Perplexed Farmer:** How is he to meet Alien Competition? By GEORGE VILLE. Translated from the French by WILLIAM CROOKES, F.R.S., V.P.C.S., &c. Crown 8vo. 5s.

VIRGIL.—**Publi Vergili Maronis Bucolica, Georgica, Æneis;** The Works of VIRGIL, Latin Text, with English Commentary and Index. By B. H. KENNEDY, D.D. Cr. 8vo. 10s. 6d.

The Æneid of Virgil. Translated into English Verse. By JOHN CONINGTON, M.A. Crown 8vo. 6s.

The Poems of Virgil. Translated into English Prose. By JOHN CONINGTON, M.A. Crown 8vo. 6s.

The Eclogues and Georgics of Virgil. Translated from the Latin by J. W. MACKAIL, M.A., Fellow of Balliol College, Oxford. Printed on Dutch Hand-made Paper. Royal 16mo. 5s.

WAKEMAN and HASSALL.—**Essays Introductory to the Study of English Constitutional History.** By Resident Members of the University of Oxford. Edited by HENRY OFFLEY WAKEMAN, M.A., and ARTHUR HASSALL, M.A. Crown 8vo. 6s.

WALFORD.—**The Mischief of Monica:** a Novel. By L. B. WALFORD. Author of 'Mr. Smith,' &c., &c. 3 vols. Crown 8vo. 25s. 6d.

WALKER.—**The Correct Card;** or How to Play at Whist; a Whist Catechism. By Major A. CAMPBELL-WALKER, F.R.G.S. Fcp. 8vo. 2s. 6d.

WALPOLE.—**History of England from the Conclusion of the Great War in 1815 to 1858.** By SPENCER WALPOLE. Library Edition. 5 vols. 8vo. £4 10s. Cabinet Edition. 6 vols. Crown 8vo. 6s. each.

WELLINGTON.—**Life of the Duke of Wellington.** By the Rev. G. R. GLEIG, M.A. Crown 8vo. 3s. 6d.

WELLS.—**Recent Economic Changes** and their Effect on the Production and Distribution of Wealth and the Well-being of Society. By DAVID A. WELLS. Crown 8vo. 10s. 6d.

WENDT.—**Papers on Maritime Legislation,** with a Translation of the German Mercantile Laws relating to Maritime Commerce. By ERNEST EMIL WENDT. Royal 8vo. £1 11s. 6d.

WEYMAN.—**The House of the Wolf:** a Romance. By STANLEY J. WEYMAN. Crown 8vo. 6s.

WHATELY (E. Jane).—WORKS BY.
English Synonyms. Edited by R. WHATELY, D.D. Fcp. 8vo. 3s.

Life and Correspondence of Richard Whately, D.D., late Archbishop of Dublin. With Portrait. Crown 8vo. 10s. 6d.

WHATELY (Archbishop). — WORKS BY.

Elements of Logic. Crown 8vo. 4s. 6d.

Elements of Rhetoric. Crown 8vo. 4s. 6d.

Lessons on Reasoning. Fcp. 8vo. 1s. 6d.

Bacon's Essays, with Annotations. 8vo. 10s. 6d.

Whist in Diagrams: a Supplement to American Whist, Illustrated; being a Series of Hands played through, Illustrating the American leads, the new play, the forms of Finesse, and celebrated coups of Masters. With Explanation and Analysis. By G. W. P. Fcp. 8vo. 6s. 6d.

WILCOCKS.—The Sea Fisherman, Comprising the Chief Methods of Hook and Line Fishing in the British and other Seas, and Remarks on Nets, Boats, and Boating. By J. C. WILCOCKS. Profusely Illustrated. Crown 8vo. 6s.

WILLICH.—Popular Tables for giving Information for ascertaining the value of Lifehold, Leasehold, and Church Property, the Public Funds, &c. By CHARLES M. WILLICH. Edited by H. BENCE JONES. Crown 8vo. 10s. 6d.

WILLOUGHBY.—East Africa and its Big Game. By Capt. Sir JOHN C. WILLOUGHBY, Bart. Illustrated by G. D. Giles and Mrs. Gordon Hake. Royal 8vo. 21s.

WITT (Prof.).—WORKS BY. Translated by FRANCES YOUNGHUSBAND.

The Trojan War. Crown 8vo. 2s.

Myths of Hellas; or, Greek Tales. Crown 8vo. 3s. 6d.

The Wanderings of Ulysses. Crown 8vo. 3s. 6d.

The Retreat of the Ten Thousand; being the story of Xenophon's 'Anabasis'. With Illustrations. Crown 8vo. 3s. 6d.

WOLFF (Henry W.).—WORKS BY.

Rambles in the Black Forest. Crown 8vo. 7s. 6d.

The Watering Places of the Vosges. Crown 8vo. 4s. 6d.

The Country of the Vosges. With a Map. 8vo. 12s.

WOOD (Rev. J. G.).—WORKS BY.

Homes Without Hands; a Description of the Habitations of Animals, classed according to the Principle of Construction. With 140 Illustrations. 8vo. 10s. 6d.

Insects at Home; a Popular Account of British Insects, their Structure, Habits, and Transformations. With 700 Illustrations. 8vo. 10s. 6d.

Insects Abroad; a Popular Account of Foreign Insects, their Structure, Habits, and Transformations. With 600 Illustrations. 8vo. 10s. 6d.

WOOD (Rev. J. G.).—WORKS BY.— continued.

Bible Animals; a Description of every Living Creature mentioned in the Scriptures. With 112 Illustrations. 8vo. 10s. 6d.

Strange Dwellings; a Description of the Habitations of Animals, abridged from 'Homes without Hands'. With 60 Illustrations. Crown 8vo. 3s. 6d.

Out of Doors; a Selection of Original Articles on Practical Natural History. With 11 Illustrations. Crown 8vo. 3s. 6d.

Petland Revisited. With 33 Illustrations. Crown 8vo. 3s. 6d.

WORDSWORTH.—Annals of My Early Life, 1806-46. By CHARLES WORDSWORTH, D.C.L., Bishop of St. Andrews. 8vo. 15s.

WYLIE.—History of England under Henry IV. By JAMES HAMILTON WYLIE. 2 vols. Vol. I., 1399-1404. Crown 8vo. 10s. 6d. Vol. II. [In the Press.

YOUATT (William).—WORKS BY.

The Horse. Revised and enlarged. 8vo. Woodcuts, 7s. 6d.

The Dog. Revised and enlarged. 8vo. Woodcuts, 6s.

ZELLER (Dr. E.).—WORKS BY.

History of Eclecticism in Greek Philosophy. Translated by SARAH F. ALLEYNE. Cr. 8vo. 10s. 6d.

The Stoics, Epicureans, and Sceptics. Translated by the Rev. O. J. REICHEL, M.A. Crown 8vo. 15s.

Socrates and the Socratic Schools. Translated by the Rev. O. J. REICHEL, M.A. Cr. 8vo. 10s. 6d.

Plato and the Older Academy. Translated by SARAH F. ALLEYNE and ALFRED GOODWIN, B.A. Crown 8vo. 18s.

The Pre-Socratic Schools: a History of Greek Philosophy from the Earliest Period to the time of Socrates. Translated by SARAH F. ALLEYNE. 2 vols. Crown 8vo. 30s.

Outlines of the History of Greek Philosophy. Translated by SARAH F. ALLEYNE and EVELYN ABBOTT. Crown 8vo. 10s. 6d.

www.ingramcontent.com/pod-product-compliance
Lightning Source LLC
Chambersburg PA
CBHW051857300426
44117CB00006B/433